But Were They Good
for the Jews?

But Were They Good for the Jews?

Over 150 Historical Figures
Viewed From a Jewish Perspective

Elliot Rosenberg

A Birch Lane Press Book
Published by Carol Publishing Group

To Dad, Mom, Myron, Bubba
Uncle Louis, and Hesh

A Birch Lane Press Book
Published by Carol Publishing Group
Birch Lane Press is a registered trademark of Carol Communications, Inc.

Editorial, sales and distribution, rights and permissions inquiries should be addressed
to Carol Publishing Group, 120 Enterprise Avenue, Secaucus, N.J. 07094

In Canada: Canadian Manda Group, One Atlantic Avenue, Suite 105, Toronto,
Ontario, M6K 3E7

Carol Publishing Group books may be purchased in bulk at special discounts for sales
promotion, fund-raising, or educational purposes. Special editions can be created to
specifications. For details, contact Special Sales Department, Carol Publishing Group,
120 Enterprise Avenue, Secaucus, N.J. 07094.

Manufactured in the United States of America
10 9 8 7 6 5 4 3 2 1

Library of Congress Cataloging-in-Publication Data

Rosenberg, Elliot, 1937–
     But were they good for the Jews? : over 150 historical figures
viewed from a Jewish perspective / Elliot Rosenberg
        p. cm.
     "A Birch Lane Press book."
     ISBN 1-55972-432-3 (hc)
     1. Jews—History.   2. Celebrities—Attitudes—History.
3. Judaism—Relations.   4. Antisemitism—History.   I. Title.
DS117.R67   1997
305.892'4'009—dc21   97-34616
                                                  CIP

CONTENTS

5. After Napoleon and Before Hitler   138

Prince Klemens von Metternich and Emperor Francis I / Tsar Nicholas I /
The Duke of Wellington / Louis Philippe / Frederick William IV of Prussia /
Napoleon III / Italy's Founding Fathers: Giuseppi Mazzini, Giuseppi
Garibaldi, and Count Camillo Cavour / Tsar Alexander II / Richard
Wagner / Otto von Bismarck / Tsar Alexander III / Nicholas II /
Emperor Franz Joseph / Kaiser Wilhelm II ◆ OTHER VOICES, OTHER
DEEDS: Queen Victoria and son Edward VII / Crown Prince Frederick
William of Prussia / Crown Prince Rudolph of Austria / King Ludwig (the
Mad) of Bavaria / Rasputin / William Ewart Gladstone / Fyodor
Dostoevsky / Count Leo Tolstoy / Anton Chekhov / Friedrich Nietzsche /
Friedrich Engels / Charles Dickens / Thomas Carlyle / Thomas Babington
Macaulay / Emile Zola

6. Sinking Into the Abyss of a New Dark Age   213

Adolf Hitler / Field Marshals Erich von Manstein, Albert Kesselring, Erwin
Rommel, and Colonel-General Johannes von Blaskowitz / Benito Mussolini
/ Men of Vichy: Henri Philippe Petain and Pierre Laval / Hungarian
Regent Nicholas Horthy, Bulgarian King Boris III, King Christian X of
Denmark, and Finland's Carl Gustaf von Mannerheim / Francisco Franco /
Winston Churchill and Anthony Eden / Franklin Delano Roosevelt /
Pope Pius XII

7. Toward Those Broad Sunlit Uplands — With Thunderclaps   252
    Overhead and Firefights Along the Journey

Clement Attlee and Ernest Bevin / Harry S. Truman / Joseph Stalin /
Dwight D. Eisenhower / Nikita S. Khrushchev and his successors / Pope
John XXIII / Charles de Gaulle / Lyndon B. Johnson / Richard M. Nixon /
Mohandas Gandhi and Jawaharlal Nehru, Mao Tse-tung and Chou En-lai /
Anwar el-Sadat / Jimmy Carter, Ronald Reagan, George Bush, and
Bill Clinton

AUTHOR TO READER

One day, as I enthusiastically recounted King Richard the Lion-Hearted's daring exploits to my uncle Louis, he suddenly interrupted, "Yes, he was a great leader, but was he good for the Jews?"

This comment was less a question than a refrain that he had learned from my grandfather. By contrast, as a child I assessed greatness against an ecumenically broader canvas. The significant cross on Richard's crusader tunic did not detract from my desire to emulate his children's-book image, a gallant warrior seated atop his bedecked steed, advancing to do battle in the Holy Land against sinister, crafty, treacherous Saracens.

Early impressions are lasting impressions. Memories of those historical personages, a procession of kings and queens, soldiers and statesmen, still glistened as I matured. Adult-level biographies provided more realistic accounts, but scrupulous index searches for pages covering "attitude toward Jews," "position on anti-Semitism," or "Jewish policies" often came up empty. So it was not easy, even years later, to address Uncle Louis's concern, now my own. Were history's "good guys" really good? Were its "bad guys" truly villainous?

These pages are the product of a curiosity I hope is shared by many others. Revisiting centuries past, I filled in the blanks for Uncle Louis and the rest of us. The outcome is an image of celebrated and infamous Old and New World figures through six-starred prisms. There will be exceptions to the rule of writing about familiar historical figures. For example, we find Old World despots who altered the course of biblical and postbiblical Judea. That's why Antiochus and the contemptible father-son duo of Vespasian and Titus (from a Jewish standpoint) will appear.

Torquemada, Queen Isabella, and Tsar Nicholas II have received exhaustive examination in volumes on anti-Semitism, but skirting past them in the belief that readers already know them all too well would be inappropriate.

Absent from these pages, however, is any exploration of the roots, branches, and foliage of anti-Semitism. My goal is simply to skip through history's briar patch and answer the question Uncle Louis stumped me with so many, many years ago: But was he good for the Jews?

I describe sovereigns and commanders and politicians whose proclamations, directives, edicts, ukases, and laws brought relief, anxiety, or terror to their Jewish subjects, nationals, and citizens for two millennia. Some public men and women who are denied a brief individual sketch of their own may appear in "Other Voices, Other Deeds," the section closing chapters 1 through 5. Look there, also, for a grab bag of men and women honored in their time or celebrated in ours for making their mark on cultural life. The formidable number in this category better excuses most exclusions—but not all. Some—the Leonardos, Michelangelos, Dantes, and Beethovens—are omitted because of the paucity of anything revealing they had to say, if they indeed said anything, about Jews in their midst.

In chapter 1, we draw our first examples from a point on history's time line well after the dawn of Jewish existence. Early Oriental despots tended to regard Hebrews not as a unique religious minority, but as a formidable competitor for space and resources when strong, or as a target for plunder when weak. Their predatory ways were similar to those shown toward other potential rivals or victims.

It is easy to mark as a villain Ramses II, Egypt's ruler (1279?–1223? B.C.), who conscripted Hebrew slaves to construct his treasure cities of Ramses and Pithom. Modern historians describe him as the probable pharaoh of the Exodus, although the Bible itself is vague.

Another negative label can also be applied to Nebuchadnezzar, Babylon's ruler (605–561 B.C), who laid waste to Jerusalem, destroyed the First Temple, and enslaved most of Judea's population. But, like Ramses II, Nebuchadnezzar was an equal opportunity oppressor. Our arbitrary starting line will be the confluence of Western civilization with the Jewish world, with the arrival of Alexander the Great.

But first, let's close this introduction on a positive note by culling from the ancient world's despots one exemplary and recognizable figure, Cyrus the Great, ruler of Persia (550–529 B.C.). "God turns to His anointed, to Cyrus," prophesied Deutero-Isaiah, and the king delivered, conquering Babylon in 539 B.C., ending the Jews' exile and restoring much of the treasure hauled from the Temple by Nebuchadnezzar's looters.

But Were They Good
for the Jews?

1

The Age of Greek Glory
and Roman Grandeur

While Nebuchadnezzar's shadow hovered over Judea, several hundred miles across the Mediterranean, Solon appeared as Athens's celebrated law giver. Greece's city-states grew; Greek culture thrived. Generations passed. The time of Ezra and the Second Temple was also the time of Pericles and the Parthenon. But if tides spreading from Judea and Attica lapped at each other's shores, the record is spare. Whether Solon and Pericles would have been counted friend or foe, we will never know. No judgments on Jews, pro or con, can be extracted from the great orations of Demosthenes. Nor do they appear in the philosophical works of Plato. The output of Aeschylus, Sophocles, and Euripides leave no trace of a Shylock, Fagin, or Isaac of York. The prodigious labor of Hellenism's great historians, Herodotus and Thucydides, is barren in any substantive way. Herodotus merely noted a branch of Syrians who practiced circumcision, a custom presumably acquired, by his account, from the Egyptians. It is with the world-class ambitions of Alexander that our specialized celebrity hunt begins.

ALEXANDER THE GREAT, 356–323 B.C.E.

History's Conventional View

Alexander rates as antiquity's mightiest adventurer and conqueror. Early on, he wept at his father's conquests. "My father [King Philip II of

3

Macedon] will get ahead of me in everything and will leave nothing great for me to do." Young Alex need not have fretted. Though his life spanned a mere thirty-three years, the decade following his twenty-second birthday saw his warriors marching from the valleys beneath Mount Olympus, sweeping all before them. Crossing the Hellespont to Asia Minor in 334 B.C.E., Alexander conquered the Persians at Issus, swerved south along the Levantine coastline, besieged Tyre, then occupied Egypt. There he founded one of the world's great commercial and cultural centers, Alexandria. Reversing direction, he headed to Mesopotamia, where he smashed King Darius's forces at Arbela, bringing down the Persian Empire. Babylon fell, Susa and Persepolis too. Then, across Afghanistan's passes and on to India. From the Ionian Sea to the Punjab, Alexander served as a model for every empire builder in the twenty-three centuries to follow.

But From a Jewish Perspective

Alexander enters the Jewish record as a hero, partly through deed, partly through legend.

First, the facts: After his initial victory in Asia Minor, Alexander's march south to wrest Egypt took him through Judea, then a relatively minor backwater of Darius's rich domain. In a sense, the twenty-five-year-old Macedonian crossed it to get to the other side, the Nile delta, then recrossed it on his way back to Persia's heartland. Jews found their latest foreign master's policy tolerant, as did other sects who submitted to his rule. Alexander—and his immediate successors—permitted limited self-rule, along with the continuity of ancient laws administered by religious leaders. Jews were encouraged to settle in Egypt, Asia Minor, and beyond in communities governed by their own councils, with their own courts dispensing justice. Set against the record of typical early monarchs, Alexander's policy, like Cyrus the Great's, was wise and welcome.

Second, the legend: According to the Jewish historian Josephus (more on him later), the Macedonian conqueror's arrival before Jerusalem was awaited apprehensively by Jaddus, its high priest, elders, and other notables. But far from displaying royal haughtiness, Alexander immediately prostrated himself before the high priest, saying Jaddus appeared to him in a dream and prophesied his triumph over Darius's forces. Next, Alexander visited the Temple in gratitude, offering a sacrifice.

While offering no corroboration of Alexander's Temple visit, the Talmud relates a similar tale of this journey to Jerusalem. Substitute an aristocratically garbed Simeon the Just for Jaddus, and in this version Alexander descends from his chariot and kneels. "Shall a great king like you prostrate himself before this Jew?" chides one of his companions. "The image of this man wins my battles for me," Alexander replies. He asks Simeon why he has come, learns of the Jews' fear that their hostile neighbors, the Samaritans, plan to gain control of the temple and then destroy it. Alexander sides with the Jews, puts an end to their enemy's plot, and resumes his march north, leaving a now secure and contented Judea behind.

Temptation exists to fast-forward three hundred years from Alexander to Rome's Caesars. Following the warrior-king's death in 323 B.C., his universal empire quickly crumbled, with his subordinate commanders dividing the spoils. Their descendants who ruled Syria (the Seleucids) and Egypt (the Ptolemeys) held sway over Jewish life and destiny for three centuries, but not one of the thirty in their two dynasties remains a Jewish or non-Jewish household name except the last Ptolemey, Cleopatra VII, and she properly belongs as an exotic footnote in "Other Voices" at the end of this chapter. Yet one among the Seleucids towers above the others in malevolence, marking him a great villain in Jewish eyes. Despite lack of name recognition, we know him by his deeds. Antiochus IV, the son of Antiochus III and brother of Seleucus IV, is the man who made Hannukah possible.

ANTIOCHUS IV (Epiphanes)
Ruled 175–164 B.C.E.

History's Conventional View

Antiochus began his reign in Syria contesting Ptolemaic rivals for domination of their joint frontier (modern Israel) and worrying about how to pay huge indemnities imposed by triumphant Rome following a war during his father's rule. It ended when he was ambushed and slain while campaigning beyond his eastern frontier against the fierce Parthians. In between, he embarked on a massive effort to hellenize, that is, superimpose Greek culture and institutions upon his largely non-Greek subjects. He installed a Greek colony at Babylon, added temples to assorted gods and other splendors at his capital Antioch, and levied heavy taxes. As a measure of his popularity, Antiochus Epiphanes (God Manifest) also became known as Antiochus Epimanas (the Mad).

But From a Jewish Perspective

Antiochus pressed hellenization on his reluctant Judean subjects with a furious passion exceeding tyrannical norms. That's why he earns inclusion here as a major villain.

Seleucid incursions started simply enough, when Antiochus's predecessor decided to raid Jerusalem's Temple treasury. In Greco-Roman times, this holy building held not only valuable religious vessels and ornaments, and reserve funds to meet periodic ransom payments demanded in that perilous age, but also private assets stored there for safety's sake. So, in itself, Temple plundering evidenced no clear commitment to anti-Semitism. The impetus mirrored Willie Sutton's for robbing banks two millennia later—that's where the money was.

But Antiochus IV pursued a darker course, transcending mere larceny. Antiquity's greedier despots had often distributed posts of prestige to the highest bidder, but, after placing the Temple's top priesthood on his "for sale" list, Antiochus saw fit to resell the position when an even more lucrative offer came along. Ethics aside, this unpleasant form of revenue enhancement, breaching Temple autonomy, was a minor prelude. His uncompromising hellenization policy really brought Seleucid-Jewish relations to a crisis.

Following riots in Jerusalem sparked by false rumors of the tyrant's death while campaigning in Egypt, Antiochus returned, stormed the Temple, removed its eternal lamp, and constructed a great altar to Zeus, to which his fellow Greeks came in homage. Next he built the Acra, a near-impregnable citadel, within the city to house a permanent Greek garrison for enforcing decrees aimed at the annihilation of Judaism. No other faith in the polyglot Seleucid empire was similarly targeted. He demanded Jews to break with their religious laws, "profane the Sabbath and pollute the sanctuary." They should "build altars and temples and shrines for idols; and should sacrifice swine's flesh." If a man disobeyed "the word of the king, he should die."

Some Jews forced to forsake Torah law for Antiochus's New Order complied outwardly. A few even welcomed introduction of Greek institutions as their passport to Hellenistic civilization. Others chose martyrdom, and still more fled to the hills.

Guerrilla warfare broke out; frequent skirmishes took their toll on Greek forces. After a stunning royal defeat twenty miles south of Jerusalem, a newly enlightened Antiochus decreed: "The Jews shall have their own foods as before; none of them shall be molested in any way for deeds committed."

But concessions came too late. Under the leadership of Judah Maccabee, Jewish fighters regained their capital in 164 B.C.E. They discovered Jerusalem's Temple had been desecrated by Greeks during their three-year occupation. As the Jews set out to rededicate the Temple and light its altar lamp, searchers found only enough pure oil, Talmudic tradition relates, to burn *one* day. Miraculously, it lasted eight, and celebration of the event has lived on in the ceremonial lighting of candles at Hannukah.

Thus, Antiochus IV, the cause of it all, stands apart from the other six Antiochi of the Seleucid dynasty as a man deserving insertion in this chapter.

When the glory that was Greece, then Macedonia, and, more lately, a shallower Seleucid reflection, faded before Rome's growing grandeur, a mighty new host of Western gentiles came to know and be known in Jewish communities along the eastern Mediterranean. Our high school texts told us of Julius Caesar, his triumvirate partners Crassus and Pompey, his assassins Brutus and Cassius, his avengers Antony and Octavian. Biographer Suetonius (the Kitty Kelly of his day) and, more recently, Robert Graves (author of "*I, Claudius*"), explored the domestic debauchery of Emperor Augustus's successors—Tiberius, Caligula, Claudius, and Nero. Among dozens of obscure Roman rulers over several centuries, a few stand out. Hadrian, Constantine, and Justinian added pavestones to Western civilization's road, but how did they treat their Jews?

Drawing conclusions about emperors based on comparative Judean body counts alone, though, is misleading. Some slaughtered their Jewish subjects during rebellions against Roman rule, a practice acceptable according to antiquarian custom. Others mistreated subject populations in conquered provinces, regardless of race, religion, or creed. A few focused on Jews. Notice there were also a number of rulers friendly to Jews. We begin with one.

JULIUS CAESAR, 100 B.C.E.–44 B.C.E.

History's Conventional View

Julius was the foremost figure of the Roman world. During his tumultuous fifty-six years he rose from *quaestor* (prosecuting advocate) to *curule aedile* (magistrate) to *pontifex maximus* (political-ecclesiastical official), from *praetor* (commander) to *propraetor* (provincial governor), from consul (chief magistrate) to dictator. He is known for the conquest of Gaul, his pontic triumph, "I came, I saw, I conquered" (more alliteratively stunning in Latin, "Veni, vidi, vici"), *Commentaries*, his literary legacy to Latin students, and his crossing the Rubicon.

A jealous rival said Caesar was "the only sober man who ever tried to wreck the constitution." Shakespeare scripted his demise with the memorable exit line "Et tu, Brute?" as he fell beneath dagger thrusts by Brutus and his fellow conspirators, Casca, Cassius, Cinna, and Decius.

But From a Jewish Perspective

From a Roman's-eye view, Brutus may have been correct in his oration damning Caesar's ambition, but for Jews, Julius Caesar was a friend. Consider what came before him.

By the time Caesar passed through the Jewish homeland in 47 B.C.E., his ex-triumvirate partners (admittedly in a marriage of convenience) had already paid martial calls. First, Pompey's army conquered the decaying Seleucid Empire, and the hitherto practically autonomous Judea fell within Rome's orbit. Taking advantage of the Sabbath, when he knew Jews balked at fighting, he made a key move in his siege of Jerusalem.

Apart from shipping thousands of Judeans back to Rome's slave markets, Pompey burst into the Temple sanctuary, penetrating the Holy of Holies. But, according to Josephus, he left the Temple treasury untouched after slaughtering its defenders.

When Crassus, newly appointed Proconsul of Syria, passed through eight years later, he seized all the Temple's gold. This was Rome's first commission of grand larceny in the Holy Land. Mercifully for Jews, Crassus was slain fighting Parthians on Rome's eastern frontier shortly thereafter. Enter Julius Caesar, following a civil war in which he successfully chased his estranged partner, Pompey, across the Adriatic to Thessaly, and then the Eastern Mediterranean. Jews supported Caesar with men and supplies against his rival at a particularly perilous moment in nearby Egypt.

Now master of Rome and all its possessions and client states, Caesar proved no ingrate. By personal decree—or by leaning on the less than sympathetic Senate—he assured a kinder, gentler overlordship of Judea, gave it back the port of Jaffa which Pompey had detached from provincial control, and authorized reconstruction of Jerusalem's walls, necessary for defending it in antiquity. He established an annual tax rate at a reasonable 12.5 percent, with total exemption during the sabbatical year, the seventh year when fields lay fallow, and he ended the time-dishonored custom of extortion practiced by the military. While restoring Judean unity, he also permitted Jews in the Italian peninsula and throughout Rome's world to organize themselves and thrive.

So is it any wonder that when Cassius, Brutus, and the rest of those honorable men struck him down, Jews felt the loss deeply? Suetonius, the gossipy Roman biographer, wrote: "Public grief was enhanced by crowds of foreigners, lamenting in their own fashion, especially Jews, who came flocking to the Forum for several nights in succession."

AUGUSTUS, 63 B.C.E.–14 C.E.

Emperor, 27 B.C.E.–14 C.E.

History's Conventional View

Augustus came as close as any man to becoming the acknowledged master of the Western (and part of the Eastern) world. He started life relatively humbly as Gaius Octavius, son of a wealthy though not powerful family, but, at age thirty-six, emerged as Caesar Augustus, the first and greatest of Roman emperors. Adoption as legal heir by Julius Caesar, his great-uncle, helped, but the machinations of Cassius and Brutus, Antony and Cleopatra, and republicans made for a slippery climb. Said the crafty orator Cicero: "The young man must be flattered, used, and pushed aside."

Historians recognize Augustus as an administrative genius who re-organized the crumbling republic to meet new challenges of imperial responsibility. He did so cleverly, retaining traditional republican institutions while draining them of substance.

Nonhistorians may recall from school days the expression *Pax Romana,* a global strategy he made possible, which tranquilized the Roman world with fine roads, easy communication, and prosperous trade. "I found Rome built of brick; I leave her clothed in marble," he correctly boasted.

On his death in 14 C.E. the Senate entered him in the rolls of state deities. Modern man inadvertently honors him when we write checks or date letters the eighth month of our calendar year.

But From a Jewish Perspective

Augustus continued his great-uncle's policy of accommodation and moderation in Judea, allowing his friend and client ruler, Herod (whom most fellow Jews contemptuously regarded scarcely a Jew at all), wide latitude. When Herod asked permission to execute his own offspring for conspiracy, Augustus confirmed the sentence, but, aware of Jewish dietary restrictions, added in an aside to an aide that he would rather be Herod's swine than his son.

Turmoil in the wake of Herod's own death led Augustus to convert Judea into a Roman province. Instructions to his governor barred conduct likely to alienate Jewish subjects. Jews received exemption from emperor worship, spreading elsewhere as a test of loyalty. Troops were ordered not to parade through Jerusalem with eagle-topped standards bearing the emperor's portrait. Pagan altars, too, were kept out of the city.

Augustus's edicts toward diaspora Jewry reflected a spirit of tolerance. He upheld Jewry's rights in Asia Minor when challenged by less understanding provincial rulers. He assured Jews of "the inviolability of their sacred books and synagogues," the right to send funds to the Temple in Jerusalem, and exemption from posting bond or appearing in court Friday after dark or on their Sabbath.

At home or abroad, Jews fated to live under the Roman eagle could do worse than Augustus. And would.

TIBERIUS, 42 B.C.E.–37 C.E.
Emperor, 14–37 C.E.

History's Conventional View

The image of Tiberius passed down from antiquity remains that of Augustus's brooding, sour stepson, pushed to prominence and power by his conniving mom, Livia. A proven, highly competent general, he made a cold, uncongenial, and at times, even bored emperor. Tiberius came under the influence of an ambitious, unscrupulous prefect, Sejanus, who eliminated, one by one, the emperor's nearest kin. Tiberius also committed one of the ancient world's worst personnel mismatches—he named Pontius Pilate procurator to run Judea and rule Judeans.

To give Augustus's stepson his due, he practiced domestic thrift, engaged in no boondoggling public works fiascos, and avoided expensive wars. Suetonius writes: "He granted few veterans their discharge, reckoning that if they died still with the Colors, he would be spared the expense of the customary discharge bonus."

Hollywood spectacles set at the beginning of the Christian era often include him as a bit player, the laurel-wreathed figure in purple atop marble steps in his capital city. But Tiberius spent much of his reign in debauched reverie on the isle of Capri. One aristocratic Roman lady summoned there spoke of "that filthy-mouthed, hairy, stinking old man."

As a final horrendous personnel choice—or maybe an ultimate gesture of contempt—Tiberius named his grandnephew Gaius Julius Caesar Germanicus his heir and successor. We know the young man better under the name Caligula.

But From a Jewish Perspective

Sejanus, Tiberius's sinister eminence grise, was anti-Semitic, and Pontius Pilate (about whom more is said in "Other Voices") may have exceeded his instructions on occasion. But responsibility for what transpired throughout his realm ultimately rested with Tiberius. An example: When Pilate provocatively deposited shields inscribed with the emperor's name at his official residence in Jerusalem, Jewish complaints about the holy city's desecration reached Rome. Tiberius listened to a Jewish delegation, then ordered removal of the shields. Pilate sent them to Caesaria, a hellenized center. Mark this as an antiquarian instance of successful Jewish lobbying, made possible by Tiberius's good sense in avoiding flare-ups in a distant province.

At Tiberius's own capital, the emperor proved far less amenable and maybe more in character. Suetonius notes: "He abolished foreign cults in Rome, particularly the Egyptian and Jewish, forcing all citizens who embraced these superstitious faiths to burn their religious vestments and other accessories. Jews of military age were removed to unhealthy regions on the pretext of drafting them into the army."

Going a step further, Tiberius expelled *all* of Rome's Jews—temporarily. Details are hazy, but Josephus ascribes this act to imperial anger when the husband of a wealthy, aristocratic Roman convert complained that Jews plotted to defraud his wife.

Jews did not mourn this morose, bitter emperor. But soon the Age of Tiberius would seem like halcyon times.

CALIGULA, 12–41
Emperor, 37–41

History's Conventional View

"I am nursing a viper for the Roman people," Tiberius allegedly remarked in his dotage. Nephew Gaius—nicknamed Caligula for the army shoes *(caligae)* he wore while growing up in military camps—was no mere perverted relation of his granduncle. History proclaims him the ultimate tyrannical emperor. Caligula lived twenty-eight years, ruled much of the planet during the last four, then was mercifully (for his subjects) dispatched by his own Praetorian Guard.

"After his courtiers reminded him that he already outranked any prince or king," writes Suetonius, he insisted on being treated as a god, "sending for the most revered and artistically famous statues of the Greek deities and having their heads replaced by his own."

A sports enthusiast, he staged spectacular arena shows. During one lengthy period of preparation, he solved the problem of inflated meat prices for his lions and panthers by feeding them convicts instead. Caligula would feed his performing carnivores by lining up the menu and then issuing the order, "Kill every man between that baldhead and the one over there."

Caligula's promiscuous bloodletting embraced kin and associates. His victims included his father-in-law, his empress, and a cousin who dared to insult him by taking an antidote for a poison the emperor administered. Caligula routinely made fathers witness their sons' executions, and, when one excused himself on grounds of illness, he thoughtfully provided a litter.

He did love his sisters—perhaps too well: He engaged in incest with all three. And he was kind to his favorite horse, Incitatus, whom he presented with a marble stable, ivory stall, and jeweled collar. Suetonius tells us he had planned to name Incitatus to a consulship.

But From a Jewish Perspective

Although Roman-Jewish relations spiraled downward at a dizzying pace during Caligula's reign, history is on surer ground classifying him as a certifiable lunatic than as an anti-Semite. The emperor expected god worship his due, and any people bold or foolish enough not to indulge his whim risked the same retribution.

Crisis arose when Caligula ordered his colossal golden image placed in the Jerusalem Temple's Holy of Holies. Simultaneously, an outbreak of anti-Semitic rioting by Greeks against Alexandria's large Jewish population led both the rioters and the victims to rush delegations to Italy, each to plead its cause before the emperor. According to the philosopher Philo, one of its members, the Jewish group greeted Caligula with respectful bows at a villa outside Rome. "So you are the enemies of the gods, the only people who refuse to recognize my divinity," he scolded. The Jews protested that they made sacrifices for him, indeed, were first to do so after his accession.

"Yes, you make sacrifices *for* me, but not *to* me!" Caligula ran from room to room, slamming doors, the Jewish delegation trailing along. He pivoted, and asked accusingly: "Why don't you eat pork?" Explained the delegation leaders: "Each of your subjects follows his own customs." The emperor dismissed them, and, in an aside, said, "They're not so bad after all. They're just a poor, stupid people unable to believe in my divinity."

Another prominent arrival, Agrippa I, King of Judea, apparently convinced Caligula not to install the huge statue in Jerusalem. But the erratic emperor again changed his mind, and only the purposeful procrastination of Syria's governor, Petronius Publius—who risked forced suicide for defying his master—saved the situation.

Caligula's assassination in 41 relieved both Jew and gentile.

CLAUDIUS, 10 B.C.E.–54 C.E.
Emperor, 41–54

History's Conventional View

The image of Claudius comes to us partly through the historical record, perhaps more via the pen of British poet and author Robert Graves. His

I, Claudius maintains its popularity, and the subsequent *Masterpiece Theater* series based on it is periodically repeated, gaining new audiences.

A sickly and mentally afflicted child, Claudius grew up in a household where his own mother, Antonia (daughter of Marc Antony), called him a monster. Her manner of chiding an acquaintance for stupidity was to say, "He is a bigger fool even than my son Claudius." Great-uncle Augustus wrote, "The question is whether he has—shall I say?—full command of his senses."

Within the conspiratorial environment of early imperial Rome, Claudius seemed no threat to anyone. That perhaps explains his survival during the periodic murder sprees of Sejanus (under Tiberius) and Caligula, which swept away his craftier, more able kin. Following Caligula's own murder, no more acceptable male relative was still alive to succeed.

In foreign affairs, the new emperor brought Britain within the fold of Rome, a success that eluded Julius Caesar. In domestic affairs, the emperor kept an eye on Rome's infrastructure and monitored the arrival of grain shipments.

Claudius frequently sponsored chariot races, wild animal shows, and gladiatorial contests. His TV image, a stuttering, stammering, scatter-brained figure warranting sympathy is somewhat darkened by such commands as the one ordering that the throats of any gladiators who accidentally fell while performing at the arena be slit. "His cruelty and blood-thirstiness appeared equally in great and small matters," notes Suetonius.

He seemed to have good reason to execute his first wife, Messalina, thirty-five years his junior. Her extramarital dalliances with a galaxy of lovers scandalized the Roman establishment. But another May-September marriage, to his young niece Agrippina, proved even more disastrous. After persuading Claudius to adopt her son Nero, she poisoned Claudius to speed that ungrateful youth's rise to the imperial throne.

But From a Jewish Perspective

Claudius rates as a friend with a possible negative footnote. He rescinded Caligula's provocative decrees affecting Judea and reaffirmed Jewish rights throughout the rest of the Roman world. Claudius quenched anti-Semitic rampages by Alexandria's Greek community, warning it "to behave gently and kindly toward Jews... and not to dishonor any of their customs in their worship of their God."

The emperor simultaneously counseled Jews "not to aim at more than they previously had." This was not enough to satisfy hard-core bigots. One labeled Claudius "the cast-off son of the Jewess Salome." Another denounced him as a half-Jewish bastard.

Claudius maintained a lasting friendship with Agrippa, Palestine's Jewish king, and allowed relatively unhindered internal self-rule. But he stopped short of permitting further fortification of Jerusalem's defensive walls.

When Judea again came under direct Roman rule following Agrippa's death, Claudius let Jews elect their own choice for high priest and did not tamper with Temple affairs or Temple funds.

A test of Claudius's sympathies occurred following the slaying of Galilean pilgrims by a Samaritan mob. Jews demanded punishment of the murderers, but Rome's corrupt procurator, Cumanus, did nothing. His penchant for accepting bribes made him beholden to the Samaritans. Vigilante justice followed. News of this violence reached Tyre, Syria, seat of the emperor's legate, an official outranking Cumanus.

Along with Jewish and Samaritan representatives, Cumanus and a tribune whose troops assaulted Jews were ordered to Rome to explain their conduct. According to Josephus, Claudius heard all parties, pronounced the Samaritans at fault, banished Cumanus, and sent the tribune back to Jerusalem in chains, to be handed over to the Jews for execution.

Only one sentence in Suetonius's biography seemingly smudges Claudius's record regarding Jews in Rome itself: "Because the Jews at Rome caused continuous disturbances at the instigation of Chrestus, he expelled them from the city." But this incident relates to unrest stemming from nascent Christianity. So we can attribute the emperor's action to a quest for civic tranquility, not anti-Semitism. Claudius deserves no blemish on that account.

NERO, 37–68
Emperor, 54–68

History's Conventional View

It is Nero, not Antonia's Claudius, who strikes the public as a monster. His notoriety for pyromania remains fixed by legend. That he saw opportunities for urban renewal in the embers of burned Rome and initiated a fire relief fund for victims rarely receives notice. Neither does his reluctance to extend Rome's borders to include unwilling new subjects, nor his pronouncement that lawyers charge clients a fixed, reasonable fee.

Instead, his reputation is further sullied by such acts of state and personal whimsy as murdering his stepfather's real son, Britannicus, and later, his own nagging mother. Agrippina died cursing the womb that bore him, after surviving several earlier botched assassination attempts. These varied from being fed poison (she took antidotes), being taken to sea in a leaky, rickety boat (she swam to safety), and being given a bed beneath dislodged heavy ceiling panels (she avoided their collapse).

After finally disposing of his mother by sending assassins to her villa, he murdered his aunt for her money. Also among his victims: his first wife, Octavia, who bored him, and his second, Poppaea Sabina, whom he truly loved. According to Suetonius, he kicked her to death during a quarrel. Before taking a third wife, Statilia, he was obliged to murder her husband, a respected consul.

At the emperor's death, Suetonius wrote: "At last, after nearly fourteen years of Nero's misrule, the earth rid herself of him."

But From a Jewish Perspective

Open warfare eventually broke out in Judea on Nero's watch, but blame really rests with his four on-the-scene governors, as rapacious and insensitive as any in the empire. They were: Felix (52–60), Festus (60–62), Albinus (62–64), and Florus (64–66), who subjected Judea to its worst misrule since the Roman conquest. Historian Tacitus (no friend of the Jews, as we'll see in "Other Voices") writes of Felix: "With all manner of lust and cruelty, he exercised royal functions in the spirit of a slave."

Josephus regarded Felix's replacement, Festus, as a relative improvement, but called the next in line "guilty of every possible misdemeanor." Under him, official actions took the form of "widespread robbery and looting of private property," and in Judea "tyranny reigned everywhere." "Such a man was Albinus, but his successor, Gessius Florus, made him appear an angel by comparison." Florus "boasted of the wrongs he did the nation and, as if sent as a public executioner to punish condemned criminals, indulged in every kind of robbery and violence." When he demanded a huge sum from the Temple treasury, the fires of rebellion were finally ignited.

Meanwhile, back in Rome, Nero's personal record vis-à-vis Jews is mixed. On the minus side, tax extortion mounted in the provinces, including Judea, apace with the emperor's extravagances. And a municipal dispute in Caesaria pitting Jews against Syrians found Nero coming down against the Jews.

On the plus side, one must record instances of the emperor protecting Jewish interests. When tensions rose in Jerusalem because Festus ordered demolition of a newly constructed Temple wall for military reasons, Nero listened to the appeal of the Temple priests and overruled his procurator. And in the wake of the great fire that tore through Rome in 64, Jews represented a likely scapegoat. Perhaps influenced by Poppaea Sabina (the spouse he later kicked to death), Nero passed over the Jews and targeted the "followers of Chrestus" instead.

In 66, news of Judea's rebellion reached Rome. By Josephus's account, Nero stepped in after first showing "lordly disdain." He sought a general "to whom he could entrust the East in its disturbed state, with responsibility for punishing the Jewish upheaval and preventing the spread of the infection to the surrounding nations."

That general was Vespasian.

VESPASIAN, 9–79
Emperor, 69–79

TITUS, 40–81
Emperor, 79–81

History's Conventional View

Of Roman emperors, Vespasian and Titus are better known—or should be—to Jews than the wider public. This pair, father and son, ascended to god rank (both were eventually deified at their capital) on celestial stairs paved with Jewish bones. Already a successful commander in the empire's distant corners, Vespasian moved methodically to quash Judea's uprising. This conquest won him support among Rome's legions and brought him to the throne in 69, the tumultuous year following Nero's death, during which three immediate predecessors met violent ends.

Known for financial rigor (back in his younger days as African proconsul, an angry overassessed crowd pelted him with turnips), Vespasian brought order to Rome's chaotic fiscal climate by increasing taxes and cutting spending. When the marine fire brigade, constantly on the move, applied for a special shoe allowance, he instructed them to march barefoot instead.

Suetonius describes his one serious failing as avarice. He "openly engaged in business dealings which would have disgraced even a private citizen—such as cornering the stocks of certain commodities and then putting them back on the market at inflated prices." In all other respects he was "from first to last moderate and lenient," not the "sort of man to bear a grudge or pay off old scores," an emperor who "never rejoiced in anyone's death and would often weep when convicted criminals were forced to pay the extreme penalty."

His son Titus completed the subjection of Judea after Vespasian left for Rome. He assumed increasing degrees of responsibility as his father aged, succeeding him in 79.

Titus's own brief reign—two years, two months, and twenty days— was marked by a series of natural disasters. The eruption of Mt. Vesuvius destroyed Pompeii and Herculaneum (a boon for archaeologists ever after); a fire raked Rome for three days and nights, and one of the worst outbreaks of plague in antiquity raged through the capital.

Throughout this assortment of disasters, the emperor's conduct, reports Suetonius, "resembled the deep love of a father for his children." He issued comforting edicts and distributed public funds. None of his predecessors "ever displayed such generosity." Titus became "the object of universal love and adoration."

But From a Jewish Perspective

Vespasian and Titus were major enemies of the Jews. Not that we should fault their success in quashing rebellion throughout Judea. That's what capable commanders when ordered are supposed to do. But their brutality in carrying out their assignments and their subsequent severity toward the vanquished do not endear their memory.

Posterity's main source for the conflict is Josephus Flavius, formerly Joseph ben Matthias, Jewish commander of Galilee turned traitor. Surrendering after sterner comrades chose suicide over humiliation, Josephus ingratiated himself with Vespasian and Titus, joining their camp outside Jerusalem, and later their court at Rome. In time, he gained

Roman citizenship, a state pension, and bed and board at the emperor's palace. His image of father and son in *The Jewish War*, written under imperial auspices, should therefore be suspect.

But even Josephus at his sycophantic best could not sugarcoat every stark fact revealing their savagery. Consider his description of the fate befalling starved defenders of Jerusalem who left the city's safety in search of food and fell captive:

> Scourged and subjected before death to every torture, they were finally crucified in view of the wall. Titus, indeed, realized what was happening, for every day, five hundred—sometimes even more—fell into his hands. However, it was not safe to let men captured by force go free, and to guard such a host of prisoners would tie up a great proportion of his troops. But his chief reason for not stopping the slaughter was the hope that the sight of it would perhaps induce the Jews to surrender in order to avoid the same fate.

Eventually there was "no room for the crosses, and no crosses for the bodies."

The fall of Jerusalem followed, with general butchery of both disarmed defenders and women and children. Josephus puts the figure at one million (Tacitus, at six hundred thousand). But Josephus absolves his new patron of blame for torching the Second Temple. "Caesar [Titus] shouted and waved to the combatants to put out the fire; but his shouts were unheard as their ears were deafened with a greater din, and his hand signals went unheeded amidst the distractions of battle and bloodshed."

Set this against an account by the Roman historian Sulpicus Severus, believed to be based on a lost manuscript of Tacitus. He calls the Temple's destruction a premeditated act by Titus designed to break the spirit of Jewish resistance elsewhere in Judea. Not in dispute is Titus's order to turn Jerusalem to rubble, with only three towers left erect as a reminder of the Temple's grandeur.

Following the gutting of both the Temple and the city in 70, Titus marked his triumphal return home with stops at provincial cities, such as Caesaria. Again, his apologist Josephus: "While he remained there, he celebrated his brother's [Domitian's] birthday in the grand style, reserving much of his vengeance on the Jews for this notable occasion. The number of those who perished in combat with wild beasts or in fighting each other or by being burnt alive exceeded 2,500." Then, on to Beirut, where he prepared for his father's birthday "a still more lavish display.... Vast numbers of prisoners perished."

At another stop, a small positive gesture: Titus rejected a proposal by Antioch's Greek-Syrian majority that Jews be expelled from that city. Josephus ascribes this act to his humanitarian instincts, but others as merely a commonsense step to forestall unrest among Jewry elsewhere in Rome's far-flung empire.

On the report card of Titus's father, now emperor, appears one decent mark. Before handing his military command to Titus, Vespasian agreed to a request by the Pharisaic sage, Johanan ben Zahkar, whose concerned students smuggled him out of Jerusalem in a coffin. Ben Zahkar, foreseeing the doom of Judea's capital, sought permission to lead several scholars, unharmed, to the town of Jabneh. There he could "teach his pupils" and all could "observe the mitzvot" and "study the Torah." Vespasian did not intend Jabneh to emerge as a new spiritual center, filling the vacuum left by Jerusalem's fall, but that is what happened.

Although the emperor stationed the Tenth Legion on permanent garrison duty in the Holy Land (normally the presence of Roman legions was restricted to frontier provinces), he perhaps deserves opaque credit for removing auxiliary regiments raised in Caesaria and Syria. Under Nero's governors, their hostility and provocations had led to the fatal rebellion in the year 66.

Nothing in Vespasian's imperial resumé, though, really chips away from the debits he, and later Titus, and still later his younger son Domitian, amassed. Throughout the land of the vanquished, Jewish property became state property. Imperial edicts swept away communal and religious rights. Vespasian's agents tracked down and murdered families descended from the House of David, lest they become the focus of a Davidic revival.

Replacing the contribution each Jew made to the Temple with an annual tax destined for the Roman capital's Temple of Jupiter, Vespasian imposed spiritual anguish as well as financial pain. Unlike most subject peoples, Jews paid both land *and* poll taxes. In the ironically named Temple of Peace, Vespasian "laid up the golden vessels from the Temple of the Jews, for he prided himself on them," writes Josephus. "But their Law and the crimson curtains of the inner sanctuary, he ordered to be deposited in the Palace for safe keeping."

Throughout their reigns, father and son continued issuing coins commemorating the conquest of Judea. The best-known portrays a woeful, weeping Jewess beside the victorious emperor and bears the inscription "Iudaea Capta." Since Roman coins served dual purposes, the second being a medium for propaganda—the message was clear and clearly humiliating.

On a domestic note: Titus never viewed Jews as allies, but his mistress *was* Jewish. While cutting a bloody swath through her homeland, he became infatuated with Princess Berenice, sister of Judea's king. Their affair continued in Rome, but when the possibility of a royal marriage loomed, the capital's social nobility—and likely Titus's father Vespasian—recoiled at the notion of a future Jewish wife. Reluctantly, Titus sent her away.

Today, at the entrance to Rome's Forum, his major handiwork remains etched in stone: The Arch of Titus has survived 1,900 years. Widely reproduced in photos, its relief tableau shows legionnaires hauling off the Temple menorah and other treasures seized from broken Judea.

A contemporary called Titus "the darling of the human race." Talmudic literature labels him "the wicked descendant of the wicked Esau."

We now skip two reigns to reach Emperor Hadrian, for by the second century C.E. there are only three more historically celebrated Roman rulers—Constantine the Great and Julian the Apostate (fourth century) and Justinian the Great (sixth century)—who are described here. Bypassed will be such forgettable personalities as Balbinus, Decius, and Probus, and, admittedly, such better recalled ones as Trajan, Diocletian, and Theodosius. There were over seventy emperors in the West between 31 B.C.E. and 476 C.E., with more in the Byzantine Empire to the east.

HADRIAN, 76–138
Emperor, 117–138

History's Conventional View

Readers even vaguely aware of antiquity's huge cast of characters can often identify Hadrian. He built Hadrian's Wall, which stretches seventy-three miles in northern Britain. Constructed to prevent barbarian attacks, the wall is Rome's greatest feat in military engineering.

Hadrian abandoned his predecessors' policy of expansion, choosing instead to secure the borders of Rome's already extensive conquests. He traveled their length—Britain, Gaul, the Rhine, Spain, Greece, Asia Minor, Syria, and Egypt—becoming the most geographically aware of all its rulers.

He shared common soldiers' rations in the field and climbed Mt. Etna at age fifty. A builder at home as well as abroad, his magnificent mausoleum, later renamed the Castle Sant'Angelo, awes tourists in the Roman capital today. Contemporary chroniclers viewed him as a cultured devotee of Greek civilization with a consummate curiosity to understand his world.

But From a Jewish Perspective

Hadrian's relations with his Jewish subjects began amiably enough. As one of his first official acts, he executed Lusius Quietus, whose arbitrary rule as Judea's governor embittered the population. Moreover, the time-honored Sibylline Oracles had predicted that the man whose name is like the sea (Adriatic) would be good for the Jews. And Hadrian soon promised to rebuild Jerusalem as a Jewish city, clearly fulfilling the prophecy.

But then, for reasons embedded in the realm of conjecture, the emperor reversed direction. Conciliation became confrontation. He proclaimed Jerusalem's future as a pagan metropolis, with a temple to Jupiter as the city's most important religious structure. Jewish hopes were trampled. As an ex-governor of Syria, Hadrian was surely cognizant of Jerusalem's significance to the Jewish world.

Friction grew. He proclaimed a universal ban on circumcision. Although not directed at Jews alone, this decree struck them harder than any other group, for the act of circumcision establishes a male's covenant with God. As in Nero's day, discontent grew, with even grimmer consequences.

The Roman historian Dio Cassius traces unrest, and in 132, open warfare, directly to Hadrian's policies. Initial victories under the near-legendary Shim'on Bar Kochba turned to ashes as Hadrian brought fresh legions from distant corners of the empire to crush Jewish insurrection. Before the storm subsided three years later, 580,000 Jewish rebels were slain, and fifty fortified towns and 985 villages were razed. According to Dio Cassius, Roman forces left the land a bleak wilderness, jackals and wolves howling in the streets. Roman losses, too, soared, so much so that Hadrian's report to the Senate omitted the customary formula, "I and my army are well."

Now came the emperor's full fury. A sacred scroll was symbolically and ceremoniously set ablaze on the Temple Mount. Jewish structures still standing in Jerusalem were demolished and their foundation grounds plowed. Hadrian renamed the city Aelia Capitolina, rebuilt it as a pagan enclave, and forbade Jews entry except once a year to weep at the remains of their holy places. Hadrian installed two statues at the former Temple sanctuary side by side—one of Jupiter, the other of himself. He erased the very name Judea from Roman maps, substituting Syria Palaestina.

By attacking Judaism as well as Jews, he exceeded even the father-son savagery of Vespasian and Titus. Whether his motives were truly anti-Semitic or merely pan-Hellenistic, their effects matched. Obedience to Torah law was deemed defiance of Caesar's law, and systematic persecution followed. Synagogue meetings were banned, communal institutions snuffed out. Some Jews attempted to escape Rome's reach by fleeing to desert caves, there to observe the Commandments in secret. Others, as in the time of Antiochus, yielded to an implacable foreign master, renouncing their heritage.

This was also a time for martyrs. An oft-repeated rabbinic tale went:

> "Why were you killed?"
> "For having circumcised my son."
> "Why were you burned?"
> "For studying the Torah."
> "Why were you crucified?"
> "For having eaten unleavened bread."

In his own and succeeding generations, the Roman and Greek intellectual elite praised Hadrian as the friend of culture and enlightenment, but where Hadrian's name surfaces in the Aggadah, it is accompanied by such language as "the Wicked" and "may his bones rot."

(Pleasing Postscript: Hadrian's handpicked successor, Antonius Pius, revoked Hadrian's punitive edicts, allowing Jews to again follow Torah teachings. He reinstituted the ban on imperial statues in synagogues both in Palestine and the Diaspora. Alone among his subject peoples, Jews were permitted to perform circumcisions once more. Antonius Pius was clearly a friend of the Jews.)

CONSTANTINE THE GREAT, 280?–337
Emperor, 306–337

JULIAN THE APOSTATE, 331–363
Emperor, 361–363

History's Conventional View

We move forward a century to the reign of Flavius Valerius Constantinus, known later as Constantine the Great, founder of Constantinople, one of the world's great cities. Constantine stabilized a tottering empire, reorganized its civil administration, reformed its stagnant military, and reunified East and West. But casual readers of history recall him best for halting the persecution of Christians, a three-centuries-long Roman practice. According to legend, as he prepared to battle a rival for Rome's throne, he saw a cross in the heavens—*in hoc signo vinces* ("by this sign thou shalt conquer"). And conquer he did.

Reversing imperial policy, he encouraged Christianity's growth, built basilicas in leading cities, and issued militant edicts on religion, guided by church fathers. Rival faiths were targeted for extinction. (Christians may rightly regard him as their champion.)

By contrast, they label his nephew—who followed Constantine's son, Constantius, to the throne in 361—Julian the Apostate. The preceding two decades under Constantius, a case of "like father, like son," had prevailed. But "like uncle, like nephew" was not to be. Julian loathed Christianity.

In his twenty tumultuous months as ruler, Julian sought to undo Rome's religious transformation and implement a benign paganism. His efforts, cut short by assassination while campaigning in the East, earned him the hatred of contemporary Christians and an ignominious place in their historical literature.

But From a Jewish Perspective

Jews conversant with this dynasty's deeds and unrealized plans may well see Julian as "the Great One," and Constantine as unworthy of adulation. Constantine issued repressive edicts at Jews, the "impure beings," the members of "an unclean and pernicious sect." These "baleful" people were not allowed to congregate for religious services—gatherings deemed sacrilegious—nor seek to convert others to their faith, nor harass those who joined other religions. Hadrian's ban on Jews residing in Jerusalem, discarded by recent emperors, was reimposed. Only on the ninth day of the Jewish calendar month of Av could they pass through its gates to mourn the Temple's destruction.

Worse, Constantine's assaults only superficially resembled blows struck by past Roman despots. Their motivation had been mainly political—to crush dissident, potentially rebellious sects. His was religious —to obliterate all vestiges of Judaism and to force its adherents to adopt the one true faith, Christianity.

By contrast, Constantine's nephew Julian merits designation as one of the Roman world's foremost Righteous Gentiles. In one sweeping edict he declared the end to persecution at the hands of "the barbarous of spirit and presumptuous of heart," and he permitted Jews to return to their homeland. By decree, he freed them of the long-standing tax imposed under Hadrian and cancelled new taxes prepared by his predecessor to strain Jews even further. Perhaps even more significant, Julian announced his commitment to reconstruct "with great diligence the Temple of the supreme God" and "the holy Jerusalem which you have for many years longed to see rebuilt."

The emperor ordered reluctant Roman authorities on the scene to cooperate in this project, and Jews soon reopened a temporary synagogue near the Temple Mount. Shofars blew throughout Palestine in celebration of Julian's favor. Thousands of Jews in Persia and Babylon packed their belongings and began their trek homeward.

As a confirmed pagan, although an enlightened one, Julian believed paganism superior to Judaism. In his writings, he contended that Jewish law was harsh, and Jewish customs and the nature of Jewish priorities such that, consequently, Jews failed to spawn military leaders, lawyers, musicians, and natural scientists in proportion to their numbers. But, he argued, Jews were indeed the chosen people of their particular deity, one "truly most powerful and most benevolent," who "is worshipped by us, as I well know, under other names."

Julian believed Jews deserved better of the empire that, nearly four centuries earlier, had swallowed them. Unfortunately, his philo-Semitic policy was clearly out of vogue with Rome's now Christianized masses. When Julian embarked on a hazardous campaign against the Persians he was murdered, according to some accounts, by a Christian Arab.

The bright, shining moment for Jews and Judaism had passed.

Repression returned with renewed vigor throughout the Roman world. The next 165 years would see ebbs and flows. Then, with the Age of Justinian, harder times beckoned.

JUSTINIAN THE GREAT, 483–565
Emperor, 527–565

History's Conventional View

Our long leap from the mid–fourth century to Justinian sweeps us past the decline and fall of the Roman Empire in the West (476) to the pinnacle of Byzantine brilliance and power in the East.

Justinian rates "great" status on several grounds, evident in his own time and ratified by succeeding generations. During a near forty-year reign, his army reconquered North Africa from the Vandals, successfully fought Goths and Franks, and even reoccupied fallen Rome and northern Italy for a while. This was no small feat considering a nearly unbroken string of barbarian depredations.

In Constantinople he built Hagia Sophia, Byzantium's most splendid church. To the contemporary Greek historian Procopius, it was "a spectacle of marvellous beauty, overwhelming to those who see it, but to those who know it by hearsay altogether incredible." (Conquering Ottomans would later convert it into a mosque, and secular Turks, still later, would turn it into the city's prime tourist lure.)

Procopius privately explored Justinian's persona, apart from publicly extolling his official deeds: "This emperor, then, was deceitful, devious, false, hypocritical, two-faced, cruel, skilled in dissembling his thought, never moved to tears either by joy or pain, though he could summon them artfully at will when the occasion demanded, a liar always, not only offhand, but in writing."

Justinian's architectural gem is matched by his voluminous paper trail, a legal code identified with much of Europe's twists and turns through history. His Corpus Juris Civilis gathered a hodgepodge of earlier rules and regulations into one cohesive whole. Wrote Procopius, "Finding the laws obscure because they had become far more numerous than they should be, he preserved them by cleansing them of the mass of their verbal trickery, and by controlling their discrepancies with the greatest firmness." Justinian reinterpreted past edicts, added a few nuances of his own, and, if the finished product contained unpleasantries for a bare fraction of Byzantium's multitudes, few cared.

But From a Jewish Perspective

Jews were among those who did care. Justinian's *novellae* ("imperial instructions") forbade Jews to practice religious rites in lands newly reconquered from the Vandals. Synagogues there faced confiscation. Judaism, in effect, was to be eradicated. At least North Africa was quite distant from Constantinople, allowing a merciful breach between edict and enforcement. Closer to home, Justinian's legal web held Jews in its strands more securely.

Judaism retained status in Byzantium as a *religio licita* ("permitted religion"), but Justinian's codification of laws evolved under past emperors omitted some protective of Jews and replaced them with tighter restrictions. The confession of faith recited in synagogues, "Hear, O Israel, the Lord is one," was banned as a denial of the Trinity. Also forbidden was use of the Mishnah in interpreting the Torah. Discourse on oral law would also not be tolerated. And in 533, when bishops saw Torah-reading itself as a challenge to the truth of the Christian faith, Justinian obligingly barred such perceived Hebraic competition.

The emperor raised canon law to rank equal with state law. In the provinces, implementation of anti-Judaic laws emerged as the joint responsibility of civil and religious authorities. Local bishops could report the negligence of provincial governors in carrying out the letter of such laws directly to the emperor himself.

Moreover, Justinian set himself up as arbiter for internal Jewish matters, ruling that only the Septuagint or other Christian-approved versions of the Bible be used in those portions of Byzantium where synagogues employed a Greek translation. He ruled that Passover could no longer be celebrated in the years when it preceded Easter. Heavy penalties for holding seders or serving unleavened bread applied.

In civil affairs, Jews could no longer claim exemption from the financial burden implicit in service on municipal bodies. Lest this be considered a fair tradeoff by wealthier Jews, since such duty normally assured immunity from corporal punishment or exile, Justinian ruled that "Jews must never enjoy the fruits of office, but only its pains and penalties." Bold concepts in Justinian's celebrated code crystallized his policy toward Jews. "They shall enjoy no honors. Their status shall reflect the baseness which in their souls they have elected and desired."

The principle of *servitus Judaeorum* ("servitude of the Jews") was established, and the hitherto uneven pattern of persecution was systemized for a Christian civilization marching towards its Age of Faith.

Justinian—like Constantine—surely earned designation as great in gentile eyes. For Jews, he was just as clearly an enemy.

Other Voices, Other Deeds

Several Romans, noble or at least notable, merit attention as supporting players at this stage of Jewish history—Marc Antony and Cassius, whom Antony termed honorable, among them.

The lean and hungry CASSIUS (?–42 B.C.E.) found his financial appetite insatiable when he materialized in the Jewish homeland following Caesar's assassination. Gathering republican troops in the east for the civil war almost certain to follow, he moved from town to town demanding tribute. "Jews were ordered to contribute seven hundred talents [of silver]," writes Josephus. Herod earned "hearty approval" by quickly meeting his own one-hundred-talent quota, but Cassius abused others for slowness and "poured forth his fury on the unfortunate towns" (i.e., he enslaved their populations). Fortunately, Cassius did not remain long. He left Syria to link up with Brutus, and both met their fate at the Battle of Philippi, in 42 B.C.E.

When MARC ANTONY (83–30 B.C.E.), covictor over Caesar's assassins with young Octavian, emerged as Rome's newest master in the East, he decided Herod, who ingratiated himself via word and bribery, "should now be king of the Jews." Herod flattered his latest patron by redesignating a high-towered fortress dominating the Temple area Antonia in his honor.

But a Judea run by a Jew (albeit so imperfect a one as Herod) was not assured. The Queen of Egypt eyed it greedily. Josephus writes, "Antony, ruined by his passion" for CLEOPATRA (69–30 B.C.E.), "had become the complete slave of his desire, while Cleopatra had gone through her own family till not a single relation was left alive, and, thirsty now for the blood of strangers, was slandering the authorities of Syria and urging Antony to have them executed, thinking that in this way she would easily become mistress of all their possessions."

Herod, aware he figured prominently on her list of enemies, prudently built Masada's fortress as a refuge. Antony was "sober enough" to realize that some of her demands were "utterly immoral." Nonetheless, he handed parts of the Jewish homeland, including the palm groves at Jericho and a number of towns, to the Egyptian Queen. Herod leased back portions from her at an exorbitant 200 talents a year and attempted thereafter to befriend her, if he could.

This train of events should not necessarily taint Cleopatra with an anti-Jewish brush. She was simply greedy. And Antony's behavior is partially excusable, enslaved, as he was, by his lust. In any event, Antony and Cleopatra's defeat by Octavian at the Battle of Actium, in 31 B.C.E., ended the royal couple's reign.

Herod, again showing his dexterity in hopping from patron to patron, pledged his loyalty to Octavian and was given back Gaza, Samaria, and a few other choice pieces of land for his "Jewish" kingdom. He lived prosperously ever after. Some noble Romans may not have been good for Jews, but they were certainly good for Herod.

A few of Rome's intellectual and literary elite left their views on Jews and Judaism to posterity. Here, we briefly take note of better-known cultural achievers.

CICERO (106–43 B.C.E.), the greatest Roman orator ever, advanced his career by forceful advocacy at political trials. Defending a proconsul accused of diverting one hundred pounds of gold bound for Jerusalem's Temple in 59 B.C.E., Cicero dredged up all the anti-Jewish canards then extant. He denounced Judaism as a *barbara superstitio* ("barbarous super-stition"), described the Jewish race as a people born to slavery, and told Roman senators judging the case how obvious Jewish intrusiveness had become at public gatherings. "There surely can be all the less obligation upon us to respect Jewish religious observances when that nation has demonstrated in arms [uprisings] what its feelings are toward Rome."

Rome's most illustrious historian, TACITUS (55?–after 117), set aside objectivity, and occasionally a fact, when writing about Jews. Take their origins: Tacitus mentions several current theories, giving credence to one that they were plague-beset Egyptians driven into the desert by their own countrymen.

A chapter in his *Histories* describes their customs, "which are at once perverse and disgusting," yet "owe their strength to this very badness." He writes that "among themselves they are inflexibly honest and ever ready to show compassion," but regard "the rest of mankind with all the hatred of enemies."

Tacitus did not perceive Jews as the political threat that the empire officials did, but rather as a weakening agent on Roman society and moral values. He wrote, "Things sacred with us, with them have no sanctity, while they allow what with us is forbidden." And he would have preferred Jews live far from Rome's capital and environs.

JUVENAL (50–127), preeminent satirist and a contemporary of Tacitus, shared his concern about Judaism's impact. Juvenal gave vent to his prejudices through poetry rather than prose, ridiculing Romans who found positive virtues in Jewish customs and practices. He regarded synagogues as the haunt of beggars, their congregations hateful of anyone not of themselves. Jews "are trained to despise the laws of the Romans," he wrote, and "adore nothing but clouds and the divinity of heavens." Their abstinence from pork made no sense, they were unwilling to give a drink to a thirsty man if uncircumcised, and their refusal to work on the Sabbath derived from laziness. So the surviving words of Rome's great orator, historian, and satirist share a distaste for Jews.

We close "Other Voices" and this chapter with two celebrated Romans, one a prominent autocrat, the other a Stoic philosopher who also happened to be emperor.

PONTIUS PILATE (?–after 36) arrived in Judea as procurator in the year 26 and promptly infuriated Jerusalemites by his heavy-handedness. He allowed troops preparing for their winter encampment to enter the city with raised standards bearing the emperor's image. Not a man to be deterred by religious sensibilities, or ethics for that matter, he appropriated Temple funds for public works projects, again arousing the Jews.

When crowds gathered he ordered his legion to attack the protesters. Many died. Agrippa I, the puppet Jewish king installed by the emperor, complained to Rome of the procurator's "inflexible, merciless, and obstinate manner." And Philo of Alexandria, who had met Pilate, said he was consumed with "corruption, violence, and robbery," responsible for "oppression, illegal executions, and never-ending most grievous cruelty."

It is difficult to visualize Pilate, as the evangelists paint him in the Gospels, as a fair-minded, conscious-stricken upholder of justice reluctantly yielding to a surly Jewish mob following Jesus' trial. Pilate eventually overreached even his own capricious limits, directing soldiers to attack Samaritans gathered at a religious ceremony. Syria's governor, his immediate superior, removed him from office. The procurator was ordered to report to Rome and account for his conduct. Pilate never returned to Judea.

Our final figure, MARCUS AURELIUS (121–180), receives note here not because his reign as emperor was more auspicious for Jews than many others omitted, but because he rises above them in the general esteem accorded his character down through the ages. His surviving *Meditations* gave him the reputation of a philosopher-king, a gentle, moral, and erudite man. But what of his understanding of Jews? "Stinking and tumultuous!" he declared to his companions during his passage among them in Judea. He expressed preference for the company of the Teutonic barbarians he fought in the north.

In the ancient world, and even more so in the Dark and Middle Ages to follow, heroes and villains frequently change character when seen from a Jewish perspective.

2

Through the Dark and Feudal Ages

Traditional Western chronology progresses from Rome's decline and fall to the Dark Ages and Middle Ages, followed by the Renaissance, which brings Europe to a cultural zenith and a god-directed destiny to rule the world. However, such distinctive progressions had a different meaning to Jews as they struggled through the ages.

Late in the sixth century, Pope Gregory the Great set the tone for Europe's interfaith relations. Not himself unreasonable—given the context of his time—Gregory would be followed by ecclesiastical and secular princes who used harsh strictures against Jews to justify cruelty against these helpless outcasts.

In the year 590, when Gregory became pope, nineteen-year-old Muhammad was driving camels across the desert of distant Arabia, and the early impressions Muhammad formed from his association with Jewish tribes on the peninsula would plant the seed for Jewish fortune and misfortune in Arab lands for centuries to come.

Jews would find Charlemagne (Charles the Great) the last tower of Christendom tolerant of their well-being. The plight of Jews worsened even as gentile Europe emerged from its dour, dismal Dark Ages and into a world portrayed in literature as filled with fairy tale castles, gorgeous tapestries, chivalrous knights and fair maidens. Recognizable royal chess pieces emerge against this backdrop: William the Conqueror, Henry II, Richard the Lion-Hearted, King John, the three Edwards, France's

Philip Augustus and Saint Louis, and Germany's Frederick Barbarossa. Then, fifteenth-century Florence, Venice, and Rome gave birth to the Renaissance, spawning Donatello, Botticelli, DaVinci, Michelangelo, and Raphael—but also Cesare Borgia and Machiavelli. And from Portugal and Spain burst forth an Age of Discovery fostered by Henry the Navigator, Ferdinand and Isabella, Christopher Columbus, and a pride of conquistadors. All made their impact on world history. But were they good for the Jews?

GREGORY I (the Great), 540–604
Pope, 590–604

History's Conventional View

In addition to his designation as Gregory I, the Great, Gregory earned claim to such titles as *Pater Europae* ("Father of Europe") and *Consul Dei* ("Counsel of God"). When he ascended St. Peter's throne at age fifty, Rome's western empire lay in ruins. Byzantium's rulers would permit no challenge to Constantinople's jurisdiction in the east, so Gregory wisely directed his ambitions westward. Barbarian tribes north of the Alps, extending to Atlantic shores, became the prize. He even sent missionaries cross-channel to savage England, bringing that distant isle into his fold.

Gregory promoted papal influence, then elevated that influence to supremacy in church affairs. Fueled by energy and intellect, he infused the medieval church with a mixture of idealism and realism. His reform of the mass generated the Gregorian chant.

Born into Rome's aristocracy, command came easily to Gregory. A master of business administration, he centralized papal affairs and warred on corruption. He set right elements of the Roman Church he described as a "battered ship whose rotten planks are groaning in the tempest."

He saw himself as chief shepherd of men's souls, and what he did and how he did it left a long, documented record. Some 854 of his letters survive in an official register. And his *Book of Pastoral Rules* would become a guide for bishops throughout the Middle Ages:

> The conduct of a prelate ought so far to transcend the conduct of the people as the life of the shepherd is wont to exalt him above the flock...in thought he should be pure, in action chief; discreet in keeping silence, profitable in speech; a near neighbor to every one in

sympathy, exalted above all in contemplation; a familiar friend of good livers through humility.

But what did Gregory I mean to the Jews?

But From a Jewish Perspective

Thanks to that prolific written record, Gregory's position on Judaism is well-documented. He regarded it a *superstitio*, the essence of Jewish "depravity." He described Jewish understanding of Scripture as "perverse," their arguments against Christianity nonsensical. He saw Judaism as a contagion, and strictly forbade missionary activity on its part. He found it "unwholesome and accursed for Christians to be in servitude to Jews" by working under them. He barred Christians from consulting Jewish physicians and clergy from employing Jewish clerks. He accepted the letter and mean spirit of Justinian's laws as precedent:

> Jews must not hold public office. Jews must not build new synagogues. Jews must not make bequests. Jews must not spread their spiritual contamination through marriage to non-Jews. Judaism's adherents must be rescued from their false doctrines and embrace the Christ.

To those policies, Gregory the Great applied his strength, power of office, intellect, and considerable will.

But consider him in the context of his time. He could have encouraged Jew-hating zealots to attack the Jewish population. In a letter to the bishops of Arles and Marseilles, he provided rules for conversion and denounced forced baptism. "I appeal to your fraternity to preach frequently to these persons," he wrote, "and appeal to them in such a manner that the kindness of the teacher more than anything else will make them desire to change their former mode of life." To Bishop of Terracina went instructions to use "gentleness...kindness...admonition ...exhortation....It is more desirable that they should assemble with kindly feelings to hear from you the word of God than that they should tremble at the immoderate exercise of your severity."

Gregory's approach, where he exercised direct jurisdiction, included such inducements as reduction of rent and labor service, free baptismal robes for those who couldn't afford them, and, on infrequent occasions, even pensions. More importantly for Jews who intended to remain Jews, he ordered imperiously: "We will not have the Hebrews oppressed and afflicted unreasonably. According to the liberty of action justly granted them by Roman law, let them manage their own affairs as they think best and let no man hinder them."

Throughout Western Christendom Gregory's words were law.

In 591, when the Jews of Terracina, in central Italy, complained that Bishop Peter had seized their synagogue, ejecting them because their singing had been audible at a nearby church, Gregory ordered a synagogue elsewhere be given to them for services.

In 598, when Bishop Victor of Palermo broke into a synagogue and consecrated it as a church, doctrine prevented Gregory from deconsecrating it. But he reprimanded Victor and ordered him to pay full value to the Jews and also to restore their books and ornaments.

On Easter Sunday in 599, when a riotous gang smashed into a synagogue in Caralis, a port city on Sardinia's Gulf of Cagliari, and placed a cross, Virgin Mary's portrait, and a baptismal robe there, Gregory ordered Archbishop Januarus to remove the items immediately.

In yet another case, when a converted Jew of Cagliari in Sardinia entered his former synagogue and installed a crucifix and pictures of Jesus and Mary, Gregory directed the Bishop of Sardinia to remove them. "Just as the law forbids the Jews the building of new synagogues," he scolded, "it also guarantees them preservation of the old ones." A circular letter warned all bishops: "Just as it is not befitting to permit Jews in their communities to go beyond the boundaries of what is permissible by law, so also the rights they already have should not be diminished."

Throughout the Middle Ages, all protective papal bulls relating to Jews would begin with Gregory's introductory phrase: "Sicut Judaeis non debeat."

Gregory the Great was a formidable foe of Judaism, but he did not lack scruples.

MUHAMMAD, 571–632

History's Conventional View

Left fatherless under an uncle's protection, Muhammad rose from shepherd boy to trainee camel driver to caravan merchant in the service of a rich widow. At twenty-five, he married the widow he worked for. She was fifteen years his senior. He had freed himself from day-to-day drudgery and could now afford extended periods of time for leisurely meditation in Arabia's rocky hillsides. What he contemplated was a viable, unifying monotheistic faith to replace the polyglot of idols accepted as deities by desert tribes. Once the first revelation came via Archangel Gabriel, Muhammad, now aged forty, offered an increasing flow of comments and directives which his followers would later commit to writing in what became known as the Koran.

Unfortunately, Muhammad's hometown of Mecca was also home to a thriving tourist traffic tied to that ancient idolatry. So vested interests there made him a Prophet without honor and a candidate for assassination in his own land. Hence the flight known as the Hegira to Medina in 622. Here, Muhammad's organizational skill came into play, his preachings multiplied adherents, and his successful tribal wars won still more followers.

By 630, Muhammad was back in Mecca, this time as a conqueror. He cleansed the Ka'aba, its holy shrine, of false gods, thereby bringing reluctant fellow Arabs to Allah's side. Soon he was master of all Arabia. At his death in 632, Islam, which many Westerners came to call Mohammedanism, was ready to burst out of north Arabia (the Hejaz).

Muhammad's world impact would be phenomenal and lasting, and Mohammedanism would rival both Judaism and Christianity.

But From a Jewish Perspective

Muhammad altered Jewish history, first between the Red Sea and the Persian Gulf, then on the broader landscape of North Africa and southern Europe. Initially promising, relations between the Prophet and the People of the Book worsened with deadly consequences. Leaders of the three Jewish clans at Medina, clients or allies of neighboring Arab tribes, misread Muhammad's mind-set, and, self-destructively for themselves, the strength of his movement.

Muhammad never said some of his best friends were Jews. But when he fled Mecca, a town with few Jews, and arrived at Medina, whose 8,000 to 10,000 Jews perhaps made up the majority of its population, he did reach out to them, after his own fashion. His newborn monotheistic faith acknowledged their forebearers as the first people to receive divine revelation. He consulted their scholars and engaged in dialogue with them. He accepted major Jewish practices: prayer said in the direction of

Jerusalem, Saturday set aside as a day of rest, an annual fast day, Ashura, to correspond with Yom Kippur.

Perhaps indulgent Jewish leaders—not disinclined to seventh-century missionary work—saw this charismatic visionary as leading Arabia's idol worshipers en masse to Judaism. If so, they miscalculated. Muhammad did not see his nascent movement as an adjunct of Judaism. He demanded recognition of himself as a lineal descendant of Moses and all the prophets down to Jesus. He considered himself the last and greatest among them.

Learned Jews scoffed at such pretensions. They pointed to glaring errors in his narration of biblical events and ridiculed him before his admirers. In turn, Muhammad accused Jews of corrupting Holy Scripture. Muhammad substituted Mecca for Jerusalem as the place where prayers were to be directed. Friday instead of Saturday became the day for religious observance. And he replaced one day of total fasting with the month-long semifast of Ramadan. These were profound doctrinal changes from the older religion from which he now distanced Islam—but he warred on Jews as well as Judaism.

Beginning in 624, four years of relentless hostility would destroy all the stubborn Jews in his midst who denied him. Qaynuqa's craftsmen and artisans, members of the first and smallest of Medina's Jewish tribes to feel his wrath, had supposedly broken an agreement with the Prophet. They were given three days to gather their belongings, collect their debts, and leave the town of Medina.

The wealthier Nadir, the second tribe, received word to leave Medina within ten days, under threat of death, for plotting against the Prophet. Their elders had refused demands by Muhammad's lieutenant, Abu Bakr, for contributions or loans. "We are not in need of Allah whereas He seems in need of us," they answered. The original ultimatum let them keep their palm groves and return for the date harvest. They unwisely hesitated—and subsequently saw those groves burned when they eventually headed off into exile carrying their movable goods in a six-hundred-camel caravan.

The severest fate fell upon the Qurayza, accused of treacherously negotiating with the Prophet's Meccan foes. A visit from the Angel Gabriel convinced Muhammad not to lay down arms until this tribe was annihilated.

Medieval Arab historian Ibn Hisham recounts what happened next: "The Apostle of Allah—may Allah bless him and grant him peace—had commanded that every male who had attained puberty should be slain.... When they had surrendered, the Apostle of Allah—may Allah bless him and grant him peace—had them imprisoned.... Then the Apostle went to the Market of Medina... and had trenches dug. After that, he sent for them and had them decapitated into those trenches as they were brought out in groups.... These proceedings continued until the Apostle of Allah—may Allah bless him and grant him peace—had finished them off."

The largest Jewish tribe in Arabia lived ninety miles beyond Medina. At their oasis, protected by a string of mountain fortresses, the prosperous Khaybars produced grapes, dates, vegetables, and grains, and also manufactured fine silk clothing and weapons. Through assassination of key leaders and direct assault on isolated strongholds, the Prophet's men swept away all resistance by 628.

As Muhammad assessed the future, practical economics softened his extreme responses. The Khaybars' agricultural skills had benefited the Hejaz's infidels and believers alike. Leaving their oasis desolate or mismanaged would ill-serve Allah's followers. The Khaybars were allowed to remain providing they paid half of their farm output to the conquerors. Omar, a successor of Muhammad, would later produce what many regard as a spurious will attributed to the Prophet declaring there must not be *two* religions in the Hejaz. Omar used it to cleanse the Arab heartland of Jews and replaced the indigenous Khaybars with knowledgeable slaves.

Elsewhere in Islam's secure domains, Jews would find life under Caliphs infinitely more tolerable than under Christendom's kings. As long as the People of the Book paid their taxes—at exorbitant rates—they could worship freely and govern their own affairs. This protected status offered opportunities unmatched in bigotry-driven medieval Europe.

Would Muhammad himself have approved this evolution? The moderating effects of stability and success were beyond the ken of a Prophet engaged in a struggle to breathe life into his still-fragile infant faith.

CHARLEMAGNE, 742–814
King of the Franks, 768–814
Emperor of the West, 800–814

History's Conventional View

Charlemagne, king of the Franks and emperor of the West, emerges from the ninth century in Europe's Dark Age, as the most powerful figure of his time. The king of the Franks restored Rome's fallen empire in the West, an unmatched feat. His energy, skill, and capacity to command lifted the Carolingian dynasty to lofty heights. Successors bearing such designations as Louis the Pious, Louis the Stammerer, Louis the Child, Charles the Bald, Charles the Fat, and Charles the Simple could not be compared to Charlemagne.

Charlemagne's grandfather, Charles Martel, had checked the advance of Muhammad's followers at Tours in central France. The twenty-six-year-old future emperor would inherit from his father a stable throne. Modern France and Germany did not exist, but he came to rule large portions of those future states. Brittany, Gascony, Acquitaine, Provence, Burgundy, Lombardy, Bavaria, and Saxony were under his direct rule. Bohemia, Moravia, and Croatia fell under his sway as satellites.

Charlemagne recognized Saxon, Slav, and Avar submissions only after they accepted conversion to Christianity. In Rome, on Christmas Day in 800, he added the title of emperor, as Pope Leo III placed a golden crown on his head. "Defender of the Faith," "Protector of the Papacy," "God's Regent on Earth," such was his place in the making of Europe.

In our own day, though, Charlemagne's fame derives not only from his statecraft but from his patronage of learning. Aachen, his capital, became a magnet for architects, musicians, astronomers, and the rest of Europe's intellectuals and artists.

But From a Jewish Perspective

Gregory the Great would have applauded Charlemagne's devotion and readiness to advance Christianity at sword-point. But Charlemagne's Jewish policy, blind to canon law, would have appalled that unbending church father. Under Carolingian kings, Jews quietly prospered, and tenets of Gregory's inflexible faith demanded that they not. Pope Stephen IV wrote the archbishop of Narbonne a lengthy letter outlining papal frustration:

> Overcome by grief and woefully alarmed, we have received word from you that the Jewish people, who have always been rebellious toward God and hostile to our customs, live on Christian soil in full equality with Christians, calling freehold fiefs in cities and suburbs their own, and that this is done on the basis of the privileges formally granted to them by Frankish kings. Christians till Jewish vineyards and fields.

Christian men and women live under one roof with these traitors day and night, taint their souls by words of blasphemy. These unfortunates must daily and hourly humble themselves before these dogs, serving them in all their whims.... Justice alone demands that the promises given these traitors be declared null and void, so that the death of the crucified Savior shall at last be avenged.

Stephen did not dare confront Charlemagne directly. This pope and his successors in Rome knew the safety of papal property from barbarian sacking depended on the Frankish king's goodwill, so they were compelled to bide time until he passed from the scene and his son Louis the Pious, also well-disposed to Jews, moved center stage.

In 759, Jews of Narbonne in Southern France had supported Charlemagne's father Pepin during his campaign to drive out the city's Moslem rulers. The grateful Pepin granted them a portion of the city and continuation of traditional autonomy. Charlemagne endorsed this policy in his own reign, adding nuances of his own beneficial to Jews throughout his realm. Gregory the Great would have been aghast at witnessing Jews mingling freely at the Frankish Court with scholars and intellectuals, all ignoring canon law.

There were restrictions for Jews. Christians might work for Jews, but not on Sunday; this was a punishable offense. Nor could Jewish creditors demand or accept church utensils or religious objects as collateral. Disputes between Jews could be resolved in their own courts, but when Christians and Jews appeared together in general courts, a special oath was devised for Jews to clear themselves of accusations. "May God not help me," it read, "the God who gave the Torah to Moses at Mount Sinai; may the leprosy of Naaman strike me; may the earth swallow me, as it swallowed Dathan and Abiram, if I did any wrong to you in this instance."

For Charlemagne, Jews had much to offer. Greater freedom gave them greater opportunities, greater prosperity, and, consequently, greater taxation, a burden spared the indigent. Jews also provided an invaluable channel to the fabulous East. Ties to brethren in the Islamic world facilitated contact and trade—spices, fine fabrics, and gems. The dazzling Baghdad caliphate of Harun-al-Rashid (of *Arabian Nights* fame) had much to offer.

In 797, Charlemagne sent agents on a long, difficult journey to Harun-al-Rashid's Court. Five years later, one lone survivor returned—Isaac the

Jew, guide and interpreter, bringing luxurious gifts, plus the most fascinating zoological curiosity to arrive in northern Europe. Abul Abbas, swaying his elephantine trunk and long ivory tusks, amazed all.

Sturdy as the pachyderm looked, he could not survive Europe's cold. Nor could Charlemagne's Jewish policy survive the Church's hostility once the emperor died in 814.

For the two centuries following Charlemagne's demise, no well-known historical figures emerged in Western Europe. So we now move forward to the year 1066, cross the English Channel for the first time, and look at some of the best-recalled and most luminous rulers of Britain.

WILLIAM I (The Conqueror), 1027–1087
King, 1066–1087

WILLIAM RUFUS (his son), 1056–1100
King, 1087–1100

History's Conventional View

English history took a new turn in 1066, the year William the Conqueror, at the head of a Norman host, sailed from France, invaded the island kingdom, and overcame the Anglo-Saxons led by their last king, Harold.

William, son of Robert, Duke of Normandy, also known as Robert the Devil, was ambitious, shrewd, resourceful, and very lucky. The Battle of Hastings, perhaps the most decisive ever fought on English soil, might have ended in a Saxon victory if Harold's tough foot soldiers hadn't fallen for a ruse and left their hilltop defenses to pursue William's "fleeing" cavalry.

Once ruler, William brought along the Norman feudal structure and a Norman nobility to populate its upper ranks. William's Domesday Book, a detailed inquiry into the wealth of England, set forth his new kingdom's tax base. Philosopher David Hume called this part of the Conqueror's legacy "the most valuable piece of antiquity possessed by any nation." William clearly springs from history's pages as a Great Man, but his life was cut short at fifty, when he was thrown by his horse.

By contrast, William Rufus, who became king of England though not Normandy, which was reserved for his brother, has been described by historians as a man of "insatiable greed," "royal avarice," and "unnatural vices." Add shortsightedness as well, blamed for a baron's revolt in 1089.

He quashed it by expansive promises of reform, just rule, and lower taxes, none of which he intended to keep. William Rufus was slain while hunting in New Forest by a presumably errant arrow.

Not a major player in the scheme of global chronology, he is a man nonetheless deserving of brief mention here, along with his father. They were the first English monarchs under whom the sceptered isle saw the arrival of Jews.

But From a Jewish Perspective

Before William the Conqueror crossed the Channel, record of a Jewish presence in England is open to question. But with the conquest came a verifiable handful from Rouen to London, and the next two centuries, ending in 1290, saw a stream of Hebrews journeying from the continent to settle in England. Their number on the island would reach approximately sixteen thousand.

One can only guess at William's motives, if any, in allowing these pariahs of European society to infiltrate his domain. Their effect on monetary affairs and crown finances during his own lifetime appear negligible, and the Church showed open hostility. But the tough, nail-hard Conqueror was risky prey for predatory clerics. They waited for a weaker successor.

Son William Rufus was a safer target when rumors tied him to sympathy for Jews. The learned Eadmer, a Christ Church monk, accused William Rufus of accepting money from the relatives of recent apostates to force these former Jews to return to their "accursed faith."

Another, more powerful foe of the Conqueror's son was Anselm, archbishop of Canterbury, later canonized. Anselm was involved in missionary work aimed at converting Jews. The archbishop's animosity toward the king stemmed from William Rufus's perceived tolerance of them.

RICHARD THE LION-HEARTED, 1157–1189
King, 1189–1199

History's Conventional View

King of England by Grace of God and by a throw of genetic dice that left him King Henry II's eldest surviving son, Richard the Lion-Hearted simply lacked any inclination to govern. Zest for the hunt was matched by a zealous compulsion to pursue Muhammad's followers. Consequently, England's sovereign spent little time in his homeland, and even less managing its domestic affairs. During his Crusade against the infidels, he would seize Cyprus, lay siege to Saracen strongholds along the Levantine coastline, capture Tyre and Jaffa, and then languish two years in a castle prison after alienating the very Christian princes through whose territory he needed safe conduct for the long journey home.

Characteristically, Richard's domicile in England following his release was brief. He recrossed the Channel to fight on French territory and eventually fell during the siege of Châlus, a castle in France. Dying, he chivalrously—if futilely—pardoned the archer who shot him.

But From a Jewish Perspective

For Richard's coronation, on September 3, 1189, the Jewish establishment arrived to pay its respects and proffer expensive gifts. Wrote chronicler William of Newbury: They "feared that the good fortune they had under the former king might be less favorable to them under the new ... and hoped to find favor equal to the multitude of their gifts."

But they were rebuffed by an edict barring their presence. Some were manhandled by royal doorkeepers. Insults gave way to fists, then sticks and stones, and finally more lethal instruments. Thirty Jews died.

Richard himself bears no direct blame for instigating the riot, but surely some censure for remaining uninformed or indifferent to the bloodshed beyond the banquet hall's front door.

By the time he and fellow celebrants had consumed two thousand chickens, the mayhem was done. Once informed, he acted, siding with prey rather than predator. Again, William of Newbury: "The new king, being of a great and fierce spirit, was indignant and grieved that such things should have occurred at the ceremony of his coronation. He was angry and yet perplexed to know what was to be done in the matter."

The likelihood that riots would spread put Jewish lives and property at risk far beyond London. Only three Christian perpetrators were hanged, and these for crimes—arson and robbery—directed at fellow Christians.

Richard issued stern orders in letters sent to every shire in his realm commanding that Jews be left in peace. Jews forcibly converted during the upheaval were allowed to return to their own faith. There were no more riots while Richard remained in England.

He left on a Crusade three months after his coronation, not to return, except sporadically, for many years. And while the king was away, his anti-Semitic vassals could freely victimize their helpless prey.

According to William, the most memorable incident—the mass suicide of York's Jewish community inside their besieged refuge—occurred while "the king had established himself across the sea." These Jews, apprehensive as riots spread, had gathered in the local castle. It was stormed by a mob.

Richard's welcome return resulted, in no small part, from the enforced generosity of his realm's Jews. Leopold, duke of Austria, had taken Richard prisoner after his shipwreck on the Adriatic coast, then sold him to the Holy Roman emperor, Henry VI. The 5,000 marks assessed Jews for the king's ransom came to three times the rate paid by their sover ign's Christian burghers.

The royal merchandise might have been worth the heavy price had Richard decided to remain in England after 1194. But only one year of cumulative time in his ten-year reign actually saw Richard on English soil. His protracted truancy gave Jews a chance to preview the caprice and avarice of his younger brother John, already on-site, soon to be their de jure lord and master.

JOHN, 1167–1216
King of England, 1199–1216

History's Conventional View

First, anyone familiar with Robin Hood and his Merry Men knows that John, still prince, was allied with the villainous Sheriff of Nottingham. Second, even those who place no stock in the Robin Hood tale recognize John as the disreputable party in the pastoral tableau at Runnymede. Without a ruler of his ilk, the English barons—hardly a democratizing lot—would not have sought written assurances of his future conduct via the Magna Carta.

His sibling rivalry with Richard resulted in his brother languishing in Henry VI's custody longer than rules of chivalry demanded. John did not welcome him home then or later on.

At age thirty-two, the crown was his. What he did with it led to quarrels with the pope, causing his excommunication, and France's Philip Augustus (more about him later) to say nothing—and nothing need be said here—about the confrontation at Runnymede in 1215, where the Magna Carta entered history.

John was cruel, nasty, selfish, and tyrannical. He sired a son, Henry III, whose role in English-Jewish history is more notable than in English history.

But From a Jewish Perspective

Jewish life under John began uneventfully enough. After succeeding Richard in 1199, he appointed "Jacob, Jew of London" the "presbyter [of] all the Jews of the whole of England"—theoretically his expert on Jewish affairs, but, more realistically, his tax agent.

John issued a confirmation of the charter of the Jews two years later. Since Jews fell outside the feudal framework, this charter guaranteed they would be allowed to live in freedom, which was not an inherent right. Successive English rulers were free to confirm or repudiate their predecessor's policies, but since the quid for the quo of royal protection was a steady stream of funds for the king's treasury, fiscal logic argued for confirmation. The document declares:

> John, by the grace of God, know that we have granted all the Jews of England and Normandy to have freely and honourably residence in our land, and to hold all that from us which they held from King Henry, our father's grandfather, and all that they reasonably hold in land and fees and mortgages and goods, and that they shall have all their liberties and customs just as they had them in the time of the aforesaid King Henry, our father's grandfather, better and more quietly and more honourably.

As John's dependents, the Jews were also at his mercy, and John could be merciless when his purse moved him. In 1210, he locked up wealthier Jews at Bristol Castle and demanded a 66,000 mark ransom to free them. One tale spread by a monk was that the teeth of one of the richest Jewish detainees were pulled out, one by one, under John's order, pending payment to the Crown of 10,000 marks. According to this story, the man refused to make payment until the seventh extraction.

The fact that John was not a bit shy about taking assets wherever he found them led his disgruntled barons to insert a provision in the Magna Carta:

If anyone who has borrowed from the Jews any amount, large or small, dies before the debt is repaid, it shall not carry interest as long as the heir is under age, of whomsoever he holds; and if that debt falls into our hands [i.e., the king's hands, following the Jewish creditor's own demise], we will take nothing except the principal sum specified in the bond.

Under John's son Henry III, crown finances and Jewish money remained fixed in their predator-prey embrace. As a devoted son of the Church, Henry largely rebuilt Westminster Abbey, adorning it with costly gifts to the shrine of Edward the Confessor, his patron saint. And Aaron of York, who prayed elsewhere, was expected to contribute gold generously to that enterprise, and also buy a chalice decorated with precious stones for the abbey. Moreover, as construction work on his more secular Tower of London proceeded, Henry diverted a 100-mark debt owed to Aaron for that purpose.

Royal treasury records indicate extensive fund-raising among the Jews, irrespective of any medieval business cycle fluctuations: 1226—4,000 marks; 1229—8,000 marks; 1230—6,000 marks; 1233—10,000 marks. In 1239, an empty treasury was revived by forcing Jews to surrender one-third of their assets. Ten years after that, a crown decree called upon Jews to treat with their king via delegates "as well concerning his as their own advantage." In effect, the decree said, ask not what your king can do for you, but what you can do for your king.

Some 106 representatives from twenty-one "Jewries" throughout the realm were ordered to constitute themselves bailiffs and collect a tallage of 20,000 marks from coreligionists while being held personally responsible for prompt payment. A decree in 1253 declared, "The king orders that no Jew should remain in England unless he does some service to the king and that, as soon as possible after birth, whether male or female, every Jew should serve us in some way."

Other provisions pleasing to the Church showed the heavy royal hand stifling Jewish life: "...And that there be no synagogue of the Jews in England save in those places in which such synagogues were in the time of King John, the king's father...and that every Jew wear his badge conspicuously on his breast."

Jews were being prepared for the mortal blow. It would come forty years later, under Henry's own son, Edward I. But first we recross the Channel to French soil. Tarrying further in England as the 1200s shut down would do violence to chronology and leave two significant French sovereigns adrift beyond their own centuries.

PHILIP AUGUSTUS, 1163–1223
King of France, 1180–1223

History's Conventional View

Set against the competition, Philip Augustus proved a consistent thorn in the side of three generations of English Plantagenets, going back to Henry II. He established France as a leading European state, consolidated royal power, reformed finance, administration, and justice, chartered the University of Paris, encouraged trade, and brought his surly feudal lords to heel. He waged profitable wars, acquiring Normandy in one of his more notable conquests.

Philip Augustus, with a cross on his tunic, embarked on the Third Crusade in 1190 along with Richard the Lion-Hearted and Frederick Barbarossa. But Philip Augustus quarreled with Richard, left for home, conspired with John, then prince, behind Richard's back, and in 1202 eventually warred with John, now king. Later, he defeated a coalition of nobles formed against him.

But From a Jewish Perspective

Philip was an implacable enemy of his own Jews. As a child, he heard—and believed—that Jews were guilty of all manner of crimes, including the murder of Christians during Holy Week and the draining of Christian blood to prepare Passover fare. He had learned more than a score of Jews in the town of Blois had been burned in 1171 and no doubt thought well of it. Crowned at age seventeen, he was convinced Jews owned half of Paris and that priests regularly pawned gold and silver church utensils with these gross, pitiless moneylenders.

Within a year, he struck. One Saturday in March 1181, while Jews in his royal domain—Paris and Orleans—prayed, his soldiers began a sweeping roundup. Release followed payment of 15,000 silver marks. An admiring contemporary biographer, only half accurately, wrote: "He stripped the Jews as the Jews at one time stripped the Egyptians during their Exodus." Next, in a move that delighted most Frenchmen and contributed to chroniclers' assessment of his generosity, he released

Christians from debts to Jewish creditors provided they paid a portion of that debt to the royal treasury.

In 1182 he ordered all Jews expelled from provinces under direct royal jurisdiction. Their crime: deicide. They could take their personal belongings, but title to their homes, farms, fields, barns, vineyards, wine presses, and granaries now fell to a new owner—himself. He gave their synagogues to the Church for its use.

Philip Augustus's absolute power did not extend to adjacent provinces where independent-minded lords ruled, so there the refugees settled. But sanctuary was illusory. Following a Jew's slaying by a Christian in the village of Brée sur Seine, Duchy of Champagne, Countess Blanche felt justice would be served by handing the killer over to the Jewish community. He was hanged at Purim.

Word got back to Philip Augustus that the accused was given a crown of thorns before execution, mocking Jesus. Infuriated, the king ordered troops to cross his vassal's land on a punitive expedition. Confronted and trapped, the village's Jewish community received an ultimatum—convert or die. They chose death, and approximately one hundred were burned alive. Only children under thirteen were spared.

In 1198, Philip Augustus brought the Jewish exiles back to his royal provinces. Their profitable ventures had once sustained his treasury, and without them tax revenues plummeted. So he made a deal with those economically more savvy counts who had welcomed his expelled Jews. The vassals would now send the "king's Jews" back to the royal provinces. In return, the king promised not to touch the "counts' Jews."

Back in Paris, the repatriates were ridiculed. Long before England's rulers complied with a ruling by the Church's Lateran Council that Jews wear distinctive badges, Philip Augustus did. A wheel-shaped "Jew Badge" soon appeared on their outer garments.

Philip Augustus rightly earned his designation from Jews—"the Wicked King."

LOUIS IX (St. Louis), 1214–1270
King of France, 1226–1270

History's Conventional View

Considered the ideal Christian prince even in his lifetime, Louis received canonization shortly after it ended. Louis had taken the Crusader's vow in

1244, and a companion knight, John de Joinville, wrote, "From the beginning of his reign to the end of his life no layman of our time spent his whole life in so saintly a manner.... St. Louis loved God with his whole heart and it was on Him that he modelled his actions...the king was very compassionate to the poor and suffering."

De Joinville had accompanied Louis on the Sixth Crusade to the Holy Land, a pious undertaking but military disaster during which the king fell captive. Louis returned home after four years in Syria, but eventually planned a new crusade. He died in Tunis, as it was getting under way.

The *New Catholic Encyclopedia* says of him: "Despite the personal example Louis set by his devotion to the crusades, it is arguable that a greater claim to respect was his interpretation of his responsibilities as king, in the light of his faith. After the violence of the previous two reigns, Louis brought peace and promised justice."

But From a Jewish Perspective

The spiritual excellence and good works that inspired Louis's sainthood were evident to medieval Catholic minds, but not to the Jews. He despised Jews and his ill will continued without respite during his forty-four years as king. The suffering they endured under other monarchs in the feudal world was often fueled by dry, rational financial avarice, and Louis persecuted with zest and religious passion. In his France, there existed the usual popular storm against Jewish money-lending, and at one point he canceled one-third of his subjects' indebtedness to Jewish creditors. But his motives transcended such petty mortal concerns as economics.

As his Jew Badge of choice, Louis preferred red felt or yellow cloth worn on the upper garment, front and back, "so that those thus branded may be recognized from all sides." On the question of Christian-Judaic dialogue, he told his confidante de Joinville that only learned clerks should engage in such discourse with Jews. "A layman, as soon as he hears the Christian faith maligned, should defend it only by the sword, with a good thrust in the belly, as far as the sword will go."

In Louis's eyes, the only good Jew was a converted one. He personally attended baptisms of more prominent apostates and set up accounts for children newly brought into the Faith. These were then fed and lodged under the guardianship of friars, often at the king's own expense.

One act of Louis's zeal stands out among his others. In 1240, reports reached Pope Gregory IX that Talmudic writings defamed Jesus and criticized Christianity. He ordered seizure of Talmuds throughout Christendom and a thorough investigation of their contents. Spanish and English rulers ignored the order, but Louis eagerly complied.

In June of that year, the Talmud was formally put on trial in Paris, amidst much fanfare, with Queen Mother Blanche in attendance. Four rabbis defended centuries of accumulated scholarship against such charges as blasphemy. A tribunal of bishops and Dominican monks pronounced the Talmud guilty, and in 1242, punishment was carried out. Twenty-four cartloads of Talmudic writings seized or surrendered under threat of death rolled through the winding streets of the French capital. When the procession reached a public square, the wagons were emptied and these carefully crafted, irreplaceable manuscripts were consigned to flames. Two years later, smoke from a similar burning again rose over Paris as more precious Talmuds, overlooked or hidden during the first hunt, were discovered and confiscated.

This benchmark (for Jews) of Louis's reign did not match the bloodshed of Philip Augustus. But then, nobody ever claimed Philip Augustus was a saint.

EDWARD I, 1239–1307
King of England, 1272–1307

History's Conventional View

St. Louis, a contemporary of Henry III, died of the plague two years before Henry's son, Edward—"Longshanks"—inherited the English crown. So moving from Calais to Dover at this point serves chronology well. Edward came to be renowned as an innovative, progressive ruler. He set up the "Model Parliament," a putative democracy of a sort. He instituted legal and administrative reforms, earning him recognition as the English Justinian. Beyond England's borders, Edward pursued an aggressive policy. He waged genealogical warfare in Wales and Scotland to assure favorable bloodlines on neighboring thrones, one of which, the Stone of Scone, he brought to Westminster Abbey (a theft which still annoys Scots in our own century). Edward died while preparing another expensive northern campaign against Robert I the Bruce.

But From a Jewish Perspective

By Edward's succession in 1272, English Jewry's economic value was winding down. His Plantagenet forebearers had already squeezed Jewish moneylenders dry, so he suffered no noticeable financial pain when he banned their activity three years later in his Statutim de Judeismo:

> Albeit he and his Ancestors have received much benefit from the Jewish People in all Time past; nevertheless, for the Honour of God and the common benefit of the People, the King hath ordered and established That from henceforth no Jew shall lend any Thing at Usury, either upon Land, or upon Rent, or upon other Thing.

Although English Jews now had permission from Edward to engage in formerly barred activities such as commerce, handicrafts, and agriculture, this was a dubious liberation. Acquiring fresh skills in pursuits long denied was difficult, and even if they achieved mastery in a craft it availed them nothing. Monopolistic guilds could refuse them admittance, and did. And if any nearsighted Guildsman, or other Christian, could not easily tell Jew from non-Jew, Edward's regulations stated "that each Jew after he shall be Seven Years old, shall wear a Badge on his outer Garment, that is to say, in the Form of Two Tables joined, of yellow felt, of the length of Six Inches and the Breadth of Three Inches."

In 1279, an edict imposed the death penalty on Jews accused of blasphemizing Christianity. The next year, Edward ordered Jews to listen to Dominicans preaching conversion.

Despite their financial plight, Edward figured one last extortion was viable. In the spring of 1287 he arrested the heads of Jewish families and demanded their communities throughout the realm raise a 12,000-pound ransom payment.

Edward's final solution to the country's Jewish problem came on July 18, 1290. An act of expulsion gave them three months to leave England. The official reasons stated included their continued practice of usury and efforts to persuade converts to return to Judaism. The king's gains were undeniable. His decision put him in good stead with the Church, clearly Europe's most potent power broker, and with extortion from Jews no longer an alternative in perception, as it no longer was in reality, Edward could better prevail upon Parliament to enhance royal tax revenue from Christian sources. Most important, perhaps, was that no act of his reign won greater popular acclaim throughout his domain. As in the France of Philip Augustus's day, Jews could take movable goods with them, but all other property became the Crown's. Any Jew found in England after All Saints' Day, November 2nd, 1290, would be hanged.

It can be said in Edward I's favor that he wanted the expulsion of England's Jews—approximately sixteen thousand in number—conducted humanely and without violence. His July 18 instructions to the sheriff of Gloucester read: "He is ordered to cause the Jews to have safe conduct at their cost when they, with their chattels, which the king has granted to them, direct their steps to London in order to cross the sea." In another letter, on July 27, he wrote, "The king to all his wardens, officers and sailors of the Cirque Ports, greeting.... You should ensure that their passage is safe and speedy...free from danger."

The king meant what he said. When a ship's captain took passage money from a group of Jews, then left them stranded on a sandbank to drown at high tide, Edward ordered him hanged.

Edward I will be the last English monarch for many reigns to come to be given more than passing note on these pages. Such notable and notorious sovereigns as Henry V, Richard III, and Henry VIII ruled over an island kingdom that in a foreign tongue and different century would be pronounced "Judenrein."

Other Voices, Other Deeds

The personalities in this section make their appearance semi-chronologically. Identified by name alone, HENRY IV (1050–1106), emperor of the Holy Roman Empire, blends anonymously into an ocean of numerical Henrys of various nationalities and time frames. So, to justify his inclusion, let's first set him apart from his namesakes. Henry IV added the expression "going to Canossa" to the language as the essence of ultimate contriteness—royalty to rags in a literal sense. This came about during his bitter dispute with Rome. The rivals: Henry IV and Pope Gregory VII (formerly Hildebrand of Cluny). The issue: temporal versus Church supremacy, specifically, patronage power over ecclesiastical appointments. Their mutual contempt was evidenced by the manner in which they addressed one another:

The pope: "Gregory, bishop, servant of the servants of God, to Henry, the king, greeting and apostolic benediction—*that is*, if he be obedient to the apostolic see as is becoming in a Christian king."

Henry: "Henry, king not by usurpation, but by the holy ordination of God, to Hildebrand, not pope, but false monk. This is the salutation which you deserve, for you have never held any office in the Church without making it a source of confusion and a curse to Christian men, instead of an honor and a blessing."

The indelible image (1077): Henry, excommunicated, crosses the Alps in bitter winter, dressed in sackcloth, and waits three days in deep snow before the pope's palace at Canossa for absolution.

The rest of the story: Henry, forgiven, retains his throne, then renews his challenge of Church authority, this time successfully.

But what did all this have to do with Jews?

Henry's policy toward Jews was an extension of this independent-mindedness. He countered the anti-Semitism of second-tier secular and ecclesiastical authorities by insisting they came under no jurisdiction but his own—"They belong to Our Chamber."

Jews received exemption from customs duties in imperial towns and enjoyed trade and travel privileges throughout his empire. In this, Henry was first impressed, then influenced, by the example of Bishop Rüdiger of Speyer, who invited Jews to settle in his bishopric, for their presence "could only tend to the greater glory of the region." After Rüdiger introduced Henry to his town's Jewish elders, the emperor confirmed their rights and, on his journey through the Rhineland, granted similar rights to Jewish communities he passed.

Unfortunately, at the First Crusade's onset a few years later, Henry's good will availed Germany's Jews nothing. Mail-coated knights and ragamuffin mobs routinely targeted nearby Jews rather than faraway Saracens. Three months of pillage and massacre reigned, while Henry, in Italy at the time, remained ignorant of their plight. When news finally reached him, he reacted promptly with orders to dukes and bishops throughout his realm to shelter and protect them. On returning home, he allowed the Jews who had saved their lives by accepting baptism to return to Judaism. This was a no-no. The new Pope, Clement III, responded to this edict by declaring: "We have heard that the baptised Jews have been permitted to apostasize from the Church. This is something outrageous and sinful and we require you and all Our brothers to ascertain that the sacrament of the Church is not desecrated."

Henry ignored clerical protests and, moreover, ordered an investigation of Jewish murders. Convictions followed, and even an archbishop was punished for enriching himself with valuables entrusted to his care by terrified Jews.

Henry deserves better from history than mere recollection as a forlorn sinner, shivering in the snow outside Canossa.

Unlike St. Louis, ST. BERNARD (1091–1153) qualifies as both a saint and a friend of the Jews. Founder of the Cistercian monastery at Clairvaux and a powerful figure in Church politics, Bernard, as could be expected, depicted Jews in the theologically correct language of his times—a people meant by providence to live in misery until the last Day of Judgment as witnesses to their rejection of Jesus. But conduct counts more than rhetoric, and Bernard's conduct was exemplary contrasted with that of Louis IX, his near contemporary. Bernard's passion was the engine that drove Christian Europe toward the Second Crusade, but he remained mindful of the atrocities that accompanied the first. He brooked no toleration of anti-Semitic outbursts on home ground.

When a zealous monk named Rudolph incited mobs with the cry, "Let us first avenge the crime of the crucifixion on the enemies among us!" Bernard sternly warned: "'Whoever makes an attempt on the life of a Jew sins as if he had attacked Jesus himself."

Nor would he countenance wholesale seizures of Jewish property to finance the Crusade. He approved only the abolition of interest payments on credit extended to participants in the great endeavor. Given the times, this was indeed moderation. More importantly for Jewish life and limb, Bernard prepared an epistle reminding Second Crusaders of the disaster met by Peter the Hermit's rowdy band at the onset of the First Crusade. Peter's followers had cut a bloody swath through Rhineland Jewry before being themselves scattered, enslaved, or killed on the way to the Holy Land. "It is to be feared," he wrote, "that if you act in like manner, a similar fate will strike you."

Bernard of Clairvaux earned his sainthood.

HENRY II (1133–1189), king of England after 1154, was more important in English history than his son John or grandson Henry III. But not in English-Jewish history. The earlier Henry presided over quieter times for Jews, less extortionist, less cruel.

Nonetheless, Jews were unhappily given the role of keeping the kingdom financially solvent. Henry extracted an emergency tax from them in 1168, then a much larger assessment of 60,000 pounds, in 1188, to help finance the Crusade about to get under way. This amounted to one-fourth of the value of all portable property held by London Jewry. The whole of Christian England, by contrast, contributed just 10,000 pounds above this figure.

By the year that huge tax was levied, Aaron of Lincoln was dead. But since he could not take his wealth with him, his fortune reverted to the Crown. And it was plenty. Aaron had run a banking empire covering twenty-five counties of England with seventeen agents all over the island. Several hundred notables were in his debt. They owed him 15,000 pounds, equivalent to three-fourths of the Crown's normal annual revenue. Henry found it necessary to set up a special branch of his Exchequer, named the Scaccarium Aaronis, with no function other than processing his immense estate. Windfalls from other dead Jews would have been lost to the Crown had they become Christians in their lifetimes. So is it any wonder that Henry aroused the ire of church officials by discouraging the conversion of Jews?

Thomas à Becket died before Aaron and played no role in the disposal of Aaron's worldly holdings, or financial planning for military adventures in the Holy Land. And Henry II is best remembered, of course, neither for dealing with Jews nor their money, but for provoking the assassination of his erstwhile friend, later named a saint.

FREDERICK BARBAROSSA (1123?–1190), Holy Roman emperor for nearly forty years, was slated to lead the Third Crusade, abetted by fellow monarchs Philip Augustus and Richard the Lion-Hearted. But the fabled "Redbeard" departed earthly life via one of history's more significant drownings. Seven hundred and fifty years later he would become the centerpiece of gaudy Teutonic ceremonies staged by Hitler and Goebbels. Historically, however, he was a friend of the Jews.

For German Jewry, the Third Crusade could have raised havoc similar to the first. That it didn't resulted from Frederick's foresight. His timely order not to preach against the Jews, directed to monks and priests, helped, and his warnings to the Diet that anyone convicted of killing Jews would pay with his own life helped even more. Local marshals dispersed surly mobs hovering around Jewish districts, and Frederick let it be known that anyone who inflicted injury on a Jew would have his hand chopped off. At the emperor's urging, bishops in his realm threatened people who attacked Jews with excommunication. A Jewish chronicler, Ephraim ben-Jacob of Bonna, wrote, "Frederick defended us with all his might and enabled us to live among our enemies, so that no one harmed the Jews."

Another pivotal figure of the Third Crusade would likely have taken umbrage at being cited for Christian virtues. SALADIN (1138–1193), formidable foe of Richard the Lion-Hearted, is credited with gallantry and magnanimity—and Jews shared in this largesse. During the nearly century-long occupation by the Crusaders of Jerusalem, they had been barred from living in the Holy City. Then, in 1190, they were welcomed back.

The Jewish poet Al-harizi described the return: "But God raised the spirit of the Ishmaelite King [Saladin] in the year 4950 [1190, Christian Era] from the creation of the world, imbuing him with wisdom and courage. He marched with an army from Egypt, besieged Jerusalem, and God handed over the city into his hands. Then he sent out a call through all the cities: let each of the descendants of Ephraim return there from Ashur and Mitzraim [Mesopotamia and Egypt] and from all the localities where they are dispersed."

The Moslem warrior-king's wisdom extended to his personal affairs as well. The plague, smallpox, leprosy, and other diseases lurked around the twelfth-century Near East. Saladin hired Moses Maimonides, a physician, paying him an annual stipend for consultation. A generation earlier, St. Louis, who died from the plague in Tunis, probably scorned the notion of consulting Jewish physicians.

We now backtrack chronologically to three men whose writing brought them influence.

PETER ABELARD (1079–1142), French scholastic, developed a rationalistic philosophy and occupied the Chair of Logic at Notre Dame. He wooed and won his talented pupil Heloise, niece of the cathedral's canon, who disapproved, and that placed him in a star-crossed match similar to Romeo and Juliet's, of romantic legend.

It's his writings, though, not his celebrated love life, that concern us here. In Abelard's "Dialogus inter Philosophum, Judaeum et Christianum," an invented dialogue mouthed by a philosopher, a Jew, and a Christian, he first reproaches Jews by asserting that all their earthly hopes faded with the destruction of the Temple, leaving them a pitiable people. But later came an insightful dissection of their plight, circa 1135:

> Scattered among all the nations, having neither king nor secular
> prince, the Jews are oppressed with heavy taxes as if they must buy

their lives anew every day. To mistreat Jews is regarded work pleasing to God. For Christians can only explain such imprisonment as the Jews suffer as the result of God's hatred of them. The lives of the Jews are in the hands of their fiercest foes. Even in sleep they are not spared terrifying dreams. Except for heaven, they have no safe refuge. When they wish to travel to the nearest town, they must pay large sums of money to buy the protection of the Christian princes who, in truth, desire their death in order to seize their inheritance. The Jews are not permitted to own fields and vineyards because there is no one to guarantee their possession. Thus the only livelihood that remains to them is usury, and this, in turn, excites the hatred of the Christians.

Unfortunately, nothing in Abelard's cogent analysis altered the behavior of secular or ecclesiastical authorities. France was then ruled by the House of Capet, from which Philip Augustus and St. Louis would spring. Besides, Abelard's personal affairs placed him in a compromised position, scorned by the folks who counted in Paris.

By contrast, Italian Scholastic philosopher THOMAS AQUINAS (1225–1274) earned sainthood. His synthesis of Catholic theology, called Thomism, makes his *Summa Theologica* one of history's more influential works. But what did he think of Jews?

Evidence comes in a letter written in March 1274, the year of his death. He was responding to a widow's question concerning her husband's will. This was no ordinary woman in mourning. She had inherited the duchy of Brabant, comprised of much of present-day Belgium and the Netherlands. Her late husband instructed that Jews and other money lenders be expelled if they refused to drop that onerous occupation.

"It is true, as the laws declare," he answered, "that in consequence of their sin (rejecting Jesus) Jews were destined to perpetual servitude, so that sovereigns of state may treat Jewish goods as their own property, save for the sole proviso that they do not deprive them of all that is necessary to sustain life."

In his writings, Aquinas also decried the murder of Jews, contending that they should be preserved as eternal witnesses to the truth of Christianity. As had Gregory the Great six centuries earlier, he opposed sword-point conversions, preferring friendly persuasion as the means of winning converts. At no point does Aquinas mirror the latent sympathy for Jews that can be extracted from the words of Abelard.

Clearly, Aquinas was no avant-garde theologian. But neither was he the mortal enemy that Jews found among less learned ecclesiastical and secular men of action before and after him.

GEOFFREY CHAUCER (1340–1400) looms foremost among pre-Shakespearean literary figures on the English landscape. That merits consideration, but not necessarily guarantees inclusion here. Had he remained mute on Jews and Judaism, he would not appear. The England of his day certainly argued for silence. The last Jews were expelled from English soil nearly one hundred years before he wrote *The Canterbury Tales.* Nonetheless, we find "The Prioress's Tale," one of twenty-three accounts he presents by way of pilgrims assembled at Tabard Inn. The plot: While wandering through the Jewish section of town singing hymns of his faith, an eight-year-old Christian child is murdered.

Here is a sample in plain, updated English of how Chaucer spun his tale:

> Thenceforth the Jews conspired
> to hurt this innocent out of this world;
> for this purpose they hired a murderer,
> who had a hiding place in an alley,
> and when the child was passing by,
> this accursed Jew seized him and held him fast,
> and cut his throat and cast him into a pit.

The frantic mother uncovers the crime when she hears her newly buried son singing "Alma Redemptoris." Justice is sternly served when the Jewish community is wiped out in retaliation.

Now, an abrupt change, culturally and geographically. VLADIMIR (956?–1015), prince of Kiev, ruled over a barbarous land, now a large portion of present-day Russia. A pagan potentate, he searched for *any* religion to clothe his whole domain—and that's why he's included here.

If history in the tenth century had been different, the later Jewish Pale and Romanov-inspired pogroms would never have come about. Medieval Russia, not twentieth-century Israel, would have become the postbiblical Jewish state.

According to the Russian chronicle, part history, part myth, there came a point in time when Vladimir sent forth word he would select his God by a "test of faiths." Precedent for this sort of spiritual challenge existed in Eastern Europe's backwaters and indeed may be the basis for the story of how the Khazar Tartars living in southern Russia chose to become the Khazar Jews two centuries earlier. (Khazar power had been broken in 969 by Kiev's growing might while Vladimir was still a child.)

According to the chronicle, when the prince decided to abandon paganism, representatives of Western Christendom, Greek Orthodoxy, Judaism, and Islam appeared before him. From the start, the contest went badly for the Jewish emissary.

"Why are not Jews living in Jerusalem, their own country?" Vladimir asked.

"God was angered at our ancestors," replied the Jew, "and scattered us throughout the world for our sins and delivered our country to the Christians."

Vladimir narrowed his options, responding, "Then how can you teach others when you yourselves were repudiated and scattered by God? If God would love you, you would not be dispersed in alien lands. Do you intend to inflict such troubles on us?"

The pioneer Jewish historian, Simon Dubnow, believed the theologically-driven Russian chronicle put undue emphasis on Vladimir's reaction to Judea's fall rather than the collapse of the Khazar state, an object lesson of closer proximity. In any event, realpolitik probably guided Vladimir's hand more than religious motives. By choosing Greek Orthodox Christianity, he smoothed relations with the once-potent eastern Roman Empire to his south, and by positioning himself to marry the Greek emperor's sister, he saw himself and his rising young state as the natural heir to fading Byzantium in the Eastern world. But with the new religion came the virulent anti-Semitism of the older empire. Centuries ahead, this would curse Russian Jewry with the likes of Nicholas I, Alexander III, and Nicholas II.

Historically, Prince Vladimir became Saint Vladimir, but for Jews he could have done a more saintly thing had he chosen differently back in 989.

Closing this section, we note PEDRO IV (1334–1369), ruler of Castile from 1350 until his untimely demise. Spain's clergy and grandees labeled him Pedro the Cruel, presumably because he periodically stooped to murder and mayhem for political ends. He was, however, very good for Jews.

Lacking the accepted religious scruples, he surrounded himself with Jewish advisers and employed Jews alone as his tax collectors. One became master of his treasury, another his personal physician and astrologer. Jealous Christians frowned at his "Jewish court." When the Cortes asked that he repeal the autonomous Jewish courts of arbitration, he responded, "Jews are a weak people, and if they were subjected to the general court of arbitration, they would always suffer injustice."

Unfortunately, Pedro's favor would cost Jews dearly. More than any other stratum of Spanish society, with good reason, they unstintedly backed his cause against bastard brother Henry de Trastamara's effort to seize the throne. Building popular support, Henry chided Castilians for allowing themselves to be ruled by a Jew. In the ensuing civil war, as besieged cities fell, one by one, Jews emerged as Pedro's final defenders, and they paid the price in blood and treasure.

The end came at Toledo in 1369. More than eight thousand Jews were consumed by fire or downed by sword, and Pedro was taken prisoner. Face to face at last with his half-brother, Henry mocked, "This is the Jew, the son of a whore, who calls himself King of Castile." Pedro was decapitated.

From Rome came Pope Urban V's congratulatory message: "The believer can only rejoice over the death of such a tyrant who arose against the Church and had defended Jews and Saracens."

So we end this chapter on another "what if": What if Pedro, dead at age thirty-five, had triumphed, and *his* descendants sat on the Spanish throne for centuries to come? From Henry de Trastamara's side of the family came a girl, born in 1451, and we know now what the coronation of Isabella as queen portended for Jews.

3

Renaissance, Reformation and Beyond

Leaving behind the Dark Ages and the medieval world, we move through the Renaissance, the Reformation, and the Age of Kings, those neatly self-defining subdivisions in world history textbooks. But for Jews, the two hundred years that saw modern Europe emerge with the beginning of the fifteenth century meant an extended dark night punctured by a few twinkling stars.

Let us start with Queen Isabella, who merits a chapter to herself in Jewish historical accounts.

ISABELLA, 1451–1504
Queen of Castile after 1474, and Aragon after 1479

History's Conventional View

As children we first meet Isabella in fanciful illustrations, the heroine-savior of Christopher Columbus's dream to find a westward route to the Indies. She is portrayed as regal, wise, and bejeweled, although willing to part with those gems to pay for his journey. Later, we learn she had inherited Castile, husband Ferdinand had inherited Aragon, and together they ruled a united Spain, save for the southern tier, Granada, still under fading Moorish aegis. Once the Moors were removed in 1492, Spain would enjoy a magnificent future. She would also exile Spain's Jews. In greater depth, the *New Catholic Encyclopedia* explains:

She was devoted to the religious and political unity of Spain, the modern history of which begins with her reign.... Together the reyes católicos (Catholic monarchs) suppressed civil war and banditry; reformed the law, the judiciary and the administration; encouraged sheepbreeding and trade; built a regular army; reconquered Granada (1481–1492); strengthened the monarchy vis-à-vis the nobles, the cities, and the Church.... They reformed the secular and regular clergy, anticipating the Counter-Reformation, and founded universities to encourage the revival of learning.

But From a Jewish Perspective

Two events seal Isabella's place in Jewish history—the Inquisition and the Expulsion.

A "national" Inquisition came to Spain at Ferdinand and Isabella's insistence. The Vatican was reluctant to place control in the royal couple's hands, but in the end yielded. Not long after, a solemn procession preceded the first burning—six men and women accused of desecrating Jesus' image—as Seville held an auto-da-fé. After 1481, nearly a dozen tribunals would blot the peninsula.

Torture became commonplace in obtaining confessions from Marranos, baptized Jews suspected of reverting to their former religion or "judaizing" others. In Inquisition dungeons, flogging, the burning of flesh, dislocation of limbs, and stretching on racks usually achieved the desired results. Resisters would be burned at the stake. Even those who eventually admitted to apostasy might fare no better if they held out *too* long, trying the patience of their tormentors. Mercifully, some last-minute penitents could anticipate being strangled *before* consignment to the slower-working flames. As a not inconsiderable windfall, the property of Inquisition victims enriched Isabella's treasury.

At one point, reports about her administration of the Spanish Inquisition led Pope Sixtus IV to complain in a brief to her: "It seems to Us that the Queen is urged to institute and confirm the Inquisition by ambition and greed for earthly possessions rather than by zeal for the faith and true fear of God."

Isabella rejected his plea that she treat Marranos more humanely. Nor would she accept on Spanish soil papal representatives to listen to Marrano appeals.

The 1480s were busy years for Spain's peculiar institution. Seville registered at least one auto-da-fé per month. Tallies of victims vary. Apart from the thousands consumed by flames, many were sent to a living death as oarsmen chained beneath decks of galleys. Others rotted in underground dungeons.

The Inquisition targeted backsliding converts—"secret" Jews—but did not touch openly professing Jews. To cleanse Spain totally of Jewish taint, Isabella needed to do more. She chose expulsion.

On March 31, 1492, the royal couple issued their "General Edict on the Expulsion of the Jews From Aragon and Castile." In part, it read:

> there is no doubt that intercourse of Christians with Jews, who seek to mislead them to their damnable religion, causes the greatest harm.... It has led to the undermining and debasement of Our holy Catholic faith.... We have therefore resolved to expel all Jews of both sexes forever from the borders of Our kingdom. We herewith decree that all Jews living within Our domains, without distinction of sex or age, must depart by no later than the end of July of this year from all of Our royal possessions and seigneuries.... And let them not dare set foot in the country again, for the purpose of settlement, or transit, or for any other purpose whatsoever. If, however, disregarding this command, they shall be caught in Our domains, they will be punished by death without trial and with confiscation of their wealth.

Under such duress, some chose baptism as an alternative, risking at some future point the probing eye of the Inquisition. But the overwhelming majority, two hundred thousand, departed. Many sought haven in neighboring Portugal rather than chance a perilous sea voyage to distant ports. They erred in thinking themselves beyond Isabella's reach. When she betrothed her daughter, the Infanta Isabella, to Portugal's king, Dom Manuel, she demanded their marriage contract contain a provision that he expel both those forlorn emigrants and indigenous Portuguese Jews as well. Against his own better judgment, Dom Manuel agreed to this ultimatum.

Isabella pressured Christian princes around the Mediterranean rim to deny refuge to her former subjects, and she met some success. But in the distant Ottoman Empire, home to many, Sultan Bayezid II "marvelled greatly at expelling the Jews from Spain, since this was to expel its wealth," according to a chronicler. He viewed Isabella's decision as impoverishing her own realm while enriching his.

* * *

We cannot leave Spain's queen without reference to Tomás de Tor-quemada (1420?–1498). His voice and deeds were so intertwined with Isabella's as to make them one.

This Dominican prior of noble lineage became the queen's confessor (later Ferdinand's as well), and her guiding hand in matters of Faith, with its concomitant cruelty. Appointed first inquisitor general for the realm at age sixty-three, his was the executive genius behind its implacable and efficient machinery of persecution. He has been described as austere, rigid, arrogant, and a fanatical bigot.

The story is told that the royal couple wavered before taking the drastic step of expulsion. Leading Jews, close to the court, appealed to them. Isaac Abravanel, collector of the crown's sheep tax, and Rabbi Abraham Senior, Castile's chief treasurer, offered a 30,000-ducat gift to defray debts incurred by the long war to subjugate Granada. At that moment Torquemada supposedly stormed into the palace chamber, held high a crucifix above his head, and scolded his sovereigns: "Judas Iscariot sold his master for thirty pieces of silver. Your Highnesses would sell him anew for thirty thousand."

Whether these powerful words banished doubt from Isabella's mind, if indeed they were uttered, and, indeed, if she harbored a conscience capable of raising doubt, belongs to conjecture. The deeds of Isabella and her inquisitor general speak plainly. Spain now had "one flock with one shepherd."

MARTIN LUTHER, 1483–1546

History's Conventional View

Here stands Martin Luther, roaring engine of the sixteenth-century Protestant Reformation, a charismatic, bold, bullying, unyielding man of faith in his beliefs and cause. There is the indelible image of this man of action posting his ninety-five Theses on the door of Wittenberg's Castle Church on October 31, 1517, opening a permanent tear in Western Christianity. His assault on Rome's doctrine of salvation by works and the sale of indulgences ultimately scattered one flock into many and aroused its shepherd, the papacy, to strike wildly. Religious turmoil, attack and counterattack, would embroil Jews. Early on, Pope Adrian VI bade one powerful German prince close to Luther to "put a muzzle on his blasphemous tongue." The wrath of that tongue seared more than his fellow Christians.

But From a Jewish Perspective

Luther wrote prolifically in an age when Gutenberg's recent invention could spread his words rapidly within Germany's many princely states and across frontiers. With time, his language, for Jews, regresses from evocations of promise to disappointment and uneasiness, and then to outright hatred.

In the beginning, as the former Augustinian friar, priest, and professor discarded Roman Catholicism's dogma to forge his new path, he saw Jews as a people ripe for conversion. Like Muhammad nine centuries earlier, he apparently believed that if he could choose the right words, they would flock to his cause.

In 1519, two years after posting his Theses challenging the existing order, Luther denounced the long-standing doctrine of *servitus Judaeorum*. He scoffed, "Absurd theologians defend hatred for the Jews," and said they "are slaves of Christendom and the emperor.... What Jew would consent to enter our ranks when he sees the cruelty and enmity we wreak on them—that in our behavior towards them, we less resemble Christians than beasts?"

In his essay "Jesus Was Born a Jew," Luther wrote: "Were I a Jew and saw what blockheads and windbags rule and guide Christendom, I would rather be a pig than a Christian. For they have treated the Jews more like dogs than men. Yet the Jews are kindred and blood brothers of our Saviour. If we are going to boast about the virtues of race, Christ belongs more to them than to us."

Two decades earlier, in Isabella's Spain, such sentiments would have earned Luther a trip to the bonfire. Critics labeled him a half-Jew.

But Luther's milder, gentler approach had an agenda: "My advice, therefore, is to deal kindly with the Jews and to instruct them in the Scriptures so that they come over to us.... How can we hope to win them over and improve them if we forbid them to live and work among us and to trade and mingle with us, and force them into usury! We must welcome them into our midst."

Jews accommodated Luther's spirit of good feelings and responded in kind, speaking well of Protestantism. But they rejected his appeal to conversion. By 1526 he was complaining of Jewish intransigence in remaining loyal to Judaism. The 1530s saw him referring to "stiff-necked Jews, ironhearted, and stubborn as the Devil."

Luther was clearly not a man who suffered rebuke. By the 1540s, Jews were "venemous and virulent," "thieves and brigands," and "disgusting vermin." His 1544 pamphlet "Concerning the Jews and Their Lies" set forth a comprehensive program for dealing with them:

> Set their synagogues on fire, and whatever does not burn up should be covered or spread over with dirt so that no man may ever be able to see a cinder or stone of it.... Their homes should likewise be broken down and destroyed.... They shall be put under one roof, or in a stable, like gypsies, in order that they may realize they are not masters in our land, as they boast, but miserable captives.... They should be deprived of their prayer-books and Talmuds.... Their rabbis must be forbidden to teach under the threat of death.

German Jewry's foremost figure, Joseph Ben Gershon of Rosheim, described Luther's work as "such a boorish and inhuman book, containing curses and vilifications hurled at us, hapless Jews, such as by the will of God can truly never be found in our beliefs and Judaism generally." Luther's proposals were of a gravity never uttered by any scholar, "that we Jews ought to be treated with violence and great tyranny, that none was bound to honor any obligation toward us."

Were Luther a cloistered theologian happily divorced from the real world his words—patently provocative—might have been forgotten except by other theologians. But the secular rulers of Saxony and Hesse, tutored by him, saw Luther's program as a guide for their own conduct of public affairs. His 1546 sermon "Admonition Against the Jews," repeating accusations of ritual murder, poisoning of wells, and black magic, stirred up even more trouble.

Martin Luther died that same year. But his legacy of hatred proved lasting. Because of his polemics, the *Jewish Encyclopedia* notes:

> The Lutheran Church, unlike that which owed its foundation to John Calvin, retained all the superstitious abhorrence of the Jews inherited from the medieval Catholic Church. Indeed Luther's attitude was worse, for he recognized no duty to protect the Jews. Throughout the subsequent centuries, Luther's ferocious castigation of the Jews

provided fuel for anti-Semites and the vicious force of that legacy was still evident in Nazi propaganda.

THE MALIGNED RENAISSANCE POPES
(late fifteenth, early sixteenth centuries)

History's Conventional View

To devoutly Christian eyes, those heirs of St. Peter, men neatly pressed together as Renaissance popes, merit history's critical view of them. Protestants revile the various Renaissance popes for simony, nepotism, crass materialism, spiritual emptiness, and a penchant for intrigue in expanding papal possessions. Roman Catholics find them difficult to defend for much these same reasons.

SIXTUS IV, pope from 1471 to 1484, was not above setting family and Holy See territorial ambitions on a higher plane than ephemeral religious affairs. As added baggage, ALEXANDER VI, the corrupt Borgia pope from 1492 to 1503, carries forward guilt-by-parenthood, having sired the notorious siblings Cesaré and Lucretzia. JULIUS II, pope from 1503 to 1513, taxed and spent to be elected pope. He also hired Raphael to do his walls, and Michelangelo his ceilings. Julius assumed the role of warrior-pope, taking the field against Venice and France.

During LEO X's tenure, 1513 to 1521, the continued sale of indulgences, which could purchase salvation, spurred Luther's rebellion against Rome. Leo was Rome's great patron of the arts. CLEMENT VII, pope from 1523 to 1534, a scion, like Leo, of the powerful Medici family, shared his kin's good eye for art and blind one for frugality. He also meddled in quarrels between Francis I, king of France, and the Holy Roman emperor, Charles V (about whom more shortly). Championing Francis proved a disastrous blunder, for a peeved Charles let his troops sack Rome in response. PAUL III, the last of the major Renaissance popes, from 1534 to 1549, emerged from the wealthy and ambitious Farnese family. He was characteristically worldly, as were his predecessors, and shamelessly engaged in nepotism. After him came the seeding of the Counter-Reformation.

But From a Jewish Perspective

Except for Alexander VI, a moral leper, these Renaissance popes were collectively some of the Jews' warmest supporters between St. Peter's times and the advent of John XXIII in the twentieth century. The very absence of narrow religious fervor in their makeup bade well for the adherents of Judaism in their age. Historian Cecil Roth placed them "among the leaders of Italian humanism," and Jews benefited from the "benign atmosphere" in papal domains.

Although Sixtus IV authorized the Spanish Inquisition, he did so reluctantly under intense pressure from Ferdinand and Isabella, and soon condemned the royal couple's merciless persecution of Marranos. Sixtus tried to mitigate the Inquisition's harshness in distant Castile. Within his own papal domain, however, moderation prevailed. He enjoyed amicable relations with leading Jews, employed a Jewish physician, showed interest in Jewish literature, and employed Hebrew copyists in the Vatican library. He rejected "blood libels" purporting that Jews drained the bodies of Christians and, in 1475, refused to canonize Simon of Trent as a holy martyr. Simon's militant supporters had said the youth was a ritual murder victim.

Even Alexander VI allowed so many Marranos fleeing Spain's Inquisition into Rome that the city's refugee population doubled during his reign. When Ferdinand and Isabella protested, he ordered the new-comers to state their pro forma Christian loyalty. He reduced the size of the mandatory badge worn by professing Jews, but burdened them with an additional 5 percent charge, above the customary taxes, to defray Turkish war costs. For his personal amusement, he extended the distance of the annual race in which humiliated Jews ran naked through the city so that he could view it from his Castel Sant'Angelo residence. Nonetheless, for the sake of Jewish survival in the Mediterranean world of the late 1400s, better this Borgia's eclectic depravity than Torquemada's single-minded principles.

Julius II, who consigned the Sistine Chapel ceiling to Michelangelo's paintbrush, entrusted his personal health to Samuel Sarfatti, a Jewish physician, as had Alexander before him. More importantly for Jews at large, the pope's mind-set, along with his temporal and aesthetic concerns, did not include attacking Jews. Benevolent neglect was indeed welcome.

The worldliness of the first Medicean pope, Leo X, son of Lorenzo the Magnificent, fostered tolerance of Jewish learning as another aspect of the Renaissance cultural scene. During his papacy, a drawn-out dispute involving the Talmud came to a head. It had begun when a turncoat Moravian Jew, Johann Pfefferkorn, had accused Talmudic writings of blaspheming Jesus and Christianity. Johann Reuchlin rose to the Talmud's defense. He was one of the few Christian scholars in central Europe capable of reading Hebrew. Soon religious orders and university professors throughout France and Germany were caught in the dispute, which reached Rome for a decision. Rather than condemn and burn the Talmud, a popular course that would have pleased St. Louis, Leo encouraged a Christian printer to publish its entire text, uncensored.

On another occasion, Leo reconfirmed privileges accorded Jews in a French papal territory despite the vigorous protests of the bishop there, who wanted them exiled. Moreover, Leo ended the Jewish badge requirement in his French domains and let this obligation fall into disuse within Italy. To Martin Luther, Leo was the functioning head of a "kingdom of Antichrist." For Jews, Leo's was a peaceable kingdom.

Clement VII, the second Medicean pope, earned accolades as a "favorer of Israel" and a prince gracious to Israel from contemporary Jewish writers. Jews gained admission to his circle, and his physician was one. He allowed Marrano fugitives to settle in the Adriatic seaport of Ancona, then went a step further: He let them profess Judaism openly. In Rome he sanctioned control of Jewish internal matters by Jews themselves. In instances of disputes between Jews and Christians, he established a special court under a Roman cardinal vicar, bypassing the civil court, prejudiced against Jews. Jews could expect no better pope—and would get none—for centuries to come.

During Paul III's fifteen years in the papacy, Jewish fortunes in the Roman Catholic center began their downward spiral. Blame the times, not Paul himself—he was a good man. Complained one exasperated French cardinal, who vainly sought his permission to expel Avignon's Jews: "Christians have never received from their popes such privileges and favors as the Jews receive from the current high priest, Paul III; they are not only secured, but also armed with all these rights."

But strains were building in the church edifice because of threats, real or perceived, to the Holy See. Paul approved creation of the sternly disciplined Jesuit Order and yielded to pressure, allowing Inquisitorial fury to erupt in Portugal. He permitted the resulting stream of Marranos to settle in Ancona, as had his predecessor. Clearly, though, power in Rome was shifting inexorably to forces of repression.

After his death, Inquisitor General Cardinal Giovanni Pietro Caraffa ordered all copies of the Talmud found in the city seized, and Paul's successor, Julius III, upheld the ruling, and then let hundreds of "harmful" books be burned. Julius was no enemy of Jews, having earlier confirmed their rights in Ancona. He had condemned the blood libel and forbade baptism of Jewish children without parental consent. But he could not check the reactionary cardinal's now-dreaded Holy Office.

In 1555, Caraffa himself was elected pope. By midyear, he issued a bull erasing all the tolerant practices of the Renaissance popes in years past:

> Since it appears utterly absurd and impermissible that the Jews, whom God has condemned to eternal slavery for their guilt, should enjoy our Christian love and toleration only to repay our graciousness with crass ingratitude and insults, and, instead of bowing their heads humbly, to strive for power: Furthermore, in view of the fact that their imprudence, which has been brought to our knowledge, goes so far in Rome and other places lying within the domains of the Holy Roman Church that Jews venture to show themselves in the midst of Christians and even in the immediate vicinity of churches without displaying any badge, rent houses in the finest quarters of the city, purchase estates, employ Christian nurses and other servants in their households, and in various other ways trample underfoot Christian honor, we find ourselves compelled to institute the following measures.

When the long recital of stringent rules ended, Jews would find themselves locked nightly in ghettos, restricted to one synagogue in each community (all others would be torn down), required to wear a yellow hat if male, a yellow kerchief if female. Henceforth, the only occupation open to Jews would be peddling old clothes.

As for Ancona, that long-term safe haven for Marranos on Italy's west coast, Caraffa—as Paul IV—abruptly cancelled letters of protection granted by past popes. Agents of the Inquisition acted swiftly, and twenty-five victims fell to the flames.

CHARLES V, 1500–1558
King of Spain, 1516–1556
Holy Roman Emperor, 1519–1556

History's Conventional View

As grandson of Ferdinand and Isabella, and a Habsburg heir, young Charles V inherited much of Europe. To this he added Mexico, Central

America, and the lion's share of South America. Among Americans, he may best be recalled as the sovereign commanding Cortez, Pizarro, de Soto, and the rest of Spain's roving conquistadors. But his Old World role was more complex. His election as Holy Roman emperor in 1519, at age nineteen, placed him in the maelstrom of central European politics, as well as the emerging Reformation. For more than three decades he was the most powerful man in Christendom.

But From a Jewish Perspective

Toward Jews, Charles V wore two faces, a Spanish kingly face and a Habsburg Holy Roman emperor's. Often, he wore them simultaneously.

On Iberian soil and on overseas terrain held by Spanish arms, he indeed reflected the policies and principles of Queen Isabella, his grandmother. As King of Spain, Charles fully endorsed Inquisitorial severity. He rejected a 400,000-ducat gift by Marranos shortly after mounting the throne because it carried a condition—that he curb holy tribunal practices, such as acting on spurious evidence produced by witnesses whose anonymity guaranteed their immunity from challenge. Pope Leo X had prepared a papal bull proposing reforms, but Charles insisted his tribunals were saving sinful souls.

The Spanish king sent apostolic inquisitors to the New World to replicate Old World practices. In 1528, Mexico City staged its first auto-da-fé. Three "judaizers," including a Marrano conquistador companion of Cortez, died in the flames. Only in the Spanish Netherlands were Marranos offered a measure of safety denied them elsewhere in Charles's vast inheritance—but only temporarily. When Spanish troops crossed the Mediterranean and captured Tunis in 1535, all its Jews were sold into slavery.

By contrast, central European Jews found themselves under a different Charles, less threatening and even benign. When crowned Holy Roman emperor at Aachen, he refrained from exacting the customary coronation tax and issued a general letter of protection for Germany's Jews. He made no effort to institute the Inquisition or even tamper with privileges extended by past emperors.

At one point, Charles instigated a debate between an apostate Jew and German Jewry's spokesman, Joseph ben Gershon (better known as Josel of Rosheim). Josel won, resulting in the disgraced convert's expulsion from Augsburg and renewed protection for Jews in the Holy Roman Empire.

Nonetheless, Josel was wary about approaches to Charles. In 1532, a bizarre visionary arrived at Regensburg, where the emperor had convened the Diet. This much-traveled visitor told Josel of his plans. "At this time a foreign proselyte named Solomon Molcho has appeared with strange notions to rouse the emperor so that he will summon all Jews to battle against Turkey," wrote Josel. "When I heard what he had in mind, I warned him against stirring up the emperor's heart, lest the great fire consume him."

Molcho ignored the warning, insisted on an audience with Charles, and later "was placed in iron chains," according to Josel's diary, "taken to Bologna, and there burned."

At Diet sessions in Regensburg (1541) and Speyer (1544), Charles reaffirmed Jewish privileges. Contemporaries regarded the Speyer document "the most liberal and generous letter of protection ever granted to Jews." When Luther's preachings led to anti-Semitic outbreaks Charles intervened, prompting Josel to describe him as the "defending angel" against Luther. Nor would Charles brook ritual murder charges. "Only on the basis of popular superstition," an imperial edict stated, "Jewish men and women must not be tortured and executed. One must look for the real motives of the crimes and, in the event of doubt, such issues are to be referred to the emperor, who is the supreme judge of the Jews."

When Spanish troops entered Germany in 1546 during the Emperor's campaign against rebellious Protestant princes, they brought along ingrained peninsular intolerance. Josel complained that his people "who had previously suffered from Lutherans were now suffering from the Spanish Catholics" despite charters of immunity. Charles responded promptly, issuing an order to his army not to molest Jews.

Whether the real Charles was the one who wore the Holy Roman Empire's crown or the one who became the brutal king of Spain is arguable. Perhaps the politics of culture, custom, and geography determined which face he wore. The two realms had established patterns in their treatment of Jews, and Charles upheld the traditions of each.

No such ambiguity attended decision-making by his hard-bitten son Philip, who saw something of the wider world in his youth but later withdrew and ruled from his palace and monastery, El Escorial, outside Madrid.

PHILIP II, 1527–1598

King of Spain, 1556–1598

History's Conventional View

Philip, an only son, inherited Spain, the Spanish Netherlands, and an immense overseas empire, though not the title of Holy Roman emperor, which fell to his uncle Ferdinand. During Philip's reign, Spain retained its rank as Christendom's foremost military power.

Narrow-minded, a religious bigot, and not overly bright, this six-teenth-century Spanish king emptied his treasury and squandered gold and silver shipments brought from Mexico and Peru on hopeless Crusades to crush Turkish power, to suppress Protestantism in the Low Countries, and to bring back heretical England to the Catholic fold. For this last "great enterprise" he constructed and provisioned the Spanish Armada, a lavish expeditionary force aimed at conquering England, only to be defeated by Lord Howard and Sir Francis Drake. Philip was arrogant, aloof, cold, stubborn, intolerant, and dangerous.

But From a Jewish Perspective

A Josel of Rosheim, at ease in the presence of cosmopolite Charles V, would have found son Philip an impossible sovereign to approach. Philip detested Jews. His enthusiasm for Inquisitional activity was boundless, and only less expansive geographical parameters than those ruled by his father kept him from extending his terror.

The Inquisition in the Spanish Netherlands, diminished in Charles's day, revived under Philip. As Lutherans increased in numbers in the Low Countries along with other sects, Jews suffered retaliatory Catholic fury. In 1571 Philip's ruthless agent, the duke of Alva, ordered all Arnhem's Jews seized. That same year, across the Atlantic, Philip revived Mexico's slumbering Inquisition, putting its tribunals to work on a regular basis. He set as his goal "freeing the land which has become contaminated by Jews and heretics." New World auto-da-fés now became routine. The most celebrated of Marrano burnings featured the governor of Neuvo Leon province, his mother, and five sisters.

Some twenty-one tribunals of the Holy Office covered the Spanish Empire during Philip's reign, fifteen of them on Iberian soil. This made possible the king's physical presence at those climactic pageants of faith where, following colorful processions, the doomed were ritually sentenced. He attended at least five auto-da-fés and apparently enjoyed them. In 1586, before a trip to Toledo, he wrote his secretary: "...although I have heard nothing about it, it is possible that there will be one this year. It is really worth seeing for those who have not seen one. If there is an auto [da-fé] during the time I am there, it would be good to see it."

In 1590, Philip ordered Spanish Lombardy's nine hundred Jews expelled. Local officials in this northern Italian possession, more aware of the economic benefits of a Jewish presence than their royal master, ignored the order. In 1596 he wrote his lieutenant in Milan demanding that the order be carried out "most straightly and without further delay or objection and without awaiting any further orders from me." Philip's handwritten postscript threatened, "If this is not done at once, it will be necessary to send someone from here to do it." Finally, in January 1597, the persistent monarch warned more firmly that if his order remained unexecuted, "we shall seek out and punish whoever has caused these delays." Seventy-two Jewish families were forced to leave.

This was probably Philip's last vengeful act against Jews, but his demise the following year came too late for all those lives disrupted by expulsion or destroyed by flames.

SULEIMAN THE MAGNIFICENT, 1496?–1566
Sultan, 1520–1566

History's Conventional View

On the world stage, Suleiman rivaled his contemporary, Charles V, and for a decade, Philip II. The greatest of Ottoman sultans ruled a vast Islamic domain in the East and advanced Turkish power into North Africa and continental Europe. He ruled Belgrade and Budapest as well as Algiers and Rhodes. European states adjacent to his realm did not treat lightly complaints or demands transmitted by his emissaries, a matter of some consequence to his Jewish subjects.

Suleiman's lengthy reign also brought administrative reform to Constantinople's sprawling possessions. Under his aegis, the arts and sciences prospered. The imposing wall surrounding the Old City of Jerusalem that awes tourists in our day was built at his command.

But From a Jewish Perspective

Suleiman, like his predecessors Bayazid II and Selim I, and his own son Selim II, welcomed and encouraged a Jewish presence in Turkey. Jews fueled commerce, engaged in manufacture, and taught Turks the workings of cannon and gunpowder. At Court, Jewish physicians were in great demand.

When Suleiman captured Rhodes in 1523, he sent 150 Jews accomplished in commerce from Salonika to that undeveloped island. (His son Selim would do the same on an even larger scale when he captured Cyprus in 1571. Selim relocated one thousand Jewish families of artisans there despite protests it would damage their former residence's textile industry. "In the interests of the said island, my noble command has been written," he proclaimed. Reluctant Jewish migrants received a twenty-year tax exemption, plus free housing.)

Jews called Suleiman King Solomon for his wisdom, and a measure of that wisdom took the form of admitting to his circle Jewish advisers in foreign trade, statecraft, and diplomacy. The influence of his personal physician, Moses Hamon, transcended medical matters. In 1532, when a ritual murder charge emerged against the Jews of Amasia, in Asia Minor, Hamon induced the sultan to order an inquiry. Officials responsible for pressing this libel were identified and punished. Future such cases would be tried in the sultan's own court, not by the provinces.

Jews could count on Suleiman's intervention when he was apprised of injustices. At Hamon's request, in 1552, the sultan sent an emissary to the Venetian republic demanding freedom for a prominent Marrano widow and her nephew. He also insisted they be restored their substantial fortune, which had been confiscated by mercenary officials. Venice dared not refuse.

On reaching safety at Constantinople, the pair returned to Judaism, and the young man, under a newly adopted name—Joseph Nasi— entered government service. He became indispensable to both Suleiman and Selim as a political and diplomatic counselor, gaining power and prestige. Literary proof is seen in the manner he was empowered to begin his correspondence: "We, Duke of the Aegean Sea, Lord of Naxos..." Suleiman's Ottoman Empire was a land of opportunity.

More important for the average Jew was the support Suleiman elicited for them in troubled times. The sultan had arranged so-called capitulation agreements with European sovereigns, assuring the rights of their respective subjects in each other's realms. Some Christian rulers, though, regarded Jews and Marranos a class apart, fair game for persecution and periodic burnings. With Nasi at his elbow, the feared sultan made clear that Jews who immigrated to Turkey, then happened upon Christian soil for commercial or sundry reasons, were to be regarded protected persons.

Even the fierce holy tribunals would not dare risk the sultan's displeasure. In a noteworthy case, Pope Paul IV was checked in his pious effort to annihilate Ancona's Jewish and crypto-Jewish population. A sternly-worded message to him demanded that Jews claiming Turkish status be released from the Inquisition's dungeons. They were.

In 1564, an ageing Suleiman gave his loyal Jewish counselor the once prosperous, now decaying, city of Tiberias, plus several surrounding villages, as a Palestinian haven for impoverished European Jews. A wall was constructed around the city and rebuilding began. Settlers arrived from Ancona and Venice in Turkish ships. Mulberry trees were planted to inaugurate the raising of silkworms. Nasi imported wool from Spain for a planned textile industry. But opposition from surrounding Arabs and pirate attacks on supply vessels waylaid the ambitious project. Not even a benevolent Suleiman the Great, via his gift to Joseph Nasi, could sire a sixteenth-century Jewish state in the Holy Land.

IVAN III (the Great), 1440–1505
Grand Duke of Muscovy, 1462–1505

IVAN IV (the Terrible), 1530–1584
Grand Duke of Muscovy, 1533–1547
Tsar of all Russia, 1547–1584

History's Conventional View

These two Ivans rank among Russia's great tyrants. Ivan the Great earned that description by ending the Tartar domination stemming from the days of the Mongol Empire. Ruthless and clever, he warred against Lithuania, conquered Novgorod, and expanded Russia's borders into Siberia. By marrying Sophia Paleologa, niece of the last Byzantine emperor, he could lay claim to that fallen empire's global renown. Under

Sophia's influence, Ivan became the stern Orthodox Church's foremost champion. On the positive side, she imported scholars, painters, and architects, placing a civilized veneer over her husband's still semibarbaric realm.

The dismal reputation of his grandson, Ivan the Terrible, derives from his perceived disdain for moderation when massacre seemed a viable alternative. Young Ivan reigned before he ruled, having inherited his extensive share of the world at age three.

After Ivan IV had been crowned Russia's first Tsar, he rightfully saw the nobility as a threat to one-man tyrannical progress. When he thought Ivan, his son and heir, was becoming too friendly with those backward-looking aristocrats, he killed him in a fit of rage. But Ivan IV showed remorse for this domestic homicide.

But From a Jewish Perspective

Ivan the Great had little contact with Jews. "The prevailing xenophobia of both the Russian masses and their rulers," wrote historian Salo W. Baron, "kept out the Jews and other foreigners." In the wake of Muscovy's divorce from Tartar domination, he did make use of several multilingual Jews in diplomatic dealings with the Golden Horde's Khan. A Jew dwelling in the Crimean harbor of Kaffa even tried communicating with Ivan in Hebrew, but he was told to use another language—Russian or Mohammedan (Arabic)—to make himself understood at Court.

One Kievan Jew settled in the commercial center at Novgorod and began spreading Jewish religious thoughts. These concepts took root, and Greek Orthodox defectors began a movement that rejected icons and saw the messiah as a being yet to arrive on the scene. Rumored sympathizers included Ivan's own daughter-in-law, Helena, and his chancellor. Alarmed, the metropolitan of the city of Novgorod sparked repression of this Judaizing sect. Many apostates were burned at the stake.

At some point in his reign, Ivan the Great became aware of the high ratings given Jewish physicians in the West. He invited one such highly respected practitioner in Mantua to travel east to care for the royal family. Although serving Muscovy's master entailed rewards, risks also existed. When the overly boastful doctor failed to cure Ivan's ailing son, the duke had him summarily decapitated.

Better for Jews near Muscovy's borders would have been a prematurely fatal ailment befalling Ivan's grandson, the Terrible one. This well-earned appellation only marginally affected Jewish life at the beginning of his reign. That's because there were still few Jews in Russia and little prospect of more arriving.

An exchange of correspondence between Ivan IV and Poland's king, Sigismund Augustus, in 1550 explains why. Sigismund relayed complaints to his royal peer made by Polish Jews trading in Russia. They had been arrested and their merchandise confiscated. Naturally, they stopped crossing this hostile frontier, and Polish treasury revenues dropped as imports declined. Sigismund wrote: "Therefore, our Brother, order that our Jewish merchants should not be barred from entering freely your country with their wares, just as other merchants of ours and yours proceed in our and your kingdom."

Ivan's response illustrates what he believed:

What you wrote to Us, that We should allow your Jews to travel Our principalities as in ancient times—well, We wrote you more than once before, informing you of the bad deeds of the Jews, of how they had misled Our people from Christianity, poisoning potions were introduced by them into Our kingdom, and they played dirty tricks on Our people. . . . In other countries, likewise, wherever the Jews sojourned, they brought about great evil; and for those deeds they were expelled from those countries, and some of them were even condemned to death. We will not have the Jews visit Our principalities because We do not wish to see any evil here; We only wish that God grant My people to live peacefully without any disturbance. As for you, Our Brother, you need not write to Us in the future about the Jews.

Barring Jews from Russian soil at least spared them physical harm. Then in February 1563, Ivan's troops were on the march. They stormed into Polotsk, a Lithuanian city where large numbers of Jews resided. Ivan gave them an ultimatum: Embrace Russian Orthodoxy or die. He was as good as his word. Holes were drilled through the Dvina River's thick shell of ice, and some three hundred men, women, and children were hurled through them into the freezing waters beneath.

That winter day, in Jewish eyes, Ivan earned his title.

The House of Tudor's Superstars

HENRY VIII, 1491–1547
King, 1509–1547

ELIZABETH I, 1533–1603
Queen, 1558–1603

History's Conventional View

The swagger, splendor, and sheer massiveness of Henry VIII, so evident in portraits by court painter Hans Holbein the Younger, come to us replicated in countless cinematic portrayals. Henry VIII is noted for his six wives (two of whom he beheaded) and an exercise of royal authority that brooded little criticism and less dissent. Politics was a hazardous calling under this king. Even so clever a man for all seasons as Sir Thomas More ended his life at the block when conscience barred any acquiescence to his royal master's divorce from wife number one, Catherine of Aragon, his subsequent marriage to Anne Boleyn, withdrawal of allegiance to Rome, and the Act of Supremacy fostering an independent Church of England. Henry personified ruthlessness, yet he did have a soft side. Rather than subject his second wife to the capricious swings of an ax wielded by a journeyman, Henry sent for a finely crafted Flemish sword and an executioner of proven merit.

Henry's daughter by the unfortunate Anne Boleyn gave her name to an age, Elizabethan, and her lengthy reign is the stuff of history, legend, and the arts. We see Elizabeth's England as a procession led by Good Queen Bess herself, with a stellar supporting cast featuring Shakespeare and those adventurous spirits, Drake, Hawkins, and Raleigh.

But From a Jewish Perspective

Jewish life in Tudor England was virtually nonexistent. Jews had been expelled in 1290, so Edward I bears partial blame. So does Henry's father, Henry VII. While Henry VII was arranging the future Henry VIII's marriage to Catherine of Aragon with Ferdinand and Isabella of Spain, he promised never to allow Jews into his domains. Isabella had made it quite clear, if he refused the oath, the marriage was off.

Nonetheless, a few crypto-Jews slipped in, as they did elsewhere, in the guise of new Christians, and since London was not Madrid, no

Inquisition rooted them out. The hazy record suggests a Marrano colony of thirty-seven houses by 1540, probably followed by dispersion.

A bizarre turn had brought Jews and Jewish law before Henry VIII's troubled mind a few years earlier. When Vatican reference to Church doctrine blocked his bid to divorce Catherine, he turned to a higher authority—the Old Testament—and who better to interpret it than learned rabbis? Catherine had originally been betrothed to Henry's older brother, Arthur, who died shortly after the marriage. And was not coveting one's brother's wife forbidden?

Henry's agents approached leading rabbinical figures in Italy and won some support, but seemingly conflicting texts in different books of the Bible left the question unresolved. Looming in the background was the fearful spectre of papal retribution. The rabbis dared not alienate Vatican clerics for the sake of alleviating a distant monarch's domestic woes.

Henry did not get his way with Rome. Excommunication by Pope Paul III followed, for Henry moved ahead on his own. His messy divorce spawned the growth of Hebrew studies in England as a by-product, with Marranos imported from the Continent as teachers.

Elizabeth's contact with Jews was nearly as circumscribed as her father's. Marranos were present, but few; openly-professing Jews, not at all. But foreign affairs thrust Jews of one type or the other onto the Tudor landscape.

Don Solomon Aben-Jaish, an adviser to Turkey's sultan—later to be elevated by his sovereign to duke of Mytilene—established ties with Elizabeth's own close adviser, William Cecil Lord Burleigh. The Jew and English Lord shared a common foe, Spain's Philip II, and Don Solomon sent envoys to negotiate with the Queen.

In 1588, a secret Jew, Dr. Hector Nuñes, gave Burleigh and Walsingham, Elizabeth's spymaster, invaluable intelligence—news of the Spanish Armada's arrival at Lisbon on the first leg of its fateful mission north. In 1590, an English warship captured a Marrano-filled vessel sailing from a Portuguese port for haven in the Netherlands. Among passengers taken prisoner, according to a story passed down in Jewish accounts, was one Maria Nuñes, whose beauty so enchanted an English captain that he proposed marriage. Eventually Elizabeth asked that she be brought to Court. Impressed by Maria at their meeting, the tale continues, Elizabeth drove through London's streets with her in an open carriage. Later, Maria and her fellow passengers were released to complete their interrupted journey to Amsterdam, where they openly resumed their Jewish faith.

Small Marrano communities had settled in London and Bristol during the last years of Elizabeth's reign, but an unpleasantry marked her relations with the one crypto-Jew closest to the throne—her personal physician. Whatever his medical credentials—and he had become a member of the College of Physicians and served the earl of Leicester before coming to Elizabeth's attention in 1586—Dr. Roderigo Lopez's political activism overshadowed his professional merits. First, he plotted with the erratic Dom Antonio, pretender to the Portuguese throne, who maintained a shadow Court in London. Philip II had seized the throne; Dom Antonio wanted it back. Lopez then had second thoughts, withdrew this support, and worked for an understanding with Philip instead. Suspiciously, he did not reject outright suggestions from Madrid that he assassinate this exile who would be king. Complicating matters further, he became involved with, and then ran afoul of, the earl of Essex, Elizabeth's favorite.

Clearly out of his depth in the swirling world of palace intrigue, Lopez was arrested, charged with conspiring to murder Elizabeth herself. Did he really intend to poison his royal patient? Sir Robert Cecil, a rival of Essex, championed the Marrano's cause, but Elizabeth, unconvinced of his innocence especially after his confession under torture, let her physician be executed at Tyburn.

The unfortunate physician's ordeal led to new productions of Christopher Marlowe's *The Jew of Malta*, and a competitive William Shakespeare began writing *The Merchant of Venice*.

The early Stuarts—James I and Charles I—followed Elizabeth to the throne. In English history, their reigns were eventful—but not for Jews. So we now skip past this pair to their successor, one civil war removed, commoner Oliver Cromwell, Lord Protector of England, a pivotal figure in the course of Jewish history.

OLIVER CROMWELL, 1599–1658
Lord Protector, 1653–1658

History's Conventional View

Contemporaries respected or hated Oliver Cromwell. His modern image owes much to a legendary stern demeanor during his five-year reign. A man of puritanical fervor and fury—not an unreasonable view, since Puritans were puritan in those days—he banned fun and frivolity from London. Royalists, wedded to divine-right rule, would not budge from their principles. An enemy of royal prerogatives, Cromwell became lord protector of the commonwealth of England, Scotland, Ireland, and the dominions thereof. Other Dissenters may have had better-versed theological minds or parliamentary acumen in the long struggle with Stuart divine-right sovereigns, but when civil war erupted between these irreconcilable forces, it was Cromwell who installed the order, discipline, and religious enthusiasm in his military formations called Ironsides, molding them into a smooth fighting machine.

Cromwell insisted on the execution of the deposed Charles I, for which he bears the label "regicide." Impatient with Parliament's interminable bickering, he appointed major generals to run the country and infused English life with a severity many found stifling. After his death, Cromwell's body was disinterred, and then hung in chains. His place in history, Thomas Carlyle would write two centuries later, has been a "place of ignominy, accusation, blackness, and disgrace; and here this day who knows if it is not rash in me to be among the first that ever ventured to pronounce him not a knave and liar, but a genuinely honest man."

But From a Jewish Perspective

Historian Carlyle was not the pioneer he declared himself in reasserting Cromwell's good name. Jews saw him as a friend and ally. He invited openly-professing Jews back to England after a three-and-one-half-century absence. That the manner of the return did not match his, or their, ideal cannot be traced to any stinting on his part.

For Jews, the names Oliver Cromwell and Manasseh ben Israel are happily blended. Manasseh, a prominent scholar and rabbi in the Amsterdam community, had taken heart at Charles I's overthrow and reckoned that Puritan adherence to Old Testament beliefs might soften England's new men to a Hebraic reentry. He initiated correspondence with Cromwell, even suggesting a disarming theological rationale for admitting them. Not until the dispersal of Jews reached every corner of the known world—including England—could the venerable prophecy of a Messianic era begin. On a more prosaic secular level, both Manasseh and Cromwell gauged the economic implications of Jewish merchants plying their trade from British, rather than Dutch, ports across the Channel.

Cromwell invited Manasseh to England, but untimely hostilities between England and Holland temporarily delayed his appearance on British soil. When he did arrive, in October 1655, as guest of the lord protector, the rabbi grew disappointed at the opposition he found. Rumors spread about his real motives and those of his coreligionists. One gossip-monger spread a story that Jews intended to buy St. Paul's Cathedral and convert it into a synagogue. In December 1655, Cromwell, clearly supportive of Manasseh's goal, convened a special conference at Whitehall in London of members of the government council. But he failed to sway these leading luminaries, theologians, and merchants.

To the clergy, Cromwell had said: "Since there is a prophecy of the impending conversion of the Jews, we have to aspire to that goal by preaching the Gospels; but that is only possible when they would be permitted to live where the Gospels are being preached." Excellent logic on Cromwell's part, but it didn't succeed. Ecclesiastical figures responded that the conversion of Jews—whether from afar or on-site—was unlikely. They expressed concern that admission would lead to a flurry of "judaizing" by the newcomers instead.

No less significant was the opposition of London's influential merchant class. It wanted no competition from Jews. Cromwell argued, "You say that the Jews are the lowest and despised people; but how can you seriously fear that those despised people would gain the upper hand in industry and credit over the noble English merchantry, which is esteemed throughout the world?"

The lord protector failed to move them; nor could he reach out for support of royalist sympathizers who detested him: He ended the sessions. Formal measures for readmission had failed.

A favorable resolution of the issue came about in a backhanded way the following year. The on-again, off-again sea war between England and Spain led to the confiscation of property belonging to one Antonio Robles, a Marrano considered by legal definition an enemy alien. The irony of punishing a refugee whose very presence derived from the perils he faced in his homeland was not lost on London's sharper minds in political and legal circles. So this time around prospects seemed brighter when London Jews presented another petition asking to be allowed to live freely according to their religious beliefs. As before, Cromwell was

sympathetic: "Oliver P.—Wee doe referr this Petician to the consideration of ye Councill. March ye 24th 1655/6."

In July, the Council of State acted. Exactly in what manner is
unknown, for pages of the council records containing its deliberations
were mysteriously ripped out. But observable facts are better than lost
words. By judicial decision Robles got back his property, and openly
professing Jews were quietly allowed to trickle back to the island. Formal
legislation never came about, nor was there a need to press for it again.

In 1657, London's Jewish population felt confident to purchase a home
to establish a synagogue. Having departed for Amsterdam, Manasseh
died that year. The lord protector's life ended in the next.

The Seventeenth-Century Bourbons of France

LOUIS XIII, 1601–1643
King, 1610–1643

LOUIS XIV, 1638–1715
King, 1643–1715

History's Conventional View

During the first half of the seventeenth century, while England's Stuarts
and Parliament bickered, France surpassed a fading Spain and became
Europe's leading power. Two Bourbons reigned; one of them actually
ruled.

Louis XIII wore his French crown for thirty-three years, but the first
seven were under the regency of his mother, Marie de Medici. For almost
all the rest, Cardinal Richelieu, his chief minister, molded French policy,
centralized state authority, and pursued the "natural frontiers of Gaul,
the Pyrennes, and the Rhine." France's involvement in the Thirty Years
War was inspired by Richelieu, and this crafty prelate, not his royal
master, comes to us as the nemesis of Dumas's *The Three Musketeers*.

Louis XIV—"the Sun King"—mounted the throne at age five, sat there
until 1661 under the tutelage of Richelieu's successor, Cardinal Mazarin,
and then, at age twenty-two, began to rule as well as reign. Absolutism
became his trademark: "L'etat c'est Moi!" ("I am the State!"). Colbert, his
finance minister, developed mercantilism, a state-guided national economy, and a tax system that weighed heavily on the petty bourgeoisie and
peasantry. Louis built the money-consuming palace of Versailles, symbol

of his power and a gathering place for France's now-unoccupied, dandified nobility. He also spent lavishly as a patron of the arts and dipped even deeper into his treasury to finance interminable border wars. These conflicts added new territories but helped bankrupt France.

But From a Jewish Perspective

Louis XIII and Louis XIV get space here because the whole of seventeenth-century France is difficult to ignore in light of its rise to world prominence. Absent the first decade, they reigned through to the end of the century. On the other hand, their ninety-year reign caused some perturbations, but no great difficulties, for the Western Jewish world.

Back in the fourteenth century, Philip the Fair and his successors had completed the labors spiritedly pursued by Philip Augustus and St. Louis in making life miserable, and then impossible, for Gallic Jews. Theoretically, no Jews remained when Louis XIII ascended the throne, and none should have been observable when he left—but there are always exceptions.

The case of Elijah Montalto, a Portuguese Marrano who settled in Venice, was one. His fame as a medical man extended to Paris, reaching the ears of Maria de Medici, the king's mother. She offered him the post of court physician. Montalto set two conditions for taking the post: He must be allowed freedom to practice his religion and he must be exempted from his duties on the Jewish Sabbath. The queen-regent agreed to these terms. (Later, when Montalto died at Tours while accompanying young Louis, the queen-regent took care to have his body embalmed and transported to Amsterdam, where he could receive a proper Jewish burial.)

Once young Louis XIII was declared of age, he reaffirmed the expulsion order long in effect. His April 1615 royal decree read:

> We say, declare, wish, ordain, and it is our pleasure, that all the aforesaid Jews who dwell in this, our kingdom, country, domain and seigneuries under our command, shall under penalty of execution and confiscation of their property leave and depart from here forthwith, and this within the times and terms of one month after the publication of these presents.

But there may have been less to this declaration than met the eye. The decree was prompted by an effort to oust Jews who had come to Paris with Concini, formerly one of his ministers. Concini had been assassinated, possibly at royal command, and the measure swept away his entourage. Even the minister's hapless widow was tried for sorcery and practicing Judaism. Whether his 1615 decree was implemented or lay inert in metropolitan France, its fate in France's overseas colony of Martinique was indisputable: Local officials there ignored it. Jews played a vital role in the island's economy, and colonial administrators, insulated from royal reprimand by distance, chose to close their eyes.

Facts of economic life could not be overlooked closer to home, either. After French arms took the fortress city of Metz, Louis granted its Jews a letter, in 1632, declaring their presence in the city a necessity. Maybe Richelieu or an obscure palace factotum wrote the letter, but it bears his approval.

Fifteen years into son Louis XIV's reign, when he was age twenty in 1658, Church officials sensed victory. They pressed for, and won, a king's order restricting all Jewish colonial commerce. Martinique was again the focal point, and sensible colonial governors ignored it, just as they had his father's decree. Economic facts prevailed over smothering directives.

By 1671, Colbert's mercantilist policy led Louis to issue a charter of liberty for Jews under royal authority. Marseilles merchants, upset over the king's declaration of their port as an open harbor where Jews could freely trade, complained at Court. Colbert answered for his royal master:

> Commercial envy will always impell the Christian merchants to persecute Jews. But you should be above such motives that issue from personal interests. You should take into consideration the benefits the government derives from the industrial activity of the Jews, which comprises all the parts of the world, thanks to their association with their coreligionists.

This sort of Cromwellian explanation carried more force than the lord protector's at Whitehall, thanks to French absolutism. But again, times changed. As the 1680s progressed, Colbert's influence waned. In a royal decree issued May 2, 1682, the king ordered the immediate expulsion of Jews not only from Marseilles but from the whole of surrounding Provence. Jesuits next convinced him to order Jews expelled from French overseas possessions. So, in March 1685, Louis issued his Code Noir decree, which formally banned Jews from Martinique, Guadelupe, and St. Christopher:

It is our wish and we decree that the edict of the late King of glorious memory, our greatly honored lord and father, dated April 23, 1615, be carried into effect in our Islands and, by these presents, We command all our officers to chase out of our lands all Jews who have established their residences there whom, as declared enemies of the Christian faith, We command to get out in three months...upon penalty of the confiscation of their bodies and property.

This was merely a paper victory for reactionaries at Court though, because absolutism stopped at metropolitan France's borders. In the New World, local authorities still looked the other way. Molasses, sugar, and Jews intertwined, and any measure to disengage them could only hurt the islands. Meanwhile, back in metropolitan France, even Louis himself was not overly rigid. He granted Lettres de Naturalité to favored Jews, thus investing them with the rights of ordinary Frenchmen.

But the Sun King was certainly no friend of Jews. Late in his reign, waging war, tinkering with his beloved Versailles, and living the life of a grand monarch spared him little time to give Jews much thought. When he did, what he said was not to their liking.

After their expulsion, Jews had quietly drifted back to Provence with the connivance of economics-minded provincial officials. But word leaked back to Paris. In 1710, Louis—grown pious at age seventy-two— issued a special decree. He annulled the permission granted Jews by Provence's Parliament to transact business in Marseilles, Toulon, and other cities. He ordered Jews "to leave the kingdom without any belongings," and told local officials to take any and all means to expel the Jews "because that is our wish."

Meanwhile, in Russia, under questioning, Louis's near contemporary, Peter I, had given some thought to Jews early in his reign but never came up with a fresh idea after he emerged as Peter the Great.

PETER THE GREAT, 1672–1725
Tsar of Russia, 1682–1725

History's Conventional View

Peter gets credit for turning Russia from a backward, isolated state on Europe's eastern flank into a modern power. Just ten years of age at his accession as Russia's coruler, he grew into the position of reigning monarch. While in his twenties, he toured Europe for seventeen months, absorbing all it had to offer. The blossoming world of technology he found in Germany, Holland, and England fired his imagination. Back home, he tackled corruption, reformed government administration, and crippled the rebellious Streltsy, the Tsarist military corps. He expanded industry, set up the Academy of Sciences, and founded the city of St. Petersburg as Russia's "window on Europe." After a long war with Sweden, the new Russia supplanted that Scandinavian land as the dominant Baltic power.

Peter sought to westernize Russia in detail as well as by grand sweep. He ordained an end to old customs, ending the tradition of long, flowing beards worn by boyars, Russia's aristocracy. "Russia must be coerced!" he declared. For a country barely a century removed from Ivan the Terrible's barbaric despotism, Peter the Great's progressive despotism promised an enlightened future.

But From a Jewish Perspective

In 1698, before he became Peter the Great, he set forth his position on Jewish participation in the new Russia: No Jew would be allowed to live there. It happened during his stay in Holland when his friend, Burgomaster Witzen, at the behest of Amsterdam Jews, asked that some of their number be permitted to cross the Russian frontier as merchants and experts. A chronicler recorded his response:

> You know, my friend, the character and customs of the Jews; you also know the Russians. I, too, know them both, and believe me, the time has not yet come to unite these two peoples. Tell the Jews that I thank them for their offers and I understand the advantages I might have derived from them, but I would have pitied them for having to live among the Russians.

Whether this almost apologetic logic was sincere or merely polite camouflage in addressing his civilized host, the aftermath is less disputable. No Cromwellian invitation was to be issued during his long reign. In time though, territorial expansion would bring Russia to the Jews, if not the Jews to Russia.

Yet men of Jewish ancestry—even early in his reign—reached his inner circle. Vice Chancellor Shapirov, a converted Polish Jew, began his rise by entering royal service as a gifted linguist—he spoke six languages.

Two Jews—Meyer and Lups—assisted in his financial operations. Even closer to Peter was Jan da Costa, another versatile linguist descended from Portugese Marranos. He reached St. Petersburg by way of Hamburg. In 1714, Peter appointed him court jester, a post giving him free reign to ridicule the customs of Old Russia to the delight of his high society audience. After hours, the tsar reportedly enjoyed conversing with the keen-minded da Costa on theological matters.

"Whether a man is baptised or circumcised," Peter is quoted as saying in an Imperial Russian Archives document, "it is all the same to me provided he is a man of honor and knows his business."

For Jews, though, that applied only to those fortunate enough to gain access to Court. Toward Jews in general, Peter's attitude remained constant. When he promulgated a manifesto in 1702 inviting foreign artists to come to Russia, he excluded Jews.

But they could not be ignored after Russia annexed Baltic territory, and even less so when Peter conquered parts of the Ukraine ruled by Poland. In 1708, on discovering that Jewish traders had taken root in scattered cities of this new domain, he ordered that henceforth they would be admitted only in Kiev, and to dispose of their wares wholesale—not retail.

Farther north, when the northern war against Sweden raged across Jewish-populated sections of Poland, Russian soldiers eagerly pillaged Jewish property. According to historian Simon Dubnow, "only one pinkas [Jewish communal archive] recorded an instance in which Peter I intervened on behalf of a Jew."

This intercession occurred in White Russia, in 1708, when the Russian garrison at Amtcheslav began plundering local inhabitants. Dubnow wrote, "On the 18th of Elul, the sovereign, the tsar of Muscovia, named Peter, the son of Alexei, arrived here with his army that was beyond count. Marauders and robbers of his people attacked us, without his knowledge, leading almost to bloodshed. We would not have escaped it if God would not have made the tsar come to us in the synagogue. We are grateful to Divine Providence in that the tsar delivered us and wreaked revenge by ordering the immediate execution of thirteen of them; and the country calmed down again."

Peter's response to Burgomaster Witzen years earlier may have been prescient. Had he wished to, Peter could not have erased anti-Semitism with the ease that he sheared off beards. Tension over a Jewish presence in Smolensk, a commercial hub between White Russia and Moscow, and even more so in Cossack-inhabited areas farther south, proved troublesome to the tsar during the final years of his reign. Two years after Peter the Great's death, his widow, the Empress Catherine I, issued an edict settling matters:

> The Jews of masculine sex and those of feminine sex who are found in the Ukraine and in other Russian cities are to be expelled at once beyond the frontiers of Russia. Henceforth, they will not be admitted into Russia upon any pretext and a very close watch will be kept upon them in all places.

Or so she thought.

The rest of humanity may praise Peter for extracting Russia from its dark ages and bringing it into the newly enlightened world of the eighteenth century. But not Jews.

Other Voices, Other Deeds

A royal anticlimax opens this concluding section. Commoner Oliver Cromwell survived the first trickling back of Jews to England by just two years. Shortly thereafter, the Stuarts, who hated him and his works, returned from continental exile. Would one of those works—his Jewish policy—be undone during the Restoration? Under CHARLES II (ruling from 1660–1685), the answer was no.

Technically, the 1558 Act of Uniformity, which labeled any rites other than those of the Church of England unlawful, remained in force. But while still in the Netherlands, Charles had assured Amsterdam Jews that their coreligionists had no reason to fear his reemergence in England. Jewish bankers secured that promise with a generous financial contribution. The 1656 commission given to one Lt. General Middleton to act as Charles Stuart's agent in brokering a deal with rich Jews read:

> That whereas the Lt. General had represented to His Majesty their good affection, and that they had assured the Lt. General that the application which had been lately made to Cromwell in their behalf by some persons of their Nation had been and was absolutely without their consent, the Lt. General is impower'd to treat with them, that if in that conjunction they shall be ready to assert by any contribution of money, arms or ammunition, they shall find that when God shall restore His Majesty that he would extend that protection to them

which they could reasonably expect, and abate that rigor of the Law which was against them in his several Dominions, and repay them."

When put to the test, Charles was as good as his word. London merchants had grown hostile at the notion of Jewish competition. Their aldermen repeatedly petitioned the king "to shut the gates of the country, so that the religion and the welfare of all subjects should not be jeopardized." The targeted Jews, in turn, sought the Crown's protection "as loyal and law-abiding subjects." This he granted "so long as they demeaned themselves peaceably and quietly with due obedience to His Majesty's laws and without scandal to his government."

A further test came in 1673, when a grand jury at Guildhall responded to anti-Semitic rabble-rousing by indicting Jewish communal leaders for worshiping in public. When Jews threatened to leave England rather than endure loss of religious freedom, Charles had an order in council issued to halt the legal proceedings. He also warned the prosecutor "not to cause any more anxieties to Jews."

Charles's brother and successor JAMES II (ruling from 1685 to 1688) also traveled a benign path regarding Jews. In 1685, thirty-seven prominent Jewish merchants—technically Marranos—were arrested for failing to pay the mandatory tax imposed on those who failed to attend the established church. James, a Catholic at odds with Anglican conformity, put an end to this archaic regulation affecting Jews, "His Majesty's intention being that they should not be troubled upon this account, but quietly enjoy the free exercise of their religion." Three years later, his unhappy subjects deposed James II, chasing him into another exile across the Channel. But by now the Jewish position in England was reasonably secure, and since the new sovereign, WILLIAM, PRINCE OF ORANGE (king from 1689 to 1702), was of Dutch extraction, prospects remained favorable after the Glorious Revolution of 1688. Historian Cecil Roth noted that William's expedition was inspired by Englishmen, executed by Dutchmen, and financed by Jews. The prince was advanced two million crowns by a Hague Jew, interest free, and prayers were uttered in Dutch synagogues for his success.

Thanks to service as an army contractor, Solomon de Medina received a knighthood from William, the first openly-professing Jew to win that distinction from an English monarch. More important for the overall Jewish population, though, was communal exemption from penalty in

1698, when Parliament passed a bill suppressing blasphemy. By century's end, Jewish life in England was on a steady, if not always serene, course, safe from future royal or parliamentary caprice. English rulers play a smaller role on upcoming pages.

We now turn to a few cultural icons who crossed the stage during the centuries covered by this chapter, 1492 through the Renaissance, the Reformation, and into the age of absolutism. Striking omissions occur, but remember, men of arts and letters were unlikely candidates to be backed against a wall and questioned closely, "Are you now or have you ever been a friend (or enemy) of Jews?"

SIR THOMAS MORE (1478–1535), Tudor-era scholar and humanist, author of *Utopia*, is a case in point. For his lengthy (562-page) biography of More, author Richard Marius futilely sought literary evidence of More's position. He reported ". . . the startling fact that we find no hostile remark or metaphor about contemporary Jews in all the works of Thomas More."

The absence of derogatory comments, he logically concluded, showed More's leanings toward tolerance. Others in More's England were wont to use such expressions as "It would make a Jew repent," "worse than a Jew," "as false as any Jew," and "as vile as a Jew." These were conspicuously absent from More's vocabulary. Evidence is scant or nonexistent for many literary lights of those times.

By contrast, we need seek no subtle message in the words of Elizabethan dramatist CHRISTOPHER MARLOWE (1564–1593). A few lines from his 1590 play *The Jew of Malta* fix his position:

> We Jews can fawn like spaniels when we please
> And when we grin, we bite, yet ere our looks
> as innocent and harmless as a lamb's.

And:

> As for myself, I walk abroad a-nights,
> And kill sick people groaning under walls.
> Sometimes, I go about and poison wells.

The true mind-set on Jews of Marlowe's greater contemporary WILLIAM SHAKESPEARE (1564–1616), has been explored ever since *The Merchant of Venice* was first performed at The Theatre in 1576. The great Bard bequeathed anti-Semites an arsenal of expressions, among them "shylock" (as in Shylock) and a "pound of flesh."

Although Shakespeare hardly made Shylock the moneylender someone would turn to as a first resort, he did make him human, a step upward from traditional sixteenth-century stereotypes. Shylock declaims:

I am a Jew. Hath not a Jew eyes? Hath not a Jew hands, organs, dimensions, senses, affections, passions? Fed with the same food, hurt with the same weapons, subject to the same diseases, healed by the same means, warmed and cooled by the same winter and summer as a Christian is? If you prick us, do we not bleed? If you tickle us, do we not laugh? If you poison us, do we not die?

In the 1930s, *The Merchant of Venice* would emerge as a Nazi favorite, enthusiastically performed in the Third Reich.

The vehicle for JOHN MILTON's (1608–1674) literary greatness insulated England's towering seventeenth-century poet from any need to cater to accepted tastes. Such an epic work as *Paradise Lost* found a different audience. Milton wrote as a Puritan in the England of Cromwell's heritage, and from a Jewish perspective, he was a good man. He respected the Hebrew Bible, read it each morning until his vision failed, and, as he aged, turned more and more to the precepts of Mosaic law.

In his more worldly capacity as Cromwell's Latin secretary, he may have had a hand in the negotiations that led to the return of Jews to England. If so, speculates Milton biographer A. N. Wilson, his contact with the few Jews then in London may have contributed to his Judaic sympathies.

In the generation after Milton's, JOHN LOCKE (1632–1704) made his mark as a philosopher and political scientist, becoming a beacon of the Enlightenment. Thomas Jefferson acknowledged his intellectual debt to Locke, describing him in a letter to painter John Trumbull as one of the three greatest men in history. Jews had good reason to think well of Locke. In his 1689 "Letter Concerning Toleration," Locke wrote, "Neither Pagan, nor Jew, ought to be excluded from the civil rights of the commonwealth because of his religion."

Britain's New World colonies were taking shape during Locke's time, and Locke proposed a very liberal constitution for South Carolina. Trade between that colony and the Barbados had led Christian merchants to complain that "the Jews so swarm" as to be a menace to the English. Locke saw bigotry, not Jews, as the real menace, and inserted a clause in his draft for the protection of "Jews, heathen, and other dissenters." The basic document adopted was not exactly as he wrote it, but conveyed his spirit.

We conclude this section by turning time backward briefly and crossing the Channel to the Low Countries, then moving fittingly on to Spain, where the chapter began.

The most respected humanist of the decades when the Renaissance lapped at the Reformation was DESIDERIUS ERASMUS (1466–1536) of Rotterdam. The biting wit of *In Praise of Folly* delighted Europe's civilized elite. Unlike his friend and fellow humanist Thomas More, Erasmus spoke out in defense of the Jews and Judaism. "If it is Christian to hate the Jews, all of us are only too good Christians," he wrote. Although he had little, if any, personal contact with them, he was not reluctant to comment on the Jewish threat: "Jews are very numerous in Italy; in Spain there are hardly any Christians. I am afraid that when the occasion arises, that pest, formerly suppressed, will raise its head again."

Because of his renown, Erasmus might have proven a potent ally to the lesser revered (except by Jews) German humanist Johann Reuchlin, when he single-handedly took on the dogmatic Talmud-burners in central Europe. Instead, Erasmus merely gave Reuchlin lukewarm support as a sort of professional courtesy by describing his colleague's nemesis, Johann Pfefferkorn, as "a criminal Jew who had become a most criminal Christian."

Whatever his accomplishments on European civilization's broader canvas, Erasmus deserves no place of honor in Jewish thought.

In 1616, the year Shakespeare died, so did MIGUEL DE CERVANTES (1547–1616). But if we assume *Don Quixote's* creator, born and bred a Spaniard in the century of Inquisition, would thrash Jews more soundly than the Elizabethan Englishman, we are wrong. Cervantes showed his tolerant spirit to the minor extent of taking as his mistress the descendant of a converted Jew, and to the major extent of letting no anti-Semitic canards infiltrate his prose. True, he avoided writing passages that could be interpreted by any stretch as philo-Judaism, but this was Spain.

In one lesser work, *Los Alcaldes de Daganzo*, he did express a notion that Inquisitional authorities might have found questionable. He cleverly derided the belief that the finest qualification for public office was an untainted bloodline. Such purity of descent ruled out not only Jews (who when found were prospects for bonfires), but sincere converts as well.

Should we deny attention to CHRISTOPHER COLUMBUS (1451–1506)? Perhaps. Mystery surrounds his origins, leading some scholars to speculate he was a Marrano. The *Jewish Encyclopedia* says the family name

Colon was not uncommon among Italian Jews. Moreover, his embellished signature evokes Hebraic symbolism. He refers to the Second Temple as the Second House, the way a Jew of his times might. He dates its destruction in the year 68, the same according to Jewish tradition. Of necessity, we will assume he was an observant Christian.

That done, what could be said of Columbus and the Jews? This is less a question of what the great sailor thought of Jews than of what Jews—or, more accurately, Marranos—thought of him. Luis de Santangel, keeper of the privy purse for King Ferdinand (then sovereign of Aragon), took an interest in Columbus's overseas project, later helping raise the two million maravedis necessary to convert the stuff of dreams into seaworthy ships manned by real crews. Another royal treasurer and ex-Jew, Gabriel Sanchez, also participated in the great financial venture. (The myth about Queen Isabella pawning her jewels to raise the necessary funds gained currency two centuries later.) Other Court personalities of Jewish extraction lobbied for the Italian navigator's scheme, including Ferdinand's first chamberlain. Astronomical tables in Abraham Zacuto's *Perpetual Almanac* helped Columbus chart his way westward. When he reached Asia, Luis de Torres, a Jew hastily baptised just before departure, was appointed interpreter; the man knew Hebrew, Chaldean, and Arabic.

In reviewing his grand project, Columbus began, "Therefore, after all the Jews had been exiled from your realms and dominions, in the same month of January, Your Highnesses commanded me that with a sufficient fleet I should go." Apart from that brief note, according to Samuel Eliot Morison, whose *Admiral of the Ocean Sea* won a Pulitzer Prize, "Columbus did not once mention in his writings a tragic movement that was under way at the same time as his preparations, one that must in some measure have hampered his efforts and delayed his departure."

Columbus's second voyage, in 1493, was financed by royal treasury funds derived from the sale of confiscated Jewish property, as were his third and fourth trips across the sea. Silent on moral issues—which he could do nothing to influence—Columbus took the (Jewish) money and sailed.

That the New World became a haven for Jewish refugees centuries later was not to Columbus's credit. But it is reason enough to place him in "Other Voices, Other Deeds."

4

The Age of Enlightenment

L ouis XIV's severe seventeenth-century absolutism mellowed into eighteenth-century benevolent despotism. But not everywhere, or for everyone. True, Austrian, Prussian, and Russian monarchs invited philosophers to their courts. By century's end, the French Revolution would redirect European—and Jewish—history.

MARIA THERESA, 1717–1780
Archduchess of Austria, 1740–1780

History's Conventional View

Maria Theresa's reign could have ended scarcely months after it began in 1740—and nearly did. Maria Theresa was the first female to rule the sprawling Hapsburg lands. Despite assurances given Charles VI, her father, that they would accept the young woman's right to the throne, Prussia, Bavaria, and Saxony swiftly advanced claims on their huge but apparently vulnerable neighbor.

The ensuing War of the Austrian Succession saw Frederick the Great (whom we meet shortly) gobbling up Silesia, while troops of his formidable ally, France, plus Bavarian forces, marched on Prague and Linz. But Maria Theresa forged alliances of her own and—save the loss of Silesia—retained sovereignty over her polyglot empire.

Her forty-year reign sparked a resurgence of Austrian prestige on the world stage; she was adept at power-politics well. Despite her moral protestation that "Trust and faith are lost for all times!" she partook in the First Partition of Poland. Galicia, with its huge Jewish population, passed into her chubby hands.

Maria Theresa bore sixteen children, one of whom grew up to be France's extravagant Marie Antoinette. Her own personal tastes were baroque, and they're still lavishly evident to tourists in Schoenbrunn Palace, the imperial residence she rebuilt. It is there that six-year-old Wolfgang Amadeus Mozart concluded his recital by jumping on the archduchess's lap and kissing her. She laughed and hugged him. On occasion, she would show motherly affection to youngsters—provided they were Christians.

But From a Jewish Perspective

The Jewish historian Heinrich Graetz called Maria Theresa "the most Catholic Empress, who was at once good-natured and hard-hearted." Another Jewish historian, Simon Dubnow, wrote, "The only woman on the Austrian throne caused more trouble to the Jews than had all preceding emperors."

This Hapsburg offspring ("empress" in all but legalistic dynastic jargon) learned anti-Semitism from her father, then displayed her own bigotry on a much larger scale. Her rationale was alleged Jewish cooperation with Frederick's forces during their occupation of Hapsburg territory. Her mind was fixed regarding these "internal enemies."

In December 1744, without first consulting her more knowledgeable representative in Bohemia, she sent him an order: "Because of many important reasons, we have adopted the supreme resolution that in the future no Jew is to be tolerated in our inherited duchy of Bohemia." By January 31, 1745, all Jews were to depart Prague; by June's end, they were to be gone from the entire province.

Local officials transmitted pathetic appeals to Vienna asking for postponement. They said the many thousands to be evicted, some ailing, some with infants, could not possibly leave by month's end amidst midwinter snows.

Even Count Kolovrat, Maria Theresa's chosen agent to carry out this expulsion, pled with her to drop her deadline. She agreed, "most graciously," to a one-month delay, but only for sick residents and for women who had just given birth.

When the deadline expired, Prague's university rector witnessed the sad procession to the city gates. "It was an awful sight to watch the people leave the city with their children and sick." Of the two thousand Jews still left in Bohemia's capital, some were community leaders held semihostage until 160,000 guildens in uncollected taxes were paid to Hapsburg officials.

Maria Theresa now found herself beset by requests to annul the June edict. Bohemian bureaucrats foresaw their province's economic affairs in shambles. Moreover, diplomatic pressure by Austria's European allies— England and Holland—descended on Vienna. The Dutch ambassador warned ominously that not even sovereigns were immune from accounting to the Almighty for their deeds.

Maria Theresa angrily objected to foreign interference in Austria's internal affairs, but such intervention, supplementing the alarm of local officials who moved to carry out her orders with more deliberation than speed, eventually had their effect. In December 1748, four years after her initial decree, she reversed her position. Jews could return to Prague and remain in the rest of Bohemia another ten years. For this privilege, Jews were assessed "tolerance money," a not very subtle form of extortion. The amount was increased when the initial ten-year period was extended. (In her Hungarian possessions, such assessments were called *malke-geld*, or "queen's money.")

Reducing the number of Jews in her domains, though, remained an obsession throughout Maria Theresa's reign. The year 1752 saw renewal of a law limiting marriage opportunity to one son in each family. Jewish households in the empire were thus held down in both Bohemia and Moravia. Periodically, a census safeguarded against any rise in their number.

Meanwhile, at the imperial core, in the same Vienna that cultivated Mozart's genius, "tolerated" Jews existed under a stifling array of decrees and "Jew ordinances." Historian Dubnow recited them:

> that young men should not enter into matrimony without the special approval of the authorities; that the Jews coming to Vienna temporarily were to have a pass and could stay no more than four days; that Jewish factories were to employ Christians also; that Jews should live apart from Christians; that married Jews were not to trim their beards, and that in general all Jews were to wear headgear with the

traditional yellow band.... The empress took into account everything except for the fact that she was not living in the Middle Ages.

That a small number of Jews was tolerated at all in Her Majesty's capital attested to their business acumen, hence their financial worth to the empire. For example, over a twenty-five-year period, Diego D'Aguilar raised ten million florins for the imperial treasury, plus an additional three hundred thousand to help Maria Theresa refurbish her beloved Schoenbrunn. (He eventually fled to London while his sovereign considered a Spanish government demand for his extradition as a "judaizer.") Another Jew, Israel Hoenig, was so successful in running the state's tobacco monopoly in Bohemia and Moravia that he was offered similar concessions in other Hapsburg lands.

No matter. The archduchess ruled that Jews "bring the state more harm than good." Maria Theresa held this view to the end of her days. In 1777, three years before that end came, she maintained, "I don't know any worse pest for the government than this nation—because of its deceit, its usury... and all the other evil deeds which an honest person detests. They should be kept at a distance or their number should be curtailed as much as possible." When it became necessary to grant a Jew an audience, she is reputed to have done so from behind a partition.

Within her lifetime, her empire emerged with the largest Jewish population in all Europe. With the stroke of the pen that detached Galicia from Poland and added it to the Hapsburg realm, the number of Jews doubled: She now had one-hundred-fifty-thousand more Jews. How to deal with them? That problem would fall to Maria Theresa's son, Joseph II, successor to the Hapsburg throne.

JOSEPH II, 1741–1790
Holy Roman Emperor, 1765–1790

History's Conventional View

Young Joseph had received the Holy Roman Empire's hollow crown on the death of Maria Theresa's consort in 1765, as well as titular status as Austria's coruler. But while his strong-willed mother lived, Joseph remained impatiently in the background. His concept of enlightened despotism was slightly ahead of his own times and far in advance of hers. In the developing Age of Reason he favored rational answers to Austria's question-marked future. They included such precocious notions as religious toleration, great leaps forward in secular education, limits on Vatican influence, and an end to the long-standing legal and fiscal privileges enjoyed by the nobility. These views aroused the ire of entrenched interests, and Maria Theresa thwarted radical change.

Once in command, though, Joseph moved with dispatch. Thousands of ordinances poured from government printing presses to work his will. And if success ultimately eluded him, at least he could argue that Europe's later convulsions spread from a *French* Revolution, not an *Austrian* one.

But From a Jewish Perspective

Joseph II's new order suggested a refreshing change after his mother's suffocating reign. When he had broached the subject of including Austria's Jews as part of the mainstream, she wrote him that without a "dominant religion...tolerance, indifference" would spread and "these were just the means to undermine everything." Only after 1780 could he pursue his Jewish policy free of his mother's restraint. Unfortunately, as we will shortly see, progress carried a heavy price.

On the positive side, Joseph immediately abolished the archaic practice of forcing Jews to wear a yellow badge. He canceled the humiliating body toll charge imposed on Jewish travelers as well as their animals. The stated aim of his series of decrees issued between May 1781 and January 1782 was to liberate Jews from "humiliating and oppressive laws" and to assure all Austrian subjects could contribute to the public welfare "without any distinction in regard to nationality and religion." All were to enjoy liberty before the law and an opportunity to earn a livelihood.

His Toleranzpatent, a statute on Jewish rights issued on January 2, 1782, was the first of its kind in Europe. Doors moldy and creaking from centuries of disuse would theoretically swing open. Henceforth, Jews would have the right to send their children to elementary schools. University admission was expressly permitted, which meant that for the first time such professions as law and medicine could be practiced without the sham of conversion. Jews could enter all trades and handicrafts, turn to agriculture, establish factories, and engage in large-scale commerce on a par with Christians. Intellectuals and businessmen likely to benefit from government-fostered assimilation viewed Joseph's plans favorably. With the sweep of a pen, he would achieve for them what they were unable to achieve themselves.

But outside this relatively small cosmopolite Jewish strata, concerns, even fears, arose. The future of Jews, as Jews, seemed at risk. German-language instruction would be mandatory in Jewish schools. Two years after promulgation of Joseph's decree, Yiddish and Hebrew were to be eliminated in contracts and public records under penalty of annulment. Judicial autonomy within the Jewish community was to be abolished. Although the body tax collected at city gates had been scrapped, a compensatory tax replaced it in the same amount. And in a dubious liberating gesture, Jewish youngsters were now eligible for military conscription.

The emperor's goal was obvious, and in fairness to him, he never tried to hide it. Joseph II wanted to turn Jews into Germans, thereby rendering them more useful to the state. If this transformation bled Jewishness from their spirit, all the better, for Austria's sovereign saw Judaism as the "quintessence of foolishness and nonsense." Discussing a report regarding a new ordinance for Galician Jews, he wrote:

> Their customs that do not contradict the laws of the state may be preserved; but with respect to the other customs one will have a choice: either he will renounce the religious customs that do not correspond to the spirit of the time and conditions, or he will forfeit all the privileges and, upon payment of the emigrant tax, will depart from the country.

From across the Prussian border, the Jewish philosopher Moses Mendelssohn commented on the emperor's reforms to an Austrian friend: "Thank you kindly for the tolerance, which is extended with the ulterior motive about uniting the faiths.... Such a tolerance, from under which the systems of merging faiths peeps out, is even a more dangerous play in tolerance than open persecution."

For better, as some Jews thought, or worse, as did others, Joseph II's views and new direction would infiltrate European states beyond the Hapsburg frontiers. Mendelssohn recognized one danger, Austria's reactionaries quite another. They likely fretted little when Joseph passed away at age forty-nine before he could take further bold steps.

In 1925, a century and a half later, an Austrian, Adolf Hitler, wrote in

Mein Kampf: "Today it must be regarded as a good fortune that a Germanization as intended by Joseph II in Austria was not carried out. Its result would probably have been the preservation of the Austrian state, but also the lowering of the racial level of the German nation."

FREDERICK II (The Great), 1712–1786
King of Prussia, 1740–1786

History's Conventional View

Hunched Frederick II stands tallest in the procession of numbered Fredericks and Frederick Williamses across the Prussian and German historical landscapes. Adolf Hitler, thankful that Joseph II's measures of assimilation failed, considered Frederick II a "heroic genius." Joseph Goebbels, Nazi propaganda minister, made a diary entry noting Adolf Hitler's lavish praise: "...and Frederick the Great! He towers above every other figure in Prussian and German history. He, and he alone, succeeded in turning Prussia into a historical entity. We should all grovel in the dust in the face of his greatness."

Contributing to this stature was his single-mindedness in expanding Prussian power via its well-drilled army, and the amoral ruthlessness he employed. Take Silesia from Austria; later cooperate *with* Austria to dismember Poland. In the cutthroat world of European diplomacy and duplicity, Frederick was always ready to dip his pen or unsheath his sword. On one occasion, luck saved him. During the Seven Years War, his capital, Berlin, was nearly overrun by his bearish, bigger neighbor, Russia. The timely death of its implacable tsarina, Elizabeth, ended the threat.

Frederick has been described as a philosopher-king, but Jews, we'll see, might alter that view. His childhood attraction to music and art struck his brutal father, Frederick William I, as frivolous. On succeeding to the throne, he invited philosophers—Voltaire, among them—to his palace, San Souci. His own collected works, written in French, his preferred language, fill more than thirty volumes. The king composed chamber music that is still played today. But closest to his heart was the army around which his state was built.

All resources of the state were mobilized to feed and nourish that army. Frederick saw himself as the "first servant" of Prussia. Johann Wolfgang von Goethe regarded him "self-willed" and "incorrigible." His unfortunate neighbors found him shrewd and ravenous.

But From a Jewish Perspective

At one point, friction between young Frederick and his father led to Frederick's flight from Berlin, but he was caught and punished by Frederick William as a "deserter." Father and son, however, were of one mind about Jews. Both detested the presence of these aliens in their midst. As a Jewish scholar put it, "It seemed as if only the name of the ruler had changed, not the principles of his government." These principles became a spider's web of rules, regulations, and restrictions certain to bring a Mona Lisa smile to Maria Theresa's lips.

Early in Frederick's reign, Breslau Jews protested when regulations reintroduced in 1744 limited them to ten "protected" families, with all others ordered to depart. Frederick responded, "They may retain the rights concerning their trade, but they cannot be permitted to bring masses of Jews into Breslau and transform it into a complete Jerusalem."

Collection of "protection money" from Jewish communities continued. So did a tax on confirmation of representatives chosen by those communities. There was a special stamp tax, a silver tax, and a passage tax when Jews crossed the border from one Prussian province to another. Frederick cautioned bureaucrats not to avoid liberality in granting new letters of protection and ordered retention of regulations enacted in 1730 regarding collective responsibility for acts committed by members of local Jewish communities.

Ten years into his reign, Frederick issued his most far-reaching ordinance, the Revidiertes General Privilegium und Reglement vor die Judenschaft. It placed Jews under the king's guardianship and subdivided "protected" Jews into two categories. Jewish historian Simon Dubnow explains:

> The first group was comprised of the privileged heads of families who possessed the hereditary right of domicile and could transmit it to that one of their children who was privileged to marry. The extraordinary enjoyed only the personal right of domicile, but could not bequeath the right to children, who could not marry. In that way, the Jews had the alternative: either abstain from marriage or leave Berlin. And that indeed was the noble intent of the lawgiver.

Beyond "ordinary" protected Jews and "extraordinary" protected Jews, Frederick left no room in his Prussia for those assigned to neither classification. Trade was open only to "ordinary" protected Jews, and for them, even dealings in such commodities as pelts, tobacco, and wool were off-limits. Entry into handicrafts was forbidden where Christian guilds existed, and since they produced most wares, little was left. Agriculture was definitely closed.

Jews needed a special concession for opening a factory, purchasing a Christian's home, or building one of their own. Frederick especially took care to keep Berlin ethnically pure. Jewish home ownership in his capital was limited to forty structures, and any Jews appearing at the city's gates were questioned, their legal documents scrutinized.

Until stresses of the Seven Years War prompted modifications, enforcement followed the letter of the law. The king held to an "inviolate principle," wrote Dubnow, that only one family member be granted the "letter of security" permitting domicile. He "rejected mercilessly" pleas for extensions. Moreover, a Jewish merchant who descended into bankruptcy forfeited his status and "the king was overjoyed whenever it was possible to strike out a Jewish family from the list of 'ordinary' Jews."

Only the mounting costs of Frederick's military machine led him to relent—and that at a hefty price. In 1763, he permitted a second child in "ordinary" protected families to marry, a concession for which Jewish communities were assessed 70,000 thalers.

Some Jews *did* prosper during the crucible of the Seven Years War as the result of Frederick's patronage. Their talent in finance proved crucial to his war-making. They provided risk capital, provisioned the army, organized war loans, and handled the government's minting operations. Never one to be bothered by moral or ethical constraints, Frederick freely debased coinage—his own and those of foreign allies—using the Jewish Berlin firm of Ephraim and Sons as his instrument. The resulting coins, "Ephraimites," aroused general scorn:

> Pretty on the outside, worthless within;
> On the outside Frederick, Ephraim within.

One Jewish name more often associated with Frederick's than others is Moses Mendelssohn, a sometime visitor at San Souci. Here, presumably, was the philosopher-king at his best, engaging in profound, cosmic conversation with the philosopher-Jew universally acknowledged as the beacon leading his people into the Enlightenment. But Frederick's nature made no allowance for genius. When the Berlin Academy of Sciences voted Mendelssohn admission to its select circle, he rejected its decision. The presence of a Jew in that prestigious academy repelled him. Instead, Frederick offered the opening to a less gifted intellect, Catherine II of Russia.

Only through persuasion would the king even grant Mendelssohn the coveted status necessary for permanent domicile in Berlin. The French Marquis d'Argens, then residing at Frederick's Potsdam court, inscribed on Mendelssohn's petition: "A philosopher and a bad Catholic begs a philosopher and bad Protestant to grant protection to a philosopher and a bad Jew."

Frederick's generosity knew bounds, however. He granted lifelong, not hereditary, privileges. So Mendelssohn could not pass them along to his children, and thence to their children, one of whom would become his grandson, the composer Felix Mendelssohn.

Royal extortion continued. Aside from "protection money," Jews were required to pay "recruit money" in lieu of military service. A "silver donation" was also extracted. Beginning in 1766, Jews were forced to deliver 12,000 silver marks annually to the royal mint. This sum was increased to 25,000 marks in 1768.

Documents carried a seal tax, and no Jew could safely travel without his precious papers. Marriage certificates for the first child in each family cost 100 thalers; for the second, 150. In the latter case the newlyweds' parents were required to export royal factory manufactures valued at 1,500 thalers even if they were certain to lose money in the transaction.

In 1769, Frederick introduced his porcelain tax as a refinement. Henceforth, marriage, purchase of a house, or any other major milestone in a "protected" Jew's life were to be tied to the purchase of a quantity of porcelain, often of inferior quality, from the royal factory. Frederick, in effect, was running a royal protection racket throughout Prussia.

Bad as things were for theoretically privileged Jews, they could have been worse for the unprotected Polish Jews he inherited in the wake of the First Partition of Poland. These were poor, hence worthless for financial extortion, so his initial intention was to expel them from his newly annexed provinces. Impracticality halted that solution. Instead, such "beggar Jews" were quarantined in those areas where they resided. Movement was barred, lest it contaminate the rest of Prussia.

In 1780, responding by letter to a suggestion that he better the lot of Prussia's Jews, Frederick wrote: "I have long known that you unfortunately cherish a secret inclination for the miserable Jews. But for my part, I think differently.... Away with the usurious vermin who multiply so infamously...note it well, you adorer of these wretches."

Defenders of Frederick's Jewish policy fall under two headings. Those like Hitler found in him a kindred spirit and applaud his conduct. More scholarly apologists point out he cynically hated all mankind, Jews merely more than the rest. His last testament, in fact, instructed that he be buried on the garden terrace at Sans Souci next to his fine greyhounds, the only creatures to whom he gave affection.

Jews living under Frederick, on the other hand, would surely agree with the French statesman and future revolutionary, Honore Gabriel Mirabeau, who remarked after visiting Berlin that Frederick's decrees were "worthy of a cannibal."

ELIZABETH PETROVNA, 1709–1762
Tsarina of Russia, 1741–1762

History's Conventional View

Less a household name than her father's, Peter the Great, or the wife of her nephew's, the future Catherine the Great, Elizabeth's impact on what Catherine could or could not do about altering Russia's Jewish policy merits her inclusion in these pages.

Elizabeth hated Jews. She also hated Frederick the Great and almost toppled him during the Seven Years War. Her own death at the inopportune moment when Prussia was soundly whipped let Frederick survive, recover, and prosper another quarter of a century.

By those who think well of her, Elizabeth is remembered for founding the University of Moscow and the Academy of Fine Arts at St. Petersburg. She is remembered by others for lavishing funds on theater, opera, banquets, and herself. She loathed to wear a dress more than once, and is said to have lost four thousand in a 1744 palace fire. Nonetheless, fifteen thousand more were left in her wardrobe at the time of her passing.

Masquerade balls every Tuesday became de rigueur during the winter season. Because she looked well in men's clothing, both sexes at these weekly extravaganzas were expected to cross-dress.

Intrigues and conspiracies marked court life. Ignoring her advisers' recommendation that a treasonous general, his wife, and their son be broken on the rack, she commuted their death sentences and instructed that they merely be flogged, their tongues cut out, and their property confiscated before they were shipped off to Siberian exile.

But From a Jewish Perspective

Elizabeth was a religious fanatic and Jews suffered the consequences. In an ordinance issued in 1742, her first year as tsarina, she invoked the memory of her "most beloved mother," Catherine I, referring to that sovereign's 1727 order expelling Jews. Elizabeth rued the decree had not been truly executed. She wanted to make amends:

> Since we heard that Jews still dwell in our empire, particularly in Little Russia, and that they invade in various ways, presumably to engage in trade or maintain inns and taverns; and since nothing good accrues from the haters of Christ our Messiah, except the worse harm for our loyal subjects—therefore it is decreed . . . to immediately expel all Jews across the border, and in the future not to admit them under any circumstances, unless some of them would be willing to profess the Greek Orthodox faith, in which event, the baptised would be granted domicile in our empire, but are not to be released from our country.

Suspecting some local officials might look the other way as in the past, she demanded they "keep a sharp eye, under threat of arousing our utmost wrath and extreme corporal punishment, against failing to carry out the command."

With "this wicked decree," wrote Dubnow, she had "with one blow" denied Jews both permanent and temporary residence in her huge realm. Petitions from the Ukraine and Lifland led the Russian Senate to send Elizabeth a report that Jews be allowed to cross the border for trade, arguing they should be permitted to do so for the sake of the state's commerce, to help increase royal treasury revenue, and for the economic well-being of her Christian subjects in border provinces. But Elizabeth's mind was closed. "From the enemies of Christ, I wish neither gain nor profit," she scribbled on the report.

Among the deportees was one Antonio Ribera Sanchez, a former Portuguese who had practiced medicine in St. Petersburg since 1731, headed the army's medical department, and served as Elizabeth's own personal physician. When his Jewish origins became clear, even he was forced to move on.

A 1753 document points to thirty-five thousand Jews ousted during the decade as Elizabeth worked her will, although this statistic may be high. Whatever the future, though, Elizabeth bequeathed to her successor a Russia nearly devoid of a Jewish presence.

CATHERINE II (the Great), 1729–1796
Tsarina of Russia, 1762–1796

History's Conventional View

One popular mental image is of an aging Catherine the Great, floating down the Dneiper in an elegant barge, smiling approvingly as she passes picturesque hamlets, flocks of sheep grazing contentedly along the river bank, and peasants waving at their sovereign. Behind her stands her chief minister, Potemkin, architect of this elaborate charade.

Not quite accurate. True, she had a dozen or more lovers, and Potemkin was one of them. But naïveté did not earn her the title, the Great. Catherine, not her amorous partners, was the driving force in affairs of state.

This was the first tsarina to embrace the Enlightenment then infiltrating from France. But she did so selectively. She corresponded with Voltaire and regarded herself a disciple of the Encyclopedists. Their leader, Denis Diderot, was an honored guest. She collected art on a grand scale. St. Petersburg's Hermitage owes much to her cultural bent.

Whatever political illumination began to bathe the West was a light that failed in Catherine's Russia. Letters of Majesty sent to her nobility granted them ever greater power over the wretched lives of their serfs. Protests by the downtrodden evolved into a full-scale rebellion, which was brutally suppressed. Of more concern to us, Catherine engaged in an aggressive foreign policy both to Russia's south and northwest. By tearing off, and then absorbing, sections of Polish Lithuania, she suddenly found herself—as had Maria Theresa—with a Jewish Problem.

But From a Jewish Perspective

The course of Catherine's early Jewish policy, before this explosion, was unfortunately guided by the dead hand of Tsarina Elizabeth. Despite "her own more rationalistic attitude," wrote historian Salo W. Baron, Catherine "proceeded gingerly." She hesitated to depart drastically from her predecessor's hard line.

This conservative approach stemmed at least in part from Catherine's shaky legal title to the throne. A Prussian princess by birth, no Romanov blood flowed through her veins. She had seized power upon the assassination of her hopelessly inept husband, Tsar Peter III. Throw in questions about her own complicity, if any, in his assassination, then add a zeal to mollify powerful and rigid dignitaries of the Russian Orthodox Church, and her reticence to reverse past decisions makes sense. Good sense demanded caution.

The new tsarina *did* slightly relax prohibitions by means of administrative benign neglect. Whereas Elizabeth chased away Jews going about their private affairs in the still young commercial center of St. Petersburg, Catherine quietly welcomed back contractors, businessmen, and physicians. She told city officials to overlook the presence of "useful" Jews. A viable Jewish community soon emerged in this northern hub.

Slight adjustments to the status quo could not suffice, though, following the massive population shift of the First Partition of Poland. To her west, both Maria Theresa and Frederick the Great's inclination was to oust this newly acquired and clearly perceived Jewish rabble from their realms. By contrast, Catherine's solution was humane. Her order of August 11, 1772, read: "Jewish communities residing in the towns, cities and territories now incorporated in the Russian Empire shall be left in the enjoyment of all those liberties with regard to their religion and property which they at present possess."

Following mercantilist principles and aware that Jews enhanced commerce wherever they dwelled, Catherine's manifesto allowed them to join one of the Russian merchant guilds or, if they chose, to become town burghers. Moreover, Jews were to be admitted to municipal governmental bodies on the basis of equality.

However, petty authorities and powerful provincial governors alike worked to sabotage such liberalization. Orders issued at the empire's center went unimplemented. Worse, a change gradually came over the tsarina herself, Catherine's own candle of enlightenment flickered. In 1790, Moscow's Orthodox merchants complained that their Jewish competitors imported higher quality goods and sold them at lower prices. The next year, a decree stated that Jewish admission to guild membership and burgher status applied only to newly acquired territories, not to old Russia.

The net now tightened. After 1794, Jews were to be taxed at double the rate of Christians, and while their area of permitted residence extended to the provinces of the Ukraine east of the Dneiper River, it halted there. Thus, in Catherine's last years—and at her direction—the Pale of Settlement (a term yet to be coined) was taking form. "Inner Russia" was to be closed to Jews.

It is time to return to France, intellectual vortex of the Age of Reason. Voltaire deserves a special place denied his peers, for he was the leading figure of the Enlightenment. Moreover, Voltaire was a welcome guest at Frederick the Great's Court and a faithful correspondent of Catherine the Great. His caustic, sharp-edged pen outweighed many a dull sword, and this exemplary moralist, champion of free thought and ultimate man of reason chose to wield it unreasonably and savagely against Jews.

French historian Léon Poliakov understandably subtitled one volume in his scholarly *The History of Anti-Semitism* "From Voltaire to Wagner." In his carefully researched *The French Enlightenment and the Jews*, Professor Arthur Hertzberg contends that Voltaire's writings "were the great arsenal of anti-Jewish arguments for those enemies of the Jews who wanted to sound contemporary," and that "an analysis of everything that Voltaire wrote about Jews throughout his life establishes the proposition that he is the major link in the Western intellectual history between the anti-Semitism of classic paganism and the modern age."

FRANCOIS MARIE AROUET (Voltaire), 1694–1778

History's Conventional View

Voltaire's apostolic status in the intellectual ferment of eighteenth-century France goes unchallenged. We see him as a sage, robed as a classical philosopher, smiling—wryly, of course—from the marble statue by Houdon. He scathingly exposed the iniquities of France's dissolute ancien régime, ridiculed the rituals of the Church, and prudently bought a house near the Swiss border to assure a place to which he could flee if authorities moved against him.

While still a youthful critic, he was imprisoned in the infamous Bastille. But his growing prominence among enlightened men in high places, at home and abroad, later rendered him virtually untouchable. Philosopher, poet, playwright, moralist, historian, novelist, and pamphleteer—the nemesis of arbitrary power and injustice everywhere.

Flowing from his pen were such diverse works as the *Philosophical Dictionary*, histories of the reigns of Charles XII of Sweden and France's Louis XIV, an epic, *La Henriade*, a look at comparative politics, *Letters Upon the English*, a philosophical novel, *Zadig*, and a tragedy, *Brutus*. Yet their author's assessment of Dante may apply to himself. Voltaire said Dante's reputation kept increasing because he was never read.

Ask intelligent folks today to fit Voltaire on history's time line, and they will likely insert him among the great writers and thinkers. Ask them to name three of his works they read, and they are just as likely to begin and end with his satirical *Candide*, that timeless tale of a young man educated to believe "all is for the best in the best possible of worlds."

But From a Jewish Perspective

Voltaire hated Jews. Whether the vitriol in his writings poured from pure contempt of Jews as Jews, or was a derived, contaminated, contempt is still discussed by scholars. He detested the Bible and saw Judaism as the precursor of Christianity, another and more formidable target.

The evidence left by some men of state regarding Jews is often in the form of documents prepared by underlings, then wax-sealed in the royal name. But Voltaire's writings are his own.

According to French professor Léon Poliakov, thirty or more of his *Philosophical Dictionary*'s 118 articles attack Jews. Writing of Abraham, he called biblical Jews "a small, new, ignorant, crude people." The longest entry in the work is "Jews"—thirty pages. But the assault continued under headings as unlikely as "Anthropophagi," "Soul," and "Torture."

Voltaire's judgment was harsh and relentless. "You will find in them," he wrote, "only an ignorant and barbarous people who have long exercised the most sordid avarice and detestable superstition, and an insurmountable hate for all peoples who have tolerated and enriched them."

Of the Jews of Spanish-Portuguese extraction, who had proven an economic asset to France in his own time, he wrote in a 1773 letter: "I know that there are some Jews in the English colonies. These Marranos go wherever there is money to be made.... They are nonetheless the greatest scoundrels who have ever sullied the face of the globe." On the matter of persecution, he could, of course, have no sympathy for Jews: "The only difference is that *our* priests have had you burned by laymen, and that your priests have always sacrificed human victims with their sacred hands."

Voltaire's anti-Semitism has sometimes been attributed to two personal episodes. The first occurred when Voltaire was thirty-two. In 1726 he crossed the Channel armed with a 20,000-franc letter of credit drawn on a Jewish banker. "On my coming to London," he later explained, "I found the damned Jew was broke. I was without a penny, sick to death of a violent ague, a stranger, alone, helpless in the midst of a city where I was known to nobody."

The second found Voltaire, now an acclaimed philosopher, in a shady currency and diamond transaction with a Prussian Court Jew. This led to a nasty squabble and subsequent legal proceedings from which the great man of the Enlightenment artfully extracted himself by having highly placed friends influence the court. Nonetheless, the crassness of his conduct embarrassed even his royal host, Frederick the Great, certainly no font of ethics himself. Frederick sent for the court records, read the incriminating evidence, and was aghast. Voltaire left Berlin shortly after the incident.

But Voltaire denied his attitude toward Jews was influenced by personal factors: "I have forgotten about much larger bankruptcies by good Christians without complaining." On one occasion, the philosopher saw fit to answer in civil, if condescending, tone, the criticisms of Isaac de Pinto, a learned Jew. This Amsterdam scholar had sent the great man a copy of his own book with a flattering cover letter. De Pinto wrote: "Is harm done by the pen less injurious than the flames of the pyre? Is the evil not more consuming than fire, since it is passed on to posterity? What can this unhappy nation expect of the rabble if barbarous prejudices are shared even by the most glorious genius of our enlightened age?"

Voltaire responded by letter in July 1762: "The lines you are complaining of, Monsieur, are violent and unfair. There are amongst you men who are very educated and very worthy of respect. Your letter quite convinces me of this. I will take care to make an insertion in the new edition. When one is wrong, one must make amends, and I was wrong to attribute to a whole nation the vices of several individuals." But the sorry fact is that Voltaire never altered a line in the revised edition.

Nevertheless, a watchful Jewish contemporary of Voltaire was willing to turn the other cheek. Scholar Zalkind-Hourwitz said: "...the Jews forgive him all the ill he has done them, in consideration of the good he has done them, although involuntarily, perhaps even unknowingly, because if they are enjoying a little peace for a few years, they owe it to the advance of the Enlightenment, to which Voltaire has certainly contributed more than any other writer, by his numerous works against fanaticism."

While spewing venom at Jews throughout his *Philosophical Dictionary*, Voltaire had taken care to add that "Nevertheless they should not be burned at the stake." As for his overall output regarding Jews, the founder and director of the Institut et Musée Voltaire, housed in Voltaire's Geneva home, offered this defense in his lengthy biography: "Voltaire's language was the language of his times and we must not expect even the greatest of men always to rise above their environment."

But Professor Hertzberg's harsher judgment—from a Jew's perspective—seems more on the mark. Voltaire abandoned religious attacks on Jews as Christ-killers, according to Hertzberg, and "proposed a new principle on which to base his hatred of them, their innate character." Other icons of the Enlightenment believed that, once free of persecution, Jews would cast off the rituals of Judaism and melt into mainstream culture. Voltaire, writes Professor Hertzberg, believed Jews were "subversive of the European tradition by their very presence, for they are the radically other, the hopeless alien. Cure them of their religion and their inborn character remains."

A generation after the philosopher's passing, his constant pounding at Jews puzzled an American president. In an 1808 letter to a friend, John Adams, then retired, wondered, "How is it possible this old fellow should represent the Hebrews in such a contemptible light?"

LOUIS XVI, 1754–1793
King of France, 1774–1792

History's Conventional View

Great-great-great-grandson of Louis XIV and grandson of Louis XV, Louis XVI closed a long line of Bourbons against whom Voltaire railed for more than half a century. In a blossoming Age of Reason, he remained unreasonable. Against the era of the Enlightenment, he wore blinkers. Louis XV (or his mistress, Madame de Pompadour) had said, "Aprés nous le déluge" ("After us the deluge"), and upon his successor it poured.

Louis XVI is best remembered for continuing the long-established misgovernance of France. His queen, Marie Antoinette, frivolous daughter of Maria Theresa, possessed the social conscience of a moth. She quickly earned the contempt of her subjects as "that Austrian woman." While her royal husband toyed with watches, his hobby, she engaged in more expensive pastimes.

In May 1789, as France plunged in a free fall toward bankruptcy, Louis summoned the three-tiered Estates General. The first two, clergy and nobility—hopelessly reactionary—refused to extend parity to the much larger Third Estate, vehicle of France's growing middle class. The consequences need no elaboration here.

Even after the Bastille's fall, a sensible sovereign might have saved the day, the crown, and his head by a strategic retreat. But Louis XVI was neither sensible nor flexible. And Marie Antoinette didn't help by her memorable aside that, lacking bread, starving Parisians should eat cake.

History's broader view of Louis XVI ends with the narrow blade of the guillotine, beneath which thousands of the privileged nobility eventually fell, including the queen and one Chretien Guillaume de Lamoignon de Malesherbes, about whom more is said shortly.

Lest glaring domestic errors stamp France's last pre-Revolution king, United States history textbooks acknowledge great overseas deeds, or, failing that, offer a footnote recording his assent needed to set them in motion. Without French financial, military, and naval aid, George Washington's beleaguered forces might have failed in their mission, and Benjamin Franklin, Thomas Jefferson, and John Hancock could have hanged separately.

But From a Jewish Perspective

An improvement in the lot of Jews could hardly have been expected from a monarch whose ossified mind would eventually cost him his own neck. Maintenance of the status quo, with a slight nod to justice here and a deep bow to darker motives there, marked the decade before deluge.

Back in 1723, when Louis XV succeeded Louis XIV, Jews living in southern France "received into the kingdom under the title of Portuguese or New Christians" had won new patent letters confirming past privileges. Perhaps, not coincidentally, this followed a 110,000-livres payment in honor of "the joyous event of His Majesty's coronation."

Similar enthusiasm at Louis XVI's elevation safeguarded against backsliding. The established, financially comfortable Sephardim of Bordeaux, Bayonne, and Marseilles had no reason to fear Paris. But the position of the Ashkenazim in France's northern and eastern provinces was far more precarious. Their customs and language, very similar to Jews living across the French-German frontier, marked them as alien. They lived in territories wrested from German princes during Louis XIV's wars of expansion in the 1600s. In Alsace, anti-Semitism was easily stoked among the peasantry by the nobility, clergy, and especially the burghers of Strasbourg. Overtaxed and overregulated Jews sent representatives to the capital, pleading for relief. Louis granted just one concession in a January 1784 decree:

> We have heard that in Alsace and especially in the environs of Strasbourg the Jews are required to pay a body tax that places them upon the same level as cattle. Since it contravenes the good will that we cherish without distinction to all our subjects to permit a tax offensive to human dignity to remain in force for one group of them, we have found it good to abolish this same tax.

This seemed a notable step forward at a time the French capital itself still maintained a special Inspectorate for Jews and Swindlers. Inclusion of Jews in the expression "Our subjects" even implied the king deemed Jews Frenchmen, not foreigners.

But Louis had not suddenly been stricken by the Enlightenment. Six months later, he issued a second, more general, decree that signified a longer stride backward:

> Those Jews who are scattered over the province of Alsace and who, at the time of the promulgation of this law, have no definite domicile and do not pay the king any taxes for their protection...are required to leave the province within three months, even in those instances where they pledge to pay those taxes in the future.

New regulations were invoked to hamper trade in grain, cattle, and moneylending. Towns and villages were forbidden to shelter alien Jews, and under threat of expulsion, marriage among Jews was prohibited without special royal permission. By enjoining rabbis from performing marriage ceremonies without a permit, the number of Jewish families could be controlled.

Louis XVI's decree evidenced further retreat. It referred to "Jews of Our province of Alsace," and proposed to reconcile "to the degree that it seems possible to Us, their interests with those of Our subjects." Jews apparently were no longer counted as "Our subjects."

Still, there was hope for a brighter future. Louis was not a wicked soul, merely weak and easily swayed by advisers and nobles not always of noble nature. In 1785, the Metz Royal Society arranged a competition on the subject, "Is there any way of rendering the Jews more useful and happier in France?" Some useful ideas were put forward in essays. Maybe they leaked back to Versailles. In any event, in 1788, Chretien Guillaume de Lamoignon de Malesherbes, who had earlier headed a royal commission charged with mitigating civil disabilities affecting Protestants, was charged by his sovereign with a similar mission regarding Jews.

Professor Poliakov mentions a remark alleged to Louis when he met with his agent: "Monsieur de Malesherbes, you have made yourself a Protestant and I am making you a Jew!" But de Malesherbes, one of the few competent men still holding the king's ear, was stymied. Discord between Sephardic and Ashkenazi representatives appearing before his commission led to deadlock. There would be no second chance. Time was running out on the Old Regime.

Men of the Revolution

THE COMTE DE MIRABEAU, 1749–1791

THE MARQUIS DE LAFAYETTE, 1757–1834

MAXIMILIEN ROBESPIERRE, 1758–1794

History's Conventional View

There were other famous figures of the French Revolution—Danton, Carnot, Marat, Desmoulins, and Saint-Just. They do not concern us here. The Jewish question merited little interest for them and their attentions lay elsewhere. So, indeed, the same was true of Mirabeau, Lafayette, and Robespierre. But their voices, at least, enter the record.

Others chose to speak during assembly debates on Jewry's future. It was Stanislas Clermont-Tonnerre who declared, "Everything must be denied to the Jews as a nation, and everything granted to them as citizens!" But the author of this oft-paraphrased formula is not a marquee name, nor are those of Rabaut de Saint Etienne and the Abbé Grégoire, who also addressed France's legislative body on the subject.

For the first two years of the Revolution, Count Mirabeau was perhaps its most important figure. Statesman, orator, foe of the royal court, he had attended the Estates General as a deputy from the Third Estate, not the nobility to which he was born. When an aide of Louis ordered the members to disperse, Mirabeau roared, "Go and tell your master that we are here by the will of the people and that we shall not budge save at the point of a bayonet." Named president of the National Assembly formed later, he died prematurely, at age forty-two in 1791.

The Marquis de Lafayette, already a hero on both sides of the Atlantic for his role in the American Revolution, sacrificed court favor by working for a constitutional monarchy. He commanded the national guard from 1789 to 1791, while the following year saw him leading troops through Jewish-inhabited areas of eastern France. Lafayette's disenchantment with the direction taken by the Revolution by its new, more radical leaders led to his being declared a traitor. He fled the country and was, for a time, held captive in Austria.

Maximilien Robespierre—"the Incorruptible"—is best recalled for putting Dr. Guillotin's mechanical device in overdrive. Determined to "purge" the Revolution of dissent, he used the Committee of Public Safety to shed the blood of guilty and not-so-guilty countrymen as "enemies of the state." The Reign of Terror ended when Robespierre himself was arrested by fearful associates and executed.

But From a Jewish Perspective

Count Mirabeau was good for Jews and could have been lots better if he had lived longer. Having traveled widely in Europe during the pre-Revolutionary decade, he had come into contact with educated Jews. He admired Moses Mendelssohn, to whom "humanity and truth seemed much dearer" than "the dark phantoms of the Talmudists." Although Mirabeau was unsympathetic to any rituals, he did not consider Judaism an immoral religion and advocated improving the lot of its practitioners. In a 1787 treatise, he wrote:

> You desire the Jews to become useful citizens. Then banish from social life all humiliating distinctions; give the Jews access to all sources of livelihood. Instead of forbidding them to engage in agriculture,

handicraft and the mechanical arts, urge them to take up these occupations.... Confer upon them the enjoyment of civil rights and they will enter the ranks of useful citizens.

These are the ideas he carried forward past the Bastille's fall. In August 1789, during the historic debate leading to the Declaration of the Rights of Man, he clashed with conservative deputies who wanted Catholicism recognized as the state religion, with all others merely being "tolerated."

"Dominant religion!" he shouted. "May this despotic phrase disappear entirely from our legislation. Unlimited religious liberty is to my eyes so sacred that even the word *tolerance* sounds tyrannical to me."

He didn't get his way. The status of Jews remained unclear, and success elusive when the assembly returned to the matter of enfranchisement in December. Protestants gained their equality without difficulty, and even actors and hangmen received civic rights. But clerical objections and the adamancy of deputies from Alsace barred full emancipation for Jews. Realizing he did not have the votes, Mirabeau was forced to table the resolution that would have achieved it.

One month later came what some described as a partial victory. Bordeaux and Bayonne's long-assimilated Sephardic communities got their way. A motion to permit such Jews, previously enfranchised, to continue with that right passed by a 374 to 224 vote. When the Marquis de Lafayette cast his vote for the resolution the Left applauded and cheers filled the gallery. But the Ashkenazim of northeastern France were untouched by this advance.

Lalkind-Hourwitz (who, remember, offered a specious defense of Voltaire) approached the prestigious Lafayette in behalf of his ignored coreligionists. He complained that the Rights of Man should apply to all men, not denied some "who pray to the Supreme Being in Hebrew." Lafayette allowed his visitor to announce publicly that he agreed that the Jews of Paris and elsewhere in France "merited approbation." Of course, such an endorsement was welcome, but Lafayette, unlike Mirabeau, played no vigorous role in pressing for their full citizenship. And Mirabeau was soon to die.

Later, while commanding troops in the east, near Metz, Lafayette assured local Jews of their religious freedom, but even this edict was suspended during the Reign of Terror, in 1793 and 1794, instituted by Robespierre. Synagogues were shut, religious property vandalized. In fairness to Robespierre, he did not single out Jews for special persecution; he insisted his revolutionary Cult of Reason supplant *all* religions, and he struck at Christianity with comparable fury.

The Incorruptible deserves no condemnation as an anti-Semite without an asterisk. In fact, early on, he could be counted among those friendly to Jewish aspirations, if not the Judaic religion. During the abortive, early debate on Jewish rights, he declared;

> How can you blame the Jews for the persecution they have suffered in certain countries? These are, on the contrary, national crimes that we must expiate by restoring to them the imprescribable rights of man of which no human authority can deprive them. . . . Let us give them back their happiness, their country and their virtue by restoring them their dignity as men and citizens.

Robespierre's appeal to the National Assembly was unequivocal: "The vices of the Jews are born of the abasement in which you [Christians] have plunged them. Raise their condition and they will speedily rise to it!"

The Robespierre speaking in December 1789, like Mirabeau, was not potent enough to force through equality for Jews. When he was, by 1793, that goal had been theoretically achieved—at least on paper. Soon, with the rise of Napoleon, it was *only* on paper.

Not long after the rigidly "Incorruptible" Robespierre passed from the scene, France fell into the hands of the corrupt Directorate. The unsettled status of Alsace's Jews remained precarious during its four-year stewardship, from 1795 to 1799. None of its members rate recognition here for good or ill. We skip past them and move on to a man who needs no introduction, but will get one anyway, albeit briefer than his place in history warrants.

NAPOLEON BONAPARTE, 1769–1821
Emperor of France, 1804–1814 and 1815

History's Conventional View

Cartoon portrayals of copycat dictators or lunatics, their right arms held stiffly beneath their coats, say much about Napoleon's image as the classic despot. Labeling someone a Little Napoleon, sometimes in ridicule, sometimes in awe, is a reminder there once strode over Europe the real authoritarian figure.

Just twenty when the Bastille fell, Bonaparte's career was meteoric. At twenty-six, already a general, he defended the Tuilleries against an unruly Parisian mob, dispersing it with "a whiff of grapeshot." At twenty-seven he conducted a brilliant campaign against Austria's army, conquering northern Italy for France. At twenty-nine he sailed for Egypt, won the Battle of the Pyramids, and invaded Syria. At thirty, he overthrew the loathsome Directorate in a coup d'état and installed himself first consul.

A dazzling string of martial and diplomatic triumphs lay the heart of Europe at his feet. In 1804, aged thirty-five, he cast aside the sham of republican government and named himself emperor. More successes followed. Victories over Austria and Russia sent his reputation for military genius soaring—and his arrogance and vanity rose apace. Soon the thrones of conquered lands were being filled with his relatives, and he looked for new worlds to master in the East. But, as Winston Churchill noted more than a century later, Napoleon forgot that it snows in Russia.

The emperor's disastrous retreat from Moscow in the winter of 1812 bled France's manpower, eventually leading to his first abdication. After brooding in exile at Elba, he made a last stab at recapturing the past, stumbled at Waterloo, abdicated again, and then faded away on the dismal, isolated Atlantic isle of St. Helena.

But From a Jewish Perspective

During the fourteen years of the Napoleonic Era, Bonaparte's edicts and whims touched every Jew in France and across each frontier where French troops marched. But what did Napoleon think of Jews?

Historian Léon Poliakov writes that the emperor's comments "placed end to end would provide the material for a small anti-Semitic catechism." Standing erect, he was five feet, two inches tall and overlord of a continent. When he spoke of Jews, this is what he said:

"The Jews are an objectionable people, chicken-hearted and cruel."

"They are caterpillars, grasshoppers, who ravage the countryside."

"The evil primarily comes from that indigestible compilation called the Talmud, where their true biblical traditions are found side by side with the most corrupt morality."

This mind-set must remain in focus while reciting actions taken by the emperor. Unfortunately, many Jews—then and now—associate him with one extravaganza, more show business than substance, memorialized in paintings and engravings, and even passed down in the folklore of eastern European Jewry: his convening of the Grand Sanhedrin at Paris. For this he gets undeserved praise, since his motives were devious, not noble. But that's getting farther along the time line than we should at this point.

Napoleon's first impact on Jews came while campaigning against Austria's forces defending northern Italy. Still a soldier in the service of the Revolution and its ideals—liberty, equality, fraternity—he commanded troops that broke centuries-long shackles confining Jews to medieval-type ghettos.

The year 1798 found him in Alexandria, with wild visions of cutting the route from England to India and severing the British Empire. He devised a strategy to rally Near Eastern Jews to his colors. The bait: a national homeland in the Holy Land once he had conquered the place. But local Jews refused to accept his offer. They remained loyal to their Turkish masters, comfortable under the benign neglect practiced by the Sublime Porte.

Failure of his grandiose plans, thanks to the British Royal Navy's victory over his supporting fleet, led to Napoleon's hasty return to Paris and taking command of the French government. Now, along with other domestic concerns, the future of French Jewry would come to his desk for a decision. At first, Napoleon ignored this minority because resolution of Catholic and Protestant questions seemed more essential. "As for the Jews," he reportedly said, "they are a nation apart, and their adherents do not mix with any others; we will therefore have time to concern ourselves with them later."

When that time came, at first he toyed with the idea of proving himself superior to past absolute monarchs: "It was the practice of feeble rulers to persecute the Jews. I shall better their lot." But after listening to complaints from provincial communities about this "nation within a nation," he decided on a dramatic measure. Again, the vortex was Alsace.

In March 1806, he dictated a note: "... to date from January 1, 1807, Jews who do not possess property will be subject to a tax and will not enjoy the right of citizenship." Members of his Council of State led him to put aside this plan. However, he would not ignore complaints about extortionate interest rates that he heard while passing through Strasbourg. In May 1806 he issued an imperial rescript suspending debt payments owed to Jewish moneylenders by Alsatian farmers.

More comprehensive weapons to work his will were needed, so Napoleon followed this edict by summoning the leaders of Jewish society—eminent businessmen, financiers, rabbis, and scholars—to an assembly of Jewish notables. Here, the whole question of whither the Jews would be dealt with. Napoleon's stated purpose was "to revive among the Jews...the sentiments of civic morality that have unfortunately been moribund among too large a number of them by a state of abasement in which they have long languished."

Other notions, expressed privately over the years, were probably not far from his mind: "I do not intend to rescue that race, which seems to have been the only one excluded from redemption, from the curse with which it is smitten, but I would put it in a position where it is unable to propagate the evil." And, "good is done slowly and a mass of tainted blood only improves with time.... When one in every three marriages will be between a Jew and a Frenchman, the Jew's blood will cease to have a specific character."

When the 112 handpicked delegates arrived in Paris, they were received at the Hôtel de Ville with fanfare as an honor guard beat a drum tattoo. But the welcoming speech of Napoleon's representative, Count Louis Mathieu Molé quickly took a dangerous turn. He put to them twelve specific questions that were a mixture of the innocuous, the embarrassing, and the dangerous.

It was easy to answer a test of patriotism: "Do the Jews...regard France as their homeland and do they feel an obligation to defend it?" "Yes, to the death!" But others contained booby traps. Did Jewish law encourage Jews to practice usury among their own community? Among Christians? What police jurisdiction did rabbis exercise? Would marriage between Jews and Christians be permitted?

Tactful, reassuring responses—though, in the case of intermarriage, an evasive one—pleased the emperor. But he wanted their statements to have the force of communal law and for this he needed the sanction of a higher authority. Thus the convening of a Grand Sanhedrin, set for March 1807, the first in eighteen centuries. Seventy-one rabbis, scholars, and experts in Jewish law were to participate, the number identical with biblical times.

Whether the idea originated with Napoleon or was planted there by an assimilated German Jew is still unclear. The event proved a propaganda coup, pinning the loyalty of Jews to the Napoleonic eagle. Some saw it as equivalent to the French leader's concordat with Rome.

The gathering's first session opened with great pomp and pageantry in a secularized chapel renamed the rue du Grand Sanhedrin. At the government's direction, participants wore black mantles and black hats. Those on the presidium wore wide-sashed velvet or silk cassocks and fur-lined hats. Seating, arranged by seniority, took the form of a semicircle around the presidium. Napoleon wanted an arresting show and he got one.

Before the first session, a solemn service had been held in a Paris synagogue during which the Sanhedrin's chairman uttered a special prayer "for our immortal emperor," and for the victory of his army. Another rabbi paid homage to Napoleon as "the creative genius, who, of all mortals in the world, is the best created in the image of God." Jews would have to demonstrate themselves deserving of his grace by sending their sons to serve "under the glorious banners of Napoleon the Great."

Some of the delegates no doubt saw behind the emperor's mask. Prudence dictated panegyrics, not critical analyses. None of them had seen the emperor's secret instructions to his interior minister, dated September 3, 1806. Simon Dubnow describes them:

> "An impressive assembly has to be created, that should fear losing its fortune [that is, equal rights]—a council of Jewish leaders—who would not want to be looked upon as responsible for the tribulations of the Jewish people" (if they were to adopt such resolutions to which the emperor would take objection). The firm majority "should drag along the vacillating rabbis, and should influence the fanatics, if the latter were to prove adamant; they should see to it that they must adopt those resolutions (of the assembly of notables), under threat of expulsion of all the Jews."

The bountiful praise heaped on Napoleon by Judaism's most prestigious gathering—through which he tightened control over France's Jewish population—impressed Jews beyond its frontiers, as was his intention. The apparent respect shown by the emperor for their religion's ancient traditions was talked about in faraway ghettos and shtetls. And this paid handsome dividends when logistics problems hampered his forces advancing through former Polish territory.

The retreating foe had burned or carried off all provisions, and Polish Jews, dependable middlemen, came to the rescue with grain, oats, and barley. The Grand Armée marched on its stomach; they kept it well fed.

Even while campaigning in the East, Napoleon followed Sanhedrin proceedings. He received news and issued orders to the commissioners overseeing its deliberations by a chain of fleet couriers.

Professor Howard Morley Sacher writes: "Polish Jewry knew nothing of Napoleon's motivations. They knew only that he treated his Jews—in Poland as well as in France—like human beings; while Prussian and Austrian authorities treated them like dogs. Jewish contractors and peddlers by the hundreds willingly undertook the responsibility of provisioning the French army in the Duchy of Warsaw."

Despite the exuberance ignited by its revival, the Sanhedrin's life was brief. After rubber-stamping the assembly's decisions in accordance with Napoleon's will, the gathering was dissolved within one month, never to be reconvened. The emperor may have been influenced by adverse reaction from non-Jews with long memories. Historian Léon Poliakov points to the link in Christian minds between the Grand Sanhedrin and deicide. Napoleon would not have been flattered when his secret police seized an underground pamphlet depicting him as "The Lord's Anointed, who will save Israel." Nor when an emigré journal published in London imputed Napoleon was himself a Jew!

Moreover, a note shown him by his cunning police chief, Joseph Fouché, described negotiations between French royalists and Portuguese Jews between 1791 and 1793, indicating their past disloyalty to the Revolution. When Jews were next faced with a major Napoleonic initiative, it was his decree of March 17, 1808, that caused the stir. They soon labeled it the infamous decree.

Although it left Jews in the Seine region and southwest France with their established rights largely untouched, it set up special laws, department by department, through the rest of France. These edicts struck a blow at freedom of movement and livelihood. Jews who had temporarily left the border provinces now found themselves forbidden to return to their homes. Jews engaged in any business activity would henceforth need a "patent" from the local prefect. New regulations made the legal collection of debt payments difficult, and, in the always contentious Alsatian sector, nearly impossible.

These provisions remained in effect throughout the rest of the

Napoleonic era, disappearing only in 1818, when the restored Bourbon, Louis XVIII, refused to renew them.

Another Napoleonic decree, issued simultaneously, established thirteen regional consistories for administrative convenience. Jewish heads of family would pay dues to their consistories, but these were attuned to state, not communal, interests. Officials were "to ensure that no assembly for prayers should be formed without express authorization, to encourage Jews in the exercise of useful professions and refer to the authorities those who do not have an acknowledged means of livelihood, and to inform the authorities each year of the number of Jewish conscripts in the area." The duty of rabbis was to "call for...obedience to the laws, especially...those related to the defense of the fatherland...and, in particular, every year, at the time of conscription, to induce the Jews to consider their military service as a sacred duty." By these interlocking edicts, Napoleon revealed himself better than by arranging the theatrical setting at the rue de Sanhedrin.

Still, Napoleon was clearly good for Jews outside France, but in a manner Zalkind-Hourwitz earlier and mistakenly had applied to Voltaire—"involuntarily" and "perhaps unknowingly." Where French troops marched, ghetto doors were flung open. Though this freedom stemmed from principles rooted in the Revolution, the acts of emancipation derived from Napoleon's performance as a military commander. Jews in Prussia and elsewhere welcomed his legions.

As French troops occupied towns, army engineers leveled long-standing walls surrounding Jewish quarters. Music blared, fireworks lit the sky, and soldiers cheered. To the inhabitants, Napoleon seemed an agent sent by the Lord to deliver them. Holland's new sovereign—Napoleon's brother Louis—treated Jews well and abolished the ancient court oath they found humiliating. He even ordered the transfer of fair days from Saturday to Monday in deference to the Jewish community.

Another brother, Jerome, named king of Westphalia, granted full emancipation to Jews in his new kingdom, and, moreover, put immigrant Jews on an equal footing. On February 9, 1808, when a large Jewish delegation visited Jerome to express their thanks, the king replied, "Tell your brothers to enjoy the rights that were granted to them. They can depend upon my protection on a par with the rest of my children."

Back in Paris, Napoleon read an account of this reception in the official Westphalian newspaper and promptly upbraided his younger brother.

"There is nothing more ridiculous than the audience you granted Jews," he wrote. "I undertook the task of reforming the Jews, but I never wished to attract new Jews to my duchies. Moreover—I always avoided every thing that could testify to respect for the most despicable people."

While the spirit of tolerance touched some members of the Bonaparte family, it did not inspire the emperor.

ALEXANDER I, 1777–1825
Tsar of Russia, 1801–1825

History's Conventional View

Alexander I is regarded the principal agent in Napoleon's downfall, absent Nature's contribution—the Russian winter. When the Grand Armée rolled relentlessly and invincibly toward Moscow, he continued the uneven struggle rather than bargain for the terms of a forgiving peace. "Napoleon or I," he had said earlier. "From now on we cannot reign together." In Russia's darkest moment, he said the burning of Moscow "illuminated" his soul. Russia would survive.

Among decorations at his Monticello, Virginia, home, Thomas Jefferson owned busts of both Napoleon and Alexander, his contemporaries in a tumultuous era. Jefferson may have admired the tsar's reform-minded, liberalizing tendencies early in his reign, an expressed desire to remake Russia into a modern, enlightened state. The young sovereign was impressive—strong, handsome, humane, unfailingly courteous, full of vigor. Charles Maurice de Talleyrand, Napoleon's duplicitous former foreign minister, once set about flattering the tsar: "Sire, the French people are civilized, their sovereign is not. The Russian sovereign is civilized, his people are not. The Russian sovereign should be the ally of the French people."

But Alexander was mercurial and rash. At the Congress of Vienna he strutted about bemedalled in magnificent uniforms, the most important figure in Europe. But soon, a new Alexander would emerge, mystical and morose, rigid and reactionary. By his end, a decade later, Russia's masses—and Russia's old allies—would see no cause to mourn.

But From a Jewish Perspective

Since Poland's partition, half of world Jewry was sheltered in the unwelcome abode of a stern, unloving step–Mother Russia. In 1801, when Alexander rose to the throne, following the dispatch of his erratic father Paul I, Jews awaited clues as to whether this new Romanov would differ from the old. The year before, Paul had received a report from his agent, the poet Gabriel Derzharin, sent to western provinces to investigate conditions. The result was neither poetic nor ambiguous: "An Opinion on How to Avert the Scarcity of Food in White Russia Through the Curbing of the Jews' Avaricious Occupations, Their Reformation, and Other Matters."

Proposals were in keeping with the tone of its title, but Alexander chose not to act on them. Instead, in 1803 he appointed a commission to explore Jewish affairs anew and then offer useful recommendations. Its most level-headed member said the wisest course would be to "unshackle their hands" and "prohibit as little as possible and to grant as much freedom as possible." But Alexander chose a more abrasive route. His decree issued December 9, 1804, "The Statute Concerning the Organization of the Jews," was Russia's first fundamental law pertaining to Jews.

The law upheld Jewish admission to municipal councils and general courts while allowing maintenance of communal bodies, or kahals. Schools up to university level were opened to Jewish students. As an alternative, kahals could operate their own schools if they adopted the general curriculum.

Alexander's decree also mandated that rabbis and communal elders learn Russian, German, or Polish, the three languages in which Jews were soon to be required to conduct all legal and commercial affairs. Secondary students and Jews traveling temporarily outside the Pale, the restricted area beyond which Jews could not reside, were to abandon traditional garb. These were steps toward assimilation, welcome to the few, threatening to the many.

Worse, the decree promised a major catastrophe not far off. For years, tension simmered between peasants and Jews in rural areas. Alexander's solution was simple: to remove the Jews, thereby ending the strife. Unless they chose to become farmers themselves, they would be uprooted from villages and hamlets and sent to towns and cities. Like most simple solutions to complex problems, it was a bad one. Urban centers within the Pale were already overcrowded. Adding the three hundred thousand members of sixty thousand families would create horrendous conditions. Nonetheless, resettlement was slated to proceed.

Then news from France put a halt to this madness. In 1806, the restless Napoleon was again on the move, this time uncomfortably close to the Russian frontier. His convening of the Sanhedrin aroused European statesmen. Klemens von Metternich, then Austria's ambassador to Paris, wrote home to Vienna, "There is no doubt that he will not fail to present himself as a liberator to the Christian people of Poland and as a messiah to its immense Jewish population." The same conclusion settled in the mind of Alexander and his circle in St. Petersburg. If Napoleon's troops reached Russian soil, why shouldn't Jews, like those in Austrian and Prussian territory, joyously welcome their freedom?

Alexander was unstable, but not stupid. In February 1807, the same month the Grand Sanhedrin's preparations were under way, he sent an official to his western provinces with orders to discover the extent to which "the military circumstances and the present conditions of the border provinces as well as the economic ruin of the Jews, which is inevitable if their expulsion be enforced," made resettlement difficult or impossible.

Given the wording of his instructions, the Tsar's agent knew what he was expected to report. Resettlement was suspended. But, unexpectedly, a dazzling reconciliation of Napoleon and Alexander—the famed "meeting on a raft" on the Nieman River near Tilsit, at which the two tyrants planned the division of Europe between them, removed the rationale for suspending resettlement. They would have resumed. However, friendship between the French and Russian despots could not last.

The interlude between war and peace, and peace and renewed war, served as bridge-building time for Alexander toward his Jews. The tsar's propagandists worked to wean them from any inclination to choose the modern Cyrus that Prussia and Austria's Jews had found so appealing during "the Little Corporal's" earlier thrust eastward. As war clouds descended—1812 was approaching—Alexander fretted about wholesale defections of his disenchanted Jewish subjects.

His fear was unwarranted for reasons that may have been beyond his mind to grasp. They were prophesied by Rabbi Shneor Zalman, leader of the Hasidim in White Russia, who had earlier been arrested on suspicion of political disloyalty. "If Napoleon should be victorious," he said, "the Jews would become richer and their situation will advance, but their hearts will drift away from Father in heaven. But if our Tsar Alexander were to triumph, Jewish hearts would draw nearer to our Father in heaven, although Jews would become poorer and their status lower." Russia's Orthodox Jews were not about to trade their ties to God and tradition for the uncertainties of a brave new world.

When Napoleon's invasion took place, Jews were quick to express their loyalty and show their patriotism to the tsar. From grimy resistance chiefs to his elegant governor at Vilna, Alexander received word of "their faithfulness" and "special devotion" during the occupation. At great personal risk, they smuggled food to harassed partisans and kept a watchful eye on French troop movements. Two Jewish deputies functioned at army headquarters in a dual role—as provisioners for the Russian forces and as intermediaries with the tsar to protect Jewish interests in the combat zone. If ever there was a time for a Russian tsar to show his appreciation for Jewish loyalty, this was that moment.

In June 1814, Alexander directed the two deputies at his army headquarters to convey to the "Jewish kahals his gracious disposition," and assurance he would soon reach "a decision concerning their Jewish wishes and requests to improve their lot." The Congress of Vienna marked the high-water mark of the tsar's glory and power. Vienna police, who spied on all dignitaries of note, made reference to "Tsar Alexander's two Court Jews."

After French troops evacuated the "free" city of Lübeck, its senate voted to expel Jews. Alexander protested this violation. He similarly intervened on behalf of Frankfurt's harassed Jews.

It was easier to describe Alexander's actions than look into the mind that motivated them. In 1817, Alexander came under the sway of an English missionary, Lewis Way, who worked diligently to enfranchise Jews for the purpose of eventually drawing them to Christianity. "It is vain to invite them to become Christians," Way argued, "without treating them as men and brothers." The tsar, finding Way's notion appealing, had him draft a plan for his foreign minister to bring before the Concert of Europe. It called for complete emancipation.

But nothing came of it. With Napoleon's specter vanished, diplomats of the other great powers had grown suspicious of any initiatives by their impetuous and all-too-powerful former ally.

The tsar's comments led another visiting missionary, John Patterson, to believe "Emperor Alexander has been particularly interested in their [the Jews] favor for their fidelity to him in the time of the French invasion." The French ambassador at St. Petersburg, La Ferronays, wrote home in February 1820, "The emperor is doing a lot to make much of the Jews. Prince Golitzen is taking particular care of a certain biblical rabbi who is probably involved in the great work." Patterson and La Ferronays misconstrued much of what the tsar was up to. Alexander, now moving into his mystic, fanatically religious phase, was intent on saving the Jews from themselves, not Russian arbitrary injustice.

In 1817 the Society of Israelite Christians had been formed under his personal patronage, but this outreach program, imprudently continued beyond the experimental stage, was backfiring. It recruited a few dozen members, but a new "judaizing" sect, the Subbatniki, proved far more effective in pulling in the opposite direction. Shocked at such leakage, Russian Orthodox authorities cracked down on this "sect of Yids" in their midst.

When the Congress of Verona convened in 1822, writes Léon Poliakov, Alexander "politely got rid of Lewis Way, who had come along to remind him of his promises." One by one, Alexander excluded liberal advisers from his circle, replacing them with old-school reactionaries. Whatever glow for reform still flickered in his mind was finally extinguished. For Jews, his transformation from Jekyll to Hyde was complete.

Expulsion from rural districts, decreed back in 1804, suspended while Napoleon strode center stage, and shelved when Alexander recognized Jewish loyalty during the war, was now resumed by order of the tsar. As a beginning, on April 11, 1823, he decreed that all Jews in two western provinces be removed from villages by January 1, 1824. Over this nine-month span, some twenty thousand were deposited in overcrowded cities of the Pale, with no plans having been made for their accommodation or employment. This irrational decree created such destitution that even the tsar's own insensitive ministers realized it had to be undone. In 1825 deportations were suspended, and many of those already deported were allowed to return to their former villages. Alexander, broodingly pious and embittered, died that same year before he could inflict further damage. Unfortunately, his younger brother, Nicholas I, would energetically pick up the torch of bigotry and ignite it anew.

Other Voices, Other Deeds

JEAN-JACQUES ROUSSEAU's (1712–1778) references to Jews are skimpier than Voltaire's, as would be any contemporary writer's, and his impact certainly less. If not an outspoken friend, he certainly was no bigoted foe. Evidence of unwarranted Jewish travail in unenlightened Europe could not have escaped Rousseau, famous for the line that men were born free but were now everywhere in chains.

In his fourth book of *Emile*, he made a plea for understanding. "We shall never know the inner motives of the Jews," he wrote, "until the day they have their own free state, schools, and universities where they can speak and argue without fear. Then, and only then, shall we know what they really have to say."

Voltaire read *Emile*, made several contemptuous annotations in his copy, and declared, "this absurd novel is unreadable."

Rousseau chose not to widen the arc of his understanding to encompass Jews of biblical days. These he saw as "the vilest people, perhaps, who existed then, or, flatly, as the vilest of peoples." Such a perception led him to admire Moses all the more, for Moses

> planned and carried out the astonishing undertaking of setting up into a national body a swarm of wretched fugitives, without arts, without weapons, without talents, without virtues, without courage, and, who, not having a single inch of ground in its own right, made a strange troop on the face of the earth. Moses dared to make this wandering and servile troop into a political body, a free people, and while it wandered in the deserts without a stone on which to rest its head, he gave it that institutional form which has stood the test of time, of fortune and of conquerors which five thousand years have not been able to destroy or alter and which still continues to exist today in full force even when the national body no longer exists.

Professor Léon Poliakov acquired unpublished pages of Rousseau's most celebrated work, *The Social Contract*, from the Neuchatel Library reinforcing the philosopher's wonder at Jewish survival:

> The Jews provide us with an astonishing spectacle.... Athens, Sparta, Rome have perished and no longer have children left on earth; Zion, destroyed, has not lost its children. They mingle with all the nations and never merge with them; they no longer have leaders, and are still a nation; they no longer have a homeland, and are always citizens of it.

In a lesser work, Rousseau dismissed the attention given defectors who turned violently against Judaism. "You may convert some poor wretch, whom you have paid, to slander his religion," he wrote. "You get some wretched old-clothes-man to speak, and he says what you want; you may triumph over their ignorance and cowardice, while all the time their men of learning are laughing at your stupidity."

The fact that Jews were often condemned apparently upset Rousseau, for in another work he wrote:

> Do you know many Christians who have taken the trouble to inquire what the Jews allege against them? If anyone knows anything at all about it, it is from the writing of Christians. What a way of ascertaining the arguments of our adversaries! But what is to be done? If anyone dared to publish in our day books which were openly in favor of the Jewish religion, we should punish the author, publisher, and bookseller.

DENIS DIDEROT (1713–1784) poured twenty years of his life into *L'Encyclopédie*, which eventually reached twenty-eight volumes, six supplementary volumes, and two volumes of tables. Many of the engravings we see in histories of the eighteenth century are reproduced from that timeless work. In earlier writings cited by Professor Poliakov, he depicts Jews as soldiers of an army which had been "strongly recommended" by Moses "to show their enemies no mercy and to be large-scale usurers, two commandments which they fulfilled excellently." (Diderot obviously didn't call in Rousseau as a consultant.)

In fairness to Diderot, he despised Christianity and other religions with equal fervor. In his eyes, the pope was no less villainous than Moses. His *L'Encyclopédie*, moreover, was not harnessed as a vehicle to run over Jews, as Voltaire used his *Philosophical Dictionary*. Diderot's long, rambling article on the philosophy of the Jews provided ample opportunity. He didn't take it.

What he did do was tone down his animus toward Christianity—at Judaism's expense—by revising passages to squeeze past the censors. Jesus, an "obscure and fanatical Jew" in his original draft, emerges in the published version as the more politically correct "Son of God." The lessons drawn from his similes and parables are "always beautiful and satisfying," whereas the Talmudists apply their comparisons in a "puerile and frivolous way."

In correspondence with Catherine II, Diderot drafted questions on Russia's economic condition, asking, first, the size of its population, second, the number of its monks, and third, the number of its Jews. However, Professor Poliakov records that he made no similar reference to Jews in another note written for the tsarina. Characterizing Jews as avaricious extortionists had always been a fashionable technique of Jew-baiting, employed years earlier by the then youthful Diderot. But here, despite the subject matter of the note being usury, the mature Diderot let the chance pass.

Diderot also let pass more than one opportunity to show any understanding of what Jews had endured for nearly 1,800 years. In his exhaustive study of Jews during the French Enlightenment, Arthur Hertzberg points out that Diderot constantly attacked the Church and its Inquisition without mentioning the persecution of Jews at their hands.

"There was only one such passage in defense of the Jews," writes Professor Hertzberg, "and not a very warm one, in all his writings." The case he cites comes from an article on the Crusades in *L'Encyclopédie*. It reads: "They massacred them [Jews] whenever they could find them; these brutish and imperious people believed that they could properly avenge the death of Jesus by slitting the throats of the little children of those who had crucified him."

CHARLES LOUIS DE SECONDAT MONTESQUIEU (1689–1755) is best remembered for *L'Espirit des lois* (The Spirit of the Laws), a 1748 landmark in political theory. Constitution-makers across the Atlantic were indebted to it when they devised the separation of powers for the central government of the infant United States.

Two decades before he published his masterwork, Montesquieu, quite uncharacteristically, was guilty of one attack against Jews. It appears in *Lettres persanes*: "Know that wherever there is money, there are Jews. Thou inquirest what they do here? Just what they do in Persia: nothing can be more like a Jew of Asia than a Jew of Europe."

In the same work, he showed the kind of sensitivity regarding Judaism's relation to Christianity and Mohammedanism never shown by Diderot. Montesquieu described the People of the Book as "a mother that has brought forth two daughters who have stabbed her with a thousand wounds." Justice and humanity concerned him. While noting the "difference between tolerating a religion and approving it" in his *L'Espirit des lois*, he insisted states must oblige various religions to leave each other in peace. In one chapter of this classic, he makes a plea on behalf of Jews: "I cannot help remarking by the way how this nation [the Jews] has been sported with from one age to another: at one time their effects were confiscated when they were willing to become Christians; and at another, if they refused to turn Christians they were ordered to be burnt."

Montesquieu explained that the burning of a nineteen-year-old girl at a Lisbon auto-da-fé impelled him to write another chapter. His indignation comes through to readers as a Jew addresses his inquisitors:

> We conjure you, not by the mighty God whom both you and we serve, but by that Christ who, you tell us, took upon him a human form, to propose himself for an example for you to follow; we conjure you to behave to us as he Himself would behave was he upon earth. You would have us be Christians, and you will not be so yourselves.

Perhaps as a reasonable man in an Age of Reason, Montesquieu expressed optimism. He died in 1755, 134 years before Hitler's birth, and that fact excuses the most off-key prediction he made: "The Jews are at present saved; superstition will return no more, and they will no longer be exterminated on conscientious principles."

JOHANN WOLFGANG VON GOETHE (1749–1832), creator of *Faust*, occupies a significant place among eighteenth- and early nineteenth-century Teutonic men of letters. In autobiographical accounts, he admitted that anti-Semitism came to him early on and explained why:

> The abhorrence of the Jews that stirred in me in my earliest youth was really rather timidity in the face of enigma and ugliness. My contempt was more the reflection of the Christian men and women surrounding me. Only later, when I made the acquaintance of many intellectually gifted, sensitive men of this race did respect come to join the admiration I cherish for the people who created the Bible and for the poet who sang the Song of Songs.

The mature Goethe would say he "never had been an enemy of the Maccabean family," and after a fashion, possible even believed it. He regarded himself a cosmopolitan above "patriotic narrowness." If, at one point, he disparaged Jews in *Faust*, at another he ridiculed fellow Christians. A line about the Jews' inclination to obtain dubious property is balanced by another that King and Church were similarly so disposed.

He found biblical Jewish heroes admirable, but "as those Jewish heroes step into the present time, we are reminded that they are Jews and we feel a contrast between the forefathers and the descendants which confuses and irritates us." This preference for the past's dead Jews to the contemporary world's live ones was reflected in his attitude toward Jewish emancipation in his homeland. He loathed the notion.

The great poet felt more comfortable with "diversified subordination which, from the highest to the lowest, from the emperor to the Jew, seemed to unite rather than divide individuals, and favored the general well-being." For Jews to move up a rung or two in the social order would violate long-standing tradition, an indication of "disdorder worse than injustice."

When reform nonetheless threatened in the wake of French Revolutionary ideas lapping at the Rhine, Goethe's reaction was furious. "The most serious and most disastrous consequences are to be expected," he wrote, "...all ethical feelings within families, feelings which rest entirely on religious principles, will be endangered by these scandalous laws." He pinned some of the blame on the "omnipotent Rothschild."

Goethe avoided going out of his way to attack Jews, but he was eager, not merely content, to leave ill enough alone.

England's literary lions, too, could be mean-spirited, although in intellectual circles the nature of anti-Semitism there tended to be more genteel than on the Continent. But there were exceptions.

DANIEL DEFOE (1660–1731) made much of "the execrable Jews, crucifying the Lord of Life." Their absence from Robinson Crusoe's fabled isle left Jews unscathed in his most famous work. But elsewhere in his writings, Defoe did not shrink from such culturally acceptable phrases as "that cursed Jew," "the malicious Jew," "that dog of a Jew," and "that traitor of a Jew."

In his 1724 novel *Roxanne, or the Unfortunate Mistress*, written five years after *Robinson Crusoe*, Defoe vividly describes the heroine's ordeal when, jewels in hand, she comes face to face with a member of that community:

> the Jew held up his hands, looked at me with some horror, then talked Dutch again and put himself into a thousand shapes, twisting his body and wringing up his face this way and that way in his discourse, stamping with his feet, and throwing abroad his hands, as if he was not in a rage only, but in a fury. Then he would turn and give a look at me like the devil. I thought I never saw anything so frightful in my life.

Scholar Montagu Frank Modder speculated on the cause for this vitriol. In 1692, before reaching his pinnacle as a writer, Defoe had gone bankrupt. Was there a Jewish moneylender in his past? Even if so, Voltaire remember, denied that such personal contact sparked *his* animosity. Maybe Defoe simply was giving readers what they expected, the comfortable stereotype Elizabethan audiences found pleasing back in Will Shakespeare's day.

Poet ALEXANDER POPE (1688–1744), whose *Rape of the Lock* remains a staple of English literature, offered the following "prayer" in a less acclaimed work: "Keep us we beseech thee, from the hands of such barbarous and cruel Jews. . . . And that we may avoid such like calamities, may all good and well-disposed Christians be warned by these unhappy wretches' woeful example, to abominate the heinous sin of avarice."

A contemporary of both Defoe and Pope, satirist JONATHAN SWIFT (1667–1745) authored *Gulliver's Travels* and was a political activist in high social circles. He helped Court rivals of the mighty duke of Marlborough bring about his downfall.

Swift would have turned back the clock to pre-Cromwell, pre-Manassah ben Israel times. He wrote: "What if the Jews should multiply and become a formidable party among us? Would the dissenters join in alliance with them likewise, because they agree already in some general principles, and because the Jews are allowed to be a stiffnecked and rebellious people?"

Through Swift's prose ran such financially explicit terms as "rich as Jews," "as rich as a Jew," "richer than a Jew," and "as rich as fifty Jews," according to Modder.

Although GEORGE III (King from 1760 to 1820) did not shrink from ruling (or meddling) as well as reigning—such diverse figures as Ben Franklin and Lord North will affirm that to be so—the evolution of Jewish life in the sceptered island proceeded without much impact from this Hanoverian sovereign.

In October 1803, George III reviewed a parade of East London volunteers in Hyde Park. This patriotic outpouring followed the chief rabbi's call for Jews to support king and country when Napoleon was again threatening invasion. George commented on the large number of men bearing animals names—Wolf, Bear, Lyon—passing before him. ". . . what, what!"

If taking note of this shows a tint of condescending social anti-Semitism, we may justifiably make the least of it. George III was no threat to Jews.

George's grandfather, GEORGE II (who ruled from 1727 to 1760) even merited a gold star, six-pointed, for saying yes when concerned British Jews sought help for their coreligionists in Prague. Maria Theresa, the Austrian empress, had just issued her brutal expulsion decree. At their audience, members of London's Great Synagogue explained what was happening, and their king showed considerable sympathy, repeating, "It is not right that the innocent shall suffer with the guilty."

George II issued instructions to his ambassador at Maria Theresa's court to join his Dutch colleague in a vigorous protest. "This was probably the first instance in modern history," wrote historian Cecil Roth, "of diplomatic intervention by a European Power on behalf of an alien minority on purely humanitarian grounds."

5

After Napoleon and Before Hitler

Some of the figures populating the following pages are perhaps quite familiar to a smaller number of readers descended from those who fled tsarist Russia's anti-Semitic cauldron. Alexander II, a lesser evil, Alexander III, a greater evil, and the two Nicholases, of matched wickedness, get space, although not nearly as much as deserved based on their infinite capacity for inflicting misery.

Montesquieu, a man of reason, would ultimately be proven misguided in his civilized assumption that "the Jews are at present saved; superstition will return no more, and they will no longer be exterminated on conscientious principles." But he should not be faulted for inept stargazing. The century before 1914 would see retraction of many of the clues pointing at horrors to come in presumably enlightened western Europe.

Anti-Semitism had not disappeared from the palaces and chanceries of Paris, London, Berlin, and Vienna, but it devolved into more civilized guises, marked by political, economic, and social restrictions. My choices for important figures of the times hinged on two questions: Did they wield power over Jews? Did they use that power?

Several pages back, any eminent crowned head automatically qualified. No longer. Thus, Queen Victoria, like grandfather George III, merits only back-section attention. On the other hand, several of her prime ministers could not escape the issue of Jewish emancipation, and the Duke of Wellington replaces the House of Hanover as a leading subject for discussion. Successors Sir Robert Peel, Viscount Melbourne, and Viscount Palmerston faced the same gnawing issue after the great duke, but they lack household name status at least on one side of the Atlantic.

Some readers will note the absence of a section on Benjamin Disraeli, who is celebrated as one of Britain's greatest statesmen. This is no oversight. True, he rose in the House of Commons to support a resolution permitting Jews entry in Parliament by declaring, "Yes, it is as a Christian that I will not take upon me the awful responsibility of excluding from the legislature those who are from the religion in the bosom of which my Lord and Savior was born." But Disraeli was born a Jew and raised as one until the age of thirteen. In later years, Prince Otto von Bismarck would refer to him as *Der Alte Jude*, and, as he displaced arch-rival William Gladstone as prime minister, Mrs. Gladstone complained to her eldest son, "Is it not disgusting after all Papa's labor and patriotism and years of work to think of handing over his nest egg to that Jew."

By the same rule of thumb, Karl Marx must be excluded. Although this apostle of atheism was virulent in his anti-Jewish harangues, he was Jewish. In his stead appears collaborator Friedrich Engels, a bona fide gentile Communist who—as far as Jews should care—behaved as a lesser scourge.

Any rogues' gallery of nineteenth-century Jew-haters would dedicate a wall to the likes of German superpatriot and historian Henrich von Treitschke, the race-obsessed Englishman-turned-German Houston Stewart Chamberlain, and Vienna's rabble-rousing politician Dr. Karl Lueger. But tip-of-the-tongue status eludes them in our day, so look for them instead in more scholarly works on anti-Semitism.

As with Voltaire in the preceding chapter, one writer makes the cut for pride-of-place, and for the same reason. Composer Richard Wagner was also a man of letters—and pamphlets and articles. Far better for Jews had his right hand lost its cunning, or at least stuck to making musical notations instead of wandering off into the alphabet. Young Adolf Hitler would find his furious prose as well as soaring music a source of inspiration.

But the most powerful language in the nineteenth century still lay at the disposal of monarchs and officials, expressed in decrees and orders. We begin with the adroit, manipulative diplomat whose shadow hovered over Europe for three decades after Napoleon's fall.

PRINCE KLEMENS VON METTERNICH, 1773–1859

FRANCIS I, 1768–1835
Emperor of Austria, 1804–1835

History's Conventional View

Metternich did not rule the European continent, nor even his own country—but he was arguably the dominant figure to emerge from the 1814–15 Congress of Vienna. The thirty years that followed—labeled the Age of Metternich—saw his policies, adopted at home and abroad, as a grand effort to gag liberalism and set history's clock-hands in retrograde motion. Metternich and "reaction" make a seamless fit.

Trained for diplomatic service, he played the role of Europe's puppeteer from his perch as Austrian foreign minister, a post he held for nearly forty years. His early success in keeping Austria out of Napoleon's grasp (by a clever dynastic marriage) and then getting Austria into the victorious Allied coalition, when the Corsican faltered, demonstrated impeccable timing. Francis I rewarded him by naming him a hereditary prince of the Austrian Empire.

The Metternich System entailed strict police supervision, diligent censorship, and firmness in stamping out any trace of dissent. He guided like-minded reactionary royals in ending any threat, real or imagined, to the existing order. As a power broker, he never doubted himself. "Error never had access to my mind," he boasted. He saw himself as a "rock against which the waves of disorder beat in vain." Among contemporaries, Metternich's vanity and conceit became legendary. He remarked, "The behavior of people toward me is rather that of sponges, anxious to absorb ideas."

The prince's place in history was assured not by royal birth but from the cunning and wiliness that prompted his conceit. He set Europe's course through less intellectually gifted sovereigns—his own, Francis I, and Russia's erratic tsar, Alexander I, whom Metternich said was incapable of pursuing a consistent line of thought. He had the brains; they had the power.

Domestic affairs within the Austrian Empire were less susceptible to Metternich's management. His sovereign leaned on other conservative advisers and, moreover, had ideas of his own. The political credo of

Francis I reads: "Govern and change nothing." His uncle, Joseph II, had seen the empire's Jewish population as an untapped resource and prospective "plus" for Austria's future. Francis saw no advantage.

But From a Jewish Perspective

Jewish concerns never made the agenda of Metternich's grand designs for Europe, either at periodic international gatherings or at one-on-one summits with the rich and powerful. At the Congress of Vienna in April 1815, Jewish notables of Vienna and Prague unwisely counted on Europe's "coachman" to intercede with Emperor Francis to carry out a promise of equality made back in 1797, when French Revolutionary spectres haunted the Hapsburg realms.

Two months earlier, Metternich had shown willingness to step forward when approached by a Jewish delegation protesting the withdrawal of equal rights by ruling bodies in Frankfurt, Lübeck, and Bremen, so-called free states in the German confederation. Violations there would have ignored guarantees made by the Congress. Metternich sternly warned those Hanseatic cities that "the influence of the Jewish banks and commercial firms must be taken into account." A natural conservative inclination to maintain economic stability and financial order, not humanitarianism, likely motivated his intervention. In any event, support for harassed Jews beyond Austria's frontiers never translated into sympathetic attention to Austria's own Jews—except in small matters and for moneyed Jewish acquaintances.

The Viennese Rothschilds became a financial pillar of the empire, and Metternich took care to humor them. Two members of the banking family were named Austrian consul generals, and the prince and his wife showed up as guests when Salomon Mayer Rothschild sent out dinner invitations. Salomon wanted an old embargo on Jewish industrialists engaging in mining and metallurgy lifted. A Rothschild wish could not be lightly ignored—except behind his back.

On one occasion, Metternich wrote the Archduchess Marie Louise's husband: "I myself have committed the great offense of making it impossible for the Rothschild family to obtain an Austrian decoration. If he [Salomon] thought I was implicated, he would regard me as a positive cannibal."

On large matters affecting the mass of Austria's Jews, he engaged in similar Machiavellian-style princely lying to obscure fact with fiction. In an 1818 memorandum he affirmed that Joseph II's liberalizing edicts were "in full force," that Jews could choose between public and private schools for their children, that all trades were open, that opportunity beckoned even in the military, except the cavalry branch, which still required a Christian oath. Advances needed no "precipitous reforms."

Jewish historian Heinrich Graetz, writing within memory of the Metternich era, painted a more somber picture: "What was done by Austria itself, which displayed such righteous indignation against Lübeck on behalf of the Jews? Francis I and his ruler, Metternich, completely forgot the benevolent intentions [*sic*] of Joseph II, and kept in mind only the hateful laws of Maria Theresa against the Jews."

The Alpine province of Tyrol was closed to them, as were many upland cities and villages in Bohemia. Relegation to ghettoes, though, remained the preferred method of containment in much of the sprawling, polyglot empire. According to Graetz, "everywhere there were Jew streets; the restrictions imposed on the Jews of Austrian had become proverbial, whilst in Galicia, they met with greater oppression than in the Middle Ages."

Vienna represented a special case. Although the capital was Metternich's home base, and what he knew and when he knew it was beyond dispute, the greater villain here was his royal sovereign, the lesser man. Francis I's imperial motto ran, Justice is the Foundation of Kingdoms. Regarded by his Germanic subjects as "good Emperor Francis," he paid closer attention to internal matters than foreign policy.

The emperor ordered his Judenamt (Office of Jewish Affairs) to strictly enforce regulations on Jewish settlement in Vienna. Legal status was granted to only two hundred "tolerated" families, Austrian Jewry's thin upper crust. All the rest, numbering thousands, were categorized as "aliens" subject to abuse by Judenamt police, especially if bribe money was not readily available. Out-of-town Jews coming to the big city for trade could remain only a fortnight after paying a "ticket tax," obtain a two-week extension, and then face expulsion. Capricious raids by authorities on Jewish homes resulted in tenants being dragged off to police headquarters for verification of papers. Even residences of officially "tolerated" Jews— and synagogues—suffered intrusion by police seeking "illegals."

At first, Francis denied domicile in Vienna to all foreign Jews except

Turkish subjects covered by a long-standing pact with the Porte, but when several European governments protested and France's ambassador threatened retaliation if French Jews remained barred, Francis backed down.

Direct approaches to the emperor by the Jewish elite—those financiers and industrialists Metternich tactfully granted small, usually personal, favors—achieved nothing of value. In November 1816, community representatives humbly presented a petition to their sovereign. "Would it not be compatible with truth and justice," they proposed, "to resolve to remove the yoke that still oppresses half a million useful citizens—and to grant Jews all their civil rights, without restrictions?" Then, a fallback position: "But if it is impossible to carry out such a general measure, then perhaps it could be done gradually, in individual states, commencing with Lower Austria, where its local followers of the Mosaic faith are already deserving of the emperor's grace and attention, because they evince civic responsibility and are law-abiding and educated, and because their commercial and industrial enterprises are beneficial to the State."

Francis instructed his privy council to consider the matter. "The bureaucrats," wrote historian Simon Dubnow, "debated endlessly as to whether Jews could more quickly be 'rendered harmless' through repressive or liberal measures." A year later, they presented their sovereign with a majority report favoring continuation of restrictions and separate dissenting positions. Francis absorbed all this. Then, in January 1820, he finally made his decision: "Jews shall not be permitted to multiply and disseminate; they are not to be tolerated by any means, except in those provinces where they were admitted heretofore." He promised further review of provincial laws regarding Jews, his goal being to "render Jewish customs, the Jewish mode of life, and Jewish vocations harmless."

Francis I died in 1835, but Metternich survived to witness the European system bearing his name collapse. One deed to his credit marked those latter years. In 1840, the prince pushed his considerable political weight around to defend Jews, though, once again, a crisis involved foreign Jews, not Austria's own. This was the infamous Damascus blood libel affair, given more attention later when we reach Louis Philippe, "King of the French." Suffice it here to note that Metternich instructed his representatives in Damascus and Alexandria to pressure a barbarous Egyptian overlord into halting the persecution of Syrian Jews. Austrian-French rivalry in the Near East perhaps exaggerated this indignation over imprisoned and tortured Jews, since a French agent instigated their arrest, but let's give Metternich his due, or at least the benefit of doubt.

A generation later, Heinrich Graetz speculated that the Austrian minister's intervention may have been influenced by the desire to please the house of Rothschild, which had been extremely "zealous" on behalf of these beleaguered coreligionists. The aging prince and his aging banker, Salomon Rothschild, continued their close relationship as the era of reaction waned. Both made enemies. In January 1848, with upheaval imminent, Metternich warned Salomon, "If the devil catches me, he gets you, too." Two months later, Austria's perennial chief minister fled Vienna, aided, perhaps, by his old ally, for safe haven in London.

NICHOLAS I, 1796–1855
Tsar of Russia, 1825–1855

History's Conventional View

After succeeding his brother Alexander I (because another brother rejected the crown) Nicholas quickly made his mark as a ruthless military ogre who regarded his wide-ranging domains as barracks. His grim, stern thirty-year-reign went unbesmirched by any redeeming societal value. Soviet historian Sergei M. Soloviev summed up his personality— "despot by nature, with an instinctive aversion for every movement and expression of individual freedom and independence."

Nicholas adopted "orthodoxy, autocracy, and nationality" as his program. When he paid a call on young Victoria in England, she found him an "uncivilized mind." Back home, poet Alexander Pushkin regarded his tsar "an execrable sovereign but distinguished colonel."

Nicholas devoted his considerable energy to saber and cannon, thrived on military parades and reviews, and deigned to mold the Russian army into a world-class fighting force. He recalled his predecessor, Alexander I, had brought the Russian army all the way to Paris in 1814. "My greatest pleasure," he remarked, "is to talk to my beloved soldiers, to know their needs, to assure myself of their training and progress— nothing interests me so much." But even by Nicholas I's military agenda, he rates a failure. In the Crimean War, his vaunted army failed in the battle against France and England.

Until then, "the Iron Tsar" earned a fearsome reputation as "Gendarme of Europe," squashing liberal movements and bullying dissatisfied nationalities. In 1830 he crushed a bid for Polish freedom. "Sire, Warsaw is at the feet of Your Majesty!" reported his army commander. Nicholas proved characteristically merciless to the defeated foe. Displaying royal fellowship in 1848, he dispatched Russian troops to help neighboring Austria smother a Magyar uprising.

For Russia itself, he created a "Third Section" within his imperial chancellery. This dreaded precursor of modern secret police agencies blotted out any form of dissent. Pervasive fear led a visiting French aristocrat to comment, "One does not die, one does not breathe here, except by permission or by imperial order."

But From a Jewish Perspective

Nicholas I did not throw Jews into the Dvina to drown, after the manner of Ivan the Terrible. Nevertheless, Jews could describe this Romanov as a most despicable tsar, and all the more so, for Nicholas, though not a man *of* the nineteenth century, was surely aware he was ruling *in* the nineteenth century.

Distrusting state bureaucracy, Nicholas I entrusted sensitive state affairs to organs over which he exercised direct personal control. Hence, Jewish misery could not be attributed to faceless officials acting without their master's consent. Russia was Nicholas; Nicholas was Russia.

The Pale of Settlement, the holding pen for Russia's Jewish population, which was already leading a de facto existence, did not get its name coined until his reign. Back in 1816, the twenty-year-old Grand Duke had noted in his diary during an educational tour of Russia's western regions: "The ruin of the peasants in these provinces are the Zhids.... They are full-fledged leeches sucking up these unfortunate provinces to the point of exhaustion."

On becoming tsar, Nicholas resolved to end this infestation of "Zhids." In 1827 he imposed restrictions in Kiev, the largest city in southwestern Russia, where a thriving Jewish community had grown from its beginnings in 1794. Newcomers were barred; old settlers were slated for eviction: "Their presence is harmful to the industry of the city and the crown proper."

In 1829 Courland was removed from the Pale. The tsar next deemed the Jews of Sevastopol "inconvenient and harmful." In 1835 Jews were excluded from Astrakhan and the Caucusus. Historian Simon Dubnow summarized the results of Nicholas I's population upheavals: "Thus, people were hurled at random from villages into cities, and from some cities into others, from one province to another, as though it were a matter of moving a herd of cattle."

A temporary halt came in the wake of Poland's 1830 rebellion. Nicholas granted a three-year postponement of expulsions from Kiev when that city's governor warned St. Petersburg of the risk that Jews, backed to the wall, might join the Poles in common cause. But in 1833 the governor could not similarly get Nicholas to let Jews remain after pointing out that prices would soar if efficient Jewish merchants were ejected from the city. He rejected economic arguments and would concede a delay only until the comprehensive Ordinance Concerning Jews came into effect in February 1835.

Meanwhile, Nicholas instituted a policy more historically damning than compulsory expulsions, which, however brutal, lacked the malign uniqueness of his new scheme. After all, Maria Theresa and Frederick the Great also practiced expulsion on a grand scale. Greater infamy attaches to the tsar's machinations to snuff out Jewish life using, as his weapon of choice, military conscription.

Until 1827, Jews avoided army service through payment of a special recruitment tax. In other European states, an end to army exemption suggested a step forward toward acceptance and equality: new obligations, new rights, and an elevated status. Not so in Russia.

His ukase of August 1827, mandating twenty-five years of service for many non-Jews as well, contained a special provision applying only to Jews: "Jewish minors, that is, those below eighteen years of age, are to be sent to special training institutions for military service." To parents of boys as young as twelve, that meant an additional six years' separation added on to the quarter-century separation from home and family, designed to wean them from their Jewish identity—if they survived.

Jewish communities were directed to furnish their quota of youths. When they failed to do so, raiding parties descended on their villages to kidnap the prescribed number. Children wrested from their loved ones faced shipment to faraway garrisons, often never to be heard of again. Their anguish can be imagined, and enough narratives exist to evoke the effects of these cruel measures. Our concern here, is Nicholas, the man and his methods.

Early on, several high officials tried to dissuade their sovereign from so radical a measure. According to Dubnow, the tsar was "irked by the sluggish implementation of his favorite project." A confidential palace memo prophesied, "the chief benefit to be derived from the drafting of Jews is the certainty that it will move them most effectively to change their religion."

However, the tsar's wishes would not be realized. Russian revolutionary Alexander Herzen came across a group of pathetic young draftees, or cantonists as they were called, and questioned their transport officer:

"Whom are you escorting and to where?"

"As you see—a horde of damned little Jews, eight to ten years of age—had been assembled. At first, they were to be driven to Perm; then the order was changed: We're driving them to Kazan. I took charge of them for a hundred versts. The officer who handed them to me said, 'It's a misfortune—a third of them stayed on the road (the officer pointed his finger downward). Not half will reach their destination. They die like flies.'"

At one point, Jewish pleas convinced a majority of the tsar's own government council (certainly no philo-Semites) to recommend the draft age for Jews be raised to eighteen, matching all other recruits. Nicholas personally rejected such equality, ruling cantonist practice would "remain as before."

Beginning in 1835, codification of earlier Jewish statutes in the Charter of Disabilities, preceding a tsarist decree, again cleansed Kiev of Jews, as well as the provincial countryside. A scheme to settle thousands of Jewish families in the far eastern outposts of the empire failed shortly after inception. Nicholas called a halt "to protect the native population of Siberia from the Jews."

The only positive element associated with the tsar's geographical redistribution of the Jewish population was an end to village expulsions in some provinces. But that, only on grounds of impracticality.

Jews were forbidden to marry before the age of eighteen, to use Yiddish in public documents, or to build synagogues near churches. A censorship campaign against Jewish books—biblical, talmudical, rabbinical, or hassidic—tried to squeeze perceived subversion from their printed pages. After thousands of volumes were forwarded to St. Petersburg, with many thousands more to come, Nicholas granted provincial governors permission to burn them on the spot, passing on only one copy of "purged" books to his ministry of internal affairs.

After a decade, the tsar's repression seemed to subside. "For a while," writes Dubnow, "the government tired of beating Jews."

In 1840, Nicholas established the Committee to Determine Ways and Means for the Radical Reformation of Jews in Russia. One measure zealously pursued set up government-authorized schools as alternatives to community education. As an attraction, graduates would be assured a shorter term in military service. A young German-Jewish scholar was engaged as an emissary to spread word of tsarist benevolence to his coreligionists throughout the Pale. But the tsar's real motive, contained in a secret directive, reached the Jewish community: "The aim of the education of Jews is in the rapprochement of Jews to the Christian population, and in eradicating of the prejudices which the Talmud instills in Jews."

In December 1844 came a new decree—"to subjugate Jews in cities and in towns to the general administration—and to invalidate the kahals," those self-governing communal systems historically a bulwark of Jewish survival. Their future skeletal duties would be carrying out conscription orders and collecting special levies, such as the candle tax. On official holidays, rabbis would deliver sermons lauding their sovereign.

Another edict by Nicholas brought more woe. It instructed his police "to deport all Jews who dwell within fifty versts of the Prussian and Austrian borders [about thirty miles]. Homeowners are allowed two years to dispose of their property. The order is to be carried out without any excuses."

Thousands of families in the Ukraine and Lithuania were affected. According to Dubnow, "some nineteen communities declared they did not know where to go, and that they intended to mark time until they would be expelled by force." French, German, and English newspapers carried articles criticizing the "new Spain."

Further touches of torment were promulgated by this Romanov tsar. He promulgated a law banning Orthodox Jews from wearing traditional garb and sidelocks. As a supplementary measure, "His Imperial Majesty enjoins Jewish women from shaving their heads on the eve of marriage." Jewish businessmen abroad lost Russian nationality if they failed to return within the time frame set by their passports. Plans were afoot to segment Jews into five classes based on their "usefulness" to the state. For those at the bottom—lowly tradesmen and the poor—their lives of desperation would now embrace the constant threat of mass conscription.

When Nicholas visited London in 1844, Sir Moses Montefiore, businessman, philanthropist, and longtime acquaintance of Queen Victoria (he knew her as a youngster), used the occasion to present him with a memorandum on Jewish travail at home. Two years later, Sir Moses journeyed to St. Petersburg, was received courteously by Nicholas and allowed to visit Jewish communities. Tsarist officials received instructions to show him every respect. Nevertheless, he returned home empty-handed.

Foreign opinion left Nicholas unmoved. Following the Montefiore mission, an 1847 document reported that he told the British ambassador he "had no great feeling for the Jews and was resolved not to change the law of Peter the Great."

Over the course of his long reign, Nicholas actually went far beyond the decrees of his ancestor Peter. And, undoubtedly, he would have found new ways to bring grief to his Jewish subjects if he had not blessedly passed into history in 1855, the same year his beloved army foundered in the Crimea.

In western Europe following the French Revolution, Jews could begin a quest for a life of dignity and equality. Some luminaries helped, others hindered. And the most important figure in either category during the years following Napoleon's defeat belonged to the man idolized for ending the French emperor's reign.

SIR ARTHUR WELLESLEY
Duke of Wellington, 1769–1852

History's Conventional View

Everyone knows the Duke of Wellington as victor of Waterloo, the man who defeated Napoleon. Less well-known is his successful command of the expeditionary force sent to Iberia to fight French invaders in Spain. (A beaten enemy general said his performance "raises Lord Wellington almost to the level of Marlborough.") Even less well-known, some of Wellington's greatest influence took place as a politician following his military career.

Stay the "soldier of Europe," his associates had advised him.

Bemedalled, weighed down with honors, treated with awe at home and on the continent—why chance failure now?

But Wellington termed himself "the retained servant of the monarchy" and marched off to political wars bearing the Tory standard. Like Metternich, his contemporary, Wellington rates as an arch-conservative, but England had no repressive anti-Semitic measures in place, guarded by a strong-willed emperor who ruled as well as reigned. Nor was "the Iron Duke" a monster like the Iron Tsar, a still young Nicholas I in 1828, the year Wellington became prime minister.

During his tenure, Wellington turned back no clocks. However, he did stifle the winds of change. Only with the greatest reluctance—to prevent rebellion in Ireland—did he finally press for a Catholic emancipation bill extending equal rights to Rome's adherents.

In November 1830 he was forced from office after stubbornly resisting those great democratic reforms designed to extend suffrage, thereby making Parliament a more representative body. Detractors smashed windows at Apsley House, his London residence. Later, nostalgia elevated him to the role of elder statesman. Selective memory filtered out all but his masterful generalship on Europe's battlefields.

But From a Jewish Perspective

Better for Jews had Sir Arthur Wellesley stayed a soldier. Once in command of the House of Commons, Wellington listened to a proposal by Nathan Meyer Rothschild that Jews be allowed to own freehold property and vote in parliamentary elections. The banker's access to the hero at Waterloo came not merely from prominence in the financial world, but also from his role in providing funds for Wellington's campaign in Spain when others would not risk capital. The prime minister refused to support his proposal.

Similarly, when Isaac Goldsmid, a prominent railroad builder, came to Wellington concerned lest his son be denied admission to the bar because indemnity against taking a Christian oath had been invalidated, Wellington again proved unhelpful. On the more decisive issue of Jewish "emancipation" raised earlier, at one point members of the Jewish Board of Deputies came away with the impression he was "not unfavorable," though he felt obliged to postpone Jewish equality. They misread his intentions.

At a meeting in early February 1829 between the prime minister and wealthy Jews, Rothschild went beyond the financial agenda and once more raised the question of Jewish disabilities. Again Wellington dodged adroitly.

Later in the month, Rothschild, Goldsmid, and Moses Montefiore met the prime minister to press the issue scheduled for action in Parliament. Montefiore emerged with "no doubt the duke would take no part against them." More skeptically, Goldsmid envisioned a darker scenario. He sensed Wellington would oppose Jewish equal rights "to win back some of the ground they [the duke and his ally, Robert Peel] had lost with the High Tory party by reason of recent concessions to the Roman Catholics." Goldsmid suggested circumventing the duke instead of working through him. He hoped publicizing their cause and winning over public opinion would be more fruitful, but high-placed Christian supporters of Jewish emancipation feared confrontation, trusting instead to parliamentary maneuvering. It seemed the safer course.

Early in 1830 they introduced a bill stating, "all civil rights, franchises and privileges... offices, places, employments, trusts" that had been opened to Roman Catholics would now "be opened to Jews." The first reading went well, as it passed, 117 to 97. But stiffening opposition before the second reading led Rothschild to call on the prime minister.

The banker asked Wellington to release government ministers from party discipline and allow members to vote their conscience. The prime minister refused. On May 17, 1830, the bill met defeat on its second round, 228 to 165.

Jewish concerns dropped from view as the Great Reform Bill, extending suffrage rights to Britain's growing industrial and commercial classes, and the swirling controversy around it, moved front and center. It became the unbending Wellington's undoing: He fell from power. In the spring of 1833, when the issue of Jewish emancipation surfaced in the House of Commons, the duke sat in the House of Lords. So this time the Jewish bill moved swiftly through the lower house without rancor—but then it moved on to the House of Lords. Wellington rose to oppose this "needless liberal invention." The philo-Semitic Lord Holland, listening closely, recorded his reaction: Wellington

delivered one of the worst and perhaps most injudicious speeches we have yet heard from him; every word of it implied or avowed that no relaxation of exclusive laws should ever be made but under pressure of necessity, i.e., intimidation, and that repeal of the test act as well as of Catholic disabilities had been granted to the formidable number of petitioners and their determined manner of demanding relief, not to the reason of justice of their cause. The burden of proof lay, according to his Grace's notable philosophy, on those who claimed, not on those who refused constitutional rights.... His theory of human society is truly that of an enemy.

The bill was defeated. Jews would have to wait another quarter of a century, until July 1858, before one of their number could take a seat in Parliament without doing so "in accordance with the true faith of a Christian."

The Britain of Wellington's time held seven million Roman Catholics and only thirty thousand Jews—not nearly enough to intimidate Napoleon's conqueror.

LOUIS PHILIPPE, 1773–1850
"King of the French," 1830–1848

History's Conventional View

The most striking image of Louis Philippe comes from caricature rather than elegant state portraits. It is a roundish, pear-shaped, blandly garbed figure, comical, and definitely unregal. Alexis (*Democracy in America*) de Tocqueville noted his "lack of refinement and noble bearing," but poet Heinrich Heine suspected his common gray hat concealed a crown beneath, and the scepter of absolutism hid inside his innocent-looking umbrella. If his "Citizen King" mannerisms masked the real man, they kept him on the throne for seventeen years.

Louis Philippe came from the Orleanist rather than the Bourbon side of the family, which put him in a politically correct position during the French Revolution as "Philippe Egalité," although he eventually fled when the Terror put all aristocratic heads at risk. After wandering through Europe—Sicily, Switzerland, and England—and spending several years in America, the call to power accompanied the 1830s July revolution. Haughty Bourbon cousin Charles X had outworn his legitimate welcome.

Louis Philippe agreed to rule within the law rather than float above it.

During the Orleanist reign, the army insignia dropped the ancient fleur-de-lis for the blue, white, and red of 1789. The new king's goals for France were stability and political calm. Only a colonial war in Algeria (where the French Foreign Legion's legend began) and a nasty scare in Syria (which aroused Jews more than the mass of Frenchmen) siphoned attention abroad. Otherwise France remained, to the chagrin of more bellicose souls, mired in peace.

Louis Philippe relied on the capitalist class for support. They, in turn, fed greedily on his laissez-faire benevolence. The rich got richer. Corruption in the king's circle of wealthy friends led to ridicule of the Orleanist monarch as "the king of the three-percenters," "the protector of bankers," and "the mediator of stockbrokers."

High hopes that inspired the revolution of 1830 flickered and burned out. Louis Philippe and his regime were perceived as part of France's lingering problem. Moreover, set against eighteenth-century Bourbon splendor, the excitement of the French Revolution, and the glory of Napoleon's empire, the reign of the Citizen King was both boring and hated. Bourbon legitimists saw him as a usurper. Republicans viewed him as a royalist. Bonapartists detested him. Wage earners recognized him and his cronies as an enemy. Only the wealthy bourgeoisie stuck by him.

The end came during the revolutionary year of 1848. Hastily departing the fluid—and dangerous—Paris scene, Louis Philippe fled into a London exile, appropriately enough under the alias Mr. Smith.

But From a Jewish Perspective

Louis Philippe's response to Jews was mixed. When the July revolution installed its Citizen King, Jewish emancipation had already advanced closer to established fact than it had across the Channel. Napoleon's "Infamous Decrees" of 1808 lapsed in 1818, never to be renewed. French Jews could regard themselves Frenchmen, not aliens among the Gauls. Still, some work remained, and Jews welcomed Louis Philippe as an accommodating monarch likely to give them true equality.

His first year as king saw Judaism reach financial parity, as rabbis joined other clerics paid from the state exchequer. Doors opened widely in the business world, the army officer corps, and at universities, this at a time when professing English Jews still could not enter Eton, Rugby, Oxford, or Cambridge.

During Louis Philippe's nearly two-decade reign, the "More Judaico," a humiliating oath containing self-imposed curses for falsehoods mandated for Jews testifying in court, was abolished. Historian Howard Morley Sacher wrote, "Nowhere on the continent of Europe, save perhaps in the little Kingdom of the Netherlands, was Jewish emancipation reasserted so early, so bloodlessly, so undramatically." Jewish communities joined in praising "this king, elected by the nation, risen from the barricades, who has enlarged our liberties."

In 1835, under archaic legislation, the canton of Basel, Switzerland, banned an Alsatian Jew from settling there. France's envoy protested, pointing out that Swiss citizens of any faith enjoyed full rights on French soil. He was ignored.

Adolphe Cremieux, a prominent lawyer and Jewish communal leader, appealed to the king, who issued a royal decree invalidating a French-Swiss treaty because of this "disregard for international rights." Heading an appreciative delegation, Cremieux called at court to directly thank his sovereign. Reviewing the incident, he commented, "This Jew, who was extradited from Switzerland, said defiantly: 'I am a French citizen!' And the king of France severed all diplomatic relations with the canton. . . . Yes, the Revolution of 1789 established the principle of equality for all citizens; but until *you* ascended the throne, the consequences of this principle were apparently feared."

Louis Philippe replied he was "happy to show an example of full emancipation for Jews," adding his wish that "the canton of Basel will act in the spirit of the century in which we live."

On a day-to-day basis, James de Rothschild, head of the family bank's Paris branch, became a royal intimate. "My brother had occasion to see His Majesty quite casually," Vienna-based Salomon told Metternich's chief aide. "He goes to the palace whenever he wishes." Aside from acting as the regime's financial pillar, James handled Louis Philippe's personal investment account. The July Monarchy's slogan was "Enrichissez-vous!" ("Enrich yourself!"). Both men did so unabashedly.

In 1840, an incident at the far end of the Mediterranean ignited Jewish communities throughout Europe and across the Atlantic. Appeals for justice united such diverse rulers as England's Victoria, Austria's Metternich, and even the Russian Empire's tsar, Nicholas I, in condemnation of atrocities committed against Jews in a corner of the Moslem world. Only France and its Citizen King made no protest. Details of the "Damascus Affair" fill thin books and thick chapters in longer volumes. Our simpler purpose here is to extract Louis Philippe, relate his role in the scandal, and attach or detach blame.

In February, Father Thomas, a Capuchin friar, and his Arab servant disappeared a day after being seen in the Jewish Quarter. Since the Capuchins came under French protection, the French consul, Ratti-Menton, was brought into the investigation and swiftly became its key player. At his instigation, the old blood libel was produced and several Jews arrested, including a bewildered barber. Under torture he confessed, implicating seven Jewish community elders. They, in turn, were brutalized and imprisoned.

When word spread westward their coreligionists were aghast. In London, Sir Moses Montefiore easily won Foreign Secretary Lord Palmerston's support, and Victoria's offer of aid followed. From Vienna, Metternich instructed Austrian consular officials in both Damascus and Alexandria (seat of Mehemet Ali, overlord of both Egypt and Syria) to protest vigorously. In Paris, Cremieux saw Prime Minister Adolphe Thiers, who professed no knowledge of Ratti-Menton's involvement.

Undaunted, Cremieux turned to the king. Louis Philippe's response, early on, was promising: "I do not know anything about the occurrence, but if anywhere there are unfortuante Jews who appeal to the protection of my government, and if anything can be effected by its means, I will conform with your wishes."

The monarch was being less than truthful. More was at stake than the lives of a few Turkish Jews: French influence in the Near East dangled in the balance.

France had thrown its weight behind Mehemet Ali, a shrewd, ambitious brigand eager to supplant a phlegmatic sultan, his nominal overlord in Constantinople. Mehemet Ali, in turn, backed his subordinate, the cruel governor in Syria, and France backed its consul in Damascus, who was egging him on.

A Jewish mission to the Moslem world was arranged. Sir Moses Montefiore received full support from his government; Cremieux received none from his. "France is against us!" he lamented.

Despite French intrigue to thwart the mission in Alexandria, Mehemet Ali yielded to significant power pressure and allowed the British,

Austrian, Prussian, and Russian consuls to investigate the charges. The "evidence" was quickly discovered to be sheer invention. The imprisoned Jews—those who survived their torture—were released.

The Jewish mission moved on to Constantinople, where Sir Moses secured a firman, or royal decree, granting protection for Jews from the sultan, who now regained control over Syria. In the wider orbit of dipomatic power plays, England, Austria, and their client, the Ottoman "sick man of Europe" Empire won; France and its client, the upstart Mehemet Ali, lost.

Homeward bound by sea, Montefiore reached Paris before Cremieux, who followed a more circuitous route. The British ambassador arranged an audience for Sir Moses with Louis Philippe, giving the Jew an opportunity to personally hand the Citizen King a copy of the sultan's firman verifying the groundlessness of the blood libel accusation, with its tacit condemnation of the French consul's behavior. The firman further forbade molestation of Jews throughout his domain. According to historian Heinrich Graetz, Louis Philippe "was compelled to swallow this humiliation and assume a gracious manner for the sake of appearances, and congratulate Montefiore on the success of his journey and his mission."

Montefiore's 1884 biographer (while Sir Moses still lived) speculated: "That a Jew should read a lesson on toleration to a French monarch was itself bad enough, but that he should read this lesson on the authority of a Turkish sultan, who had just got the better of France in a political struggle, must have been extremely awkward."

That may explain why Cremieux, having received enthusiastic receptions from Jewish communities in Corfu, Venice, and Frankfurt, encountered a curiously muted response from his own. French Jews were wary of giving offense to their sensitive Citizen King and his prime minister, Thiers.

The "honor of France" became entwined in the incident. Louis Philippe was backed into a corner by his belligerent prime minister. Thiers had been a leading figure in the revolution that put Louis Philippe on the throne back in 1830. It was probably the high point in their relationship, for the franc-watching king grew to detest his adventurous prime minister.

Seven years later, a similar incident in Syria ended quickly. Again the blood libel charge was raised in Damascus—now in the wake of a

Christian child's murder—and again French consular officers joined in the investigation, telling Ottoman police it had been credibly established that Jews sought Christian blood for their Passover.

But this time, Thiers—long since dismissed—was no longer in power. The current prime minister, Francois Guizot, arranged an audience for Sir Moses with Louis Philippe, who agreed the charges were outrageous. More significantly, action backed his words. The consular officials involved in the plot were censured.

The next year, the Citizen King passed from the scene, making way for a republic, then a second Napoleonic empire, to which we return shortly—after slipping across the frontier for a quick visit to Germany.

FREDERICK WILLIAM IV, 1795–1861
King of Prussia, 1840–1861

History's Conventional View

Matched against other selectees "up front," Frederick William IV seems misplaced. No catchy phrase such as "the Great," "the Conqueror," or "the Bold" enhances his roman numeral. He lacks not only instant name recognition but recognition aided by resort to all deliberate speed as well.

So what justifies his appearance here? Credit a frozen moment in history when he weighed an offer that the tenderers hoped he couldn't refuse, then turned it down flat. The time was March 1849, just months after Europe's year of revolution, 1848, had shaken dynastic thrones, tipping over their occupants.

Frederick William IV, son of Frederick William III (also lacking ID colorfulness), succeeded to the throne in 1840 enamored of German romanticism. Artistically inclined, he enjoyed landscape gardening, a harmless pursuit, and wanted to return Germany to the feudal rule of the Middle Ages. Convinced he had been called upon by God to rule as well as reign, he disdained representative government and regarded constitutions as "a scrap of paper."

Frederick William IV rejected the imperial crown proffered by commoners in their national assembly at Frankfurt-on-the-Main. He would not accept it unless it came from those of royal blood. He made sure Prussia's new constitution vitiated any value it might have had as a brake on autocracy.

In 1858 Frederick William IV suffered a reported stroke, and later was declared insane. His younger brother took over as regent, then as kaiser, eventually ruling all of Germany as well as Prussia.

But From a Jewish Perspective

While the future Frederick William IV was still a child, Frederick William III promulgated severe restraints on Jews, justified by the notion they "constituted, as it were, a state within a state." Jews, he contended, must prove themselves "worthy of citizenship."

Early in his reign, Frederick William IV agreed with his father, while framing his own policies more idealistically. He assured Jews he did "not adhere to the blind prejudices of previous centuries." The king proposed to treat them as a "separate nation" within his borders, reestablish ghettos of a more user-friendly sort, exempt Jews from onerous military service but also bar them from public office, and benignly place them under his own special protection. This would have the effect of "proving to the Jews the benevolence of which they are the object." He insisted that reversion to a medieval lifestyle was in their own best interest.

Assimilated Jewish representatives tactfully disagreed. After probing for a weak link in his argument, eighty-four communal organizations "patriotically" protested their deprivation of the honor to serve in Prussia's army, and because at this stage of his reign Frederick William IV was a romantic reactionary, they received no sharp rebuke—just a muted one. He again emphasized Jewish communal independence.

"His Majesty wishes that this improvement be conditioned upon the sentiments of a Christian state," the internal affairs minister informed them. "In such a state, it is impossible for Jews to function as administrators over Christians; in general, Jews should not enjoy such rights that could prove detrimental to a Christian social order." A new "law about Jews" was promised.

This edict failed to allay fears. When, after a lengthy delay, new regulations were confirmed by Frederick William IV in July 1847, provision was made for the right of autonomy in Jewish communities, but only for spiritual affairs. On the matter of equality, this charter was ambiguous. "Our Jewish subjects are accorded, throughout our monarchy, under equal responsibilities, equal civil rights on a par with our Christian subjects, *if no other norms* are designated in this law." Plenty of "other norms" were, in effect, barring Jews from any worthwhile government, university, or military post.

Europe's year of revolution followed, with its attendant opportunities and risks. Several Jews sat in the Frankfurt body that now prepared a more comprehensive Jewish emancipation. These measures were buried in a patch quilt of liberal reforms, which Frederick William IV found loathsome and managed to ignore. Once turmoil subsided, reactionaries regrouped and dejected reformers dispersed.

If Prussian commoners wanted a constitution they would have the document, but one remodeled at the direction of the king's men. This more conservative "scrap of paper" nonetheless provided several positive features for Jews. They could now vote, own land, and enter the professions—decided advances over both Frederick William IV's medieval fantasies back in 1840 and his preupheaval law of 1847. However, Crown offices remained closed. The attorney general ruled that Jews were unfit for judgeships. How could a Jew's conscience, went the rationale, allow him to administer the Christian oath to litigants and witnesses? Ministry of justice officials—apparently with the king's approval—stopped Jews from taking bar exams, effectively keeping them out of the legal profession. Bureaucratic department heads, given authority to reject job candidates on grounds of "personality," easily found Jews wanting.

Privately, the king himself railed against Jews. He deplored "the influence of that despicable Jewish clique with its tail of silly and foolish yelpers" who were a "misfortune for Prussia. . . . The insolent rabble, by word, letter, and picture, daily lays the axe to the root of the German character."

This was not a man free of "the blind prejudices of previous centuries." In fairness, the Prussia of Frederick William IV came nowhere near the oppression of his neighbor to the east, Tsar Nicholas I's Russia, but it was still a giant step behind the France of his post-1848 contemporary to the west, Louis Napoleon.

NAPOLEON III, 1808–1873
Emperor of France, 1852–1870

History's Conventional View

France's second empire, a gaudy, Can-Can reflection of the first, was scripted, produced, and directed by Napoleon's nephew, son of his brother Louis.

The New World best remembers Charles Louis Napoleon Bonaparte for his grandiose scheme to offset the loss of Louisiana during the first empire by annexing Mexico. The disastrous Maximilian Affair ended with his Austrian choice for Mexico's throne falling before a Mexican firing squad. When he allowed France to be drawn into war with resurgent Prussia, he effectively ended his flamboyant career.

That career sprouted from an idolized name, his most notable asset. De Tocqueville described him as "an enigmatic, sombre, insignificant numbskull." An abortive effort to overthrow Louis Philippe led to prison confinement, albeit a comfortable one befitting his pedigree. He then bided his time, confident destiny was on his side.

Elected president of the Second Republic following the Orleanist collapse, he traded that office for imperial status as the result of a coup d'etat. (The new constitution had barred an incumbent from succeeding himself.)

He muzzled the press, modernized Paris, encouraged railroad building, and maintained popularity as France's economy prospered. The Empire Means Peace became a recurrent, though hardly accurate, theme. He marched France into the Crimean War as a matter of honor rather than national interest, then conspired with Piedmont's prime minister to engage Austria for a less savory but more reasonable motive—the concession of Nice and Savoy. Napoleon III committed troops to protect papal authority in Rome, a woeful development for Jews. Then, of course, there was the drain of manpower and treasure in far-off Mexico, and in even farther-off Cochin-China and Cambodia. Unwittingly he laid the groundwork for the Vietnam War of a future century.

Although a dictator, by contemporary standards Napoleon III was relatively easygoing. Had he remained in Paris flinging himself into public works, fostering industrial progress, and gradually decreasing by degree the authoritarianism of his earlier reign—as he had already begun—he might have lasted into the 1870s. Instead, the empire dissolved in a flash as he led a besieged French army at Sedan into Prussian captivity.

But From a Jewish Perspective

In metropolitan France, Napoleon III did not have to enhance Jewish legal rights to prove himself. Equality already existed. However, in the ever-contentious province of Alsace, peasants and townsfolk in that hotbed of anti-Semitism saw his election as president in 1848 as an opportunity for hooliganism. This view did not reflect Napoleon the man but Napoleon the name. Memories ran deep, and they regarded the earlier Bonaparte's repugnance for Alsatian Jews a likely belief of his nephew. They were wrong. As Jews prepared to flee across the border to Switzerland, the Lower Rhine's prefect received orders from Paris to energetically suppress any budding pogrom and warn troublemakers that "individuals in the government may change, but the principles remain intact, and no government in the world can ignore them."

Anti-Semitism in the second empire existed, to be sure, but was not of the emperor's making. His government did nothing to aggravate it, and took measures to eradicate the spectre. Toward this end the machinery of an authoritarian regime could, at times, be more effective than in a democracy. In 1858, police seized a viciously written tract hailing the Inquisition and advocating the widespread slaughter of Jews. Its author went to prison.

Imposition of theater censorship also had, for Jews, an upside. The portrayal of Shakespeare's Shylock was softened, for example, and a reference to "Jews, the scum of humanity, shameful reprobates of mankind," was immediately deleted by the censor from a lesser playwright's dialogue. No soul-searching about freedom of speech denial, no lengthy court process.

As for his official and personal relations with Jews, Napoleon III showed none of neighbor Frederick William IV's antipathy to their company, or to bringing them into higher government circles, especially if they were privately successful and displayed shrewd financial minds. Achille Fould—described by Simon Dubnow as "a half-hearted Jew, but a good monarchist"—became a pillar of the Second Empire, occupying several cabinet posts.

Baron James de Rothschild was a special case. An intimate of the ousted, hence discredited, Louis Philippe, Rothschild's relations with France's new ruler were naturally cool. But if money talks, lavish credit converses loudest. And a time came when Napoleon wanted to attach his hose to the banking house pump.

Rothschild family biographer Frederic Morton describes the day in 1862 that the emperor "paid a state visit to Rothschild I, King of the Jews," at the Baron's estate, Ferrieres: "At the emperor's entry, the imperial banners were hoisted together with the Family colors on all four towers of the chateau. Surrounded by a liveried army of lackeys, pedestaled on a thick green-velvet carpet embroidered with gold bees, James de Rothschild greeted the monarch. He led His Majesty through Renaissance pavilions hung with Van Dycks, Velasquezes, Giorgiones, Rubenses. . . ."

Napoleon planted a young cedar in the gardens, a chore expected of all visiting crowned heads, ate off Sevres porcelain painted by Francois Boucher, listened to music specially composed by Gioacchino Rossini, and hunted game. At night, when he departed, "his coach rode through an espalier of Rothschild torches lighting up the sky on the very edge of the estate." Some royal figures lately disdained *any* mingling with Jews, even cosmically wealthy ones. Not so Napoleon with a Rothschild.

Unfortunately for a community of Jews beyond France's borders, the emperor stood as a buffer between Italian patriots and their goal of ending papal rule of the Eternal City. French arms alone assured Pope Pius IX of his temporal power. After ascending St. Peter's throne, he had moved from a promising policy of liberality before insurgents took over the city and soured him on reform. He denied Jews the right to live beyond ghetto walls, acquire land, engage in trade, or to enter some professions. In another throwback to centuries past, he forbade Jewish doctors to attend Christian patients. This, then, was the nature of the clerical regime Napoleon III kept from collapsing throughout the 1850s, while the rest of Italy molded itself into a nation.

As Pius IX's protector, the emperor was drawn into an international effort to convince the pontiff to reverse a notorious decision involving a six-year-old Jewish child. Like the Damascus Affair, this case stirred Jews everywhere, and the details are recited in many books on anti-Semitism.

In June 1858, young Edgar Mortara was kidnapped by papal police after a Catholic domestic confessed to a priest that she secretly had him baptized, while ill as an infant, to save his soul. Authorities refused to return the child to his distraught parents. Instead, he was sent to an institution to be raised as a Catholic.

Despite widespread condemnation of this violation of human and parental rights, the pope remained adamant. Franz Joseph, the Austrian emperor, protested. Officials of many still independent German states expressed dismay, but had little influence at the Vatican. The Protestant-led British government, too, found the pope's position deplorable, but felt

Catholic powers were better positioned to intercede. France, therefore, took the lead. Napoleon III instructed his representative in Rome to press for a reversal. Initial efforts made no headway. The French ambassador, the duc de Gramont, informed Paris of the pope's intransigence and was told to press on. He did. Eventually the papal secretary of foreign affairs, Cardinal Antonelli, told the diplomat that "of all the arguments I presented to the pope, the one to which he has been most sensitive has been the one concerning the rift the affair has made between Napoleon III and himself." Nonetheless, Pius IX would not budge.

Napoleon III, perhaps at Rothschild's urging, took on another impossible task when the Congress of 1858 reorganized the Rumanian principalities of Moldavia and Wallachia. He worked to secure Jews civil rights and an end to long-borne disabilities. Hatreds in that corner of Europe, though, were too deeply imbedded to be cast aside for the sake of accomodating civilized sensibilities—but credit Napoleon III for trying.

Human rights violations affecting their coreligionists around the world led more fortunate, assimilated Jews to form an international organization—the Alliance Israelite Universelle—to protect Jewish interests. Where better to base its operations than in the politically receptive climate of Napoleon III's Paris. In 1860, midway through his Second Empire, it began its work.

When Louis Napoleon had begun his rise, a devious Thiers sneered at this "cretin whom we will manage." But that cynical manipulator of the Damascus scenario was wrong. Napoleon Bonaparte's nephew proved no pliant puppet. If he eventually proved hopelessly overmatched against the diabolical von Bismarck, as were other European men of affairs, at least he cannot be faulted for his benign record on Jews.

Italy's Founding Fathers

GIUSEPPE MAZZINI, 1805–1872

GIUSEPPE GARIBALDI, 1807–1882

COUNT CAMILLO DI CAVOUR, 1810–1861

History's Conventional View

Mazzini, the patriot and agitator, Garibaldi, the revolutionary and guerrilla fighter, and Cavour, the statesman and diplomat, were the prophet, brawn, and brains of Italian unification. That they did not always agree, or even respect each other, does not detract from their monumental achievement.

The Risorgimento, or rebirth, progressed first through the fervor of Giuseppe Mazzini, who believed "the tree of liberty grows stronger when watered by the blood of martyrs." In 1831 he founded young Italy, a radical, violent movement pledged to national unity. Since the Austrian authorities dominating northern Italy, papal agents ruling Rome (under French protection), and the restored Bourbons in the south were not amused, Mazzini spent much of his adulthood in exile. After uprisings shook the peninsula during the general European unrest of 1848, Mazzini set up a Roman republic, lasting a few months, until Napoleon III's troops arrived. His ally, Garibaldi, accepted the presence of the French army and chose to fight another day.

Giuseppe Garibaldi, during his early revolutionary career, was pursued at one time or another by the gendarmes of Austria, France, Spain, and Naples, necessitating lengthy stays abroad. He passed 1850 laboring as a candle maker at New York's Staten Island. He is remembered for his idealism, honesty, incredible bravery, and recklessness, but most notably for leading "the Thousand"—his motley red-shirted volunteers—in the liberation of Sicily and the southern mainland from hated Spanish Bourbon overlords.

After a short stint as dictator, he handed his conquests (thereby arousing Mazzini's disgust) to Sardinia's king, Victor Emmanuel II, eventually to become part of the new Italian nation. The peasants that Garibaldi championed came to regard him a secular saint. After battle, scraps of his bloodstained clothes were saved and revered as holy relics.

Meanwhile, Camillo di Cavour, the king's legal-minded prime minister, had been manipulating unification more methodically. Since a large Austrian army clung tightly to Lombardy and supported satellite principalities in Parma, Modena, and Tuscany, Cavour arranged secretly with Napoleon III to hurl France's even larger army into the drama.

Victory by combined French and Sardinian forces left Rome and its environs, still ruled by the pope, wedged between liberated northern and southern ends of the peninsula. (It was in territory under Pope Pius IX's jurisdiction that the Mortara case occurred.) Fate, though, in the form of the spiked helmet form of Prussia, stepped in to give the Messrs.

Mazzini, Garibaldi, and Cavour a hand. In 1870, Napoleon III pulled his troops from Rome, leaving Pius IX to retreat, grumbling, behind Vatican walls. King Victor Emmanuel II's army marched into the city. Unification was complete.

Mazzini, ever the republican, saw the waving banner of the House of Savoy a betrayal of principle. "I had thought to evoke the soul of Italy," he complained, "but all I find before me is a corpse." The country, in his eyes, had become "rotten with materialism and egoism." Mazzini detested Cavour, who died prematurely in 1861, and the Sardinian-Piedmontese statesman, in turn, regarded Mazzini's idealism as "silly nonsense."

Garibaldi distrusted Mazzini and hated Cavour. At times, he equated this devious prime minister's policies with cowardice. Once, both men's faces reddened with rage on the floor of Parliament as Garibaldi pointed at Cavour and charged, "You were planning to wage a fratricidal war!" No matter. Each of the trio carried out his part in history's grand design. Together they made Italy something more than a "geographical expression."

But From a Jewish Perspective

The labors of Mazzini, Garibaldi, and Cavour were indeed a blessing for Italian Jewry. Historian Howard Morley Sacher puts it this way:

> In 1848 there had been no European country save Spain where the restrictions placed upon Jews were more galling and more humiliating than in Italy. After 1860, there was no country on the continent of Europe where conditions were better for Jews.

Mazzini's Young Italy attracted thousands of Jews who fought for Italy's—and their own—freedom during the abortive uprisings of the 1830s. In northern Italy, a Jew became his chief aide, and a Turin Jewish banking firm financed his futile 1833 expedition to Savoy. While a fugitive in exile, Mazzini formed long-standing relationships with Jews sympathetic to his planned future forays. His most ambitious venture resulted in the short-lived Roman Republic of 1849. Three Jews were elected to its Constituent Assembly before French troops put an end to this experiment in democracy, a fact not unnoticed by Pope Pius IX when restored to power.

Gardibaldi stood tall for equality. Several Jews were among "the Thousand" at his side as they liberated Sicily and southern Italy. One, Allessandro Levi, volunteered for a daring reconnaisance mission to Naples disguised as a fisherman. Arrested by Bourbon sentries and sentenced to death, he was saved by the timely arrival of Garibaldi's forces.

While Jews flocked to Mazzini and Garibaldi bent on overturning reactionary regimes by force of arms, the constitution assuring their emancipation (not a mere "scrap of paper" of the kind ridiculed by Frederick William IV) was drafted in the kingdom of Sardinia-Piedmont. "I am a son of Liberty, and to her I owe all that I am," Cavour wrote to a friend. This constitution he championed, guaranteeing civil rights and enfranchisement to all, would eventually embrace the entire peninsula under the House of Savoy's reign.

Early in his prime ministry, Cavour had complained to friends about the cost of doing business with Baron James de Rothschild and sought to shake Piedmont's treasury loose from "this Jew who strangles us." That was more a comment on Rothschild the tough banker than on Rothschild the Jew. In any event, the pair continued their symbiotic association. Rothschild funds furnished financial fuel for an impending war with Austria under cover of a project to cut a tunnel through the Alps. (The banking house traditionally denied governments credit for strictly military ventures.)

Like his sometime rivals Mazzini and Garibaldi, Cavour enjoyed good relations with less exalted Jews working in common cause, and he had no hesitation about appointing Jews to sensitive positions. Among his Jewish appointees: the supervisor of finances and public works for Tuscany; the director of his political publication *Opinione;* and closest to him of all, Isaac Arton, his confidential secretary and "faithful lieutenant." Cavour ignored clerical opposition to a Jew so near the source of state power.

On the broader scene, Jews had supported revolutionary movements and come up empty, merely substituting a lesser evil for the greater. This was not the case in emerging Italy. Mazzini, Garibaldi, and Cavour rate high on any Jewish scorecard.

ALEXANDER II, 1818–1881
Tsar of Russia, 1855–1881

History's Conventional View

Alexander II was the "Tsar-Liberator" who freed the serfs, though their quality of life hardly improved through this good deed. As he candidly explained earlier to Moscow's assembled nobility, it was prompted by less than exemplary goodwill. "It is better to abolish serfdom from above," he said, "than wait until it begins to abolish itself from below."

Alexander came to the throne in 1855, when Russia was reeling from defeat in the Crimea. The vaunted army of Nicholas I had proven flawed. The new tsar's upbringing had featured those stern principles responsible for his father's notoriety as the Iron Tsar. Alexander proclaimed his intention to rule in the tradition of "Peter, Catherine, Alexander the Blessed, and Our unforgettable parent."

Nonetheless, his early reign emitted signs of enlightened liberalism. During the Era of Great Reform—apart from ending serfdom for forty-million Russians—Alexander oversaw the restructure of state finances, the reform of the judiciary, steps toward greater local self-government, and reorganization of the conscription system. Benjamin Disraeli called him "the kindliest prince who has ever ruled in Russia."

Even Americans, circa 1865, could think well of this tsar. During the Civil War, Russia's fleet appeared outside New York harbor on a "good will" mission, taken as support for the Union cause. Some saw our subsequent purchase of Alaska—ridiculed by some critics as "Seward's Icebox" after the secretary of state responsible for the acquisition—as payback for Alexander's friendly gesture. (Later evidence put a different spin on his conduct. It appears the tsar's advisers feared that Russian warships would fall easy prey to Britain's superior navy if they were trapped in the Baltic during a crisis, so sailing them across the Atlantic kept them out of harm's way.)

The luster of Alexander II's early reign disappeared after Polish insurgents attempted to break free of Russian control once more. The tsar turned back to repression. Then, at home, restless liberals found his reforms too little and too late. More ominously, a nihilist movement took root: Violence begot violence, and police measures stiffened. In 1879, People's Will was formed, with assassination of government officials high on its agenda.

On March 1, 1881, Alexander II, returning by coach to his Winter Palace from a military review, was targeted by terrorists along the route. Two bombs were thrown—the second blast killed him.

But From a Jewish Perspective

For the first half of his reign, Alexander II was better for Jews than any tsar before him. And despite the repression to come, he was still infinitely better than the last pair of Romanovs who followed.

One measure, taken in 1856, outranks all others in earning Jewish goodwill. He called a halt to the cantonist system that separated youths from their families, a staple of his father's anti-Semitic program. Henceforth, only Jews of draft age would serve, and under the same rules as all other Russians.

Alexander also toned down the conversionist policies practiced by Nicholas and banned all conversions of youngsters under fourteen if done without the consent of their parents. Decrees in 1864 and 1866 banned the practice of reducing Jews' criminal sentences if the accused embraced Christianity and ended the money bonuses given Jewish soldiers who accepted baptism. Universities now admitted Jews, and so did the legal profession. Craftsmen and businessmen now moved freely beyond the Pale of Settlement, and within the Pale—cities formerly closed to Jews, Kiev being the largest—were now open.

Perhaps Alexander was motivated by a touch of humanity, something never evident in the Romanov bloodline. But this virtue should not be exaggerated. For example, the first time it was suggested to him that Jewish soldiers, demobilized after twenty-five years' service, should be allowed to settle wherever they chose rather than being thrown back into the Pale, his response was unequivocal: "Under no circumstances!"

Although some of the monarch's decrees bore a progressive stamp, he was no liberal. Nor was he unmindful that a better image in Jews' eyes abroad might attract needed capital to strengthen Russia's creaky financial foundation and also her infrastructure, for the great age of railroad building had begun.

In a public relations sense, the tsar's new Jewish policy was clearly a success. In 1872, Sir Moses Montefiore, aged eighty-eight, made an arduous journey once more to Russia, this time to present Alexander II with a special address of homage on the second centenary of Peter the

Great's birth. Twenty-six years earlier, he had tried to influence Nicholas I's rigid mind. The apparent thaw since then amazed him.

Sir Moses saw Alexander on July 24, then noted in his diary: "His Imperial Majesty, who conversed most fluently in the English language, received me with the utmost grace and kindness.... Nor can I here omit to record my grateful appreciation of His Imperial Majesty's consideration in having come from the seat of the summer maneuvers to the Winter Palace expressly to spare me fatigue in consequence of my advanced age."

On a more substantive note, this champion of Jewish rights reflected, "Looking back to what the condition of our coreligionists in Russia was twenty-six years ago, and having regard to their present position, they have now abundant reason to cherish grateful feelings towards the emperor, to whom their prosperity is in so great a measure attributable."

For one brief, shining moment, the Russia of Tsar Alexander II seemed at last ready to hearken to the better angels of mid-nineteenth-century tolerance. It was illusory. The later years of Alexander were overtaken by bitterness. Liberal measures had won him no love among the Russian multitudes, but, by smoothing the path for free thought, it bred dissent aloud and conspiracy under cover. Nihilism took root. The few Jewish names associated with radical movements gained official ill will for their apolitical coreligionists.

The tsar's policy toward Jews now took an unpleasant turn. Some yeshivas were ordered closed. A quietly practiced quota at first, a more conspicuous one later, barred Jewish advancement in the military. When complaints about Jewish competition and reports of blood accusations reached the capital, the all-too-familiar machinery for government inquiries began functioning.

At the 1878 Congress of Berlin, among the "Great Power" representatives, Alexander's chancellor alone opposed legal equality for eastern European Jews. "The Jews of Berlin, Paris, London, and Vienna—who certainly deserve equal civil and political rights," he said, were unlike the Jews of Serbia, Rumania, and Russia, "who are a veritable scourge for the indigenous population."

The bright cumulous puffs in the morning of Alexander's reign turned to a sinister nimbus at its dusk. Some three million Jews, mostly poor, mostly Orthodox, languished in the Pale on the day of his assassination. Worse was soon to come when his powerfully built and unambiguously anti-Semitic son mounted to the throne as Alexander III.

* * *

Rather than advance past Alexander II directly to son Alexander III, thence to grandson Nicholas II, completing the Romanov dynasty in one seamless sweep, we shift attention to Germany, thereby making our time line consistent. Alexander III was still a child, and Nicholas was unborn, when Richard Wagner and Otto von Bismarck, coming next into view, were already leaving their first impressions on the historical record.

Richard Wagner, 1813–1883

History's Conventional View

Opera lovers are well acquainted with Wagner's monumental "Ring" cycle—*Das Rheingold, Die Walkure, Siegfried,* and *Götterdämmerung*—as well as *Tristan und Isolde, Die Meistersinger, Lohengrin, Tannhäuser,* and *Parsifal.*

As a man the great composer courted controversy. Marital scandals followed him, and his penchant for profligate spending was never matched by the bourgeois notion that money borrowed is money owed. His personal idiosyncrasies, added to his poisonous political ideas, have occupied nonmusicologist biographers.

Wagner's stormy activism, not his sonorous motifs, brought him to the attention of Saxony's authorities. The year was 1848, and Europe was in turmoil. Wagner wanted revolution. Instead, he got his name inserted in an arrest warrant for treason. Not until 1859 would he dare return to Germany from exile.

During an extended stay in Switzerland, he wrote his most violent prose and built up his reputation as an anti-Semite. He met the respected conductor Hans von Bülow and his wife, Cosima, daughter of composer Franz Liszt. Wagner got to know them well, particularly Cosima, with whom he had an affair.

As Wagner's financial debts mounted and creditors hounded him, he needed a savior of operatic proportions. He found one—erratic King Ludwig II of Bavaria. Summoned to Munich by Ludwig, the young king assured Wagner that "the petty cares of everyday life I will banish from you forever; I will enable you to enjoy the peace you have longed for so that you will be able to spread the mighty wings of your genius undisturbed in the pure air of your rapturous art!"

King Ludwig supported Wagner at Bayreuth, and in 1876 the complete

Ring cycle was performed for the first time. Those who held the composer in awe could come annually to pay homage to Wagner while he was alive, and thereafter to his memory.

Not every Wagner fan stayed the course, however. "Wagner is a neurosis," philosopher Friedrich Nietzsche, once a partner in mutual admiration, declared. He reassessed the musical genius was "a cranky desperate decadent." Nietzsche wrote: "Already in the summer of 1876, when the first festival at Bayreuth was at its height, I took leave of Wagner in my soul. I cannot endure anything double-faced. Since Wagner has returned to Germany, he has condescended, step-by-step, to everything I despise—even anti-Semitism."

What Nietzsche found most repulsive in the composer, Adolf Hitler would find most alluring. In *Mein Kampf*, the struggling prison inmate and future Reich chancellor placed Wagner in his pantheon of Teutonic role models.

Hitler wrote, "The great warriors of this world, who, though not understood by the present, are nevertheless prepared to carry the fight for their ideas and ideals to their end.... To them belong not only the truly great statesmen, but all other great reformers as well. Beside Frederick the Great stands Martin Luther as well as Richard Wagner."

But From a Jewish Perspective

For many years, the Israel Philharmonic refused to perform *Rienzi*, *Tannhauser*, *The Flying Dutchman*, or any other work by Richard Wagner. Some of the many Holocaust survivors would have found doing so painful. To Wagner, Jews represented the dominant force in a degenerate Western society, especially in its arts. In his lifetime he did little direct harm to Jews, save those in his immediate circle. But the composer's haunting spirit guided the heart and hand of Adolf Hitler, born six years after his death. "I regard the Jewish race as the born enemy of pure humanity and everything that is noble in it," wrote Wagner to his patron, King Ludwig. "It is certain that we Germans will go under before them, and perhaps I am the last German who knows how to stand up as an art-loving man against the Judaism that is already getting control of everything." As Wagner saw it, "not our princes, but our bankers and the Philistines are our lords now."

Father-in-law Franz Liszt described Wagner's obsession in a letter to a mutual friend, Princess Wittgenstein: "...he flung his arms around my neck, then he rolled on the ground, caressing his dog Pepi and talking nonsense to it, in between spitting on the Jews, who are a generic term with him, in a very broad sense."

During the revolutionary turmoil of 1848, Wagner had actually *supported* Jewish emancipation in Germany, for which he was apologetic in his more mature years. He blamed this youthful error on being hoodwinked. "Jewry has been able to take root among us solely by exploiting the weakness and faultiness of our conditions.... When we fought for the emancipation of the Jews, we were in actuality fighting more for an abstract principle than for the concrete case. Indeed, all our liberalism was a not very clear-sighted intellectual game in which we waxed sentimental over liberty of the people without knowing these people."

Wagner's first major foray into anti-Semitic prose came in 1850, via his essay "Judaism in Music," published under the thinly disguising pseudonym Karl Freigedank (Freethinking). Wagner wrote, "...in spite of all our oratory and writing in behalf of the emancipation of the Jews, in actual contact with Jews we always felt instinctively repelled." Jews were not Germans, he contended, and never could be made over into Germans.

In his own field, Wagner declared true music beyond the capacity of Jews. Their limitations allowed them "only to imitate, to copy, not to originate or create works of art." Principal targets were Felix Mendelssohn (who, though converted to Christianity, could not escape his racial origins in Wagner's eyes) and Giacomo Meyerbeer: "Mendelssohn has shown us that a Jew may have the amplest store of specific talents, may possess the finest and most varied culture, the highest, most impeccable integrity—yet is not capable, not even once, of producing in us that deep, that heart-searching effect which we expect from art."

Meyerbeer's grand operas, too, could only mirror the shallow surface of Western art, never revealing greatness. The rule that Jewish blood was forever corrupted was absolute.

The attack on Meyerbeer piled ingratitude upon anti-Semitism. Respected and influential from Paris to Dresden, the older man had helped his young countryman by lending him funds and easing his entry into the Parisian musical community. Wagner had written, "I implore you to show me the way to the hearts of the Paris public through recommendations and support." His debt was clearly affirmed in a letter he later sent Robert Schumann, urging him not to disparage Meyerbeer: "Don't pitch into Meyerbeer so vigorously. I have that man to thank for everything, and more especially for the fame shortly to be mine."

But in 1851, now more secure, Wagner could write Franz Liszt of his benefactor, "I do not hate him, he is infinitely repugnant to me. This everlastingly amiable, complaisant fellow reminds me of the most muddy, I might almost say the most degraded period of my life, when he used to make a show of protecting me."

As for his overall purpose in publishing "Judaism in Music," he pointed out, "I have cherished a long-repressed resentment about this Jew business, and the grudge is as necessary to my nature as gall is to the blood. An incentive came when their accursed scribblings annoyed me intensely, so at last I let fly."

Five years later, he attributed his unpleasant reception as guest conductor of the London Philharmonic to his assault on Mendelssohn. "Mendelssohn is to the English exactly what Jehovah is to the Jews. And Jehovah's wrath now strikes me, an unbeliever." He dismissed press critics as " a rabble of Jews."

When Wagner reissued his essay under his own name in 1869, he dedicated it to an aristocratic lady who had ingenuously asked why journalists constantly berated him. The press was in the hands of Jews, he responded by way of a postscript to his original essay, naming Edward Hanslick, his most vociferous critic. To "the Master," Hanslick's "gracefully hidden Jewish origin" explained all.

In February 1878, Wagner began publishing his own periodical, *Bayreuther Blatter*, a muddled exposition of his reflections on art, culture, and race. In an article called "What Is German?" he contended that the virtues of German spirit had been sullied, that "the Jews came in from underneath in large numbers to take charge of 'business' and to dish out alcohol instead of things of the spirit to the Folk, in order to dissipate their phlegm." Thus, Jews ran not only the press, but the theater and, pretty much, the nation. In another article, "Modern," he blamed Jews for everything wrong with contemporary society—worthless music, a venal press, a ruined German language, and false cultural values. They had infiltrated politics and science as well.

Wagner expressed the certainty that Jews planned to destroy Germany "through the power of the pen," yet he refused to add his name to a heralded anti-Semitic petition ceremoniously presented to the Berlin Reichstag. His excuse: An earlier petition he had signed regarding vivisection achieved nothing; thereafter, he pledged never to sign another. To impresario Angelo Neumann, who managed extensive—and profitable—tours of Wagnerian operas, he gave another reason: "I stand completely aloof from the current anti-Semitic movement." This was a plausible position, despite his dossier. Neumann was a Jew, a valued associate, and not the only one in the composer's circle. Whether self-hating, such as the pianist and aide Joseph Rubenstein, who bemoaned his racial inadequacies when introducing himself to "the Master" ("I am a Jew. That tells you everything.") or loyal to their heritage, such as the conductor Hermann Levi, the son of a rabbi, who stoically endured Wagner's racial taunts while rebuffing efforts to push him toward the baptismal waters, both were drawn to Wagner, the artistic genius. Cosima noted in her diary: "R and I speak of the remarkable fascination he exercises on individual Jews; he remarks that Wahnfried [their home] seems to be turning into a synagogue."

In fact, a rumor spread by detractors (he earned many among fellow anti-Semites) alleged that he was himself of Jewish origin, the child of an illicit affair. Caricatures depicted him with an extravagantly-sized "Jewish" nose, and a nickname emerged, the Rabbi of Bayreuth. Many years would pass before Wagner's safe parentage was established with finality via a finely conducted genealogical investigation by Nazi racial specialists in the 1930s.

Unfortunately for Wagner's psyche, he lacked comparable resources for such meticulous detective work and might have been plagued by uncertainty. In a detailed, carefully researched biography, Derek Watson speculated, "His irrational hatred of the Jews may have increased in the later 1870s as a gesture of self-defense, a vigorous attempt to prove his Aryan purity."

Paper money he saw as a "diabolic plot." All Western civilization was a "judaico-barbaric jumble." In "Religion and Art," a *Bayreuther Blatter* article, he found everything in the world rotten, especially Jewry. In "Know Thyself," he visualized humankind's only hope for salvation was in exorcising the Jew, "the demon of man's downfall." Even "commixture of blood does not hurt him; if a Jew or Jewess intermarry with the most distant of races, a Jew will always come to birth."

In 1882, an interview granted to the impressionist artist Auguste

Renoir, who merely wanted to paint his picture, turned into a multi-faceted monologue during which the Frenchman could squeeze in little beyond "Yes, dear Master," and "Of course, dear Master." It ended, Watson points out, in "a tirade against the Jews."

The composer's death, at seventy, came a year later, but his tenacious widow Cosima kept the Wagnerian legend and the Bayreuth Festival alive. She outlived him by fifty years, and Wagner expert Ernest Newman described her "as venomous an anti-Semite as Germany could show at that time." Adolf Hitler would later come to pay respectful calls on her, Wagner's son Siegfried, and daughter-in-law Winifred, at their Wahnfried residence, and then lose himself in the Teutonic splendor of the Master's Ring cycle.

Berlin correspondent William L. Shirer overheard the Fuehrer say, "Whoever wants to understand National Socialist Germany must know Wagner." The best case a Jew can make for the Master is that he did not know National Socialist Germany or its Fuehrer.

OTTO VON BISMARCK, 1815–1898
Prime Minister of Prussia, 1862–1890
Chancellor of Germany, 1871–1890

History's Conventional View

The world sees Bismarck as a colossus astride nineteenth-century Germany. Only Wagner comes as close. An image of "the Iron Chancellor" forms: stern, penetrating eyes peering from beneath bushy eyebrows under a Prussian spiked helmet. Bismarck is the implacable Junker, the Prussian aristocrat who almost single-handedly forged the Second Reich—gruff, tough, shrewd, an autocrat who neither suffered fools nor dissenting wise men (nor, for that matter, Wagner, whose flattery—in pursuit of lucrative court patronage—he brusquely turned aside, thereby assuring the composer's ill will).

In 1863, Bismarck's first address as minister and president of Prussia set the tone for his route to national unification. "Germany does not look to Prussia's liberalism but to its power," he said. "The great problems of the times are not solved by speeches and majority decisions but by iron and blood."

Count (later prince) von Bismarck carefully crafted alliances of convenience, neutralized potential opponents, and committed his king to the right wars at the right times against the right foes: Denmark (1864); Austria (1866); and France (1870). When he was done, William I (Frederick William's younger brother) was proclaimed German emperor at the palace of Versailles. Bismarck's own place in European history was thus already secure.

Unification achieved, Bismarck's new script for Germany entailed building its economic might while maintaining a world-class military machine. He offered himself as "honest broker" to settle differences between Britain and Russia over the future of the strategic straits then controlled by fast-fading Turkey, "the Sick Man of Europe." At the Congress of Berlin, in 1878, he won new diplomatic laurels.

As chancellor of the German Empire, Bismarck was beholden only to his sovereign. Conservative principles dominated, the army's needs were deemed paramount, and pressures for democratization disdained. Nevertheless, Reichstag members could—and did—prove a nuisance.

Checkmating established or incipient rivals occupied much of the Iron Chancellor's time. He saw Rome's influence a threat, particularly after Pope Pius IX (who approved the Mortara kidnapping) fostered the doctrine of papal infallibility. Bismarck embarked on his Kulturkampf, a struggle against the church. It ended in one of his few defeats, with anti-Catholic legislation being withdrawn. Against the growing Social Democratic movement, he employed a daring gambit by co-opting its major programs: sickness insurance (1883); accident insurance (1884); and old age insurance (1889). Thus, the old arch-conservative found himself administering Europe's most progressive social program.

But Bismarck could not buy off the working class so easily. Colliding interests, with left-leaning labor, Catholic centrists, greedy industrialists, and a reactionary landed class—Junkers—in the political swirl of an increasingly restless Reichstag, made the Iron Chancellor's last years in office difficult and unsettling. Pragmatically, without being held in restraint by moral inhibition, he realigned his support base. He tolerated, even encouraged, right-wing extremists who saw Jews as their misfortune—a handy scapegoat. It was a marriage of convenience against liberals and their allies, and during the decade of the 1880s it worked.

Finally, in March 1890, the aging Bismarck was forced to surrender the helm of state, dropped as "pilot" by William II, his young, impulsive new master, better recalled, even in English-speaking countries, as the Teutonic Kaiser Wilhelm II.

But From a Jewish Perspective

"I am not an enemy of Jews, and in some instances, I even love them," Bismarck, then a thirty-two-year-old politician, declared in a June 1847 parliamentary debate on Jewish emancipation. "I would bestow on them all rights, but not the right to hold administrative office in a Christian state. I confess that I am full of prejudices against Jews—which I imbibed with my mother's milk—and I have a sense of humiliation at the mere thought that a Jew can serve as a representative of the people."

About Jews, he said he shared "this feeling with the mass of the lower strata of the people and was not ashamed of their company." In his diary, he noted, "Yesterday long Jew debate....I gave a long talk against the emancipation, said many bitter things." Emancipation failed that year, and for many thereafter.

Bismarck was the helmsman in 1869 when Jewish emancipation *did* come: "All still existing limitations of the...civil rights which are rooted in differences of religious faith are hereby annulled."

Much had happened in between. Questioned one day by his Jewish physician, he explained cryptically, "Man grows with his goals." Among those goals: Austria's elimination as Prussia's rival for German leadership. That meant war, and war meant the need for large amounts of money. Bismarck's source for financing his military buildup had been Gerson Bleichroeder, a Jew and Bismarck's personal banker. When opponents in the Reichstag later attempted to embarrass the chancellor by bringing up his Jewish connection, he stood firm:

> It is true that Bleichroeder brought me in the year 1866 the means for waging war which nobody else wanted to advance to us. This was a deed for which I was obligated to feel gratitude. As an honest person, I don't like to be spoken ill of, nor have a Jew say that I have used him and then held him in contempt, in spite of services rendered which I, as a statesman, had to value highly.

Bleichroeder was raised to the nobility. Some capable Jews rose to head departments under Bismarck, and he employed others as lawyers and his own physicians. During the 1870s, emancipation and assimilation seemed to be working for the new Germany's benefit, and for the recently reviled Jew.

Bismarck freely discussed the question of intermarriages. The results

of Jewish-Junker marriages "were not at all bad." He thought well of the
notion that "brought together a Christian stallion of German breed with a
Jewish mare. There is no such thing as an evil race and I really don't
know what advice I might one day give my sons." As he saw it, "the Jew
brings to the mixture of the different German tribes a certain sparkling
which should not be underestimated."

As noted earlier, at the 1878 Congress of Berlin, Alexander II's
representative defended Rumanian anti-Semitism on grounds that superstitious, close-knit eastern European Jews bore no resemblance to
cultured, assimilated Jews in the West. In response, Bismarck pointed
out that Jewish wretchedness in the East owed its very existence to the
political and civil restrictions holding Jews down.

Two years later, within the Reich itself, an anti-Semitic petition
bearing two hundred fifty thousand signatures (Richard Wagner's *not*
among them) reached the imperial chancellor. It demanded dismissal of
Jews from responsible public posts and teaching positions, and strong
measures against future Jewish immigration. Bismarck never acknowledged it.

The preceding paragraphs point to an apparently mellower, even
benevolent Bismarck far removed from the reactionary Junker of 1847
who could not accept Jews serving in the name of his "holy majesty."
Bismarck changed when circumstances changed; at any given phase of
German history, pragmatism guided his hand. Jews had helped him in
the struggle to unify the nation and supported him even more vocally
during the Kulturkampf against the Church. Through a series of
controversial laws, the chancellor sought to bring it under state control.
Jews were useful to Bismarck, and he responded in kind. The 1880s
brought a new set of dynamics. Shifting political currents pushed
Bismarck sharply to the right, and his Jewish supporters in the Reichstag
moved away from him.

Formerly allied in common cause with the chancellor, they now
became identified with the opposition. Simon Dubnow puts the worst
possible face on Bismarck's maneuverings:

He was infuriated by criticism form the "Jewish" liberal press. He
racked his brain for ways to curb the Jews; but as head of state he
could not speak against the emancipation which he had personally
championed for Rumania, Bulgaria, and Serbia at the Congress of

Berlin in 1878. Bismarck was thus highly delighted with the new anti-Semitic propaganda in the German community, and gave it his unofficial support.

The imperial chancellor's target of choice was not the Jew, but the Social Democratic movement. His motives were political, not racial. Discussing the liberal challenge in 1881, he told his aide Moritz Busch:

> I make a distinction in the case of the Jews. Those who are wealthy are not dangerous; they are not going on the barricades and they pay their taxes promptly. The ambitious ones are those who do not yet have everything, especially those of the press, yet even here Christians are probably the worst, and not the Jews.

Chief agitator in the renewed cycle of anti-Semitism was Adolf Stoecker, an imperial court chaplain and founder of the Christian Social Workers Party. His movement attracted petty bourgeois, clericals, small tradesmen, and others long hostile to elevation of Jews to equality. He railed against an omnipotent "Jewish International" and the Jewish press, so bothersome to Bismarck. But Stoecker and the chancellor were not friends, nor even on amicable terms.

Stoecker accused Bismarck of cowardice for not cracking down harder on Jews, especially journalists, and blamed "the very struggle against Judaism" for Bismarck's "enmity" toward him. Bismarck, for his part, believed the preacher's anti-Semitism was "inconvenient and went too far," that he had a "big mouth which cannot be shut up"—but that he was also courageous. The notion that anti-Semitism was morally unacceptable under any circumstance never came into play in the chancellor's mind.

Despite his personal disgust with Stoecker, Bismarck did nothing to halt Jew-baiting, and, by his inaction, did much to encourage it. Unlike Richard Wagner, he probably would have repudiated the Nazi racial legislation a half century later and the genocidal policy it spawned. Nonetheless, he contributed, by opportunism rather than deliberate design, to all that followed in the twentieth century.

Those consequences were beyond the horizon when he prepared his memoirs after being turned out of office. In *Thoughts and Reminiscences*, historian Alfred D. Low notes that Bismarck wrote at length about Catholicism, Jesuits, and the Kulturkampf, but "he had nothing at all to say about Judaism—an interesting contrast to Hitler's *Mein Kampf*. Obviously, the role which he assigned to the 'Jewish question' in German life was a subordinate one to him, it was just one of numerous problems. The emancipation of 1869 was in his view the last word to be said on the subject."

ALEXANDER III, 1845–1894
Tsar of Russia, 1881–1894

History's Conventional View

At the outset of his twelve-year reign, Alexander declared: "The voice of God commands us to rule with faith in the power and the truth of the autocratic authority, which we are called upon to confirm and preserve." He never took a step back from that medieval resolve, nor one forward into enlightened nineteenth-century thought.

Most readers would find it difficult to identify him in an uncaptioned class photo of European royalty, but he was huge. A British correspondent described him as "built like a butcher."

Following Alexander II's assassination he came to the throne, according to Russian historian Michael T. Florinsky, with "an instinctive, elemental attachment to the idea of the unfettered supremacy of the crown." One of his first official acts was to cancel the measure, signed on the last day of his father's life, giving elected representatives at least a small voice in modeling state policy. Instead, Alexander III embarked on a campaign of repression, employing a secret police apparatus second to none on the continent. A network of spies and informers webbed the realm.

Terrorists were dispatched, but so were liberals among the intelligentsia, socialists among the workers, and anyone else who harbored thoughts of change for Mother Russia. Siberia was huge enough to welcome them all. (Among those sent to the gallows was one Alexander Ulyanov, whose vengeful younger brother assumed the alias Lenin.)

As in the days of Nicholas I, autocracy, orthodoxy, and nationalism became signposts from St. Petersburg leading to every province of the realm. A vigorous policy of "Russification" was enforced, as Alexander set out to break regional and ethnic loyalties to language and folkways. Ukrainians, White Russians, Lithuanians, Poles, and Balts would adhere to the tsar's edicts—or else.

When the Industrial Revolution made a belated appearance in Russia, a restless and surly exploited working class would find understanding allies among the downtrodden, but passive, peasantry. But the storm beginning to build would not appear during Alexander III's reign. The tsar, his family, and their orbiting nobility thrived, and the jewelry firm of Fabergé found a ready market for gem-encrusted Easter eggs at royal palaces.

But From a Jewish Perspective

Alexander III deserves billing as the most monstrous of Romanovs, which is saying a lot when we recall Nicholas I's cantonist policy. But even Nicholas made some pretense at bettering the Jews' circumstance through an alternative educational system financed by the government, albeit his covert motive was winning its graduates for Christendom. In contrast, Alexander III committed his government to unrelenting terror.

While still heir apparent, his views were sharply sculpted by Konstantin Pobedonostsev, his tutor, later his closest adviser, and eventually procurator-general of the Holy Synod. On one occasion the future tsar rewarded a pamphleteer for bringing to his attention "On the Use of Christian Blood Among Jews."

Russian scholar W. Bruce Lincoln notes the tsar "disliked Catholics, distrusted Protestants, and despised Jews with a passion that was all pervasive." Not surprisingly, therefore, when an ingenuous bureaucrat sought promotion of an underling, the tsar rejected the request, commenting, "He is a rotten, lousy Jew."

The first year of Alexander III's reign brought on the era of the pogrom. It began in the city of Elisavetgrad, in southern Russia, and then spread like a wildfire through the Pale. Not only small, backward villages were targeted. Jews in large cities such as Kiev could expect to encounter hooligans running loose through the streets. Police merely looked on unless the savagery spread to gentile sections. Austria's consul in Kiev wrote: "The entire behavior of the police leads one rightfully to the conclusion that the disturbances are abetted by the authorities." Occasionally a hooligan would be taken into custody, to Alexander's distaste, for he deplored moves to prosecute "patriotic Greek Orthodox subjects for the disturbances."

At a mass meeting in London, the elite of British society sought to move the tsar by way of "moral weapons." Lord Shaftesbury implored him "to be for the Jews a Cyrus—and not an Antiochus Epiphanes." But foreign appeals accomplished nothing. He told the Western world that pograms were a popular response to Jewish "exploitation." A delegation of Jewish notables admitted to his presence departed from their audience bearing a similar rebuff. "On the souls of the Jews, too, a sin is burning," he scolded them. "They are said to be guilty of exploiting the Christian population."

Pursuing a "give no quarter" policy, Alexander fired his liberal (in a Russian context) interior minister and replaced him with an outspoken anti-Semite who immediately set about imposing new, even more onerous, restrictions on Jewish life.

In 1882 came the so-called May Laws, technically temporary measures that remained until World War I. Jews were forbidden to settle anew in villages or outside their own towns. Diligent officials even used the law to stop Jews in neighboring cities who had left home for the high holidays from returning.

Those specially classified Jews allowed to settle legally outside the Pale during the thaw under Alexander II were not reexamined and, if found unworthy by current standards, forced to return to the Pale. The severity of Alexander II's policy was mitigated only by the corruptibility of local police when tendered bribes proved sufficiently enticing.

In 1883 the tsar appointed the High Commission for the Revision of the Existing Laws Relating to Jews. When its work was done, five years later, Alexander was confronted with a majority report proposing an end to repression coupled with "gradual and cautious" reform. The autocrat of all the Russias could ignore unpleasant majority reports, and did. "The efforts of five years," notes Simon Dubnow, "were thus buried in the archives."

Alexander III did not simply seek to make life more difficult for Jews in his domain; he intended to make it impossible. Konstantin Pobedonostsev would one day candidly admit to a Jewish delegation hoping for relief that the regime expected one-third of Russia's Jews to emigrate, one-third to accept baptism, and one-third to perish. Since Pobedonostsev was the tsar's mentor, friend, and most respected adviser, apart from his official post as procurator-general of the Holy Synod, he and his sovereign were of one mind.

As the 1880s progressed, the legislation prohibiting Jews from moving to villages—inside as well as outside the Pale—assured the slow death of shtetl existence. A Jew could no longer even take his widowed mother from her village to his, inherit property in another village, or seek medical care beyond his own community's boundary. To make matters even worse, provincial authorities received their sovereign's permission to arbitrarily redesignate thousands of small towns as villages, shutting them to new Jewish settlement.

As the 1880s progressed, shtetl life faded into memory, resurfacing nostalgically later in twentieth-century memoirs and novels. More than one hundred thousand Jews fled Russia during the decade, mainly to the United States, where the processing hall at Castle Garden would soon prove inadequate to deal with so many immigrants.

In 1887 legislation set spartan quotas for Jews at secondary schools and universities: 10 percent within the Pale; 5 percent outside the Pale, except St. Petersburg and Moscow, which were held to 3 percent. Some students, halfway through their education, found its continuation impossible on Russian soil. In 1889 admission of Jews to the bar was halted unless special permission was granted by Ministry of Justice bureaucrats. A suspected cause was the success of Jewish lawyers in defending their coreligionists against capricious acts by local officials.

When one court dignitary submitted a memorandum on Jewish travail and urged curtailing repressive practices, Alexander noted on its margin: "But we must never forget that the Jews have crucified our Master, and have shed His precious blood."

Again, as in 1882, a broad spectrum of Britain's elite met, this time at London's famed Guildhall, to make a direct appeal to the implacable Romanov. "I cannot imagine," said the Lord Mayor, "that the Russian tsar, as a good husband and tender father, should not be considerate of all his subjects. The hopes of the Russian Jews are now concentrated upon His Majesty, the tsar of Russia. With one stroke his pen can annul the laws that oppress them so harshly."

An agreed-upon memorandum, sent to St. Petersburg, carried an emotional appeal: "Your Majesty—we who are accustomed to respect every religion, and who regard freedom of religion as a sign of true religiosity, implore You to repeal those laws that oppress Jews. Grant them the happiness of equality."

The exercise was pointless.

On the first day of Passover, 1891, an imperial ukase delivered yet another heavy blow. Except for a few longtime residents, all Jews were to be barred from Moscow. Some twenty thousand faced expulsion to the already overcrowded Pale towns. An eyewitness wrote, "Whoever failed to comply with the order of the police was subject to arrest; he would be jailed, and with criminals and all sorts of riffraff await his turn for deportation under a convoy. People sought refuge in cemeteries, during freezing weather, to escape arrest; women gave birth in railroad cars; in some instances ailing persons were brought in carts and transferred to the railroad car on stretchers."

Moscow's new synagogue, completed that year, was closed by authorities for lack of a "valid" permit. Its eye-arresting cupola, highlighted by a large shield of David, had earlier been removed. The city's new governor-general, Sergei Alexandrovitch—a grand duke, brother of the tsar, and rumored to be an even more ardent anti-Semite—wanted to reduce the already drastically diminished presence even further.

Alexander III's Jewish policy had been an international scandal for a decade when the U.S. president, James Harrison, told Congress in his December 9, 1891, State of the Union address, "this government had found occasion to express in a friendly spirit, but with much earnestness, to the government of the tsar its serious concern because of harsh measures being enforced against the Hebrews." But such representations, however tactful and respectful of his person, had no effect on this determined Romanov.

In 1892, new ordinances banned Jewish participation in local council elections despite their overwhelming numbers in many cities of the congested Pale. Another measure set criminal penalties for Jews who altered their name as a means of concealing their origins. The next year, Alexander issued an edict removing the Crimean resort of Yalta (where Roosevelt, Churchill, and Stalin would meet during World War II), from the Pale of Settlement. His imperial villa, Livadia, an ideal site for autumn relaxation, was nearby. Some residents received brief extensions to dispose of their possessions before being "mercilessly expelled," writes Dubnow, the last leaving in October and November of 1894. "The tsar was destined to die [on October 20] not far from the city that had been purged of Jews for his sake! During those days when the tsar's remains were transported by railroad to St. Petersburg, railroad cars carrying Jewish exiles from Yalta to the Pale glided along the same tracks."

NICHOLAS II, 1868–1918
Tsar of Russia, 1894–1917

History's Conventional View

The last Romanov is best recalled for his violent end. In 1918, Bolsheviks gunned him down along with his wife, four daughters, and heir apparent, a bloody coda to the dynasty's 304-year existence. The mind's-eye juxtaposes photos of the bullet-pocked wall, where the deed was presumably done, and the genteel family portrait of the seven royals before the fall.

Most characterizations of Nicholas emphasize weakness. This trait merges with another—stubbornness, and a third—ignorance. As he ascended to the throne, he publicly declared: "Let it be known by all . . . that the principle of autocracy will be maintained by me as firmly and unswervingly as by my late lamented father."

Privately, he bemoaned his illustrious fate. According to Grand Duke Alexander Mikhailovitch, his future brother-in-law, he told intimates, "What is going to happen to me . . . and to all of Russia? . . . I am not prepared to be a tsar. . . . I never wanted to become one . . . I know nothing of the business of ruling."

In years to come, apologists would apportion some of the blame for the regime's shortcomings to reactionary advisers, his stronger-willed wife, Alexandra (formerly Princess Alix of Hesse-Darmstadt), and their "friend," the rapacious monk Grigory Rasputin. But Nicholas insisted on playing the all-powerful autocrat, though he was ineptly cast for the role, rather than survive as a constitutional monarch, as more farsighted men counseled. So he cannot escape history, just as he would not escape a disastrous war with Japan in the Far East, nor a popular uprising in 1905, nor disaster in the Great War of 1914.

Nicholas II was incapable of averting Russia's collapse. Only overwhelming pressure led him to call the Duma, a democratically elected body, into session in April 1906. But he quickly dissolved it. A second Duma, put in place by a smaller, less representative electorate, met a similar fate. The tsar simply could not abide sharing power, even though he didn't have a clue about effectively ruling a country of 130 million.

While at the front during World War I, he faithfully wrote his beloved Alix, signing letters, "your poor little weak-willed hubby." In 1917 home front disorder forced his abdication, the October Revolution closed exile as an option, and the next year, a volley of shots at Yekaterinburg ended the reign of the Romanovs.

During the bleak cold war–era, some Westerners looked wistfully at the bygone times of Nicholas II and sprinkled touches of sympathy on the tsar's pathetic image. However, not the Jews.

But From a Jewish Perspective

After Alexander III's passing, Jews hoped this new tsar would be different. At his glistening coronation, Nicholas invited three rabbis to participate at public expense. However, his invitation signified nothing.

Even before his ascension, the young Tsarevitch's view on Jews was fixed. His father had seen to that. During a visit to the court of St. James (his future wife was Queen Victoria's granddaughter), Nicholas spent two days at Sandringham as a guest of the prince of Wales, whose eclectic circle of cronies included Jews. Nicholas described one party's attendees to his mother as "rather strange. Most of them were horse dealers, amongst others a Baron Hirsch! The cousins rather enjoyed the situation and kept teasing me about it, but I tried to keep away as much as possible and not to talk."

Once crowned tsar, Nicholas needed no new legal devices to ensnare his Semitic quarry. Alexander III's Temporary Laws remained in place, inexorably strangling the Jewish community politically, economically, and socially. In 1895, when the governor of Vilna suggested that Jews be allowed to relocate from his overcrowded province to less populated sites beyond the Pale, Nicholas noted, "I don't share at all the opinion of the governor."

The destruction of Jews and Judaism continued. Pogroms were more frequent, and in 1903, more systemized.

Early on, one major pogrom stirred the outside world. It occurred at Kishinev, Bessarabia, a city with fifty thousand Jews, and when it was over there were nearly 50 dead, 500 injured, and 1,500 homes and shops plundered. International censure poured down on St. Petersburg. Germany's Kaiser Wilhelm II and Austria's Emperor Franz Josef both made personal protests to their fellow monarch, but the tsar viewed increasing bloodshed with equanimity. Police, who could have halted the violence, stayed on the sidelines until it was spent, then sometimes arrested Jews for using arms to defend themselves. To his mother, the tsar explained, "The people are aroused by the impudence of the revolutionaries and socialists; and since nine-tenths of them are Jews, so the entire fury was directed at them—that accounts for the pogroms on Jews."

Nicholas encouraged the looters and the killers. In 1904, he accepted badges of honorary membership for himself and his son in the League of the Russian People, a paramilitary outfit devoted to Jew-baiting. He reportedly assured one pogrom leader, "I know the Russian courts are too severe toward the participants in the pogroms. I give you my imperial word that I should always lighten their sentences on the application of the League of the Russian People, so dear to me."

In June 1906, even as the democratically elected First Duma discussed anti-Semitic violence, a pogrom broke out at Bialystok, with ample evidence of government instigation. The Duma called for "immediate judicial investigation and the punishment of all officials, high and subordinate, without regard to their position, who were responsible for the pogroms, and the dismissal of the ministry." Nicholas did nothing to investigate the rioting, but he did dismiss the Duma the next day.

In 1907, even his conservative, often cruel prime minister, Peter Stolypin, and his cunning, unprincipled finance minister, Sergei Witte, urged him to break with the past and alleviate Jewish suffering. Witte, a practical man, saw foreign loans—much of it of Jewish origin—drying up. After a two-month wait, they had the tsar's answer:

> Despite most convincing arguments in favor of adopting a positive decision in this matter, an inner voice keeps on insisting more and more that I do not accept responsibility for it. . . . I know that you, too, believe that "a tsar's heart is in God's hand." Let it be so. For all laws established by me I bear a great responsibility before God, and I am ready to answer for this decision at any time.

Straight through to the regime's collapse, Nicholas welcomed an outpouring of anti-Semitic books and pamphlets, and he spent 12,239,000 rubles on their printing and distribution. This enabled, among other works of literature, the pamphlet "The Protocols of the Elders of Zion" to find a wide audience.

Nicholas himself was convinced that a gigantic international Jewish conspiracy intent on world rule, existed in Paris at the Alliance Israelite Universelle. Count Vladimir Lamsdorf, his like-minded foreign minister, warned it could only be overcome if he, the German Kaiser and the pope, formed an alliance against this "common foe of Christian and monarchial order." The tsar quickly responded to this memorandum: "Negotiations must be entered into immediately. I share entirely the opinions herein expressed." For once, wiser heads prevailed and this madness did not proceed. Had Nicholas followed through, the fragile Russian-French alliance would have exploded, to Berlin's delight.

Surfacing in 1911, the Beilis Case became an international cause célèbre, pitting Nicholas against the civilized world. It began when a Christian child's body was found near a Jewish-owned Kiev factory. Mendel Beilis, a manager, faced ritual murder charges, but prosecution evidence was so flawed, its witnesses so lacking in credibility, that even a jury of uneducated, superstitious peasants—clearly no philo-Semites— acquitted him quickly. They were more sensible than their sovereign, who rewarded the prosecution team with honors, promotions, and gifts.

Nicholas II once remarked, "During my reign Jews in Russia will not enjoy equal rights." To the bitter end—theirs and his—the tsar kept his word.

FRANZ JOSEF I, 1830–1916
Emperor of Austria, 1848–1916
King of Hungary, 1867–1916

History's Conventional View

The world recalls Franz Josef much as he described himself in a letter to President Theodore Roosevelt—as the last European monarch of the old school. The Hapsburg realm could not survive him. This, too, he foresaw: "God grants me this long life in order that the end of this ancient empire may be delayed a little while. After my death it is sure to come."

Franz Josef mounted his throne in Europe's turbulent year, 1848, seven years before Alexander II in Russia. Alexander III was three years old; Nicholas II would not be born for another twenty years. The last of the Hapsburgs spanned European history from the Age of Metternich to the "Age of the Automobile," a diabolical device of progress he totally rejected. (His sole reported ride in a horseless carriage came in August 1906, and then only to accommodate his guest, Edward VII of England.)

He not only ignored the telephone, he would not allow one installed within a radius of several rooms from his own at Schoenbrunn Palace.

Instead, he sent streams of telegrams daily. Every imperial residence and hunting lodge held telegraph facilities in readiness for his personal use.

The Austrian court adhered more rigidly to formality and royal etiquette than any other. The emperor insisted archduchesses dress in styles thirty years behind the times and, snickers notwithstanding, they did so. At age eighty-six, Franz Josef climbed six tall flights of Viennese stairs for a painting session at an artist's loft. He shunned the building's elevator.

Conservatism came naturally, not just with advancing age. Nearly seventy years before, in the wake of the disorder that chased Metternich into exile, he was faced with one of those new-fangled constitutions springing up around Europe. He eventually became reconciled to living with it, but he never liked it.

Defeat by Prussia in the Seven Weeks War of 1866 ended Austria's primacy in central Europe. Pieced together over centuries, this jigsaw of nationalities—Germans, Slavs, Magyars, Italians, and Jews—made an unharmonious mix. Independent Magyars won their own kingdom within the empire, and the resulting dual monarchy—Austria-Hungary—owed its stability in no small part to the presence and integrity of Franz Josef, its sovereign and symbol.

The emperor and his capital city merge in a misty, serene image, one of melodic Strauss waltzes, operetta-garbed officers, and young lovers strolling in the Vienna woods or along the banks of the blue Danube. But violence stalked Franz Josef's personal life. His brother Maximilian fell before a Mexican firing squad (in 1867). Son Rudolph shot himself at Mayerling (in 1889). The Empress Elizabeth was assassinated by an anarchist in Geneva (in 1898). And nephew Archduke Franz Ferdinand—with whom, admittedly, he shared little affection—made history's most ill-fated royal visit, to Sarajevo, in July 1914.

Franz Josef, his dynasty, his world, all disappeared in the great conflict that followed.

But From a Jewish Perspective

"I, Franz Josef I, declare that everyone is entitled to his own beliefs and religious customs. Civil and political rights are not dependent on religion. Civic duties, however, must not be obstructed by religious customs."

Not by choice did Franz Josef proclaim a liberal constitution in March

1849. Autocratic monarchism was his preferred mode of rule, so only rumblings below heralded this concession. When calmer times came, backsliding followed, but he never retreated from his commitment to religious freedom. In the eyes of Jews, he was a noble soul, and in later years, especially, a rampart against their enemies.

In practice, emancipation could not be expected overnight in a land once ruled by Maria Theresa and Francis II. Freedom to hold open religious services, the right to own property, and the opportunity to seek public office were immediate great leaps forward. The 1850s saw an end to the absurdity of denying Jews the right to hire Christian servants or, in turn, be hired by Christians as midwives. The Fundamental Law of 1867 dropped all disabilities or discriminatory practices still persisting. Looking back as they mourned a half century later, the executive body of Austrian Zionists eulogized their emperor as the "donor of civil rights and equality before the law, and their ever benevolent protector."

The year 1869 had found Franz Josef in Jerusalem where, after meeting Jewish representatives, he contributed to the construction of a new synagogue. Back home he visited Jewish institutions, freely praising Jewish virtues and devotion to family. On one occasion, as Dubnow puts it, he "dramatically" walked out of a theater when performers turned to satiric anti-Semitic songs.

While Bismarck dawdled as anti-Semites flourished across the Austrian-German frontier in the 1800s, Franz Josef accepted confrontation. "I will tolerate no *Judenhetze* [Jew-baiting] in my empire!" he emphatically told his ministers. As latent Magyar hatred poured out following the creation of a separate kingdom of Hungary, he assured worried Jews of his royal protection. Similarly, when the prospective triumph of anti-Semitic candidates in Austrian elections sent a scare through the Jewish community, he received two Jewish delegations, assuring them that support for "unconditional equality is in every respect a command of justice."

Scholar Robert S. Wistrick, author of meticulously researched works on Austrian Jewry, concludes that the emperor "increasingly appeared to Austrian Jews as their guardian angel, custodian, and patron saint against the swelling tide of anti-Semitism from below."

At an 1885 Vienna gathering, Chief Rabbi Adolf Jellinek's toast was unequivocal: "No prince of the glorious House of Hapsburg has so graciously stood by our brothers in Austria as our beloved Monarch.

What progress has been made in the liberty of our coreligionists under the exalted scepter of our sublime Monarch!...the chains which oppressed the Jews in Austria fell at the word of deliverance pronounced by our lofty regent." And when Franz Josef's fifty-ninth birthday in 1889 sparked celebrations, Jews throughout the empire once more acknowledged their debt "for the liberty which they had enjoyed during the last forty years."

The next decade would bring troubles the emperor could not end. The biggest challenge came in cosmopolitan Vienna itself, the city of Mahler and Freud, but also of an articulate rabble-rouser, Karl Lueger. While this lawyer and shrewd politician was not himself a crude racist, he knew how to appeal to a lower-middle-class constituency ever jealous of Jewish achievements. In 1895, his Christian Socialist allies won control of the city's municipal council, but Emperor Franz Josef denied Lueger confirmation as Vienna's burgomeister. The government said his past conduct cast doubt on his ability to impartially administer the capital, suppress agitators, and assure equal treatment for all citizens.

Denial of office was clearly justified, but in constitutionally run Austria, Franz Josef's power was no longer strong enough to make the decision hold. Eventually, following further electoral triumphs of his anti-Semitic slate, Lueger gained the mayoral office. (Still later, the impressionable young Adolf Hitler would find much to admire in Lueger's oratory and policies.)

Meanwhile, the path of anti-Semitism widened. In Austria's Lower Diet, several representatives accused Jewish doctors of intent to kill Christian patients by placing them in cholera hospitals. Franz Josef called this bizarre charge a "scandal and disgrace in the eyes of the world." In 1895, to the Empress Elizabeth he wrote, "Anti-Semitism is an illness spread by now in the highest circles, and the propaganda of it is incredible.... Its excesses are awful." Three years after that, as the whole empire celebrated his jubilee—fifty eventful years on the throne—and *Jewish Chronicle's* Vienna correspondent wrote: "The Jews owe a great deal to their Emperor Franz Josef, and if a day's anguish should fall into their cup of happiness in thinking of the various political retrogressive measures which they have to endure, they do not in the least blame the emperor for it."

The label of a friend of the Jews freely given to the old Hapsburg by his contemporaries (among them my grandfather, who grew to adulthood in western Galicia) perhaps needs validation for modern cynics aware of a Jewish propensity to praise Christian sovereigns for small deeds magnified and paper promises unkept. So let doubters consider how anti-Semites referred to Franz Josef—behind his back, of course. They derisively called him the "Judenkaiser."

WILHELM II, 1859–1941
Kaiser of Germany, 1888–1918

History's Conventional View

"Hang the Kaiser!" became a popular slogan for the victorious Allies as World War I wound down—and for shortcomings evident by any kingly yardstick, Wilhelm merits his ill repute.

Several generations since 1918 have perceived Wilhelm as a discreditable mix of pomposity, arrogance, willfulness, bombast, and bellicosity, crippled further by horrendous lapses in judgment. He inherited a thriving Second Reich built by Bismarck around its Prussian core and left it a shambles.

Two years after succeeding his father, who was fatally ill and reigned only three months, Wilhelm dismissed his venerable chancellor, determined to run the empire his own way. The trappings of military might became his passion, and he enthusiastically supported plans to construct a navy capable of challenging British rule of the seas. He let Bismarck's diplomatic web isolating France unravel, and virtually threw France and Russia into each other's arms by refusing to renew a pact with St. Petersburg. When war eventually came, it would be a calamitous two-front war.

Wilhelm thought big, and he picked inopportune times to say the wrong thing. By congratulating South Africa's president, Paul Kruger, on Boer success against an armed band of British raiders, he left a bad feeling in London. By encouraging German troops, embarking for China to help put down the Boxer Rebellion, with language casting them in the role of Huns, he struck a decidedly uncivilized note. By meddling in France's North African sphere—Morocco—he committed gunboat diplomacy. The "blank check" he handed Austria-Hungary—i.e., German support if its attempt to punish Serbia for Franz Ferdinand's murder led to Russian intervention—ignited World War I, "the Great War," and by authorizing "unrestricted submarine warfare" he guaranteed U.S. involvement.

When the lamps that had gone out all over Europe in 1914 were lit again, Wilhelm, last of the Hohenzollerns, was in Holland, an exile. He lived comfortably at Doorn until his death in 1941, and the one good thing that can certainly be said of him is that he privately loathed the Nazis, though probably for the wrong reasons. He kept publicly silent in return for continued compensatory payments for lost property holdings in the now Third Reich. When an honor guard ringed his chateau following the Wehrmacht's speedy conquest of Holland in May 1940, Adolf Hitler, learning of this respectful gesture, immediately ordered the troops withdrawn.

But From a Jewish Perspective

Wilhelm II was assuredly no ogre of tsarist magnitude, but neither could Jews look to him for support as they did Franz Josef. Court Preacher Stoecker, anti-Semitic and detested by Bismarck, found favor in the young kaiser's eyes, and by some accounts had a hand in events leading to the Iron Chancellor's downfall.

As Wilhelm surrounded himself with reactionaries, their racism pervaded his circle. During the final confrontation between kaiser and chancellor, Wilhelm lashed out at Bismarck for dealing with "Jews and Jesuits who are always under one cover."

True, the tsarist-inspired Bialystok pogrom led Wilhelm to join the civilized world in a chorus of protest, and at home, while complaining about the sizable number of Jews living in Germany, he might say, self-approvingly, "If I did not restrain my people, they would be Jew-baiting." But the Prussian-bred kaiser's ingrained anti-Semitism, never blatant, barred comfortable relations with Jews, except for the very rich.

Albert Ballin, long-serving head of the mighty Hamburg-Amerika Steamship line, was one such wealthy Jew, and the success of that enterprise lifted its director to high esteem. The court's drawbridge was also down for a Rothschild or two had they chosen to cross it. On more than one occasion Wilhelm sought to induce Europe's premier banking family to resume operations in its former homeland. To a young Rothschild Baron, he promised that a revived Berlin branch would enjoy status greater than those in Vienna, Paris, or London. He said he had neither racial nor religious prejudices, nor would he allow anti-Semitic conduct in court circles. But the "House of Rothschild" shunned the "House of Hohenzollern." The kaiser's magnet reached for Jewish marks, francs, and pounds, not flesh and blood. Impoverished Polish Jews who scrambled across the frontier, fleeing Nicholas II's evil empire, received shabby treatment in Wilhelmine Germany.

For all his negatives, despite even his own ignoble intentions, Wilhelm II could have become the greatest benefactor of world Jewry in Christendom. This opportunity was placed personally before the kaiser first in Constantinople, then along a dusty Palestinian road, and finally in Jerusalem itself, in October and November 1898 by Theodore Herzl.

Herzl's detailed diaries offer bountiful evidence of the highest priority he gave winning Wilhelm's support for a Jewish homeland. The land was not imperial Germany's to give; it belonged to Turkey, but Sultan Abdul-Hamid II, lording over a decaying empire as predatory neighbors gathered, had only one powerful friend left in Europe. A popular saying went, "Deutschland uber Allah." A fraternal request, or even a subtle suggestion, could sway the Moslem ruler to grant Herzl's great dream.

On learning of the kaiser's route to the Holy Land by way of Constantinople, Herzl—through a series of intermediaries—managed to arrange a private interview in Turkish capital. The Zionist founder's diary describes that first meeting with a gush of optimism, unrealistic through hindsight, but not to their zeal-driven author. Dressed in a dark hussar uniform, he writes, the kaiser "looked at me with his great sea-blue eyes. He has truly imperial eyes. I have never seen such eyes. A remarkable, bold, inquisitive soul shows in them."

Herzl pressed his scheme for a land company in Syria and Palestine, financed by Jews themselves, but under Wilhelm's protection: "He looks at you squarely and strongly—the Kaiser!—and when a remark or turn-of-phrase appeals to him, his magnificent eyes, with his lips tightly closed, say: I got you—you're my man—that's fine."

To his listener, the kaiser seemed warmly receptive—for reasons better associated with an anti-Semitic frame of mind than anything on a higher plane. This was roughly the sense of his remarks:

"There are elements among your people whom it would be quite a good thing to settle in Palestine. I am thinking of Hesse, for example, where there are usurers at work among the rural population. If these people took their possessions and went to settle in the colonies, they would be more useful."

This exchange then concluded the interview, leaving Herzl convinced of success:

"Just tell me in a word what I am to ask of the Sultan."

"A chartered company—under German protection."

"Good! A chartered company!" And he grandly gave me his hand, which is strong enough for two, squeezed it good and hard, and went outside first through the center door.

The scene next shifts to Palestine, outside Jerusalem. Herzl, informed of Wilhelm's itinerary, stands patiently at the roadside until the kaiser's entourage comes galloping into view:

"The kaiser recognized me even at a distance. It gave him a start; he guided his horse in my direction—and pulled up in front of me."

Herzl's diary records their brief second meeting:

"And how has the journey agreed with Your Majesty so far?"

He blinked grandly with his eyes.

"Very hot! But the country has a future."

"At the moment it is still sick," I said.

"Water is what it needs, a lot of water," he said from above me.

"Yes, Your Majesty, irrigation on a large scale."

He replied, "It is a land of the future."

Herzl concludes his entry by noting, "Then he held down his hand to me again and trotted off."

Their third face-to-face meeting came on November 2, 1898, a more formal affair at the imperial encampment inside the kaiser's tent. Here Herzl read his proposal:

The deputation of the sons of Israel approaches the German emperor, with profound awe, in the land which once belonged to our ancestors. ...You, Your Majesty, saw this land—it motions to the people to cultivate it. And among our brethren, there is an agonized proletariat, which is anxious to till the soil...we dare implore Your Imperial Majesty for your cooperation in this instance....The friendship of Your Imperial Majesty with His Majesty, the sultan, is so well known that there can be no doubt in the intentions of those who implore you concerning your gracious mediation.

Herzl recounted the kaiser's response in his diary: "He said roughly the following: I thank you for this communication which has interested me greatly. The matter, in any case, still requires thorough study and further discussion." The Zionist champion's confidence noticeably sagged: "He said neither yes nor no. Evidently a lot has been happening behind the scenes." Among those goings-on was the pernicious influence of Wilhelm's anti-Semitic foreign minister, and later chancellor, Bernhard von Bulow, and the passing of information to the kaiser that the response to Herzl's Zionist project, among the Jewish bankers and financiers who presumably would fund it, was tepid.

Herzl heard nothing further from the kaiser, and repeated efforts for another audience with him over many months failed. See von Bulow, he was told, and knowing that the foreign minister opposed him, Herzl realized the game was up.

Thus Wilhelm II cast aside the chance to alter the course of Jewish history, and whatever his other shortcomings, earn a place of honor in its archives. Years later, for reasons still obscure, the kaiser would deny even meeting Herzl at all.

Other Voices, Other Deeds

VICTORIA (Queen of the United Kingdom of Great Britain and Ireland, 1837–1901) receives pride of place here, having been moved aside several pages back in favor of the Duke of Wellington. While giving her name to an age, she reigned rather than ruled, so any role she played in Jewish emancipation, helping or hurting, was muted. The British constitution is unwritten, but a strong restraint.

Victoria's contact with top-strata Jews was limited, with ordinary Jews nonexistent. Early in her reign, when the Damascus Blood Libel case deepened, she conversed with Moses Montefiore, then put her ship at his disposal for the cross-channel phase of his Middle East journey. This was a personal gesture of the twenty-three-year-old queen toward a fond neighbor who had known her as a child, but it reflects, as well, her civilized consternation at Levantine barbarism, countenanced only by France's Louis Philippe.

Lionel Rothschild, a far wealthier Jew, found his route to the House of Lords blocked in 1869 by the Queen's adamancy. "To make a Jew a peer," she announced, "is a step she could not consent to. It would be ill taken and would do the government great harm." Even a personal appeal by Prime Minister William Gladstone did not move her, one of the few areas where royal prerogative could prevail over parliamentary will. Biographer Frederic Morton notes: "It was not until Suez had become British through Jewish money; not until Disraeli, baptised in faith but very unbaptised in sympathies and passions, had won her heart," that she finally consented to a peerage for Lionel's son. Yet a point in time would come when the aging queen, on visits to the continent, would, as Morton puts it, "drop in familiarly," at the French estate of a Rothschild baroness.

Beyond "the Defender of the Faith's" disinclination to accept Jews on a social level, Victoria was no Jew-hater, and were it not for her figurehead status she might have helped the most wretchedly treated Jews of all. After Tsar Alexander III made life unbearable for them, Her Britannic Majesty gave Christian Zionist William Henry Hechler, then chaplain of Britain's Vienna embassy, a letter asking Turkey's sultan to grant Russia's persecuted minority asylum in the Holy Land. It never reached the Moslem leader. British diplomatic officials refused to deliver the plea, frowning on such amateurish interference, unconstitutional to boot, by their sovereign. (A decade later, Hechler arranged Herzl's contact with Wilhelm II's uncle, the grand duke of Baden, who in turn made his initial approach to the Kaiser possible.)

Victoria's son EDWARD VII (king from 1901 to 1910), cast a broad net in filling his social circle, to the dismay of his mother and those bluebloods already in it by virtue of birth. Prosperous Jews, among them assorted Rothschilds, Sassoons, and the manipulative Baron Maurice de Hirsch, were attracted to Edward, then prince of Wales, and he to them. "If you ever become king," Victoria warned, "you will find all these friends *most* inconvenient and you will have to break with them *all*."

Several unsavory types certainly appeared, but to Lady Frances Evelyn Greville, countess of Warwick, "We resented the introduction of the Jews into the social set of the prince of Wales not because we disliked them individually... but because they had brains and understood finance. As a class, we did not like brains. As for money, our only understanding of it lay in the spending, not the making of it."

Such notions did not trouble Edward, whose carriage once rumbled through a blizzard taking him to a Rothschild wedding. He consumed kosher fare with relish and exhibited a taste for Jewish humor. Russia's

Nicholas II, while still heir apparent, was shocked by the people with which he was expected to mingle at the prince's estate.

An inclination to rub shoulders with fabulously rich Jews (atypical of course), serves as no measure to judge Edward's merit. His position on impoverished Russian Jews is a better guide. From afar he pestered Sir Arthur Nicolson, British ambassador at St. Petersburg, to address the pogrom issue in dealings with Russia's prime minister. When the occasion presented itself, he took matters into his own hands.

This happened in 1908 when Edward traveled east and met Nicholas II at Tallinin, where no Jews attended their social gatherings. Earlier, the tsar referred to him as "the greatest mischief-maker" around, a view now somewhat shared by the British Foreign Office. Edward had made known his intention to raise "the Jewish question" after getting a memo from a Rothschild colleague stressing its seriousness. Baron Charles Hardinge, a crown official, said his sovereign's intervention was not "constitutionally right or proper," and sought silence instead. Edward went ahead anyway. As expected, Nicholas did not change his ways. But credit the king of England for trying.

Edward's eldest sister, Princess Victoria, married the Prussian crown prince, FREDERICK WILLIAM (1831–88), son of William (Wilhelm) I. Already dying when he succeeded to the imperial German throne in 1888, he reigned only three months as Frederick III. Nonetheless, he deserves a few words because, from a Jewish perspective, his loss was a tragedy. Neither he nor his wife condoned the anti-Semitic movement sweeping Germany.

"In the royal family," Victoria wrote to her mother back in England, "we stand quite alone with our opinions, and in what is called society." Frederick's opposition to Junker values made him foes in reactionary ruling circles. They likened his conduct to that of an English liberal, and a Second Reich under Frederick and his thoroughly British wife would have evolved far more favorably for Jews of the realm. Their son, Wilhelm II, shared little in common with his mother and father, and much with their detractors.

Crown Prince RUDOLPH of Austria (1858–89) also had sharp differences (although not about Jews) with his father, Emperor Franz Josef. To the rest of the world, he is remembered because of the legend surrounding his mysterious death, by gunshot, at the Mayerling royal hunting lodge, possibly in a suicide pact with his seventeen-year-old love, Baroness Marie Vetsera. It is the stuff of films and novels.

For Austria's Jews, however, Rudolph could have made a difference. Worn down by age and burdens, Franz Josef, near his end, fought a losing battle against Jew-haters. Rudolph, had he lived, would surely have pursued the struggle with more youthful vigor.

The crown prince loathed nationalism, traditionalism, and clericalism, but, more importantly for Jews, he denounced anti-Semitism as the "disgrace of the century." When he openly dined with a Jewish financier in a Vienna restaurant, anti-Semites accused him of being in the pay of "the Golden International." His close ties with Moritz Szeps, editor of *Tagblatt*, won him even greater enmity, for Szeps was an even worse sort of Jew—a liberal journalist. Rudolph contributed articles to *Tagblatt*, leading Austria's premier anti-Semite, Georg von Schoenerer, to declare before a mass meeting that the "closed season on the Jewish newspaper scribblers and their associates is now past for all times." Rudolph interpreted this remark as a veiled reference to himself, and told Szeps that "to be attacked by Schoenerer is an honor."

Following Rudolph's tragic end at Mayerling, the *London Times* noted, "several of the anti-Semitic journals have behaved with great indecorum in abstaining from all words of praise for the crown prince's memory." Rabbi Adolf Jellinek, whose theatrical praise for Franz Josef we noted earlier, felt just as deeply about his son. He called him a pillar of equality in this age of hatred—he "shone forth as a model of confessional tolerance and noble humanity."

LUDWIG II (King of Bavaria from 1864 to 1886), also known as Mad Ludwig, built castles in the sky *and* lived in them. The most picturesque, Neuschwanstein, appears regularly in German tourist brochures, an enchanting never-never land.

Ludwig reigned over the second most important kingdom in Germany—after Prussia—and, as Richard Wagner's patron, financed the composer's Bayreuth showcase. Their correspondence touched a broad spectrum of subjects, Jews among them. The Master's penchant for pontificating on racial matters was well known, so when he wrote, feigning tolerance, that he didn't care whether his planned opera *Parsifal* was conducted by a Christian or a Jew, Ludwig congratulated him for making no distinction between them. "There is nothing so nauseous, so unedifying," wrote the king, "as disputes of this sort; at bottom all men are brothers, whatever their confessional differences."

Such sincere liberality apparently animated Wagner. He again wrote the young monarch, this time pointing out that Ludwig could show tolerance for Jews only because he had no personal experience of them. Bavaria's ruler found Wagner's prose less enticing than his music, so we should not taint him with guilt by association.

GRIGORI YEFIMOVICH NOVYKH, a.k.a. RASPUTIN (1872?–1916), might seem an unlikely candidate for any links to Jews given his position as a holy man and the Romanov circle's aversion to Jews. Tsarina Alexandra believed Rasputin had been sent by God to represent the mystical union between peasants and autocracy. Ironically, the debauched monk depended on a Jewish business manager. Bribes and extortions poured into the purse of this crude, illiterate charlatan, and Aron Simanovich, a Kiev diamond dealer, handled his financial affairs. An unofficial price list for his influence peddling would read: 250 rubles to free a petty forger; 2,000 to keep a man from the front lines facing German forces; 5,000 to free a political prisoner.

In one case after the outbreak of World War I, Rasputin intervened (receiving an expensive fur coat and hat in return) to protect a wealthy Jew expelled from St. Petersburg who resided there under false pretenses. Like many coreligionists, he had purchased a dental degree to guarantee domicile rights, dentists, and other professionals being exceptions to the rule barring Jewish residency. But he got caught by the police.

After the Revolution, Simanovich gravitated to Paris, later publishing his memoirs in which he claimed Rasputin was quite willing, for a satisfactory bribe, to serve rich Jews seeking to approach Nicholas II. The crafty Simanovich, not the most creditable of witnesses, displayed an autographed photo which read: "To the best of the Jews."

During the protracted campaign in England for political equality, WILLIAM EWART GLADSTONE (1809–1898), although a rising member of Parliament, was not central to victory or defeat. Eventually he became a household name and Disraeli's chief rival.

The young Gladstone was a moral man. He saw the hand of the Antichrist in the Great Reform Act of 1832, and that law did not even enfranchise Jews. So early on, his attitude toward Jewish emancipation can easily be inferred. He crisply stated his position when a bill came up in 1841 to admit Jews to municipal offices. In a parliamentary debate on the issue, Gladstone argued that the removal of municipal disabilities would inevitably lead to a Jewish presence in Parliament. He could accept Roman Catholics with some reluctance in the House, but not Jews. That would be incompatible with the Christian character of the House. Besides, Gladstone contended, the matter was unworthy of lengthy debate because the number of Jews in the realm was insignificant.

There was little reason for British Jews to expect that a stubborn man like Gladstone would change his view that "those who as conscientious men rejected Christianity" would not be capable of judging "great questions which came before them" that "were intimately associated with the distinctive principles of Christianity." But change he did. In 1847, when a bill was again moved to seat Jews in the House of Commons without taking an oath "on the true faith of a Christian," Gladstone astounded his colleagues by supporting it:

I state, with deep regret, so far as my relation to that learned body [Oxford, his constituency], that not without pain indeed, it is my intention, because I feel it is my duty, to support the measure which we are now assembled to discuss.

By his new logic, its defeat could be justified only on the unlikely prospect it be "shown that the admission of an extremely small fraction of Jews into Parliament would paralyze and nullify the Christianity of all those who sit there."

In the end it didn't matter. The backward-looking House of Lords blocked the measure.

Gladstone's personal diary's entry on December 16, 1847, reads, "It is a painful decision to come to." The next day, he wrote his father, whose aristocratic brand of anti-Semitism had not changed:

After much consideration, prolonged indeed I may say for the last two years and a half, I made up my mind to support Lord John Russell's bill for the admission of the Jews. I spoke to this effect last night. It is with reluctance that I gave the vote, but after the civil privileges we have given them already, and after the admission we have already conceded to Unitarians who refuse the whole of the most vital doctrines of the Gospel, we cannot compatibly with entire justice and fairness refuse to admit them.

Although this hardly ranks as a ringing endorsement of equality, it did take political courage. When Gladstone appeared on an Oxford platform the following year, hisses filled the gallery. He wryly noted, "My vote upon the Jew bill is on the whole unpalatable there."

Gladstone's about-face remained incomplete. In 1850 he stood aside when efforts were advanced to end Oxford's long run as an exclusively Anglican preserve. In later years, when Episcopalian convert Benjamin Disraeli became his most dangerous parliamentary rival, with the prime ministry seesawing between them, Gladstone's inherent suspicion of Jews occasionally surfaced. A case in point: When British and Russian interests clashed over the Turkish Empire's future, Gladstone wrote to a colleague in 1877:

> I have watched very closely [Disraeli's] strange and at first inexplicable proceedings on this Eastern question; and I believe their fountainhead to be race antipathy, that aversion which the Jews, with a few honourable exceptions, are showing so vindictively towards the East-ern Christians. Though he has been baptised, his Jew feelings are the most radical and the most real and so far respectable portion of his profoundly falsified nature.

Liberal Gladstone would have distrusted Conservative Disraeli in any event, but Disraeli's Jewish origin gave political quarrels an additional dimension. William Gladstone, for all his independence of mind, could not escape being his father's son.

Turning from public figures to writers and thinkers, we begin with three Russian literary giants whose views on Jews or Judaism, apart from fictional dialogue, are on the record.

FYODOR DOSTOYEVSKY (1821–1881), one-time tsarist army officer and author of *Crime and Punishment* and *The Brothers Karamazov*, evolved from a nebulous anti-Semite into a sharply-defined one, sustained by a measure of hypocrisy.

Jews never fit, nor could fit, into his vision for Russia. Evidently too low on his action agenda to warrant much attention early in his career, he began tentatively attacking Jews in 1873. By 1876 he was on the attack against "Yid" financiers for conniving to restore serfdom and bring about a "judaized world." Outside Mother Russia, he saw them already hard at work toward that end. "They would have you believe that they do not rule over Europe," he wrote, "that they do not manage, at least over there, the stock exchanges, and consequently the politics, the internal affairs, the moral life of the states."

Soon thereafter he denied any personal trace of anti-Semitism. Responding to Jewish journalist Arkady Kovner, he wrote:

> But I tell you now that I am not an enemy of the Jews at all and never have been. During the fifty years of my life I have found that Jews, whether good or bad, won't ever sit down at the same table with a Russian, while a Russian feels no hesitation about sitting down with a Jew. So who hates whom? And what sort of an idea is it that the Jews are a nation of the insulted and injured? On the contrary it is the Russians who have been humiliated by the Jews in every respect, because the Jews, besides enjoying almost complete equality of rights (they can even be officers, which, in Russia, is everything), have their own rights besides, their own law, their own statute, their own status quo that is protected by the Russian laws themselves.

This, from a keen student of crime and punishment and persecution who, in his army years, 1841 to 1844, obviously came into contact with the wretched products of Nicholas I's "cantonment" policy.

Consider a more intimate letter sent to his wife in August 1879, while he was "taking the cure" at Ems, Germany. Upset over the price of a pair of opera glasses, he wrote, "But then, in Russia, there never were such swindling shopkeepers as there are now in Germany. It is the Yids again, the Yids have taken over everything, and they cheat like mad, and I mean cheat."

From Ems he also wrote Konstantin Pobedonostsev, whose solution to Russia's "Jewish problem" was the disappearance of all Russian Jews. Dostoyevsky complained, "...and mind you, literally half of the visitors here are Yids...in my view, Germany, at any rate, Berlin, was being taken over by the Yids."

During his later years, Dostoyevsky's principal vehicle for expressing his social views among a wider audience was "Writer's Diary," a one-man review in which he sprinkled the pejorative "Yid" lavishly. The notion of letting Jews break free of the Pale of Settlement particularly rattled him, and he declared they would seize the opportunity to "invade the countryside and make life worse than under the Tartar yoke."

Jews were behind just about every attempt to disrupt Europe's order, he concluded. "The Jews have everything to gain from every cataclysm and coup d'état...and only profit from anything that serves to undermine gentile society."

COUNT LEO TOLSTOY (1828–1910) did not like Jews. But he was no Dostoyevsky. The author of *War and Peace* did not hate Jews, and such moderation on the part of a nineteenth-century Russian man of letters is itself notable. In 1881, Tolstoy even lent his prestige to a petition sent Alexander III protesting the regime's first pogroms. He signed willingly, though not enthusiastically, as he himself pointed out, as a show of confidence in activist Vladimir Soloviev, who solicited his signature. A quarter of a century later, the Kishinev pogrom *did* stir the great author, provoking him to write, "The outrages at Kishinev are but the direct result of the propaganda of falsehood and violence which our government conducts with such energy."

A private letter conveyed thoughts that, standing alone, would further endear him to Jewish minds: "The Jew is that sacred being who has brought down from heaven the everlasting fire and has illuminated with it the entire world...the Jew is the pioneer of civilization...the Jew is the emblem of civil and religious toleration."

Other extracts from his correspondence, unfortunately, show Tolstoy at less than his best. After the trial of Alfred Dreyfus, the French captain, divided Europe into Dreyfusard and anti-Dreyfusard camps, he was asked to join liberals in a manifesto asking that the French captain be freed. Tolstoy was indifferent. "It would be a strange thing that we Russians should take up the defense of Dreyfus," he wrote, "an utterly undistinguished man, when so many exceptional ones have been hanged, deported, or imprisoned here at home."

He was at his worst when he contemplated Russia's defeat in the 1905 war against Japan. "This debacle," he contended, "is not only that of the Russian army, the Russian fleet, and the Russian state, but of the pseudo-Christian civilization, as well...the disintegration began long ago with the struggle for money and success in so-called scientific and artistic pursuits, where the Jews got the edge on the Christians in every country and thereby earned the envy and hatred of all." Later, he wrote his secretary, Vladimir Chertkov, "I should like to write something to prove how the teachings of Christ, who was not a Jew, were replaced by the very different teachings of the apostle Paul, who was a Jew." Factual fuzziness aside, the hour was late, and he never got around to it.

As Tolstoy's health failed, a Slovak physician named Dushin Makovitsky became part of the Tolstoy household, treating both family members at the Yasnaya Polyana dacha and village peasants. "Dushin is a saint," wrote Tolstoy. "But since there are no real saints, God gave him a fault too: his hatred of Jews."

By noting such maliciousness as a flaw, Tolstoy, inadvertently, gives us perhaps the best evidence of its absence in his own makeup.

Although Tolstoy's positive view of Jews outweighs his negative beliefs, we would be hard-pressed to cite a Russian literary giant who deserves Jewish approval. Alexander Pushkin and Ivan Turgenev fall far short of earning that distinction. ANTON CHEKHOV (1860–1904), whose plays include *Uncle Vanya* and *The Sea Gull*, comes much closer.

The Dreyfus case again serves as a litmus test. While in Nice, France, as events unfolded, Chekhov would "devour," as he put it, all reports on the subject. "I read the papers all day long, and in my opinion Dreyfus is innocent," he wrote. "Once the French began talking about the Jews.... it meant that they were feeling uneasy and that they needed phantoms to calm their troubled conscience."

This stance—for Dreyfus and against anti-Semitism—says much about the author. When editor Aleksei Suvorin, a classic Russian anti-Semite, described Dreyfus defender Emile Zola as a mercenary in the pay of the Jews, Chekhov broke their long-standing friendship. Of Suvorin's paper, the *New Times*, he said, "It's not a paper but a zoo, a pack of hungry jackals."

Chekhov was a rare exception among the Russian intelligentsia.

FRIEDRICH WILHELM NIETZSCHE (1844–1900) put forward notions of a "superman" that became a cornerstone of Nazi ideology, enough to warrant condemnation of the erratic German philosopher who invented him. Further circumstantial evidence points to culpability. Nietzsche was long a Wagnerian, a close friend of the composer. Add to these a "cult" created and nurtured after his death by his anti-Semitic sister Elizabeth, who was married to Bernhard Foerster, another anti-Semite.

However, in writing about a superior man, Nietzsche did not intend to impose upon the world a master race. That view came from Nazi ideologues. Nietzsche's "superman" was a man in control of himself, capable of gaining power over unruly instincts and drives. His biggest criticism of Jews and Judaism was that they gave birth to Christianity, which he detested.

As for the Wagner connection, it was real, but later broken. In a late work, *The Wagner Case*, the philosopher assessed his former friend: "Wagner was something complete; he was complete corruption; Wagner was the courage, the will, the conviction of corruption."

Nietzsche opposed militarism, nationalism, and the German belief in their superiority. In *Human, All-Too-Human*, he decried, all too prophetically, schemes to "make the Jews the scapegoats of all possible internal and external troubles and to lead them to the slaughter block." He found singling out Jews unpalatable. "Unpleasant, even dangerous qualities can be found in every nation and every individual.... It is cruel to demand that the Jew should be an exception."

When one of the founders of German anti-Semitism assumed that the creator of Zarathustra would be a logical ally and willing contributor to his *Antisemitische Korrespondenz*, Nietzsche set him straight and demanded no further issues of that publication be sent to him. The philosopher parted with his own publisher, also a rabid anti-Semite. At one point he suggested that the government "expel the anti-Semitic squatters from the country."

He condemned "these latest speculators in idealism, the anti-Semites, who today roll their eyes in a Christian-Aryan bourgeois manner and exhaust one's patience by trying to rouse up all the horned-bent elements in the people."

On learning the identity of his future brother-in-law in 1885, Nietzsche wrote his sister Elizabeth, "I will not conceal that I consider this engagement an insult—or a stupidity—which will harm you as much as me.... For my personal taste, such an agitator [Foerster] is something impossible for closer acquaintance."

After the couple moved to Paraguay, there to set up a pure Germanic colony—Neuva Germania—Nietzsche, now more comfortable knowing Foerster was an ocean apart, wrote Elizabeth proclaiming himself "an incorrigible European and anti-anti-Semitic." To his mother he wrote, "the news from Paraguay is really very cheering, but I still have not the slightest wish to settle in the vicinity of my anti-Semitic brother-in-law. His views and mine are different—and I do not regret this."

Unfortunately, Nietzsche's drift into madness, followed by a premature death, gave Elizabeth, his literary executor, an opportunity to claim that his writings were something he never meant them to be. And when she was done, Friedrich Nietzsche emerged, after death, as a model for the Third Reich's racial philosophers.

When Elizabeth died at eighty-nine, Adolf Hitler ordered a state funeral. Earlier, she had presented the Fuehrer with her brother's walking stick.

Having declared Karl Marx ineligible for these pages by reason of birth, we accord several lines to his longtime collaborator, FRIEDRICH ENGELS (1820–1895). Missing from Engels' oeuvre is the incendiary message found in the collected works of his senior colleague, a self-hating Jew.

Engels was no anti-Semite, if his writings are our guide. In 1878 he even denounced "ridiculously exaggerated Jew-hating," principally because the intended target on that occasion was his collaborator. On another occasion, after Marx's death, he urged the working class not to embrace anti-Semitism. Engels believed such behavior would serve "only reactionary purposes" by distracting laborers from the path to communism. To Engels, Jews were acceptable as long as they came from the proletariat. To followers, he pointed out "that anti-Semitism falsifies the entire situation. It does not even know the Jews whom it shouts down. . . . We here in England have had during the last twelve months [the year was 1890] three strikes of Jewish workers, and now we are to promote anti-Semitism to battle capitalism?"

Engels asked himself, should socialists sacrifice Jews to win the hearts and minds of the European working class? His conclusion: "We owe the Jews too much. . . . Marx was of pure Jewish descent. . . . Many of our best people are Jews . . . if I had to choose, I would rather be a Jew than Herr von . . . !"

Crime school headmaster Fagin, overseeing an array of waifs, is second only to "pound of flesh" Shylock as a contemptible Jewish stereotype in English literature and drama. No playgoer in officially Judenrein Elizabethan England registered complaints with William Shakespeare, but CHARLES DICKENS (1812–1870) did face criticism for many years after writing *Oliver Twist*. The author of *A Christmas Carol*, *David Copperfield*, and *A Tale of Two Cities* listened and responded.

To the Westminster Jewish Free School, for example, he defended himself before a visit: "I know of no reason the Jews can have for regarding me as 'inimical' to them. On the contrary, I believe I do my part towards the assertion of their civil and religious liberty." In 1863, a letter from Mrs. Eliza Davis, whose husband had purchased Tavistock House, Dickens' London residence, led the author to make yet another defense of the pickpocket chieftain's characterization:

> Fagin, in *Oliver Twist*, is a Jew because it unfortunately was true of the time to which the story refers that that class of criminal almost invariably *was* a Jew. But surely, no sensible man or woman of your persuasion can fail to observe—firstly—that all the rest of the wicked dramatis personae are Christians; and, secondly, that he is called the Jew, not because of his religion, but because of his race. If I were to write a story in which I pursued a Frenchman or Spaniard as a Roman Catholic, I should do a very indecent and unjustifiable thing. . . . I have no feeling toward the Jewish people but a friendly one. I always speak well of them, whether in public or private, and bear testimony (as I ought to do) to their perfect good faith in transactions as I have ever had with them. And in my *Child's History of England*, I have lost no opportunity of setting forth their cruel persecution in old times.

In *Our Mutual Friend*, the following year, he created a totally sympathetic Jewish character, Mr. Riah, notable for his gentle nature and great dignity. Moreover, Dickens cast him in the role of a victim caught in the web of a *Christian* moneylender, and gave him dialogue such as, "Men find the bad among us [Jews] easily enough. They take the worse of us as presentations of the highest, and they say, 'All Jews are alike.'"

Mrs. Davis was quick to recognize this gesture at literary amends and sent the author a letter of appreciation. Dickens answered that "I hope to be, as I have always been in my heart, the best of friends with the Jewish people . . . they are a people for whom I have a real regard and to whom I would not willingly have given an offense or done an injustice for any worldly consideration." Sometime later, Dickens received a Hebrew-English Bible from Mrs. Davis as a token for "having exercised the noblest quality men can possess—that of atoning for an injury as soon as conscious of having inflicted it."

Two contemporaries of Dickens were British historians of considerable prestige, but at opposite poles from each other on Jewish issues of the day. Dickens greatly admired THOMAS CARLYLE (1795–1881), author of a monumental history of the French Revolution, who, by one account, furnished the novelist with source material for *A Tale of Two Cities*. Carlyle fostered the cult of the hero in another major work and has been described as "the most important philosophical moralist of the early Victorian Age."

Carlyle had another side; he detested Jews. Even his friend Dickens recognized that the historian had so "intensified his aversion to Jews" that he found King John an enlightened sovereign for extracting their teeth to loosen their purses. To Carlyle, the great poet Heinrich Heine was "a slimy and greasy Jew," and he said Disraeli was the only man of whom he had "never spoken except with contempt...a cursed old Jew not worth his weight in bacon."

Carlyle used his influence to sway friends in the House of Commons to vote against Jewish emancipation. "A Jew is bad," he wrote, "but what is a Sham Jew, a Quack Jew? And how can a real Jew, by possibility, try to be a senator, or even citizen, of any country except his own wretched Palestine?" He maintained that Jews contributed nothing to the advancement of civilization, being merely dealers in money, valuables, and worn clothing. One day, standing before Lionel Rothschild's great house at the corner of Hyde Park, he mused, "I do not mean that I want King John back again, but if you ask me which mode of treating these people to have been the nearest to the will of the Almighty about them—to build them palaces like that, or to take the pincers for them, I declare for the pincers."

THOMAS BABINGTON MACAULAY (1800–1859), another respected Victorian historian, was a far better man. Author of the highly praised multivolume *History of England*, he also served in Parliament during the early struggle for Jewish emancipation. He did not stand on the sidelines, compliantly following the lead of more senior members.

Macaulay could be faulted at the social level. In June 1831, after attending a ball at the Goldsmid estate, he wrote his sister Hannah: "Jewesses by dozens, and Jews by scores.... I walked home quietly but it was some time before I could get sleep. The sound of fiddles was in mine ears and gaudy dresses and black hairs, and Jewish noses were fluctuating up and down mine eyes."

Despite such a personal aside, perhaps one among several not recorded, Macaulay the public man was sincere, even fervent, in his support of Jewish rights. It was Macaulay who debated the young, still bigoted Gladstone, aghast at the prospect of sullying Christian purity in the House of Commons. And it was Macaulay who answered parliamentary opponents of emancipation who questioned Jewish loyalty to crown and country. Rulers should not be content, he said, to

> say that a sect is not patriotic. It is their business to make it patriotic. If all the red-haired people in Europe had, during the centuries, been ostracized and oppressed, banished from this place, imprisoned in that, deprived of their money, deprived of their teeth, convicted of the most improbable crimes on the feeblest evidence, dragged at horses' tails, hanged, tortured, burned alive, if when measures became milder, they had still the subject of debasing restrictions and exposed to vulgar insults, locked up in particular streets in some countries, pelted and ducked by the rabble in others, excluded everywhere from magistracies and honors, what would be the patriotism of gentlemen with red hair?

For those honorable members of the House of Commons incapable of handling analogies, he produced a more direct argument: "How was it possible to deny a Rothschild a seat on the grounds of his race when his signature on the back of a piece of paper was worth more than the royal word of three kings!"

Macaulay, elevated to a peerage, died the year after Jews won the right to sit in Commons in 1858. Carlyle, embittered in old age, outlived him by twenty-three years but fell four short of seeing, what surely would have been to his dismay, their admission to the sanctified upper chamber, the House of Lords.

On January 13, 1898, EMILE ZOLA (1840–1902) set down on paper arguably the most famous challenge of the commission of an anti-Semitic injustice. Since Victor Hugo's death some years earlier, Zola was regarded as France's greatest living novelist. He was not easily ignored.

Zola's attention had been drawn to the Dreyfus case, in which a Jewish French army staff officer had been tried, convicted, and sent to Devil's Island for passing military secrets to Germany. Since 1894, when the story swept France, it had become increasingly evident that spurious testimony, forged documents, and a huge cover-up at the highest army and government levels were responsible for Captain Alfred Dreyfus's sentence. But it took a man of Zola's stature, perseverance, and courage to press for justice.

His explosive front-page open letter to the president of France, "J'accuse" (I accuse), filled six columns. Zola reviewed the "dark cloud of tricks and expedients," the frame-up, the "arranged acquittal" of the *real* traitor, and the general staff's "managing" of these military court proceedings. He named names, and it soon became clear his purpose was to provoke libel action by War Ministry officials, thereby reopening the case.

Zola succeeded, but at great cost. Shouts of "Death to the Jews!" and "We spit on Zola!" rang out in Paris as gangs broke into Jewish homes and shops. Throughout metropolitan France during January 1898, Jewish property was pillaged. The situation in French Algeria was even worse. The Jewish quarter in Algiers was subject to four consecutive days of rioting before the tempest ceased. Quickly convicted of insulting the army's honor, Zola fled France for England. He returned the following year, fully vindicated by facts no longer capable of being suppressed—but he did not get a hero's welcome.

Zola had made powerful enemies in the government, army, and clerical circles for baring the anti-Semitism endemic in the republic. Controversy stalked his remaining years. When he died mysteriously at his Paris flat in 1902—carbon monoxide from a blocked chimney was cited—many believed the "accident" had been arranged. An investigation proved inconclusive.

Police authorities asked Captain Dreyfus not to attend the funeral in order to avoid disturbances. He came anyway. Zola's widow asked writer Anatole France, scheduled to deliver the eulogy, to describe her late husband's literary achievements, not his fight for justice. France refused, insisting on giving full recognition to his far greater deed, "a moment in the human conscience," he called it.

L'Aurore editor Georges Clemenceau, whose paper published Zola's "J'accuse," declared, "There have always been people strong enough to resist the most powerful kings, to refuse to bow before them...there have been very few to resist the masses, to stand up to the misled multitude."

In 1896, while Captain Dreyfus languished on Devil's Island but before the author took up his cause, Zola published a less widely trumpeted article, "In Behalf of the Jews." If offered a dismal description of the present and a worse prognosis for times to come:

It is several years by now that I have been observing with increasing wonder and disgust the campaign against the Jews in France. To me it seems something monstrous, going beyond the bounds of common sense, truth and justice, something which will inevitably thrust us back several centuries or bring us to the worst, the ultimate of all horrors: religious persecution.

The year Zola's plea for tolerance appeared, Adolf Hitler, age seven, was in primary school at his hometown of Linz, and Goebbels, Himmler, Heydrich, and Eichmann were yet unborn. Winston Churchill, twenty-two, was off with his hussar regiment to India's northwest frontier, Joseph Stalin, sixteen, was struggling through courses in liturgy, Scripture, and Church Slavonic at Tiflis Theological Seminary, and Franklin D. Roosevelt, fourteen, spent his summer, accompanied by a tutor, on a bicycling tour of Kaiser Wilhelm II's Germany.

6

Sinking Into the Abyss
of a New Dark Age

Top billing among the anti-Semites who strode center stage between
1933 and 1945 must be accorded Adolf Hitler. Rather than next
direct our attention to Hitler's SS agents of terror—the Heinrich
Himmlers, Reinhard Heydrichs, and Adolf Eichmanns, or the Nazi
paladins—the Hermann Goerings, Joseph Goebbels, and Julius
Streichers, we more profitably focus on headliners in the Wehrmacht.
Such men were heirs to an historical reputation for apolitical profession-
alism. So how did field marshals Erich von Manstein, Albert Kesselring,
and Erwin Rommel respond as the honor of the army faced its stiffest
test? For reasons clarified as we progress, we also look at one of their
forgotten peers, Colonel-General Johannes Blaskowitz. Then, in turn,
we move on to Hitler's Fascist partner, Benito Mussolini, Vichy collaborators Marshal Henri Philippe Petain and Pierre Laval, Hungary's
Regent Nicholas Horthy and Bulgaria's King Boris III, rulers of lesser
European states wedded to the New Order by intimidation and expediency, Denmark's King Christian X, attached by conquest, and Finland's
Field Marshal Carl Gustav von Mannerheim, united by the common
Soviet foe. Spain's Francisco Franco stands alone—a Spanish Fascist, but
one shrewd enough to keep Iberia beyond war's reach.

Our focus then shifts to leaders of the great democracies—Winston

Churchill and Franklin D. Roosevelt. This mini-survey of Holocaust-era figures closes with Pope Pius XII, whose Order of Battle contained no divisions, but whose moral authority could have crossed front lines: One in three soldiers wearing the uniform of Hitler's Wehrmacht was at least nominally Roman Catholic.

ADOLF HITLER, 1889–1945
Chancellor of Germany, 1933–1945

As We Begin, a Necessary Departure From Format

To approach Hitler under our standard headings, "History's Conventional View" and "But From a Jewish Perspective," is implicitly awkward. "The law and the will of the Fuehrer are one," proclaimed Hermann Goering, number two man in the Third Reich. "Hitler is Germany; Germany is Hitler!" shouted deputy party leader Rudolph Hess at a Nuremburg rally. Propaganda Minister Joseph Goebbels and his wife poisoned their six children rather than let them grow up in a world bereft of Hitler's guidance. But could any other than unrepentant Nazis and younger neo-Nazis have anything positive to say about "that wicked man," as Winston Churchill called him? Hitler's eulogy for slain SS General Reinhard Heydrich (known elsewhere as "the Hangman of Europe") as "the man with the iron heart" demonstrated the Fuehrer's respect for brutality. He intended the comment as high praise.

Nonetheless, renowned British historian A. J. P. Taylor created a stir in *Origins of the Second World War* (1961) by describing Hitler as an ordinary German statesman in the tradition of his Weimar predecessors, differing neither in methods nor in ideas, but only in greater patience and stronger nerves. According to Taylor, Hitler "did not make plans for world conquest or anything else. He assumed that others would provide opportunities and that he would seize them."

More recently, a less eminent but equally controversial historian, David Irving, advanced the thesis that while Hitler was "unquestionably the authority behind the expulsion operations" against Jews, the matter of "on whole initiative the grim procedures at the terminal stations of this miserable exodus were adopted, is arguable." Irving suggests the blame belongs to "Hitler's radical followers," that is, men like Himmler.

Conventional wisdom rejects such proposals. When Hitler's legions swarmed into Poland on September 1, 1939, six million European Jews were alive who wouldn't be six years later. Eight months earlier, in his rubber-stamp Reichstag, the Fuehrer had proclaimed: "If the international Jewish financiers... shall again succeed in plunging the nation into a world war, the result will be... the annihilation of the Jewish race throughout Europe."

Three years later, as the Final Solution was under way, he referred to this speech before another Nazi gathering. "People always laughed at my prophecies," he declared on November 8, 1942. "Among those are innumerable persons who no longer laugh today, and those who are still laughing will probably soon stop." And on February 24, 1943: "This struggle will not end with the annihilation of Aryan mankind, but with the extermination of the Jewish people in Europe."

In "table talk" recorded at his sinister, ever-present secretary Martin Bormann's direction, the Fuehrer mingled medicine and murder: "The discovery of the Jewish virus is one of the greatest revolutions that have taken place in the world. The battle in which we are engaged today is of the same sort as the battle waged during the last century by Pasteur and Koch. How many diseases have their origin in the Jewish virus?... We shall regain our health only by eliminating the Jew."

The question of Hitler's responsibility is relevant only for revisionists who could envisage Reich Marshal Goering, his corpulent henchman— on his own initiative—directing Heydrich to convene the January 20, 1942, Wannsee gathering at which state and party functionaries substituted continental-scale, high-tech mass murder for local, ad hoc massacres. Heydrich invoked not only Goering's authorization, but also "previous approval through the Fuehrer." In a Jerusalem courtroom eighteen years later, Adolf Eichmann testified that Heydrich told him even earlier, in summer 1941, of their Fuehrer's resolve to annihilate European Jewry. Rudolph Hoess, the Auschwitz commandant hanged after the war, said he got word of Hitler's extermination order around the same time from Heydrich's boss, Himmler.

A more valid question is whether Hitler planned the Final Solution long in advance of World War II, or implemented it under the chaotic conditions of war, minus any such grand design. There are partisans of each viewpoint. For example, some experts see the prewar Madagascar Plan for relocating Europe's Jews on a large tropical island off East Africa as evidence he opted for a geographical solution before he planned their extermination. Others see it as a ruse for what would come later.

For us, one fact stands out. The "abyss of a new Dark Age," prophesied by Churchill in event of Hitlerite victory, one "made more sinister, and perhaps more protracted by the lights of perverted science," materialized for Jews stretching from sophisticated Paris to hovels in Russia's old Jewish Pale—even as the Third Reich crumbled.

At the fateful Wannsee gathering, Heydrich had told conferees, "in the course of this Final Solution of the European Jewish problem, approximately eleven million Jews are involved." If the war against the Jews, as historian Lucy Dawidowicz called it, was Hitler's second war, he more than half won that one. But he could never have taken the field without the professional skill of a select group of army officers who, by tradition and law, were barred from even joining the Nazi party.

Three Prominent Field Marshals

ERICH VON MANSTEIN, 1887–1973

ALBERT KESSELRING, 1885–1960

ERWIN ROMMEL, 1891–1944

and an Obscure Colonel General

JOHANNES VON BLASKOWITZ, 1883–1948

History's Conventional View

Other Wehrmacht generals were close to the Fuehrer, notably Wilhelm Keitel, chief of the high command, and Alfred Jodl, its chief planner. But these intimates, both hanged at Nuremburg, were desk-bound officers. By contrast, our chosen four commanded large bodies of men in the field, and Jews were in their path.

Manstein won initial fame as the architect of the strategy that sent German armor and infantry through the supposedly impenetrable Ardennes in the swift 1940 French campaign. Later (of more interest to us) he held command of the Eleventh Army, which swept through southern Russia, operating in the former Jewish Pale.

Kesselring, a Luftwaffe commander during the Battle of Britain, won elevation to command of all German armed forces in the Mediterranean area. From headquarters at Rome, he oversaw the defense of Tunisia, then conducted a stubborn campaign, praised by military analysts, that stalled Allied advance along the Italian boot. At war's end, he was Commander-in-Chief West.

Rommel, regarded by British foes with awe, won Winston Churchill's salute as a "master of war." Under his flamboyant leadership, the Afrika Korps almost made it to Suez, Sinai, and Palestine beyond. Later in the war he prepared the French coastline defenses of Hitler's Atlantic Wall for "the longest day," the Allied invasion of Europe. Implicated in the July 1944 plot to kill Hitler, he chose suicide over disgrace, then received a cinematic cpitaph courtesy of Twentieth Century Fox's *The Desert Fox*.

Blaskowitz, oldest of the four, outranked his colleagues before 1939, commanded the Eighth Army during the blitzkrieg through Poland, and then was named commander in chief of the eastern forces, overseeing newly occupied territories. He held the post just seven months before Hitler fired him. Why justifies his inclusion here.

But From a Jewish Perspective

Jews in cities, towns, and hamlets of the Ukraine had probably never heard of Field Marshal Erich von Manstein, nor of the order he issued his Eleventh Army troops on November 20, 1941: "Jewry acts as the middleman between the enemy in the rear and the still fighting remainder of the Red Army forces and the Red leadership. More than in Europe, it holds all the key positions in the political leadership and administration, controls trades and guilds and, further, forms the nucleus for all unrest and uprising. The Jewish-Bolshevist system must be eradicated once and for all. Never again must it encroach upon our European Lebensraum." The language of Manstein's directive was in accordance with Hitler's wishes, shown by way of the Fuehrer's approval of another army commander's earlier message that soldiers must understand the necessity of "meting out severe yet fair retribution to the Jewish subhumans."

Manstein did not direct massacres through the army's chain of command. That was the job of Einsatzgruppe D, led by SS commander Otto Ohlendorf, who reported to Himmler. It murdered eighty-five thousand Jews in one four-month period. According to Ohlendorf, Manstein knew all about the killings, but Mainstein denied it. Tried by a British military court, Manstein said he was present when Hitler once described anti-Jewish measures, but believed these entailed settling Jews in an autonomous state near Lublin. Manstein's counsel argued that he could only have learned the truth from written reports (none were found) verbal reports (which left no trail) or rumor (which would have been a breach of military discipline to spread). Members of his headquarters staff defended their superior, contending that they concealed news of atrocities because they feared he would vigorously protest to Hitler and consequently lose his command, imperilling the army.

The British court was not convinced. It convicted him of disregarding his duty as a military commander to ensure public order and safety under Hague Convention standards. He got eighteen years, later reduced to twelve, then was released in 1952, having served less than seven.

Relations between Albert Kesselring, in his capacity as commander in chief of the southern forces, and Jews were even more abstract. North African and Italian Jews became pawns on a chessboard. When German troops poured into Tunisia after Anglo-American forces landed farther west, the matter arose: What was to be done with the area's eighty thousand Jews? From Rome came Kesselring's orders—mobilize Jewish labor for building fortifications. On-site subordinates were left the details, and the device they employed to enforce his directive was to enlist Jewish community leaders, on pain of death, to furnish the laborers.

The Axis ouster from North Africa spared Tunisian Jews further woe, but for Italian Jews harder times lay ahead. The German takeover following the collapse of Mussolini's Fascist regime passed wide-ranging power into Kesselring's hands. SS units rounded up Italian Jews independently of Kesselring, but not behind his back. Only suspension of disbelief permits the no see–no hear defense Manstein put forward.

At one point, SS Obersturmbannfuehrer Herbert Kappler, Himmler's man in Rome, called upon the field marshal for army personnel in the projected huge Judenaktion. Kesselring said he could not spare a single soldier for that purpose, suggesting instead the use of Jewish labor for fortification work, as in Tunisia. This may have been what passed for moderation in his mind. But when SS men murdered 335 hostages at the Ardeatine caves in March 1944, it was Kesselring who passed along, without dissent, this draconian order from Berlin. Only condemned prisoners kept alive for such an eventuality were considered eligible for slaughter, but seventy victims were chosen simply because they were Jews.

After the war, Kesselring was condemned to be shot, a sentence quickly commuted to life, then further reduced to twenty-one years. He was released in 1952, retired to a villa near Munich, and wrote his memoirs. *A Soldier's Record* reached bookstores in 1954 and conveyed advice to Jews in the form of a conversation with one of his Jewish interrogating officers:

> You have every right to demand the punishment of those who committed crimes against the Jews and reparation for what they did.... But to be guided by the idea of revenge is fatal because this mentality only leads to fresh injustice.

Field Marshal Rommel scores high among military historians for waging a "clean war." British Brigadier Desmond Young, author of a bestselling biography, *The Desert Fox*, regarded him a chivalrous opponent after spending time as a well-treated prisoner of war in North Africa: Rommel adhered to Geneva Convention rules.

One question still lends itself to conjecture. If a victorious Rommel had marched his troops through Tel Aviv, Haifa, and Jerusalem, would he have defied his master in Berlin, at the peril of his career, rather than acquiesce to the murder of Palestine's Jews? According to a more recent biographer, David Fraser, anti-Semitism played no part in Rommel's personal makeup: "He thought of Jews, when he thought of them at all, as fellow humans who he wished were Christians, who would see the light."

Rommel, nonetheless, took care to be politically correct. He attended prewar Nazi indoctrination courses and approved Hitler's War Ministry speech in December 1938 on the soldierly need to think ideologically. After lecturing a Swiss army audience, he noted, "the younger officers... expressed their sympathy with our new Germany. Individuals among them spoke with remarkable understanding of our Jewish problem."

But Rommel apparently did not grasp Hitler's solution. His son Manfred remembers that when his father, later bathed in honors, was welcomed into the Fuehrer's intimate circle, he naively suggested the appointment of a Jewish Gauleiter, or regional leader, to counteract foreign propaganda. Moments of stunned silence followed, according to Manfred, before Hitler retorted, "You've understood nothing of what I want."

During the Christmas season in 1943, Rommel learned from a friend, if he did not know before, what "resettlement in the east" really meant. His earlier suspicions had been aroused by conversations with colleagues who had seen service in Poland, notably Colonel-General Blaskowitz (about whom more will follow). When young Manfred asked parental permission to join the Waffen SS, he says his father refused.

Still unanswered—and unanswerable—is the central question for Jews, the only one that could fix Rommel's position from a Jewish perspective. Picture Rommel stepping toward the window of his suite at the King David Hotel at the sound of gutteral commands in the Jerusalem street below. He sees an SS police unit marching Jews off to an execution site. Would he have ordered his own troops to intervene? Or would he have quietly drawn the curtains, regarding this a "political matter" beyond army jurisdiction?

This brings us to Johannes Blaskowitz, the unknown soldier among our four, but the only high-ranking Wehrmacht officer who, facing this very situation, merits a measure of credit for decency in Jewish eyes. Blaskowitz, as commander in chief of the eastern forces, in the fall of 1939 dared to halt murderous conduct by Death Head's units that followed his troops into Poland: He ordered SS men court-martialed for massacres in the Poznan area, and sought to initiate proceedings against Nazi stalwart Joseph (Sepp) Dietrich, whose Liebstandarte SS Adolf Hitler formation committed atrocities before its transfer westward.

According to Third Reich values, Blaskowitz's conduct was unpardonable. Accused SS men received speedy amnesties. Blaskowitz, however, belonged to the old school. He held to traditional notions about correct treatment by conquerors of those conquered. When his initial protests reached Hitler in November 1939, the Fuehrer's army adjutant, Gerhard Engel, recorded: "He took note of it calmly at first, but then began another long tirade of abuse at the 'childish ideas'...you cannot fight wars with the methods of the Salvation Army."

Blaskowitz pressed on. He passed word of SS atrocities to high army circles at Zossen headquarters and on the Western Front. Word leaked to the neutral press. The subhead on a front page *New York Times* story of January 30, 1940, read: "Even Gen. Blaskowitz Balks at Tactics Held Aimed at Virtual 'Racial Extermination.'"

By that date, the chief of the army general staff, Franz Halder, had already noted that a breakdown of confidence in the east required personnel changes. Hitler was complaining "very indignantly" about "derogatory remarks made by senior officers concerning measures taken by us in Poland." Meanwhile, Blaskowitz had prepared another formidable dossier on SS crimes, which he handed to Army Commander Walter Brauchitsch when his chief visited Poland.

By now, Himmler felt it necessary to counter Blaskowitz's charges. In a half-hour speech before commanders and their deputies at Coblenz in mid-March, the Reichsfuehrer SS said: "In this gathering of the highest officers of the army, I suppose I can speak openly. I am doing nothing that the Fuehrer does not know." Blaskowitz himself attended the meeting, and although Himmler made no mention of his name, none was necessary. At dinner many of his fellow generals, he said, came over to congratulate him, but none offered open support.

Nevertheless, in April, Blaskowitz submitted two more thick dossiers outlining recent SS criminal behavior. Keitel refused to acknowledge its receipt. Goering's deputy went a step farther—he threatened to arrest Blaskowitz's courier.

Blaskowitz's ouster soon followed. He slipped into military limbo until late in the war, when his services were needed in France.

On July 19, 1940, the Fuehrer elevated to field marshal nine of the ten officers holding colonel-general rank at the war's onset. Only Blaskowitz was denied the coveted baton.

BENITO MUSSOLINI, 1883–1945
Duce, 1922–1943

History's Conventional View

Set against the demonic figure cut by his Axis partner, Mussolini comes down to us as something of a strutting caricature, his jaw jutting, his facial features plastic, his mannerisms threatening—a gift for cartoonists. By war's outbreak in 1939, he was waiting offstage for an opportune moment to safely jump in and pursue his dreams of glory, a revived Roman Empire girdling *mare nostrum* ("our sea")—the Mediterranean.

Originally it was Hitler, still an obscure right-wing political agitator, who saw "the Duce" as a role model. Mussolini's March on Rome had brought him to power in 1922. He waged the "Battle of Grain" to make Italy agriculturally self-sufficient, drained the malarial Pontine Marshes outside Rome, and made the trains run on time. But the dictator leaning at the balcony of the Palazzo Venezia as throngs in the square below cheered, yearned most to announce triumphs of arms.

Mussolini's conquest of Abyssinia merely whetted his appetite. He wanted more. Formation of "the Axis" around which Europe would swirl was a beginning. The May 1939 agreement with Hitler—the Pact of Steel, he called it—sealed his fate.

History's broader view of the man who marched a pathetically ill-prepared nation off to war is confirmed by newsreel film of Mussolini's body hanging by its heels from the girders of an abandoned Milanese filling station.

But From a Jewish Perspective

Mussolini was bad for Jews, but he was not like Hitler. The Duce's Fascism lacked National Socialism's sharp racial edge. Anti-Semitism could not be imposed on a population that found it alien to their nature despite, we'll shortly see, the Duce's fraternal effort.

Mussolini's early journalistic background—he had edited *Popolo d'Italia*—produced writings on a wide range of subjects, Jews among them, but consistency was never his strong suit. At one point in 1919 he attacked the "Jewish character" of Bolshevism. The next year he denied it. He wrote that Zionism was a "tool of British imperialism," then assured Chaim Weizmann that this stance was anti-English, not anti-Jewish.

The dynamics of Fascism made Jews uneasy on Mussolini's seizure of power in 1922, but until 1936 the party line denied that Italy had a "Jewish problem." More than once, Mussolini flatly declared, "Anti-Semitism does not exist in Italy." He was right about Italy, but not about himself.

Dr. Meir Michaelis, who spent a decade examining archives and interviewing surviving figures of the era, says close scrutiny shows Mussolini's attitude "was more complex than his official declarations would suggest."

Mussolini resented a perceived Jewish "separatism," Zionism, and opposition to mixed marriages. To Austria's prince, Ernst von Starhemberg he confided, "I have no love for the Jews, but they have great influence everywhere. It is better to leave them alone. His anti-Semitism has already brought Hitler more enemies than is necessary." According to Michaelis, this June 1932 statement, "embodied to perfection" Mussolini's mind during his first fourteen years of rule. The year before the Anschluss, the Duce told Austrian Chancellor Kurt von Schuschnigg, "We do not accept the Nazi racial theories, still less their juridical consequences." On another occasion he equated Fascism with "equilibrium and Latin humanity," National Socialism with "savage barbarism."

But the alliance with Nazi Germany deposited Italy's dictator at a crossroads. He could follow the path of principle or he could accommodate his Axis partner. Lacking anchor to principle, Mussolini's dilemma was simplified.

In July 1938, Italy's Office of Popular Culture issued the revolutionary "Race Manifesto" pointing in an "Aryan-Nordic direction." The document bore no signature, but Count Galeazzo Ciano, Mussolini's foreign minister (and son-in-law) noted in his diary: "He tells me that in fact he drafted almost the whole thing himself." Later, German Foreign Minister Joachim von Ribbentrop's boast of Reich success in arousing Italian racial awareness led Mussolini to deride his own work as "a ponderous German treatise translated into bad Italian."

However impure his motives, Mussolini now moved to enact and implement anti-Semitic legislation. Early in November 1938, Ciano entered in his diary, "the party has had orders from the Duce to intensify the anti-Semitic campaign," and on November 11, in the aftermath of the Kristallnacht north of the Alps, "I found the Duce more worked up than ever about the Jews. He approves unconditionally the reprisals [*sic*] carried out by the Nazis."

Mussolini's measures, pressed over objections within the Fascist Grand Council, were decreed on November 17. They banned Jews from the army, the civil service, and the Fascist party itself. Restrictions were placed on Jewish business and land ownership. However, exceptions favored war veterans, old Fascists, their children, grandchildren, parents, and grandparents—loopholes widened by lax enforcement. Naturalizations of Jews made after 1919 were declared null, and they were ordered out of the country.

As that tumultuous November ended, King Victor Emmanuel, whose signature formalized these steps, announced to Mussolini his "infinite pity for the Jews." Ciano writes that the annoyed Duce spoke of "twenty thousand spineless people" in Italy moved by the fate of the Jews. The king replied he was one of them.

Mussolini's figure of twenty thousand was a vast underestimation. Then—and for the five years to come before his fall—whenever the Duce looked backward, his countrymen weren't following. As Hitler pursued his Final Solution in 1942 and well along into 1943, peninsular Jews remained safe; Mussolini could simply not remake Italians into anti-Semites. Lack of popular support stymied all efforts to prove agreeable to his Axis partner.

Even more embarrassing than resistance at home, his military commanders in areas of France, Greece, and Croatia, which were under Italian control, blocked German efforts to seize their Jews. At Grenoble, Italian soldiers halted a transport of Jews before it left their jurisdiction. Elsewhere, Italian troops surrounded a Vichy police barracks, forcing the release of Jews kept captive there. In Greece, the Italian commander responded to his German counterpart's suggestion that he send Jews north to the killing grounds by offering sanctuary to any who could reach the Italian zone. In Croatia, General Mario Roatta flatly declared anti-Jewish actions "incompatible with the honor of the Italian army."

Mussolini, for his part, listened to German complaints and made excuses for his officers. He blamed their misunderstanding of the Jewish problem on the "logical consequence of their mode of thinking" and promised to stop such obtuse behavior. He failed.

Ironically, only with Mussolini's fall in July 1943—hailed by totalitarianism's foes around the world—began the *real* ordeal of Italian Jews and foreign Jews in Italian-held zones of occupied Europe. German troops, followed by Himmler's SS, swooped down through the peninsula and across frontier lines. In the last pathetic year of his life, Mussolini, established by Hitler as puppet ruler of the "Salo Republic," confided to intimates that he had made an error importing German racial theories into Italy. By then nobody cared what he said.

Men of Vichy

MARSHAL HENRI PHILIPPE PETAIN, 1856–1951
Chief of State, 1940–1944

PIERRE LAVAL, 1883–1945
Vice Premier, 1940; Premier, 1942–1944

History's Conventional View

A Marshal Petain gone from public life before his eighty-fifth birthday would be honored in memory as the victor of Verdun, France's hero of World War I, "the Great War." Instead, longevity offered him the opportunity to lead a fallen, truncated, "unoccupied" France through four years as an accessory to Hitler's New Order.

Millions of moviegoers who may be historically challenged by references to Vichy have gained insight into its nature through the cynical, amoral image projected by Captain Renault in *Casablanca*. For the

"Liberty, Equality, Fraternity" of more glorious times, Petain's national revolution substituted "Work, Family, Country." His policies curried favor with Nazi authorities in Paris, ruling directly over "occupied" France. Vichy gendarmes (such as the fictional Captain Renault) routinely imitated their Gestapo counterparts across the demarcation line. Remember, Italian military intervention rescued Jews from roundups by the marshal's police, *not* Himmler's.

For his collaboration, signified by a photo-op handshake with the Fuehrer himself, Petain, at eighty-nine, was sentenced to death by a postwar French tribunal. This sentence was promptly reduced to life, and he was shipped off to the isolated isle of Ile d'Yeu in the Bay of Biscay. Pierre Laval, his number two, received no such clemency. The tribunal sent him before a firing squad.

Laval's reputation as a collaborator is fixed in even darker hues than Petain, whose defenders could cite senility. All the sixty-two-year-old Laval could argue was that he played a double game in France's long-term interests. This was at least credible, for his deviousness had been established long before Vichy's emergence as more than just a popular provincial health spa. The inter-war period saw him bobbing and weaving in and out of revolving-door Parisian ministries. In the unsavory politics of the unstable Third Republic he was a survivor.

The collapse of France gave him his big opportunity, and his genius for opportunism soon made him the darling of France's new overlords. At one point, palace politics forced him out of Petain's immediate circle. Hitler insisted on his return.

But From a Jewish Perspective

One way—albeit not the only one—Laval ingratiated himself with Germans was through his willingness to sacrifice "unoccupied" France's Jews, preferably refugees rather than those native-born. Petain, at his lofty perch, avoided messy personal involvement in deal-making, but, as chief of state, signed off on arrangements made by his ambitious subordinate.

Petain *did* intervene to ask protection for individual Jews known to him personally, but this was rare. Robert O. Paxton, a leading authority on Vichy, writes that, to his knowledge, Petain never talked publicly about Jews, but the old man's sentiments could scarcely be in doubt. He was a product of the traditional French army establishment, with all the ancient prejudices endemic in the anti-Dreyfusard officer class.

In Petain's name, and certainly with his acquiescence, the first steps against Jews were taken via Vichy's *statut des juifs* in 1940. Others followed and, step by step, Jews in the "unoccupied" zone found their property confiscated, civil service posts lost, and professions and university positions closed to them. After December 1942, ID and ration cards bore a large *Juif* designation. The old marshal received many letters from proud Jewish veterans of the Great War. He was unmoved.

Native-born French Jews, veterans or not, were still safe. Of some three hundred thousand Jews on French soil, some one hundred seventy-thousand were foreigners, many stateless. From their number came the first large transports to be sent east in the summer of 1942. It departed with Laval's blessing. "These foreign Jews had always been a problem," he said. "The French government was glad that a change in the German attitude toward them gave France an opportunity to get rid of them."

Laval saw to it even youngsters made their final journey despite, ironically, some original German hesitation. With Petain present, he told Vichy's council of ministers that "in the interest of humanity [he] has obtained—contrary to the first German proposals—that the children, including those under sixteen, be allowed to accompany their parents."

Susan Zuccotti, an historian of the French Holocaust, speculates on possible reasons for his stance. He may have wanted to show ruthlessness pleasing to his Nazi master. Or, maybe, he figured French public opinion would have regarded the orphanage option less appealing. Perhaps, she adds, "he simply wanted bodies to fill his quota of Jews easily without having to touch the 'real' French."

Laval, clearly not the most trustworthy of memoirists, put his own spin on the decision while scribbling away in his postwar prison cell: "I did all I could, considering the fact that my first duty was to my fellow countrymen of Jewish extraction whose interests I could not sacrifice."

The long public record of prewar Laval revealed no deep-rooted anti-Semitism. So we may give him some benefit of doubt. He probably knew nothing—at that point in time—of the new use for a common insecticide, Zyklon B, found by the Nazis. But the Germans, for their part, made no commitment to leave native-born Frenchmen alone. If Laval had trusted to his bargaining skills, Jewry emerged the loser, for without Vichy gendarmes carrying out the roundups, transports could not have left filled. In 1942, Gestapo manpower resources were simply too thin.

The decline of Petain's mental facilities concentrated more power in his premier's hands. Although deportations didn't trouble his questionable conscience, German insistence on a mandatory Star of David for Jews above the age of six did. This was an infringement on autonomy, an embarrassment for Vichy.

Fortunately, Laval was adept at understanding the changes in the fortunes of war. While the Third Reich was winning, 42,500 were sent to their deaths in the summer and autumn of 1942—perhaps one-third "at Vichy's initiative," writes Paxton. This number declined to twenty-two thousand in 1943 as Vichy "began to drag its feet." El Alamein and Stalingrad had taken much of the steam out of the German war machine.

"One can only speculate," Paxton and coauthor Michael Marrus reflect, "how many fewer would have perished" had the Nazis been "obliged to identify, arrest and transport" Jews east without aid from Vichy authorities. After Vichy's fall, Laval said, "I tried to find out by questioning them where the Germans were sending those convoys of Jews, and their reply invariably was, 'To Poland, where we want to create a Jewish state.'" But, less ingenuously, he added, "I was well aware that this meant working there in terrible conditions, most often to suffer and die there."

Axis Europe, 1940–1944,
Supporting (and Nonsupporting)
Cast Members

NICHOLAS HORTHY, 1868–1957
Regent of Hungary, 1920–1944

BORIS III, 1894–1943
King of Bulgaria, 1918–1943

CHRISTIAN X, 1870–1947
King of Denmark, 1912–1947

CARL GUSTAF VON MANNERHEIM, 1867–1951;
Commander in Chief, Finnish Army, 1939–1944;
President of Finland, 1944–1946

History's Conventional View

Most people would be hard-pressed to match names and photos for these four European rulers, but their names may stir memories—in Christian X's case, an image as well—for they each occupy a niche in Holocaust history. They were not merely bit players, and that's why they're here.

Admiral Horthy, of old Calvinist stock, led the doomed Austro-Hungarian navy in World War I, then helped put down Bela Kun's short-lived Communist regime. Hungary's new Parliament named Horthy regent, pending clarification of who held the crown. But clarification never came, so Horthy remained at his post for twenty-four years. Through the 1930s, he generally served as a moderating force in a kingless kingdom swarming with right-wing radicals.

Given Hungary's political tilt, the country joined the Axis Tripartite Pact and sent troops to fight alongside Germany's in Russia. When Soviet troops later advanced toward Budapest, Horthy, wavering, made a bid for a separate peace. Hitler responded by sending his talented thug, SS Colonel Otto Skorzeny, to kidnap Horthy and whisk him out of the country.

The short, swarthy Boris III, husband of King Victor Emmanuel's daughter, ruled as a constitutional monarch—in theory. In fact, after 1935, a royal dictatorship prevailed, the strongest argument, we'll see, for those crediting him with the signal role in blocking Nazi efforts to grab Bulgaria's Jews. Without Boris's approval, little could happen in wartime Bulgaria.

Although its population felt more kinship to Russians than Germans, Bulgaria's geographical vulnerability, plus avarice (it saw an opportunity to regain lost territories in Thrace and Macedonia) led the country to join the Axis. Boris allowed German troops passage to the fronts in Yugoslavia and Greece, and then kept watch on its partner's Balkan flank.

Christian X's flat, defenseless Denmark fell to Hitler almost incidentally, a way-stop for Germans intent on seizing strategic Norway. Rather than flee, Christian remained in Copenhagen, quickly becoming a symbol of Danish passive resistance to Nazi ideological incursions. Hitler, for a time, left Danish internal affairs to the Danes, but when escalating tensions led to an outbreak of sabotage, the king was confined under virtual house arrest at Sorgenfri Castle.

Field Marshal Mannerheim had led Finnish forces defending their borders in the winter war of 1939–40 against the Soviet Union. Their gallant stand along the Mannerheim Line electrified the world. It was certainly no natural alliance that turned democratic Finland into a cobelligerent with Nazi Germany during Operation Barbarossa. Finns regarded this the Continuation War. Mannerheim again led the northern nation's armed forces, fighting, this time, to recover what Stalin had stolen the year before.

From 1940 through 1944, the chief political figures in Helsinki were President Risto Ryti and Foreign Minister Johan Rangell. Neither matched in prestige their fabled field marshal, whose leadership qualities had first been tested during Finland's struggle for independence a generation earlier. When Adolf Hitler arrived on his sole visit to Finland in June 1942, it was ostensibly to honor the redoubtable, bemedalled commander in chief on his seventy-fifth birthday, not to call on the men in mufti.

But From a Jewish Perspective

As limited partners in Hitler's New Order, what Admiral Horthy or King Boris could have done—or wanted to do—to impede the Final Solution has been explored by Holocaust historians for years. It is an open-ended subject, for pertinent documents were destroyed in the turmoil of defeat. In some cases the evidence survives, but in archives closed to scholars.

Horthy outlived the war, settled in Spain, and *did* set down his version for posterity. Boris never had the chance. He died mysteriously in August 1943, a subject itself deserving of suspense writers, or at least monographists. Did Hitler really grieve over the loss of his ally, who had paid him a working visit just days before? Or did he secretly order his assassination? The question interests us here because one theory still current putting Boris's demise at the hands of the Fuehrer pinpoints the king's refusal to surrender *Bulgaria's* own Jews (unlike those of newly annexed Thrace and Macedonia, who were shown no such benevolence). Hitler's mind-set could well accept a regicide or two in advancing his obsessive project—annihilation of *all* European Jewry. But first, Horthy.

Until the spring of 1944, Hungarian Jews remained unscathed by the Final Solution. Discriminatory economic and financial measures in a land rife with virulent anti-Semitism had existed since April 1938. A radical change came in March 1944, when German troops marched in. Summoned to Germany, as Horthy relates in his memoirs, "Hitler went on to lecture me on the Jewish question shouting 'the Jews must be exterminated or put in concentration camps.'" The regent says he protested deportations on humane and moral grounds, also pointing out—more appealingly to the Nazi mentality—the plan's "deleterious effect on production."

This had no effect, for Colonel Eichmann's men soon set to work. "For a long time," goes Horthy's postwar account, "I was helpless before German influence" and "lacked the means" to thwart Nazi policy. In just eight weeks, more than 437,000 Jews from the Hungarian provinces were piled into 148 trains destined for Auschwitz. Only Budapest's 200,000 remained.

By summer though, Horthy says, he "regained, though slowly and imperfectly," more room for initiative. If we are to believe Horthy, "not before August did secret information reach me of the truth about these extermination camps." At that point, he says, he took decisive action, ordering an armored division transferred to Budapest to prevent the roundup of the remaining Jews under Hungary's anti-Semitic interior minister. Acknowledgement that his "action saved the Jews still in Budapest," he writes, came from Hungarian Jewish leaders.

Truth or half-truth? Horthy *did* step in at the last moment to save Budapest's Jews, but another face can be put on his motive. As 1944 moved toward its final quarter, Allied advances through France and the unstoppable Russian steamroller along the southeastern front ended even faint notions of Axis resurgence. Horthy was deluged by warnings from the Western allies, pleas from neutrals and the International Red Cross, and, in this almost singular case, strong urgings from the Vatican. Raoul Wallenberg not too subtly pointed out the prospects for postwar punishment if he did nothing, and images of B-17 fleets pounding lovely Budapest in retribution long before that day of judgment also helped push the regent's decision-making process forward. That Horthy did not end his days collared by a noose but sitting comfortably in a Spanish villa attests that he got the message, literally and figuratively.

Horthy's humanitarianism in stopping the convoys left Eichmann unamused. That, plus the regent's decision to negotiate a separate peace, led to the kidnapping escapade removing him from the scene.

Early on, the petty bourgeois Hitler, who did not much care for royalty, accepted Bulgaria's King Boris III as a shrewd statesman and faithful ally. Sofia had enacted the Law for the Protection of the Nation as early as December 1940, providing for Jewish quotas in professions, partial property confiscation, special taxes, and exclusion from public posts. This was just the start.

A February 22, 1943, written agreement between Eichmann's man in Sofia, Captain Theodor Dannecker, and the anti-Semitic Bulgarian commissar for Jewish affairs, Alexander Belev, provided for "the deportation of the first twenty thousand Jews from the new Bulgarian lands Thrace and Macedonia into the German eastern region." They encountered a snag. When Belev found he fell six thousand short of filling the quota with Jews from outside Bulgaria's old frontiers, he turned to Jews within Bulgaria itself.

Now an even bigger problem arose. In Parliament, the deputy speaker and forty-two members petitioned the prime minister "in the name of the prestige and morale of the Bulgarian people" to block the Dannecker-Belev plan. The deputy speaker also proposed Belev's censure. This bold proposal was defeated, and its instigator himself removed from office. However grand as gestures, parliamentary outcry could not halt the trains.

The trains did halt. Deportations from Bulgaria proper never took place. Jews already arrested and processed for shipment north were summarily released. For the remainder of the war, Bulgarian Jews faced harsh restrictions, and some twenty thousand were concentrated outside the capital in labor camps. German plans for their extermination, however, were frustrated. None could be extracted from within Bulgaria's borders.

Why were Bulgaria's Jews saved? Postwar politics clouds the answer. Some writers emphasize the petition by moderates in Parliament. Once Bulgaria fell behind the Iron Curtain, Communist historians credited party cadres. Some see the influence of the royal court behind salvation. Professor Frederick B. Chary, an expert on wartime Bulgaria, notes that Queen Giovanna, her confessor Father Romano, the king's sister Princess Endoxia, the king's secretary Stanislav Balan, and the king's close advisers all acted at one time or another "on behalf of Jews, either for individuals or for the entire community."

Perhaps we can turn to an on-site Nazi for the best clue. Gestapo officer Karl Hoffmann had no political axes to grind. He was simply in Sofia in March 1943 to get a job done. When deportations were suddenly blocked that month, his report to Berlin noted that the formerly cooperative interior minister acted after receiving "a nod from the highest place." That could only have been Boris III.

There are those who see a Nazi hand in the king's death in August—within days after returning from a frustrating (for Hitler) summit in Germany. German efforts since March to get the trains moving had proven fruitless, and they not unreasonably find cause for linkage. One

American offered his opinion. Passersby on a residential street in an upscale community in Florida could hardly be expected to recognize the figure represented by a statue. Placed there by a descendant of Bulgarian Jewish survivors, it honors Good King Boris.

Wartime legends blossomed—they made good copy—recounting the sayings of King Christian X in defense of Danish Jewry. One of the most widespread went, "If the Germans want to introduce the yellow Jewish star in Denmark, I and my whole family will wear it as a sign of the highest distinction." Another had him telling Cecil von Renthe-Fink, the Occupation's German plenipotentiary, "There is no Jewish question in this country. There is only my people." Or, a variation on this to German officers complaining of his negligence in racial matters: "Gentlemen, since we have never considered ourselves inferior to the Jews, we have no such problem here." A fourth had the king threatening abdication if the Nazis introduced anti-Jewish legislation.

Henrik Kauffmann, Danish ambassador in Washington in 1940, stood foremost in popularizing his sovereign's defiant stance, and such dramatic quotes, even if apocryphal, convey basic truths. King Christian X *was* totally supportive of his country's Jews. The Danish man-in-the-street knew it; so did the Nazi man-in-the-Wilhelmstrasse and the Reich chancellery.

Actually, what they could now expect of Denmark's sovereign could have been foreseen seven years earlier. In April 1933, as the Nazis consolidated power and boycotted Jewish firms, Christian attended services at the Copenhagen synagogue's one hundreth anniversary commemoration. This gesture, appreciated by Jews, did not go unnoted by Denmark's virulent neighbor across the frontier.

When that frontier was crossed in April 1940, Hitler's notion was to turn Denmark into a model protectorate, showcasing Europe's New Order. To do so, he had to deal with the Jews. Local Nazis, anemic in numbers, tried to burn down Copenhagen's synagogue. They failed. The king promptly wrote Rabbi Marcus Melchior: "I have heard about the attempted fire at the synagogue and I am very happy that there was only slight damage." Minor incidents dotted the long calm before the machinery of extermination was ready to embrace Denmark's eight thousand Jews. The time: September 1943.

Two German ships slipped into Copenhagen harbor to receive their human cargo. Dr. Werner Best, the SS administrator conducting the action, prematurely wired Hitler: "Denmark is *Judenrein*—cleared of Jews and completely purged." Apparently, the busy Dr. Best never saw the message sent to him by the king, to be hand-delivered by Denmark's foreign minister.

Christian wrote, "I desire to stress to you not only because of human concern for the citizens of my country, but also because of the fear of further consequences in future relations between Germany and Denmark, that special measures in regard to a group of people who have enjoyed full rights of citizenship in Denmark for more than one hundred years would have the most severe consequences."

The Danish king and his people were one. More than seven thousand Jews reached Swedish refuge, smuggled there by a mini-Dunkirk under the noses of Dr. Best's men. In May 1945, they returned and found their homes and property intact, cared for by their gentile neighbors. Harold Flender, who recounted the dramatic days of escape in *Rescue in Denmark*, quotes Rabbi Melchior's reaction: "The welcome we received from the king, from everybody, is the most important event in Danish Jewish history."

Thirty-six Finnish Jews met violent death in the war years, but not at Nazi hands. They died fighting under Field Marshal Mannerheim against the Russians. The absurdity of Finnish Jews as comrades-in-arms with the "master race" was not lost on Nazi minds bent on including Finland's Jews in the Final Solution.

In July 1942, immediately after Hitler's birthday visit, Mannerheim learned that Reichsfuehrer Heinrich Himmler "requested permission to visit me, in the words of the introduction, 'to convey his belated congratulations on my seventy-fifth birthday.'"

Mannerheim wrote in his memoirs that Himmler "did not enjoy a good reputation, either in Finland or the other northern countries," but agreed to meet him. Through Goering, Himmler had earlier "agreed to make things easier in the concentration camps for some of my personal friends, and the fate of a couple of people close to me was dependent on this powerful man."

Mannerheim's memoirs are tantalizingly blank on whether Himmler got around to the Jewish question. He writes, instead, of the Reichsfuehrer's enthusiasm over Germany's new *Panzerfaust* antitank projectile.

Fortunately, Dr. Felix Kersten, the Finnish masseur (dubbed by admirers the man with the miraculous hands), whom Himmler kept constantly on hand to deal with his stomach ills, is more garrulous in *his* memoirs. The Reichsfuehrer told him before their journey north: "Hitler wants the Finnish Jews to be taken to Maidanek in Poland.... The moment is favorable to induce Finland to yield in this matter." Finland's grain supply was exhausted; it needed thirty thousand tons from Germany. "We will not make this delivery until Finland has surrendered up her Jews."

At Helsinki, Himmler went about his mission, seeing President Ryti and Foreign Minister Rangell as well as Mannerheim. It proved a frustrating experience for the SS chief. He later told Dr. Kersten, "Ryti, Mannerheim, and Rangell, that smooth eel—all three, I make no doubt of it, are Freemasons! Well, all three fine gentlemen will soon learn that it would have been wiser for them to adjust themselves to National Socialist ideas!"

For the immediate future, Hitler needed Finnish cooperation on the eastern front. He showed care not to push the envelope containing plans for Finland's mere two thousand Jews too far.

When Finland pulled out of the war in 1944, Himmler later lamented, "Oh, I'm sorry I did not have the pleasure of seeing Ryti and Mannerheim hanged—as I once wanted to do."

On December 6, 1944, Finnish Independence Day, Mannerheim came to Helsinki Synagogue for memorial services in honor of the thirty-six Finnish Jews fallen in combat.

FRANCISCO FRANCO, 1892–1975
Spain's Chief of State, 1939–1975

History's Conventional View

For a period after 1945, any list of history's most loathed rulers would have found Generalissimo Franco's name at or near the top—loathed, not feared. On that second score, he ranked well below Stalin (about whom more comes later) and lesser despots long since forgotten. Franco earned his discreditable place in contemporary history as Western Europe's last bona fide Fascist dictator.

Prudence deterred Spain's entwining in the Axis alliance, ensuring his postwar survival, but a bloody trail carved in 1936 still smeared his name. Franco owed his emergence as Spain's leader, or caudillo, to military support generously provided by kindred spirits Hitler and Mussolini. He directed rightist Nationalists against republican Loyalists in a brutal, no-holds-barred civil war. Consider him the off-camera "heavy" in Ernest Hemingway's *For Whom the Bells Toll*.

Victory came in 1939, and shortly thereafter to the good fortune of the Western democracies, Franco showed demonstrable ingratitude toward his two benefactors. Operation Felix, devised by German military strategists to seize Britain's Gibraltar stronghold and seal the Mediterranean shut, needed Franco's cooperation. Hitler didn't get it. After the two dictators met at the border town of Hendaye, the Fuehrer told intimates, "Rather than go through that again, I would rather have three or four teeth pulled."

World War II's aftermath left Franco alone and despised, an international pariah. But the cold war offered rehabilitation. The United States needed air bases on Europe's southern rim; Franco offered the real estate. He edged his way back into the international community, dulling the sharpness of his Fascist roots.

But From a Jewish Perspective

Before looking at Franco, we discount a story occasionally surfacing that Jewish blood flowed through "the Caudillo's" veins. It arises from varied clues, such as surnames suspiciously of Marrano origin, and his birth site far from Madrid in a remote region likely a past refuge for Jews fleeing corners of the peninsula more accessible to Torquemada's agents. (Remember, if we arbitrarily do not rule out such a tantalizing notion, Franco—like Marx and Disraeli—would forfeit eligibility for these pages.)

The fifteenth-century expulsion of the Jews spared Spain's dictator a minority population that would surely have whetted Hitler's appetite. At a December 3, 1943, meeting with German ambassador Hans Dieckhoff, Franco could say, "Thank God a clear appreciation of danger" caused by Jews led our Catholic kings to insure "we have for centuries been relieved of that nauseating burden." Had that "burden" still existed, would the Caudillo have loaded his Jews into trains bound for the East in a spirit of good fellowship, or, like Boris, just said no? We'll never know.

What we do know—only partly, and even that with uncertain statistics—is that thousands of foreign Jews survived the war because the rugged Spanish-French frontier along the rim of the Pyrenees, while challenging, was not impassable. Except briefly, in March 1943, under heavy German pressure, that escape hatch lay open for Jews who were capable of making their way across Occupied Europe to get there.

Some undocumented refugees—and almost all Jews passing into Spain fell into that category—bribed local police and moved quietly on to Portugal. Most were sent to a detention camp at Miranda del Ebro, near Burgos, and when that filled up, to standard prisons. Conditions were appalling, food supplied to the refugees minimal, but financial costs to the Spanish government not insignificant. No doubt, temptation existed to seal the border tightly and return "illegals" to their certain fate north of the Pyrenees. Pro-German Falangist party officials proposed doing so on political grounds alone, but escape routes remained open. Only Franco, "Supreme Chief, responsible only before God and History," could order so drastic a measure. He did not.

The Caudillo had the capacity, if his will matched, to save Jews far from Iberia by providing them with Spanish protective documents. In July 1944, a Madrid-based U.S. diplomat wrote the State Department, "all Spanish diplomatic representatives in areas under German occupation or control, including Hungary, have been instructed to render all possible assistance to Jews." Thousands received documents in Budapest including, first, five hundred children, then seven hundred adults, given visas by its legation to enter Spanish Morocco. Without "transit visas" to cross German-held territory (the kind of magic paper that created such a fuss in *Casablanca*), Jews remained in Hungary but were safe from Eichmann's hunters. As a bonus, they also enjoyed relative immunity from homegrown Arrow Cross hoodlums who were less inclined to honor protective letters issued by neutrals than by fraternally Fascist Spain.

While in Spain for an interview with Generalissimo Franco in 1970, Rabbi Chaim U. Lipschitz of the Rabbinical Alliance of America spoke to Ambassador Don Angel Sanz Briz, who had served at the wartime Budapest post. "I received a telegram from my government which was rather unusual," he said, "because generally we received our orders from our minister of foreign affairs. But on that occasion, even though the telegram was sent by the minister of foreign affairs, on it was the name of the chief of state, in other words [it was sent]...by General Franco himself in order to emphasize the importance of the project that was ordered in the telegram."

Yet, in behavior contradictory to—and impossible to reconcile with—humanity shown Jews elsewhere in Europe, Franco's consul in Athens was forbidden to issue visas on his own authority to endangered Sephardic refugees from Salonika, who could, more plausibly than any other Jews, be claimed as Spanish subjects. Each case was to be considered separately by Madrid, a time-consuming process with potentially lethal consequences.

When Spain sought reentry into world councils, Franco's established persona as a helpmate-in-ideology, if not brother-in-arms, of Hitler and Mussolini overwhelmed other considerations. Israel, herself newly admitted to the United Nations, cast a negative vote. Ambassador Abba Eban explained: "While the Israeli delegation would not for a moment assert that the Spanish regime had had any direct part in the policy of extermination, it did assert that Franco's Spain had been an active, sympathetic ally of the regime which had been responsible for that policy."

This stance would sour Israeli-Spanish rapprochement bids for many years. Franco regarded the Jewish state as ungrateful. When Rabbi Lipschitz received his much publicized audience with the Caudillo in Madrid, he first thanked Franco for World War II rescue efforts before turning to questions for a planned book. Spanish officials had warned him beforehand that the topic of Israel was off-limits. The rabbi's book, *Franco, Spain, the Jews, and the Holocaust*, eventually appeared, but its pivotal chapter bore the frank heading, "A Fruitless Interview With General Franco."

Incomprehensively, Franco passed on the chance to embellish his rescue efforts, but he has his partisans. In a 1992 magazine article, Nathaniel Weyl saw more merit than others concede in the Caudillo's refuge role. He wrote that Franco has been ignored, his contributions denigrated, as a carryover of the illusion that his civil war foes, the Spanish Loyalists, were "noble crusaders for freedom." Even so, nagging questions of motive remain. To what extent were his good deeds shaped by Allied pressure? At one point in April 1943, just after Spain closed the Pyrenees, Churchill had lunch with the Spanish ambassador in London. "I must warn your government," he said, "that if you prevent these unfortunate people seeking safety from the horrors of Nazi domination, such a thing will never be forgotten and will poison the relations between the Spanish and the British people."

Generalissimo Franco could have done more. From the leader of a democratic state—as we'll see—more should have been expected. But considering that he was ideologically no saint, the Caudillo was equally no Satan during the ordeal of European Jewry.

WINSTON SPENCER CHURCHILL, 1874–1965
Prime Minister, 1940–1945

ANTHONY EDEN, 1897–1977
Foreign Secretary, 1940–1945

History's Conventional View

Differences arise between those who regard Churchill the century's greatest Englishman and others who acclaim him the greatest Englishman ever. In 1940, his "blood, tears, toil, and sweat" leadership of a Britain alone under seige ("their finest hour"), his stirring defiance of a Hitler triumphant over continental Europe ("we will fight them on the beaches..."), marked his place in history even before "the Grand Alliance" forged with Roosevelt and Stalin turned the hinge of fate.

On America's side of the Atlantic, it was hard to understand why his fellow Englishmen voted him out of office just weeks after V-E Day. Americans couldn't fathom the parliamentary system by which prime ministers got their job and held it.

Recalling his less secure status alongside the United States president and soviet premier, he wrote: "I was the only one of our trinity who could at any moment be dismissed from power by the vote of a House of Commons freely elected on universal franchise, or could be controlled from day to day by the opinion of a war cabinet representing all parties in the state." These realities, unfortunately, become all the more relevant when we look at Churchill's war ministry not as the world at large saw it...

But From a Jewish Perspective

Churchill's commitment to a Jewish homeland extended back to the era when the Balfour Doctrine made news. Closing out his decade as an outsider—"the wilderness years"—he rose in the House of Commons in May of 1939 to oppose the Chamberlain government's White Paper. It effectively sealed Palestine against Europe's Jews seeking safety.

"As one intimately and personally and responsibly concerned in the earlier stages of our Palestine policy," he said, "I could not stand by and see solemn engagements into which Britain has entered before the world set aside...and I shall feel embarrassed in the most acute manner if I limit myself by silence or inaction to what I must regard as an act of repudiation." During his own prime ministry—except for a period after November 1944, in the wake of the Stern Gang's murder of Lord Moyne, the British minister resident in Cairo—Churchill's belief in a Jewish state remained steadfast.

Scholar Bernard Wasserstein's authoritative *Britain and the Jews of Europe, 1935–1945* states unequivocally: "No British statesman had a more consistent and more emphatic record of sympathy for Jewish refugees and support of Zionism as a solution to the Jewish problem than Winston Churchill."

When the war approached the Near East, he wanted Palestinian Jews armed, a move forcefully resisted by Colonial Secretary Lord Lloyd. Churchill found this "little less than a scandal." He favored establishing distinct Jewish units, a notion successfully blocked by fellow ministers and military commanders in the Near East. Churchill sought to get his way by making "an example of anti-Semitic officers in high places. If at least three or four of them were recalled and dismissed, and the reasons given, it would have a salutary effect." He failed. The military establishment, bureaucratic and uniformed, protected its own. When a Jewish military presence came into being under its own flag the war was well along, and Rommel had already been beaten back from the gateway to Palestine.

Since Churchill was so decidedly pro-Jewish, why did he not do more to rescue Europe's doomed Jewry? And, late in the war, why didn't British long-range Lancasters blast gas chambers and railway lines leading to Auschwitz?

Respected Holocaust historians answer these questions, but not to the satisfaction of others in their fraternity. Monty Noam Penkower's analysis of free world diplomacy, *The Jews Were Expendable*, sees Churchill relegating European Jewry to the background for the duration. For example, he notes private correspondence in which the prime minister cited "the great difficulties we are encountering and shall continue to encounter.... Transport alone [was] difficult of solution."

The White Paper remained in force throughout the war. London created no War Refugee Board similar to Washington's. Churchill's focus on a postwar Jewish state, some historians logically contend, would be of dubious value to the dead.

Such troubling questions led to Martin Gilbert's topic, "Churchill and the Holocaust: The Possible and Impossible," in an address at Washington's Holocaust Memorial Museum. Gilbert, author of several volumes in the official Churchill biography and numerous Holocaust studies, saw the prime minister stifled by limitations that Britain's "unwritten constitution" placed on his office.

Churchill was King George V's *first* minister, not his *only* minister. Cabinet colleagues with constituencies and agendas of their own could—and did—overrule him. On Jewish matters, only Minister for Indian Affairs Leopold Amery proved a reliable ally. Moreover, career civil servants administering previously formulated policy—the White Paper—deliberately avoided meddlesome politicians, like Churchill, by not sending along memoranda certain to invite hostility.

Wasserstein's study offers the decision not to bomb Auschwitz as a "notable illustration" of the capacity of lower officials "to thwart the will even of the most powerful prime minister in British history." (Although we don't know if the bombing issue reached Roosevelt's desk in the White House, we know it did reach Churchill's, at 10 Downing Street.) In July 1944 the prime minister learned of Jewish Agency requests for air assaults on the railway lines from Budapest to Birkenau to stop Hungarian deportations.

On July 7, he wrote Eden: "Is there any reason to raise this matter with the cabinet? Get anything out of the air force you can, and invoke me if necessary." Eden did so.

To prepare for this mission the Air Ministry requested topographic data, but maps promptly provided by the Jewish Agency to the Foreign Office were not passed along. They wound up in its own filing cabinets. The Air Ministry could not send out its bombers flying blind over strange terrain. So Foreign Office officials then drafted a minute for their chief explaining that the Air Ministry regarded the project as technically unfeasible—without mentioning its reason, the absence of topographical material, nor, obviously, the fact this data was tucked away by Eden's own subordinates. Churchill, out of the country when plans were eventually cancelled, may never even have been told, for in the interim, Regent Horthy stepped in to halt the trains.

We can't leave Churchill without taking some note of his long-standing heir presumptive, Foreign Secretary Anthony Eden. There would come a point in time—one Labor ministry and a second Churchill ministry removed—when the top post would finally be his, and during his brief tenure a crisis blazed across front pages that put Eden, from a Jewish perspective, in a far better light than he deserved overall. The Suez War of October 1956 dominated the attention of Jews worldwide.

True, British, French, and Israeli actions seemed coordinated to outsiders, especially U.S. government officials caught unaware. Eden, an ally of convenience, in Jewish eyes became "the good guy," America's irate leader, Eisenhower, "the bad guy."

But British and Israeli agendas differed. Israel waged preventive war to avert, at best, slow economic strangulation, and at worst, a later overwhelming assault by Gamal Abdel Nasser's Soviet-armed Egyptian army. Eden wanted back the Suez Canal, seized by Nasser, and without which British influence in the Near East sagged. Their common interest lay solely in thwarting Nasser's ambitions, threatening to both.

A less pleasing portrait of Eden emerges from an earlier palette. A longtime colleague of Churchill once told biographer Gilbert, "You have to understand, Gilbert, that Winston did have one serious fault.... He was too fond of Jews." Eden escaped this flaw. An April 25, 1943, entry in the diary of Oliver Harvey, his private secretary, reads: "Unfortunately, A. E. is immovable on the subject of Palestine. He loves Arabs and hates Jews." Still earlier, in a private note responding to a pro-Zionist memorandum, Eden wrote, "If we must have preferences, let me murmur in your ear that I prefer Arabs to Jews."

Privately held feelings *could* hold little interest for Jews, but when expressed by public men on a confidential basis, they may signal their intrusion on public policy. At the time of the Kristallnacht, Neville Chamberlain, then prime minister, wrote his sister: "Jews aren't lovable people. I don't care for them myself." The White Paper followed.

Interviewed in the early 1970s for the television documentary *The World at War*, seen by millions worldwide, Eden could speak movingly of the solemn moment of silence that followed his December 17, 1942, report to the House of Commons on German atrocities against Jews. But three months later at the White House, on March 27, 1943, he would tell Roosevelt, Secretary of State Cordell Hull, and presidential adviser Harry Hopkins (who took notes): "The whole problem of the Jews in Europe is very difficult, and we should move very cautiously about offering to take them all out of a country like Bulgaria. If we do that, then the Jews of the world will be wanting us to make similar offers in Poland and Germany. Hitler might well take us up on any such offer and there simply are not enough ships and means of transportation to handle them."

The following summer, when Regent Horthy halted Budapest deportations and offered the Allies an opportunity to spirit Jews out of the country, Eden was alarmed. He circulated a memorandum to the Cabinet Committee on Refugees quite strongly rejecting an American suggestion that the two governments announce a willingness to "undertake to care for all Jews who are permitted to leave Hungary." Colonial officials were "already much disturbed," he wrote, "by the number of Jews arriving in Palestine."

Eden was of no mind to see a drastic change of the Arab-Jewish ratio in the Holy Land's population. Years later Abba Eban would write, "More than any other British statesman," Eden "put sharp brakes on Churchill's desire during World War II to give evidence of sympathy for Zionism."

FRANKLIN DELANO ROOSEVELT, 1882–1945
President, 1933–1945

History's Conventional View

Not long after his death on April 12, 1945, most Americans would likely have agreed that if Mt. Rushmore could support a fifth chiseled presidential profile, Roosevelt's belonged there. Some suggested a Washington memorial rivaling Jefferson's. Others favored celebration of his birthday as a national holiday. Our only four-time chief executive led his one hundred thirty million downcast fellow citizens through the Great Depression. His deluge of programs and "alphabet agencies" to foster relief, recovery, and reform changed the role of government in their lives forevermore.

In 1941, as "Dr. New Deal" surrendered ground to "Dr. Win the War," he became the hope of repressed people around the globe. Political scientists of succeeding generations made him the measuring yard against which United States presidents since have been tested.

But From a Jewish Perspective

Uncle Louis, quite demanding before assigning a lofty place in history for Richard the Lion-Hearted ("Was he good for the Jews?") would be appalled at the notion that the same question could be asked of Franklin Delano Roosevelt. FDR was his hero, and not his alone. Look at all the Jews admitted to his circle—Treasury Secretary Henry Morgenthau, Supreme Court Justice Felix Frankfurter, New York Governor Herbert Lehman, speechwriter Sam Rosenman, aides Benjamin Cohen and David Niles for starters—and, of course, Zionist leader Rabbi Stephen S. Wise. The pair were on an intimate "Boss-Steve" basis. Jews of my uncle's generation never questioned the notion that "Roosevelt is with us."

That time would one day uncover Rooseveltian features less than worthy of reverential respect would have startled my Uncle Louis. He didn't read journalist Arthur Morse's pioneering *While Six Million Died: A Chronicle of American Apathy*. As later researchers extracted records long filed and forgotten, or jarred the memories of FDR associates still alive, a picture emerged of a president dedicated to winning the war against Hitler, but not, if at personal political risk, willing to keep European Jews alive to share in the victory celebrations.

Unlike Churchill, whose oratorical skills and terrible temper could goad subordinates along paths he desired only if they were sufficiently impressed or sufficiently cowed, Roosevelt's powers derived from the Constitution. Proclamations and executive orders were also his in time of crisis. And a world in chaos met that standard.

Responsibility in detail for U.S. inaction while millions died can be apportioned to shadowy figures hidden from public view in the old State Department building across the street from the White House. Assistant Secretary Breckinridge Long, refugee specialist Robert Borden Reams, and visa official Robert Alexander certainly earned no laurels. But these underlings could have been ordered by Roosevelt to act.

There are measures that FDR could have pressed before September 1939. Richard Breitman and Alan M. Kraut point out in their detailed study, *American Refugee Policy and European Jewry: 1933–1945* that "even when FDR privately assured Jewish leaders that he would act to ease the suffering of their European brothers," he disassociated himself from proposed measures "that singled out Jewish refugees." The presidential course, directed by "the political winds," employed the State Department's bureaucracy "as a trapdoor through which to drop the nettlesome issue of refugees." To placate activists, Roosevelt called for an international forum on refugees, held at Evian in 1938. It produced a mountain of pious words, nothing more.

Kristallnacht, in November of that year, evoked the expected denunciation from Roosevelt. The U.S. ambassador was recalled, but brought no Jews back with him. To challenge the mix of intolerance flavored by the xenophobia of many countrymen, Roosevelt would have had to take political risks. He was unwilling.

In May 1939, the Hamburg-American liner *St. Louis* departed Germany carrying 743 refugees seeking temporary Cuban asylum while awaiting U.S. visas. Refused permission to land, their plight made headlines worldwide. The ship's captain departed Cuba's waters but delayed return to Hamburg, where passengers likely faced a Gestapo welcome. Instead, he slowly cruised along Florida's coastline while frantic efforts were made to either induce Cuban officials to relent, or U.S. officials to accept refugees directly. Panicked passengers cabled the president. In the absence of emergency legislation overriding stern quota levels—an impossible dream—their last, best hope was an executive order from the Oval Office. Roosevelt left their telegram unanswered.

While the *St. Louis* affair dragged on, an even more protracted struggle approached climax. Back in February, two liberal legislators, New York Democratic senator Robert F. Wagner and Massachusetts Republican congresswoman Edith Nourse Rogers, introduced bills permitting prompt admission of twenty thousand children above Germany's quota. This potential crack in the ossified 1924 Immigration Act aroused strong conservative opposition.

Eleanor Roosevelt publicly aired support at a press conference, but the private views of Laura Delano, the president's first cousin—and wife of his immigration commissioner—were noted by a State Department friend: "Her principal reserve on the bill was that twenty thousand charming children would all too soon grow into twenty thousand ugly adults."

A *Fortune* magazine poll showed public opinion overwhelmingly in accord with Roosevelt's cousin, not his wife, and when the need arose for the president himself to take a stand, he wrote briefly on the paper sent to him by an aide, "File No Action." The bill died.

More would surely be done in the name of humanity, Jews reasoned, once their chief executive found persecution accelerating into mass murder. Or would it? After avoiding direct contact with Jewish groups pressing for action for the first eleven months of 1942, Roosevelt finally responded to Rabbi Stephen Wise's intimate "Dear Boss" appeal.

In *The Abandonment of the Jews* David S. Wyman points out that this December 8, 1942, gathering in the Oval Office was "the only one concerning the Holocaust that FDR ever granted to a group of Jewish leaders." Estimates of two million Jewish dead were given to him. According to Jewish Labor Committee participant Adolph Held's notes, Roosevelt responded by saying that official U.S. sources in Switzerland and elsewhere "have given us proof that confirms the horrors discussed by you."

Clearly, the president knew, but nothing came of the meeting except Roosevelt's permission to issue a press release quoting a statement he had made to a July mass meeting in Madison Square Garden: "We shall do all in our power to be of service to your people in this tragic moment."

Rabbi Wise wrote White House aide David Niles: "We ought to distribute cards throughout the country bearing just four letters, TGFR [Thank God for Roosevelt], and as the psalmist would have said, thank HIM every day and every hour."

Precious months passed. Then growing realization among Jews resulted in a sterner perception of the president's conduct, which prompted Roosevelt to arrange the April 1943 Bermuda Conference. There, in a pleasant, out-of-the-way setting far offshore, without troubling witnesses, British and American delegates discussed rescue measures.

The British had no intention of admitting large numbers of Jews into Palestine, nor the United States into its forty-eight states. Pious words by participants were a sham. Britain's chief delegate later admitted the whole affair was a "facade for inaction."

On July 28, 1943, Jan Karski, a Polish underground officer sent here to give American leaders his firsthand experiences, met face-to-face with Roosevelt in the Oval Office. Karski had actually infiltrated Belzec extermination camp posing as an Estonian guard. He described mass murder, the burning of bodies. Roosevelt's response: "Tell your nation we shall win the war!"

By now, banalities would no longer do.

Under the headline WHAT ABOUT THE JEWS, FDR? journalist Max Lerner warned, "You, Mr. President, must take the lead.... The methods are clear. Neither conscience nor policy can afford to leave them unused. And the time is now."

The newly formed Emergency Committee to Save the Jewish People of Europe had just been formed. It proposed an active agenda: a separate government agency specifically to protect Jews; pressure on Axis satellites to allow emigration; provision of food to Jews in Axis Europe;

and the urging of neutral countries to grant temporary aslyum. Eleanor Roosevelt passed along the committee's recommendations to her husband. He returned them, relates Wyman, with the comment, "I do not think this needs any answer at this time. FDR."

In the fall of 1943 he refused to meet representatives of four hundred Orthodox rabbis who gathered in Washington on a pilgrimage for rescue. "Pressure of other business" barred the possibility, they were told. "In reality," writes Wyman, "the president had a light schedule that day, and most of the afternoon was open."

When Roosevelt finally acted in January 1944, he did not do so out of moral indignation. Since the onset of the New Deal, about 90 percent of American Jewish voters regularly trooped to the polls in support of FDR. But ten months before another quadrennial November came around, Treasury Secretary Morgenthau placed before him a bombshell.

It was prepared by three Protestant subordinates under the title, "Report to the Secretary on the Acquiescence of This Government in the Murder of the Jews." Morgenthau watered down this title to "Personal Report to the President," but not its message. Eight single-spaced pages starkly outlined the State Department's indifference to the fate of European Jewry, its withholding of atrocity information, its direct sabotage of rescue efforts by Jewish agencies. Morgenthau, an old friend and Dutchess County, New York, neighbor of the president as well as a cabinet member, threatened to release the report, exposing FDR to a "nasty scandal" that election year. To induce action, moreover, he was prepared to resign.

Six days later, Roosevelt's Executive Order 9417 created the War Refugee Board, funded by $1 million from federal emergency funds, with private Jewish funding thereafter.

It was too little and far too late. Most of Europe's Jews were already dead, or would be, before its machinery was oiled and cranked up during Hungarian Jewry's ordeal. (Swedish diplomat Raoul Wallenberg was among those individuals whose work was advanced by War Refugee Board funds.)

Roosevelt's wartime conduct *has* defenders. Perhaps the most credible, because of his credentials as a highly respected historian, is Arthur Schlesinger Jr. His February 1994 *Newsweek* column, "Did FDR Betray the Jews?" argues, "The attack on FDR shows a striking disregard of historical context." He points to the tensions of the times, rampant anti-

Semitism, denunciations by right-wingers of FDR's "Jew Deal," and the popularity of Charles Lindbergh's appeals for isolation. Roosevelt, he writes, had to deal with the world "as it was."

Schlesinger contends that the War Refugee Board could have achieved little until Germany's defeat was assured, that the Holocaust became recognized only after "victory opened the death camps," that winning the war was "the only way" to save concentration camp inmates.

To Schlesinger, FDR "more than any other person deserves the credit for mobilizing the forces that destroyed Nazi barbarism." From the perspective of free men struggling to remain free, true—but not from the perspective of a trapped European Jewry. Hitler simultaneously fought *two* wars, the second to annihilate unarmed Jews from the Bay of Biscay to the Ukraine. Roosevelt only fought *one*, against the armed forces of Axis dictators.

Looking back, Congressman Emmanuel Celler saw a Roosevelt who, instead of providing "some spark of courageous leadership," had been "silent, indifferent, and insensitive to the plight of the Jews."

PIUS XII (Eugenio Pacelli), 1876–1958
Pope, 1939–1958

History's Conventional View

Pius XII stands at a balcony of the papal apartments, a reverent crowd numbering hundreds of thousands in St. Peter's Square straining for a view. Through rimless spectacles, his gaze fastens upward on the heavens. He stretches his arms, as if to embrace all humanity. Witnessing this scene, Peter Hebblewaithe, a scholar and former Jesuit, thought he "seemed to embody the very essence of the papacy as it was then conceived."

The year was 1950. Although World War II was five years distant, the cold war swept over still war-ravaged Europe. Eugenio Pacelli, pope since 1939, had guided the Holy See safely through six hellish years, its physical plant—Vatican City—untouched by violence.

Trained as a diplomat, Papal Nuncio at Berlin from 1920 through 1929, cardinal secretary of state from 1930 until his election on the death of Pius XI, he now committed his "divisions," as Stalin would have described them, in a duel with the Communist threat from the East. If popes may be justly classified as political or pastoral, Pius XII fell more readily into the former niche. In a pronouncement on June 30, 1949, he had excommunicated all those who "knowingly and with full consent defend the materialistic doctrines of communism," and, as well, those who collaborated in establishing Communist regimes "in any way." The pope spiritedly thrust his Church into the conflict for men's minds, hearts—and parliaments.

Was Pius XII a strong pope, ready to do the Lord's work battling forces of evil loose in the twentieth-century world?

But From a Jewish Perspective

The first six tragically silent years of Eugenio Pacelli's pontificate, 1939 to 1945, not the combative decade thereafter, mark the historical place of this successor to St. Peter.

Soon after World War II, the Holy See's official observer at the International Refugee Organization recalled that "His Holiness Pius XII gave asylum within Vatican City to three thousand people who were not of his faith during the occupation of Rome by an enemy power." Praise must be muted, however, when one considers a more cosmic number— six million dead. Hence, the sorrowful question Jews ask: "What did the papal father do during the war?"

Disinclined to rattle interfaith relations, Jews tiptoed around this question, emphasizing, instead, positive anecdotal stories of Jews hidden on Vatican grounds. But in 1963, a German playwright, Rolf Hochhuth, turned up the volume in his controversial play *The Deputy*. It depicted the wartime pope as a man of "aristocratic coolness," practitioner of a detached statecraft that allowed him to accept impassively the massacre of millions of Jews. Then came a flurry of questions, some yielding to diligent labor in available archives, some not. What did the pope know about the developing Holocaust? When did he know it? On learning its scope, why did he then remain silent?

Even before Hitler set Europe ablaze, there was much worth saying by "the Vicar of Christ." His predecessor, Pius XI, had already issued an anti-Nazi encyclical following Germany's racist legislation and had told visiting Belgian pilgrims, "In spirit, we are all Semites." He publicly condemned Mussolini's copycat laws as a "disgraceful imitation" of Hitler's "Nordic mythology." And he was reportedly planning further denunciations when he died suddenly, on Feburary 10, 1939.

Pius XII, by contrast, was a cool-headed diplomat, cautious, legalistic, and discreet in expression. He assured the Italian foreign minister, Galeazzo Ciano, he intended to follow a "more conciliatory policy."

How early in the European conflict did news of Reich-authorized mass murder reach Pius XII? The Holy See's intelligence-gathering network was as professionally astute and more widespread than any warring power's. Nunciatures and apolostolic delegations reported to Rome from all corners of Europe. Before long, many priests, nuns, monsignors, and even high church dignitaries in occupied countries were risking their personal safety to help Jews. The shocking scenes they witnessed were surely related to papal envoys. So, in March 1942, as anguished appeals for help were placed before Pius XII from Jews via the British minister, Sir Francis D'Arcy Osborne, and President Roosevelt's personal representative to the Holy See, Myron Taylor, comparable accounts of horror had already reached him from the Vatican's own listening posts.

An Italian priest traveling in Poland wrote his pontiff on May 12, 1942, that the slaughter of Ukranian Jews was now accomplished, and the same solution was "equally desired" by Nazi authorities for Polish Jewry. By July, further reports were flowing to Rome of massacres in Lvov, Vilna, and other Jewish centers. In August 1942, SS Lieutenant Colonel Kurt Gerstein, perhaps conscience-stricken, more likely a sincere anti-Nazi, walked into the Holy See's Berlin office and described what he had seen at the Belzec extermination camp.

On September 25, 1942, Taylor pressed Cardinal Luigi Maglione, papal secretary of state, to have the pope speak out regarding "inhumane treatment of refugees and hostages, especially of the Jews." Two weeks later the Holy See replied in an informal, unsigned note, "up to the present time, it has not been possible to verify the accuracy of reports reaching St. Peter's about severe measures taken against non-Aryans."

In his Christmas 1942 broadcast, Pius XII offered a generic condemnation of crimes against civilian populations, citing no specifics. Carefully crafted in diplomatically vague language, it made no mention of Jews. Afterward, Cardinal Maglione told the British minister, "You see that the Holy Father took account of your government's recommendation." Sir D'Arcy Osborne replied that condemnation of atrocities which could equally apply to the bombing of German cities in no way corresponded to what the British government requested.

Harold Tittmann, Taylor's assistant, cabled Washington after his own audience with Pius XII that the pope thought he "expressed himself with enough clarity" concerning German crimes. "And he seemed surprised when I told him that not everyone thought the same." According to Tittmann, the pope said he could not directly condemn Nazi killings without condemning Bolshevik conduct in the East as well.

On October 16, 1943, less than a month after Denmark's small Jewish population escaped Nazi predators, the SS launched its massive Jewish "action" in Rome. Earlier, the German ambassador, Baron Ernst von Weizsäcker, had given assurances that Vatican City's extraterritoriality would be respected. To his credit, Pius XII personally ordered the opening of the Vatican grounds and similarly protected church enclaves around the city to Jews seeking refuge. Meir Michaelis, author of perhaps the most thorough studies of this period in Italian Jewish history, came up with figures of 477 sheltered within Vatican walls and another 4,238 in Rome's monasteries and convents.

Weizsäcker wired Berlin: "The Curia is particularly upset because the action took place, in a manner of speaking, under the Pope's own windows." He warned "the people hostile to us in Rome are using this affair as a means of forcing the Vatican from its reserve. People say that when similar incidents took place in French cities, the bishops there took a firm stand. The pope, as supreme head of the Church and Bishop of Rome, cannot be more reticent than they."

But no such burst of outrage came. On October 28, a relieved Weizsäcker wired the Wilhelmstrasse: "Although under pressure from all sides, the pope has not allowed himself to be drawn into any demonstrative censure of the deportation of the Jews of Rome." Only later in 1944, in the case of Budapest's threatened Jewry, did Pius XII speak out loudly and clearly. By then Rome was safely in Allied hands, the outcome of the war assured.

Explanations abound for the pope's silence during more perilous junctions in the war. After continental Europe fell within Hitler's grasp, fears for the very survival of the Church in a German-dominated Old World was reason enough, some argue, for caution. Even well into the war, the Holy See saw risks in alienating greater Germany's own forty-five million Roman Catholics. Given the choice between Church and State, they might have chosen the Third Reich.

The pope's personal courage is unquestioned, but concern for the dangers facing Vatican City's 1,087 acres, with its priceless Michelangelo sculptures, Raphael paintings, and Bernini architecture may have weighed on his mind. Elsewhere, vengeful Nazis in retreat destroyed landmarks of culture. Hitler himself had ordered demolition of treasured monuments in Paris, one of those rare Fuehrer directives *not* carried out: Paris fell too quickly. Would he have hesitated to make a similar demand of his commander south of the Alps, Field Marshal Kesselring?

After first lauding the Church's courageous stand against Nazi euthanasia of the insane, Gideon Hausner, chief prosecutor at Adolf Eichmann's 1961 trial, later wrote, "We can only speculate heartbreakingly how many Jewish lives could have been saved by a similar stand on the part of Rome through an encyclical expressly forbidding Catholics to murder the innocent Jews."

Hausner was wistfully assaying "could have beens." But a towering Church figure—Pius XII's contemporary and, moreover, a close adviser—raised this matter at a "could yet be" point in time. In mid-1940, as Nazi systematized brutality quickened, French Cardinal Eugen Tisserant wrote a fellow cardinal in Paris of his futile urgings that the pope issue an encyclical on "the individual duty to obey the imperatives of conscience" in conflict with criminal orders. Tisserant despaired, "I'm afraid that history may be obliged in time to blame the Holy See for a policy accommodated to its own advantage and little more."

7

Toward Those Broad Sunlit Uplands—
With Thunderclaps Overhead and
Firefights Along the Journey

The more than five decades that have passed since the Holocaust offer a fresh litmus test for judging, from a Jewish perspective, the great and not-so-great leaders of the free and not-so-free worlds. Five chapters and a millennium back, our criterion could be simplicity itself: Did they kill or expel their own Jews or let them eke by, miserably perhaps, but at least safe from bodily harm? More recent chapters showed how monarchs and statesmen behaved within their kingdoms and republics, but also how they reacted to persecution abroad. (King George III's grandfather, George II, perhaps set a precedent by telling Austria's Maria Theresa what he thought of her expulsion of Vienna's Jews.)

Here we may use a new measuring rod, scarcely imaginable before Herzl's time, but a reality in our own: Israel. How did British, American, Russian, and French statesmen view the Jewish state? Did presidents, prime ministers, and premiers help or hurt during its fetal stage, its birth, childhood, adolescence, and now, maturity? We also look at other men of power and influence—Pope John XXIII, Egypt's Anwar Sadat, India's Mohandas Gandhi and Jawaharlal Nehru, and China's Mao Tse-tung and Chou En-lai.

CLEMENT ATTLEE, 1883–1967
Prime Minister, 1945–1951

ERNEST BEVIN, 1881–1951
Foreign Secretary, 1945–1951

History's Conventional View

The America of July 1945 saw the British prime minister, Clement Attlee, as that nondescript, baldheaded little man chosen by an ungrateful electorate to replace Winston Churchill, arguably the man of the century. Incredibly, the British people removed Churchill from office within weeks of V-E day. Attlee is recalled for guiding his financially exhausted country through postwar austerity, drawing it toward state socialism. With Attlee's Labour government came national health insurance and nationalized railroads, steel mills, coal mines, and civil aviation. Lacking his rival's oratorical skills, he got his message across with a simple slogan, You Can Trust Mr. Attlee.

Britain's homefront transformation took place during a six-year ministry that saw, at the international level, dissolution of the British Empire. Control of Egyptian affairs ceased, the Union Jack was lowered over the Indian subcontinent, and Burma and Ceylon received independence. But Palestine festered on and on.

Unlike his outwardly calm, well-educated Labour colleague Ernest Bevin, England's foreign secretary, rose from working-class origins to lead the Transport and General Workers Union, the largest trade union in the world. In Churchill's wartime coalition he served as labour minister; in Attlee's Labour government, as foreign secretary. Huge of frame, gruff of speech to the point of coarseness, he approached the great issues of the day with self-confident rigidity and a bullying frame of mind. "Ernie" Bevin usually got his way. For his cold war–era performance, historians generally give him high marks. Yet they cite one outstanding blemish– Palestine.

But From a Jewish Perspective

Despite Churchill's personal pro-Zionist stand, Jewish Agency leaders in Palestine, many fellow socialists, welcomed Labour's 1945 victory. The Conservative authors of the restrictive White Paper were out: friendlier Labourites were in. Better times seemed ahead.

Back in the spring of 1944, Labour's party conference, under Attlee's stewardship, had announced, "Let the Arabs be encouraged to move out as the Jews move in." They remembered the new foreign minister as an unambiguously pro-Zionist union chief in the 1930s. But that was then. After taking office, Bevin denied that his party had ever "promised a Jewish state." Moreover, "If ever it was done, it was done in the enthusiasm of a Labour Party Conference."

Of immediate concern was the fate of Holocaust survivors still unable to escape Europe. When Attlee moved into 10 Downing Street in July 1945, a memorandum already awaited him from President Harry Truman expressing the hope that Britain's government "may find it possible without delay to take steps to lift the restrictions of the White Paper on Jewish immigration to Palestine."

The prime minister's response was noncommittal. One hundred thousand Jewish refugees languished in camps as Truman pressed on. Attlee now received a report from the President's representative, who wrote of "despairing" survivors. "It is nothing short of calamitous to contemplate that the gates of Palestine should soon be closed." Amazingly, Attlee answered, "there appears to have been very little difference in the amount of torture and treatment they (the Jews) had to undergo" distinguishing them from other races in Europe. He refused to place Jews "in a special racial category at the head of the queue."

Already simmering, Palestine erupted. Irgun and Stern Gang members targeted British military installations and police posts. But Jewish Agency leaders still hoped Attlee and Bevin could be made to see reason. Chaim Weizmann met the foreign secretary, as he had so many other British statesmen at decisive points in the struggle for a Jewish homeland. "Are you trying to force my hand," Bevin snapped. "If you want a fight, you can have it!" The matter of admitting one hundred thousand refugees was closed.

The dignified Weizmann found Bevin's manner "overbearing, quarrelsome." The more pugnacious David Ben-Gurion regarded Bevin "treacherous and insensitive." The foreign minister wanted no more Jews in Palestine, nor any clustered in Britain, for that matter. During a cabinet debate regarding admission of a small number to the United Kingdom, he proposed that such refugees be trained in agriculture in order to spread them more "widely," thus discouraging a search for "openings in commerce." His coarse sense of humor allowed plays on the words *prophet* and *profit* while describing Jews. He mirrored Attlee's phraseology in the note to Truman about preventing them from getting "too much at the head of the queue."

Even Christopher Mayhew, a Bevin supporter, was moved to note in his diary, "There is no doubt to my mind that Ernest detests Jews. He makes the odd wisecrack about the 'chosen people,' explains Shinwell [Emmanuel Shinwell, a Labour cabinet minister] away as a Jew, declares the Old Testament is the most immoral book ever written....He says they [the Jews] taught Hitler the technique of terror and were even now paralleling the Nazis in Palestine."

At every step from 1945 through 1948, Bevin, with his superior's acquiescence, exposed implacable hostility to a Jewish homeland.

Consider Bevin's own November 1945 proposal for an Anglo-American Committee of Inquiry to devise resettlement options for Jews held in Europe's displacement camps. When it recommended, the following April, "one hundred certificates to be authorized immediately for the admission into Palestine of Jews who have been the victims of Nazi and Fascist persecution," the foreign secretary and prime minister flatly said no. Bevin later told a Labour party conference in Bournemouth that Americans were pressing the Palestine plan because they "did not want too many of them in New York."

Violence escalated in the Holy Land. The British retaliated by arresting three thousand Jews, including most of the senior officials of the Jewish Agency. Widespread searches for hidden Jewish arms produced even more arrests, but did not stop sabotage.

The Labour government now devised a ploy. Bevin proposed the British cabinet submit "the problem to the judgment of the United Nations." Behind this too-clever move, February 1947 was not hope for UN success, but expectation of UN failure—after which the international body would turn Palestine back to Attlee and Bevin, this time minus the strings attached to their old World War I mandate. Experts in Britain's Foreign Office were convinced a two-thirds majority could never be mustered to partition Palestine and create a Jewish state. They were wrong.

A United Nations Special Committee on Palestine diligently set about its work. Members followed the two-month ordeal of 4,500 former concentration camp inmates who arrived "illegally" from a French port aboard a converted river steamer renamed *Exodus*. Following resistance to a British boarding party (three Jews were killed, twenty-eight seriously wounded), men, women, and children were dragged off at Haifa harbor under the eyes of UN observers.

Bevin ordered these refugees loaded on British ships for return to France. French officials, however, were willing to grant asylum to those requesting it but would not disembark anyone under compulsion. So most passengers decided to stay on deck.

Bevin demanded the authorities to take them off. The French adamantly refused. Worldwide criticism descended on Whitehall. Increasingly bullheaded to the end, Bevin eventually ordered the Jews be taken to a displaced persons camp near Lübeck in Germany's British zone. He regarded detention facilities on Cyprus too close to Palestine.

When the UN eventually voted partition and a Jewish state came into existence, Bevin could partially have atoned for past behavior by accepting the embattled infant into the family of nations. On expiration of Britain's mandate, the United States immediately granted the State of Israel de facto recognition. The Soviet Union, playing one-upmanship, granted de jure recognition three days later. Bevin sulked and stalled.

Finally, in a House of Commons debate of January 1949, writes Irish statesman and author Conor Cruise O'Brien, "Bevin's Middle Eastern policy was effectively interred." Israel's own most eloquent voice, Abba Eban, described the scene as Winston Churchill "rose to his highest flights of oratory, leaving Bevin gasping for breath in the throes of parliamentary defeat." Churchill growled: "I am sure that the right honorable gentleman [Bevin] will have to recognize the Israeli government and this cannot be long delayed. I regret he has not had the manliness to tell us that tonight and that he preferred to retire under a cloud of inky water, like a cuttlefish, to some obscure retreat."

The long delay was due, he added, "not only to mental inertia or lack of grip on the part of the ministers concerned, but also, I am afraid, to the very strong and direct streak of bias and prejudice on the part of the foreign secretary."

On January 29, 1949, Bevin summoned Israel's unofficial representative in London to the Foreign Office and informed him of Britain's decision to accord Israel de facto recognition.

HARRY C. TRUMAN, 1885–1973
President, 1945–1953

History's Conventional View

Pick a point in time. When Harry Truman left office in January 1953, history's overnight verdict was severe. The Korean War—or "police action"—had dragged on interminably. President Truman had fired America's second most popular military figure, Douglas MacArthur. The first, Dwight Eisenhower, had just been elected his successor, partly on a messianic pledge to "go to Korea," partly on a promise to clean up "the mess" in Washington and get rid of those "too big for their britches, too small for their jobs, too long in office."

That was January 1953. Time has given history opportunity to reevaluate the uncommon common man from Independence, heir to FDR, and he has looked better and better as each administration since fades into our collective past.

Truman was gritty and gutsy. From his desk came decisions to stop Soviet expansion after World War II. The cold war would never have been won in the 1980s if Truman conceded it in the 1940s. Point Four, the Marshall Plan, the North Atlantic Treaty, and the movement of troops to halt Communist aggression past Korea's thirty-eighth parallel all bore his imprint.

Truman could be testy, lacking in tact, and mulish on occasion, but when contemporary national leaders hem and haw, old-timers may wistfully say, "If Truman was in the White House today..."

But From a Jewish Perspective

Some of Franklin D. Roosevelt's "best friends" were Jews. Only one of newly sworn President Harry Truman's was—his ex-partner in a failed Kansas City haberdashery. But when the critical moment for Jewish fortune came, that one would be enough.

Already, on taking office, Truman had appealed to Britain's Attlee to allow one hundred thousand Jewish survivors into Palestine. "Everyone else who's been dragged from his country has someplace to go back to," adviser Clark Clifford recalls his boss saying, "but the Jews have no place to go." Another aide, David Niles, a carryover from FDR's administration and a Jew, said he sensed in Truman a sympathy for Jewish suffering lacking in Roosevelt's makeup.

After mid-1945, the intense campaign for a Jewish homeland would wind along a tricky path, filled with back-office intrigues, super-charged pressure, threatened friendships, and allegations of political intrusions into statecraft. Truman would be at its center, and no other individual—not Attlee, not Bevin—would have greater impact than this "accidental" president.

The most immovable object he overcame—apart from the British Foreign Office—was his own State Department. FDR had assigned Jewish refugee matters to its bureaucracy and European Jewry was nearly wiped out before he was prodded to set up the War Refugee Board. State Department Near East specialists—all pro-Arab and pro-oil—opposed Jewish aspirations.

They found a natural ally at the Pentagon. The chiefs of staff said one hundred thousand American troops would be needed to protect any Jewish entity once the British pulled out their fifty thousand men. Defense Secretary James Forrestal warned partition meant that the Arabs would "push the Jews into the sea." While gloomy estimates by "striped pants" and uniformed circles reached Truman, he was buffeted by those who saw him as the instrument of delivery from Attlee and Bevin. David McCullough, author of the most meticulously woven tapestry of Truman's life, writes that he "found the mounting pressures on him by Jewish organizations extremely vexing. A good listener, he had been listening to their pleas and arguments since his earliest days in of-fice...and he had become not just worn down by it all but increasingly suspicious, increasingly resentful."

In late 1947, a deluge of one hundred thousand letters and telegrams reached his desk, and he saw striking a match to them a plausible option. At a cabinet meeting he reportedly snapped, "Jesus Christ couldn't please them when he was on earth, so how could anyone expect that I would have any luck."

But Truman intended to do the right thing, and after an Oval Office conversation with Chaim Weizmann, he decided that partition with the Negev going to the new Jewish state *was* the right thing. As the United States voted, so did a large, though not necessarily decisive, bloc in the United Nations.

The UN victory did not end Jewish pressure on the White House. In his memoirs, Truman wrote of groups and individuals asking him "usually in rather quarrelsome and emotional ways, to stop the Arabs, to keep the British from supplying the Arabs, to furnish American soldiers, to do this, that, and the other. I think I can say that I kept the faith in the rightness of my policy in spite of some of the Jews." At some point, pressure reached critical mass, and he turned Missouri mule. Early in 1948, he refused—absolutely, without exceptions—to be approached by "spokesmen for the extreme Zionist cause." This seemed odd behavior for a politician being accused by Republicans of pandering to Jewish voters as the year's presidential election campaign got under way. But Truman was Truman.

In England, Chaim Weizmann received an urgent telegram from Abba Eban to come to the United States. Eban told Weizmann he was the one hope for contact with the president. At their earlier meeting, Truman had clearly been impressed by Zionism's elder statesman. This time around, even Weizmann could not get through. No recognized Jewish spokesman got near Truman. Enter Eddie Jacobson, an unrecognized one. At the urging of a B'nai B'rith official, he flew to Washington and, on March 13, 1948, the Kansas City haberdasher walked into the White House unannounced.

Despite warnings not to touch on Palestine, Jacobson pleaded with his old friend to see Weizmann. Success did not come easily, but it came. "You win, you baldheaded son of a bitch," said Truman, "I will see him. Tell Matt [Matt Connelly, his appointments secretary] to arrange the meeting as soon as possible."

Truman and Weizmann conversed five days later in complete secrecy. State Department officials—"the striped pants boys"—were not told of the president's continued commitment to partition, a subject under renewed debate, this time at the UN Security Council. The following day Representative Warren Austin, acting under State Department instructions, backed off from partition and spoke in favor of a UN trusteeship.

Zionists called this Black Friday. Truman was furious. He believed Weizmann would surely consider him "a plain liar," according to one biographer, "a shit ass," according to another. Privately, through Eddie Jacobson, he assured Weizmann there was no change in his policy. Later, Truman sent special counsel Samuel Rosenman to reaffirm to the Zionist leader that he had not reneged and would immediately grant recognition following formation of the yet unannounced Jewish state. "I have Dr. Weizmann on my conscience," he told Rosenman.

Truman proved good as his word, even at considerable political risk.

In a tense White House showdown, according to Clark Clifford, who was present, Secretary of State George Marshall said, "They don't deserve a state, they have stolen that country. If you give this recognition, Mr. President, I may not vote for you in the next election."

General of the Army George Marshall was a formidable figure in Washington, more respected than his chief. His resignation would have torn the administration apart. But Truman stood his ground.

At midnight, Jerusalem time, May 14, 1948, 6:00 P.M. Washington time, Israel came into existence. Eleven minutes later, as promised, came President Truman's de facto recognition.

Some time later, the Israeli chief rabbi, Isaac Halevi Herzog called on Truman at the White House. "God put you in your mother's womb so you would be the instrument to bring the rebirth of Israel after two thousand years," he said. A bit overdone, thought David Niles as he looked on. But he noticed tears on Truman's cheeks.

JOSEPH STALIN, 1879–1953
Soviet Chairman, 1924–1953

History's Conventional View

"Genghis Khan with a telephone," is the way one American wit described Stalin from a reasonably safe distance.

Well before the Russian people—officially, at least—learned what a monster "That Man" in the Kremlin really was, the free world had already guessed. During the 1930s, forced collectivization of agriculture and industrialization, regardless of human cost, led to the deaths of millions.

The "Great Purges" wiped the slate of Old Bolsheviks nearly clean. Stalin's conspiratorial mind easily conjured up specters of cabals forming and reforming against him. His favored method of freeing his mind: kill off anyone proven, unproven, or even remotely visualized as a threat. Show trials at which the accused confessed their crimes against the state allowed spin-doctoring within Soviet borders, but not outside, except for the truly gullible. For a four-year spell, though, the Western public was fed a kinder, gentler, pipe-smoking statesman, sane and sagacious. From 1941 through 1945 he was "Uncle Joe," the Soviet entry at Big Three summits. Symbolic of Russian steadfast resistance to Nazi aggression, he made the cover of *Life*.

Reversal to form came with the cold war. When an "iron curtain" descended over Eastern Europe, he handled the levers backstage. When North Korean troops poured over the thirty-eighth parallel, he had given his nod. On home grounds, the grip of an already formidable police state was further tightened. New purges beckoned when, fortunately for targeted subordinates and the rest of humanity, Stalin passed into history in March 1953.

At the Soviet Twentieth Party Congress in February 1956, Nikita Khrushchev (soon upcoming) laid bare Stalin's crimes in a secret seven-hour speech. Before 1,436 Communist elite, he portrayed a reign dripping in blood, operating by terror, mass arrests, and torture. Robert Conquest's *The Great Terror* estimated twenty million dead as "the debit balance of the Stalin regime."

But From a Jewish Perspective

Thirty-eight-year-old Joseph Vissarionovich Dzhugashvili, who had adopted the name Stalin (man of steel) in establishing his Bolshevik persona, was the new Soviet Union's first commissar of nationalities in 1917, briskly promoting Yiddish cultural and educational activities, including a Moscow theater. On the whole, Jews were all right, officially. Only Bundists, religious activists, cosmopolitians, secessionists, and Zionists were bad.

On a more personal level, the *Jewish Encyclopedia* notes, he disapproved of his elder son's marriage to a Jewess and ended his daughter's romance with a Jewish film director by sending him to a labor camp. Young Svetlana learned from her father that the present generation of Soviet Jews, contaminated by Zionism, was passing it along to the next generation. His feelings evolved over the years, she would later write, "from political hatred to racial aversion for all Jews." Early on, given his views, Jews would have disappeared from Moscow and its environs and materialized in an "autonomous" region in remote Siberia. Despite heavy promotion, the ambitious Birobidzhan project petered out.

During the Great Terror, Stalin liquidated the Yiddish schools, publications, and research institutions he had founded a decade earlier. But the party's Jewish purge victims—the Zinovievs, Kamenevs, and Radeks—were denounced as Western imperialist agents, not specifically as Jews. As late as November 1936, Stalin authorized *Pravda* to print comments he made in an interview five years earlier that anti-Semitism was "the most dangerous vestige of cannibalism."

Rapprochement with Hitler after the Ribbentrop-Molotov Pact, in August 1939, led Stalin to repress news of Nazi persecutions in Poland. Jews saw no hint in Pravada or Izvestia of the ferocity soon unleashed at them. For his part, Hitler justified the pact in a message to Mussolini describing Stalin as a Russian nationalist who had rid the Soviet system of its "Jewish and Marxist" character. Foreign Minister Ribbentrop also cited Stalin's positive side: "With the removal of Litvinov [Foreign Affairs Commissar Maxim Litvinov], all the Jews have left controlling positions."

Once the Nazi invasion of June 1941 imperilled Russia, Stalin saw value in a Jewish Anti-Fascist Committee designed to win friends abroad. Emissaries were sent to visit Jewish communities in the United States and Canada and establish useful contacts in winning aid. The committee unfortunately exceeded its mandate as a docile instrument of the state. After the war, it recommended settling large numbers of returning Jewish evacuees in the Crimea. Stalin regarded this step as an act toward Zionist separatism, an opening wedge for American imperialism. Yiddish actor and director Solomon M. Mikhoels, committee chairman and de facto head of Soviet Jewry, was murdered—then buried with honors.

A pause in the downward spiral of Stalin's place in Jewish history brightened 1948, and we must give the tyrant his due. It came in May. Stalin immediately recognized the new State of Israel. With his approval, weapons from the arms factories of Czechoslovakia flowed to the infant state, but this stellar event betokened no long-term glow. It was a blow at British Middle Eastern hegemony.

Establishment of the Jewish state, if anything, accelerated his anti-Semitic policy at home. The enthusiastic welcome given Ambassador Golda Meyerson (later Meir) by Moscow's Jews reinforced his suspicion that Jews were likely agents of Zionism and capitalism. Golda Meir wrote in her memoirs, "The fact remained that Russian Jewry had shown far too great an interest in Israel and the Israelis to please the Kremlin. Within five months there was practically no single Jewish organization left in Russia, and the Jews kept their distance from us."

The Soviet dictator's obsession with Jewish-orchestrated conspiracies spilled over the Soviet Union's own borders. On his order, Czechoslovakia's Communist leadership underwent a 1952 purge. The Slansky Trial, named after chief defendant Rudolph Slansky, the party general secretary, sought to establish links between Jews, Zionism, the American CIA, and Britain's M-16.

Back home, the "Doctors' Plot" presaged greater momentum for state-directed anti-Semitism. Nine prominent physicians, including six Jews, were accused of causing the death of two party figures. The net spread to other M.D.s, presumed agents of U.S. Jewish organizations bent on medical murder. Their alleged aim: to "wipe out the leading cadres of the USSR."

High-profile Jews were induced (it takes little imagination to figure out how) to draft a letter urging Stalin to resolve matters by resettling Jews in the Far East. Release of the letter, slated for the summer of 1953, would come in the wake of "spontaneous" anti-Semitic riots certain to follow the equally assured public hanging of those unfortunate physicians in Red Square.

Stalin's own demise in March intervened; the grandiose scheme promptly collapsed. Barracks built in Siberia to house Jews, who, of course, were expected to thank Stalin profusely for rescuing them from their violent fellow citizens, went unoccupied.

There really *was* a difference between Genghis Khan and Joseph Stalin. Genghis Khan was not bad for Jews.

DWIGHT D. EISENHOWER, 1890–1969
President, 1953–1961

History's Conventional View

When war clouds gathered in Europe in 1939, Eisenhower was an unknown soldier, General MacArthur's aide in peacetime Manila. After America's entry into the conflict, North Africa's "Torch," Sicily's "Husky," and Normandy's "Overlord" would earn him five stars and etch his name in history. The White House could have been his in 1948; he chose to take it in 1952, coda to a meteoric military career.

Liberal critics found his domestic program of "progressive moderation" a bit dull, his cabinet of "eight millionaires and a plumber" heavily tilted toward big business. Periodic questioning of historians typically found Eisenhower rated below more activist chief executives. But for the public, "I like Ike" held true before, during, and after his eight-year administration. John F. Kennedy might have remained a popular Massachusetts senator if the Twenty-Second Amendment to the Constitution hadn't banned third-term presidencies.

But From a Jewish Perspective

Manila's astute Jews apparently gauged staff officer Eisenhower's leadership potential before his War Department superiors back in Washington. "An unusual offer was made to me," he reminisced in *At Ease*. Several friends offered him a job at $60,000 per year plus expenses to make a circuit across China, the East Indies, and Southeast Asia seeking refuge for European Jews. "But... I had become so committed to my profession that I declined."

When Jews next had cause to approach Eisenhower on refugees, he was commander of U.S. forces in occupied Germany. He agreed to allow Polish Jews fearful of returning to their anti-Semitic homeland to enter American sector displaced persons camps. Earlier, he had ordered German civilians from a town near a concentration camp to walk through it.

But Eisenhower, the president, not Eisenhower, the general, made a lasting impact on Jews. Halfway through his two-term tenure, the widest slash by any American presidency rent the relationship between the United States and the State of Israel.

For Israel in 1956, war with Egypt looked more and more inevitable. Gamal Nasser was bent on destroying the Jewish state, assuring his leadership of the Arab world. As a $200 million stream of weapons began pouring into Cairo's arsenal from Soviet satellite Czechoslovakia—120 MiGs, 50 jet bombers, 200 modern tanks, 150 artillery pieces, 2 destroyers, 2 submarines, and huge quantities of small arms—Israeli prime minister Ben-Gurion considered a preemptive strike before those arms could be "absorbed and digested."

Eisenhower, steering a balanced course between the threatening and the threatened, refused to sell Israel matching military hardware. He told the French premier, Guy Mollet, it was illogical to sell Israel arms, for 1,700,000 Jews could not possibly defend themselves against forty million Arabs. Mollet went ahead with the sales anyway. These arms enabled Israel to "meet the quality, if not the scale, of Egypt's Soviet weapons," in Chief of Staff Moshe Dayan's words.

For Eisenhower, the interests of Israel, with its "very strong position in the heart and emotions of the Western world" had to be weighed against a less passionate concern—black gold. "The oil of the Arab world has grown increasingly important to all of Europe," and if European economies collapsed, the effect on the United States "could scarcely be exaggerated."

In July 1956, Eisenhower and Secretary of State John Foster Dulles (his ever-hovering gray eminence) called off plans to finance Nasser's Aswan Dam construction project: He had been getting too friendly with the Soviet bloc. Nasser promptly seized the Suez Canal, British troops having departed, and announced its revenues would henceforth defray the cost of the Nile river's dam. By confronting the Western powers, he gained credence as the Arab world's superstar.

Britain's new prime minister, Anthony Eden, decided Nasser must go, or at least be soundly punished. France's Mollet agreed, for the Egyptian dictator was stirring up trouble in France's North African possessions. Israel held the key to their crackdown. If Jewish forces charged across the bleak Sinai peninsula and neared the international waterway, they could move in to "protect" the canal and separate the combatants.

For its part, Israel feared Egypt's growing war machine, as well as Nasser-inspired Fedayeen guerrilla infiltration from Gaza. Even more provocatively, he closed the Tiran Straits, a narrow passage leading to the Gulf of Aqaba and the Israeli port of Eilat.

Ben-Gurion knew a preemptive attack, justified by Nasser's illegal blockade, would arouse worldwide scorn. He was not pleased "to mount the rostrum of shame so that Britain and France would lave their hands in the waters of purity." War better now than later.

The trio expected Eisenhower, in America's own interest, would look on approvingly, or, failing that, at least benignly. A Nasserless Egypt was a Sovietless Egypt, and, quite logicially, the whole free world would be better off. But Eisenhower did not stand aside: "Foster, you tell 'em, goddamn it, we're going to do everything that there is so we can stop this thing." Donald Neff's *Warriors at Suez* quotes *New York Times* Washington correspondent James Reston's description of Eisenhower's temper: "The White House cracked with barrack room language the like of which had not been heard since the days of General Grant."

From a Jewish perspective (as well as France's and Britain's), Eisenhower's reaction defied logic. It pitted the United States and the Soviet Union (then in the process of crushing Hungary's revolution) against three proven allies for the sake of an anti-Western Egyptian dictator. As Eisenhower himself put it, "We went to town right away and began to give them hell."

Britain's Eden and France's Mollet caved in and withdrew from Egyptian soil. Ben-Gurion, with the Jewish state's future security at stake, held his ground against demands that he return the Sinai to Nasser.

In February 1957, Eisenhower sent a stiff note to the prime minister. Dulles told a Republican senator that an Israeli pullback to its own frontier was a must "to maintain the American position among the Arabs."

Eisenhower's next message contained an ultimatum: withdraw from Sinai or face a cutoff of all financial and technical aid and grain shipments, a delay in a previously approved Export-Import Bank loan, an end to all military assistance, and cancellation of export licenses for munitions shipments. Moreover, the president ordered his treasury secretary to draft changes in U.S. tax law so donors to the United Jewish Appeal and other charitable organizations would receive no deductions for funds benefitting Israel. Ben-Gurion was forced to give in.

Eisenhower wrote Ben-Gurion, "I know that this decision was not an easy one. I believe, however, that Israel will have no cause to regret having conformed to the strong sentiment of the world community." But the long-range effects: Soviet arms shipments were stepped up to Egypt, and also Moscow-friendly Syria. His confidence restored, Nasser prepared for the resumption of war, this time with overwhelming weapons superiority. When it came, Eisenhower was out of office and played no role as it unfolded.

Nikita S. Khrushchev, 1894–1971
First Secretary of the Communist Party, 1953–1964
and His Successors

History's Conventional View

A crude, roly-poly peasant pounding his shoe against a desk top at the United Nations General Assembly to signal his displeasure at the goings-on. This memorable image is part of Khrushchev's legacy, especially in America, but there was more substance to the man. He dominated Russia for a decade. His successor, Leonid Brezhnev, ruled nearly twice that time span, but it is the volatile Khrushchev, not the plodding Brezhnev, whose historical niche is the more sharply defined.

On Stalin's demise, Khrushchev ranked no higher than fifth in the Kremlin pecking order. He soon reached the hierarchical peak, pushing less clever associates to the background. Later he would add the title of premier to this posts, merely confirming that he ran Russia's government as well as its Communist party.

Khrushchev advanced Soviet military might, brought the Warsaw Pact into existence, put down the Hungarian Revolution, nourished Cuba as a Soviet outpost in the New World, and meddled in the Middle East. "We will bury you!" he once exclaimed to Western reporters, and some in the free world thought he meant it militarily, not economically. But in the end, it was the Soviet economy that did Khrushchev in, particularly a disastrous 1963 harvest. His ouster by comrades led to a permanent downsized status as state pensioner, unworthy of lengthy accolades in the Soviet encyclopedia.

But From a Jewish Perspective

Pensioner Khrushchev, in secretly recorded tapes, remembered Stalin as a "dyed-in-the-wool anti-Semite" while conceding no such flaw in his own makeup. As a Communist leader, he could deny anti-Semitism's existence in post-Stalinist Russia, then, in retirement, bemoan the difficulties in wiping it out. The elderly Khrushchev would admit admiration for Israel's military prowess, but in 1956, at the height of his power, he threatened to bomb it back to pre-Noah ages.

Khrushchev's origins were Ukrainian, and with much of his career centered there, perhaps a strain of anti-Semitism came naturally. He ruled the Ukraine in an era when Babi Yar was officially regarded no more than a ravine outside Kiev. In his shattering denunciation of Stalin's crimes at the Twentieth Party Congress, the Doctors' Plot was given a generic spin without any reference to its essential nature—a frame-up of Jews. Khrushchev would scold a fellow Communist official for crude references to *zhidi* ("Yids"), yet, in outbursts use the expression himself. He pointed to "Jewish friends" and his Jewish daughter-in-law to establish his lack of prejudice. From his recorded memoirs: "I have never been an anti-Semite, never."

Nora Levin, who traced the course of Jewish life in the Soviet Union in a two-volume work, speculates that Khrushchev's notion of anti-Semitism accorded with a narrow definition put forward by a diplomat—the "killing, beating, jailing, and ghettoization of Jews, not the milder forms of public and private discriminations and contempt." Levin points out Khrushchev denied requests by Jewish organizations to meet with him and took no steps to counteract anti-Semitism.

Khrushchev explained his misgivings about Jews in leadership roles. "This is a complicated problem," he said, because when a Jew receives an important post and surrounds himself with Jewish collaborators, "it is understandable that this should create jealousy and hostility toward Jews." During his regime, stringent quotas for Jews in the universities, the military, and in scientific and cultural institutions were maintained—just like in the bad old Stalinist years.

That Khrushchev's power might affect Jews far from Russia's borders became clear in 1955. That year, he stepped into the Middle East with a long stride, planting his feet firmly in Cairo. Massive arms shipments to Nasser began. But before two hundred new Soviet tanks, one hundred MiG fighters, and fifty Ilyushin bombers sent to Egypt could be fitted for their offensive role, Israel struck, followed by France and Britain.

A stiff note from Moscow stating the Soviet's willingness to annihilate "warmongers" via "every kind of modern destructive weapon" frightened Eden and Mollet. A November 5 ultimatum from Soviet premier Nikolai Bulganin (Khrushchev's then colleague, soon replaced by Khrushchev himself) said Israel's conduct "places in question the very existence of Israel as a state." On November 7, a CIA report attributed to the American ambassador in Moscow indicated Soviet intent to "flatten" the Jewish state.

Simultaneously, two dispatches from Eisenhower to Ben-Gurion demanding a cease-fire and Suez withdrawal warned, first, of cessation of "friendly cooperation" and, second, against expectation of U.S. help following a Soviet-assisted attack. Whether the Soviet threat was serious or just ritual bluster remains conjecture. But Khrushchev took full credit for saving Nasser's regime.

The years 1967 and 1973 would again find Egypt and Israel locked in combat. Khrushchev was gone, but successor Leonid Brezhnev was to pursue a pro-Arab, anti-Israel policy. On both occasions, shipments of Soviet military largesse to Cairo would make war possible (on the Egyptian side) and necessary (on the Israeli side). But the menace of direct Soviet intervention seemed shrill and thin, not heavy and ominous. The post-Eisenhower administrations of Lyndon Johnson and Richard Nixon made clear that they would not look on impassively as Israel was destroyed.

An internal Soviet anti-Israel policy, apparent under Khrushchev, festered throughout the eighteen-year rule of Brezhnev and was finally cured by the breakup of the Soviet Union under Mikhail Gorbachev and Boris Yeltsin.

To a French Socialist delegation in 1956, Khrushchev said, "We don't favor visits or emigration of Soviet Jews to Israel." Later, asked to comment on the denial of exit permits to Jews, he replied, "It is true to some extent and to some extent not true." Still later, he refused to discuss the subject at all.

At a Vienna press conference in July 1960, though, he could not avoid it. So he lied. The question: Why did the Soviet Union refuse even older Jews exit permits to rejoin relatives in Israel? Khrushchev denied Soviet citizens had any desire to leave. The Soviet leader was comfortably back in the secure Kremlin when Golda Meir reported to the Knesset that 9,236 Israelis had applied through relief organizations to the USSR for reunification with family members. Khrushchev had turned down all requests.

Abba Eban offered one logical explanation for Soviet behavior in *Personal Witness*. He recalls approaching Andrei Vyshinsky at a UN affair after the latter's "lavish absorption of vodka." He asked the Soviet representative about Russian reluctance to let Jews emigrate: "What does it really matter to the Soviet Union?" Vyshinsky replied: "What are you talking about? If the Jews leave, everybody will want to leave."

Such notions likely preyed on Brezhnev's mind during his long reign. Even Mikhail Gorbachev, in his proto-glasnost, preperestroika phase, was given to knee-jerk reactions on Jewish questions. At a 1985 televised press conference in Paris, he was pressed on the emigration issue and pronounced Jews are better treated in the Soviet Union than anywhere else in the world—that their 0.69 percent of the total population translated in Soviet political and cultural life to figures of 10 to 20 percent. Gorbachev, obviously statistically challenged, would later prove to be a decent man. And, mercifully, the Jewish emigration issue and the Soviet Union itself were shortly to be put to rest.

In January 1997, Brezhnev's foremost victim, Natan (a.k.a. Anatoly) Sharansky, alumnus of an eleven-year stay in the Gulag for "treason" and "espionage," returned to his former homeland as Israel's minister of industry and trade. Prime Minister Benjamin Netanyahu, too, found a Kremlin friendly to Jews on his arrival for a visit with the Russian president, Boris Yeltsin. Said Russia's first democratically elected chief executive: "Our countries and their leaders have finished a period of biased attitudes and have energetically moved toward each other."

JOHN XXIII (Angelo Roncalli), 1881–1963
Pope, 1958–1963

History's Conventional View

When a sad-faced, downcast Venetian delegation presented condolences to Cardinal Roncalli, then patriarch of Venice, soon after Pius XII's death, he listened patiently, then dispelled the gloom: "Come now, when a pope is dead they just make another one."

He may have been right that day in October 1958. But no one could say that in June 1963, after his own passing. As Holy Father, John XXIII would be one of a kind, certainly for the century, perhaps for the millennium—and for Jews, we'll see, *two* millennia.

Already seventy-seven when he ascended the throne of St. Peter's, Roncalli was chosen as a "caretaker pope" while a more appropriate successor to Pius XII, Archbishop of Milan Giovanni Montini (later Paul VI) was groomed. As yet, Montini lacked the essential cardinal's red hat. But Good Pope John, as some later called him, fooled the Church hierarchy. In the barely four years left him, he shook the institution loose form its seventh-century chain and thrust it into the twentieth.

Angelo Roncalli came from peasant stock rooted in the Alpine foothills. Ordained in 1904, he served in the Italian Medical Corps during World War I. Beginning in 1925, he moved through the Vatican's diplomatic service, making contacts and winning respect in the Balkans and southeastern Europe. Then came the nunciature at Paris, his cardinal's hat, and the patriarchy of Venice.

Once Pope, John regarded flawed precedents as ice cubes, readily melted. He promptly named twenty-three new cardinals, including an African, a Japanese, and even humble priests from third world countries. Then he raised the Sacred College's membership to ninety, most crowded in its history. In his encyclicals he welcomed aspects of the modern welfare state (which past popes and members of his own Curia still viewed with alarm) and called for peace among all nations. Even the suspicious Soviets, who disdained Pius XII as "Pope of the Atlantic Alliance," discovered in John a pope who "pays tribute to reason."

Early in his pontificate, John called for an ecumenical council, first in a century, to update the Church. Powerful conservative prelates bemoaned his election, and rumors circulated in Rome of their efforts to sabotage his actions. Biographer Pinchas E. Lapide mentions that his phones went mysteriously out of order. Mail got lost. Drafts for planned encyclicals were repeatedly mislaid.

Those fearing upheaval hoped delay—considering the pope's advanced age—might foreclose his most dramatically risky venture, the proposed Vatican Council. "A hornet's nest," one hesitant archbishop called it. But although he would not live to see it through to the end, Vatican II became John XXIII's lasting monument for Christians—and, in no small measure, non-Christians.

But From a Jewish Perspective

Not many Jews had heard of Cardinal Roncalli. But those familiar with his record had good reason to hope they could find at last a friendly figure on St. Peter's Throne in the spirit of those much maligned (though not by Jews) Renaissance popes of five hundred years back.

As apostolic delegate stationed in Istanbul, he worked closely with Jewish Agency representatives in Balkan and Eastern European rescue efforts. During the crisis of Hungarian Jewry, Roncalli "worked and toiled indefatigably on their behalf," wrote the agency's man in Turkey, Chaim Barlas. And War Refugee Board emissary Ira Hirschmann told of his producing thousands of baptismal certificates for distribution to threatened Jews. Operation Baptism it was called, although actual conversions were nil.

Time was not on the side of John XXIII, so he moved quickly. He declared:

> We are conscious today that many, many centuries of blindness have cloaked our eyes, so that we can no longer see the beauty of Thy Chosen People, nor recognize in their faces the features of our privileged brethren. We realize that the mark of Cain stands upon our foreheads. Across the centuries our brother Abel has lain in the blood which we drew, or shed tears we caused by forgetting Thy Love.

Forgive us for the curse we falsely attached to their name as Jews. Forgive us for crucifying thee a second time in their flesh.

Lapide, who, as Israeli consul in Venice in 1956, thanked the future pope for his Holocaust efforts, describes in considerable depth the revolution he attempted in Christian-Jewish relations. Early evidence came in the form of papal orders affecting the Bavarian mountain town of Deggendorf. For centuries it attracted pilgrims each September for the anniversary of the 1337 massacre of the town's Jews. They gazed at twelve highlighted pictures of that event and read inscriptions such as "the Godless Jews have maltreated the sacred host with a pointed shoehorn, until it shed the most holy blood." John ordered the pictures removed from view and the pilgrimages stopped. Local merchants and innkeepers complained about the loss of their principal tourist attraction and fought a delaying action. But John eventually got his way.

The pope took note of the Good Friday Prayer phrase *pro perfidis Judaeis*. Faulty translation into vernacular languages turned *unbelieving* into *perfidious*. As of March 27, 1959, he ordered Roman Catholics to simply pray "for the Jews.

Lapide reports that in April 1963, a bishop in Rome's own St. Peter's Basilica, by "force of habit or forgetfulness," recited the outlawed phrase in his Good Friday liturgy. John quietly halted the service and instructed the celebrant to start afresh at the intercessory prayers.

John ordered offensive passages removed from other church ritual language, including the traditional baptismal formula of abjuration: "Abhor Jewish unbelief and reject the Hebrew error." He authorized publication of books and pamphlets stripping away rock-hard prejudices that, over centuries, had infiltrated theological literature.

Following a mission to Madrid by two papal emissaries in 1959, and a second by Cardinal Augustino Bea, John's ally in Jewish matters, Spain's church hierarchy—among the most reactionary in the Catholic world— fell into line. October of that year saw the first synagogue opened in the Spanish capital since 1492. Sometime later, the Jewish community of Madrid received legal recognition. To Cardinal Bea, John entrusted a new creation, the Secretariat for Promoting Christian Unity, with the additional responsibility for forging a spirit of goodwill toward Judaism.

John's design for change encompassed more than symbolic acts produced by Papal fiat—these could be reversed after he was gone. A thorough cleansing of anti-Semitism from Church doctrine required episcopal consensus, and this could best come from the long-planned Ecumenical Council.

Though already fatally ill in 1962, John lived to open its first session, but he was gone, at age eighty-two, before its final one. If results of Vatican II fell short of what Jews hoped, John's absence must be cited. For Jews, he was the best pope since the founding of Christianity.

CHARLES DE GAULLE, 1890–1970
President, 1959–1969

History's Conventional View

Those old enough to remember World War II may subordinate de Gaulle, political figure, to de Gaulle, indomitable symbol of Free France. During the strained, soulful year of 1940, when the swastika waved above the Eiffel Tower, the tall, erect General de Gaulle inspired free men. True, his flip-side arrogance led Winston Churchill to complain that the heaviest cross he had to bear was "the Cross of Lorraine." But absent such conceit, de Gaulle wouldn't have been de Gaulle, and French postwar history might have taken a different turn.

Actually, for more than a decade it did, under revolving door ministries of the Fourth Republic. De Gaulle sulked at his village retreat, watching the political structure self-destruct. In 1958 his grand moment arrived. Recalled to power, he scrapped the Fourth Republic for a fifth, with expanded presidential prerogatives.

The reign of Charles André Joseph Marie de Gaulle was an imperial one, brooking no dispute from lesser intellects in the Chamber of Deputies or in London, Washington, or Jerusalem.

To de Gaulle, France without greatness was not France. He charted an independent course between East and West, built a national nuclear capacity, forced NATO forces from French soil, blocked Britain's entry into the Common Market, and stirred up French-speaking Quebec separatists. He also changed the course of France's Middle Eastern policy.

But From a Jewish Perspective

It is de Gaulle the implausibly implacable politician, not de Gaulle the defiantly implacable general-in-exile, who impacted on the Jewish world.

Some background: By 1967, Gamal Abdel Nasser, his 1956 military debacle behind him, was ready for another blow at Israel. Bountiful Soviet military hardware had poured into his coffers and also into Damascus. In fact, Syrian-sponsored raids on northern Israeli settlements set the clock ticking. On May 15, Nasser sent armored divisions across Suez into the Sinai peninsula. Two days later, he forced evacuation of the small but symbolic UN forces left there as a buffer following the 1956 war. On May 22, he once more closed the Strait of Tiran, cutting off Israel's Red Sea trade.

Enter Abba Eban, now foreign minister of Israel, into the Elysée Palace for an audience with President de Gaulle. Of the three Western democracies, France, the United States, and Britain, France was, until last year, Israel's chief arms supplier. Successive French governments, including de Gaulle's, enabled Israel to hold its own in clashes with Soviet MiGs. The latest agreement called for delivery of fifty French state-of-the-art Mirage V fighters.

But Eban relates that he found de Gaulle anything *but* supportive. On being reminded by Eban of France's long-standing commitment to respect Israel's right to defend itself against the outrage of a maritime blockade, de Gaulle responded, "That policy was correct, but it reflected the heat of the hour. That was 1957. It is now 1967."

According to Eban's account in *Personal Witness*, the French president began their meeting with a stark "Don't make war," reiterated it later, "...on no account should you shoot the first shell," and closed their conversation with "I advise you not to be precipitate. Do not make war."

DeGaulle was impervious to Eban's irrefutable argument that a blockade was an act of war in itself. He insisted on the alternative of "*Four* Power consultation." (Russia could later dismiss this quixotical notion out-of-hand, and President Lyndon Johnson, briefed on the de Gaulle proposal by Eban, would ask, "Who the hell are the other two?")

Seven years earlier, a very different de Gaulle had told Ben-Gurion, "Under no circumstances will we sanction your annihilation. At present, we do not possess great power, but it is growing, and we will protect you."

During the years since the Suez War, military cooperation had grown remarkably close. A joint French-Israeli committee regularly discussed mutual Mediterranean interests. French naval patrols safeguarded Israel's Red Sea traffic. French and Israeli pilots shared training programs. The

French secret service and Israel's Mossad traded intelligence data. But de Gaulle's grant of Algerian independence won plaudits along North Africa's northern rim and opened opportunities for French influence in the Middle East. If building bridges to the Arab world meant burning already standing ones to Israel, de Gaulle was willing to hurl the torches.

The French president's bombshell announcement came on May 31, when he suspended all arms deliveries to the Jewish state. Two days later, he called for his dead-in-the-water Four Power solution and said the arms embargo would continue until Israel declared its intent *not* to fight.

The effect in Israel was severe. Break in the French arms pipeline would day-by-day alter the military balance. On June 5, the day Israel struck, victory was predictable. But one month later? Or six months?

De Gaulle promptly ordered his foreign minister to denounce Israel as an aggressor, first in the national assembly, then at the United Nations. French press and public opinion opposing his stand merely stiffened his resolve. At an Elysée Palace reception on June 22, he said, "Of course, the Israelis are an admirable people. But I told them: 'Don't attack!' They have done so. And I'm annoyed with them for that."

After the war, ensuing months brought partially restored amity, and even some arms deliveries, which, incidentally, proved highly profitable to French industry. But the intimacy of earlier years was past.

Unlike commonplace U.S. presidential press conferences, a de Gaulle audience for correspondents was rare—an "event." So when he summoned the international press on November 27, 1967, coverage was extensive. One regally expressed statement shocked Jews around the world. He spoke of Jews "who had remained what they had been for all time, that is to say, an elite people, self-confident and domineering," and he wondered if this people might "once it was gathered on the site of its ancient grandeur, change into ardent conquering ambition the very moving desire that they have felt for nineteen centuries."

Criticism rained on the Elysée, including a lengthy riposte from the aging Ben-Gurion. For once, de Gaulle was on the defensive. At a January 1968 palace reception, he asked Rabbi Jacob Kaplan to remain after other guests had left, led him to a drawing room, and declared, "It was justified praise of the Jewish people. I an anti-Semite! You know what my relations are with the Jews."

De Gaulle's passing in 1970 generated worldwide tributes. Those from the western democracies emphasized the earlier de Gaulle, who held aloft the Cross of Lorraine and rallied free Frenchmen and the Resistance. For months, the Arab world had already been ecstatic about the later de Gaulle. A Cairo paper called him "the great chief," a Lebanese paper, "Napoleon of the century." Gamal Abdel Nasser called him "the only Western head of state on whose friendship the Arabs can depend."

And that certainly did *not* make him good for Jews.

LYNDON B. JOHNSON, 1908–1973
President, 1963–1969

History's Conventional View

Lyndon Johnson wanted his place in history linked to "the Great Society" he intended to build, bristling with social and economic reforms. "Let us continue," he said before Congress in the aftermath of John F. Kennedy's assassination. But Johnson did much more. His long House and Senate experience, plus skill at arm-twisting, got many more things done than his charismatic predecessor. Far-ranging civil rights legislation was passed, the costly War on Poverty begun, aid to primary and secondary education expanded, Medicare and Medicaid initiated, and an assault on environmental pollution got under way.

But Vietnam became a shroud covering all else and marking his administration tragic. "LBJ, LBJ, how many kids did you kill today?" protesters chanted as American casualties mounted. He did not start the war, but he "escalated" it, and it became a quagmire from which the United States could not extricate itself. Johnson saw South Vietnam as the first in a row of dominoes. He believed its fall would undermine other non-Communist governments by Kremlin-backed insurgents. Johnson was proven wrong, and history has been unforgiving.

But From a Jewish Perspective

During the 1956 Suez crisis, Senate Majority Leader Lyndon Johnson disputed White House condemnation of Israel. A decade later he would occupy the Oval Office himself and be put to a similar test.

Throughout his presidency, Vietnam dominated foreign affairs, and the rest of the world, while not ignored, was subordinated to Southeast Asia. Nasser's link to Moscow strengthened; Syria became a client state.

De Gaulle's tilt toward the Arabs was under way; West Germany—
under Arab pressure—stopped selling Israel tanks.

Johnson found it necessary to step up arms sales to Israel before a
dangerous imbalance arose, but lest those Arab states not under Soviet
influence be upset, the first sale of 250 modified M-14 tanks to Israel in
1965 was matched by one to Jordan, and the first A-1 Skyhawk jet fighter
sale to Israel the following year, by secret agreements to send military
equipment to Lebanon, Saudi Arabia, Tunisia, and Morocco. Johnson
hoped this hardware would not be transferred to Israel's more militant
neighbors.

From a Jewish perspective though, the president's litmus test came in
the spring of 1967, as Syrian and Egyptian provocations moved the Near
East toward renewed war. "The first necessity was to persuade the
Israelis not to act hastily," Johnson initially believed. He cabled the
Israeli prime minister, Levi Eshkol, on May 17: "I am sure you will
understand that I cannot accept any responsibilities in behalf of the
United States for situations which arise as the result of actions on which
we are not consulted."

Johnson preferred the thrust of American diplomacy be through the
UN, but events moved too rapidly. UN Secretary-General U Thant
immediately acquiesced to Nasser's demand for removal of the UN buffer
force, followed by Nasser's closing of the Strait of Tiran. Johnson called
Egypt's blockade of the Gulf of Aqaba illegal and asked Eban to come to
the White House. "All of our intelligence people are unanimous," the
president told him, "that if the UAR [Egypt] attacks, you will whip the
hell out of them." He asked for Israeli restraint while he pressed for allied
cooperation in forming an international naval escort to keep the strait
open. In his memoirs Johnson recalls, "Then I said very slowly and very
positively: 'Israel will not be alone unless it decides to go alone.'"

Foreign Minister Eban convinced his cabinet colleagues to delay
military moves, giving the president time to orchestrate a concerted naval
display. But Britain and Canada, originally supportive, backed off, and
Johnson regretfully notified Eshkol that "our leadership is unanimous
that the United States should not act alone." The Six Day War followed,
beginning June 5. "I have never concealed my regret," Johnson wrote
later, "that Israel decided to move when it did." But he would "not accept
the oversimplified charge of Israeli aggression." As predicted, Israel

needed no immediate U.S. aid in whipping Egypt, Syria, and Jordan, which joined them. But then the Soviet Union stepped in.

On June 10, the president was called to the White House Situation Room for a hot-line call from Premier Alexei Kosygin. This was a "crucial moment," with a "grave catastrophe" beckoning, warned Kosygin. Unless Israel withdrew, the Russian threatened "independent action."

From Israel's—that is, a Jewish—perspective, this was President Johnson's day of judgment. A decade earlier, under comparable circumstances, Eisenhower had told Israel to expect no U.S. support as a counterweight. Johnson's response was vigorous. He ordered the Mediterranean Sixth Fleet toward the Syrian coast, a measure certain to be picked up by Soviet monitoring stations. Rather than risk confrontation with the United States, the Kremlin backed off.

After the Six Day War, the Johnson administration—by default, in view of de Gaulle's refusal to sell Israel arms—accepted the role of Israel's principal armorer. There would be quarrels over U.S. Defense Department delays in delivery—particularly fifty top-line Phantom jets—in late 1968. But as Yitzhak Rabin, Israel's new ambassador to Washington, noted, Johnson "put an end to the whole matter by ordering that the sale be concluded without further ifs or buts."

Abba Eban wrote that the president showed "courage in departing from the syndrome of 1956." Gideon Raphael, Israel's UN ambassador, says much the same thing in *Destination Peace*, his account of those days: "When it came to the crunch of 1967, the United States, unlike ten years earlier, was firmly on Israel's side, logistically and politically."

RICHARD M. NIXON, 1913–1994
President, 1969–1974

History's Conventional View

President Nixon knew how history would view him on the morning of Thursday, August 8, 1974. At 9:00 P.M. he planned to announce his resignation, the first chief executive to do so. His alternative looked even less appealing—removal following a trial by the U.S. Senate. The bungled Watergate burglary, followed by an Executive Office cover-up, then the discovery of tape recordings depicting his role in the cover-up, did him in.

Not expunged from the record but clearly subordinated to the "long national nightmare" were foreign policy initiatives—his dramatic visit to Mao Tse-tung, the consequent "opening" to China, withdrawal from Vietnam, a Strategic Arms Limitation Treaty with Moscow freezing international ballistic missile construction, and further movement toward detente. Then there was his role when, for the third time in seventeen years, the Middle East exploded.

But From a Jewish Perspective

Can a president whose conversational vocabulary bristled with anti-Semitic canards, innuendos, and asides, possibly have been good for Jews? Richard Nixon turned this simple question into a murky one.

The answer was clearly no for Jewish employees of the Bureau of Labor Statistics. He ordered background checks to root out a "Jewish cabal" at the agency, one he suspected of undermining his administration by skewing economic statistics.

The answer was clearly no for Jewish employees of the Internal Revenue Service and Commerce Department. Aide John Ehrlichmann's notes for December 30, 1970, and March 28, 1973, indicate the president's displeasure that these departments were "overtopped" with Jews more concerned with the clock than their duties. And a muted no for those members of the Jewish legal community who regarded the seat vacated by Supreme Court Justice Abe Fortas—successor to Felix Frankfurter and Arthur Goldberg—as a "Jewish seat."

And a sharp no for "rich Jews" who filled Democratic Party coffers. Nixon wanted to make them special targets for tax investigations. "Go after 'em like a son-of-a-bitch," he told the White House chief of staff, H. R. Haldeman.

Recent taped revelations of what the president said, and when he said it, confirmed an image ex-Congresswoman Elizabeth Holtzman formed twenty-five years earlier when she achieved a national reputation for dogged questioning as a member of the House Judiciary Committee: "It deepens the portrait of a man who had very mean and ugly qualities and a contempt for the law." For American Jews, in general, Richard Nixon was never lovable, not even likable. The "Tricky Dicky" tag fit. And yet...

At his worst, Nixon caused discomfort to higher-profiled layers of

American Jewry in political and financial circles, and in the arts and media. But there was another Jewry, five thousand miles distant, across the Atlantic and Mediterranean, whose survival was at stake ten months before Nixon's resignation. His presidency was already mortally wounded when Anwar Sadat, successor to Nasser, launched an unexpected assault across the Suez Canal on October 6, 1973. Syrian troops simultaneously struck in the Golan region. The Yom Kippur War was under way. How would Nixon react?

In the uncertain period following Nixon's first presidential victory, back in 1969, Yitzhak Rabin, then Israeli ambassador, had felt uneasy. The "Jewish vote" in Nixon's bid to succeed Lyndon Johnson had gone to his Democratic opponent. He didn't *owe* Jews. "I was concerned that his attitude toward Israel might change for the worse," wrote Rabin. "But in the course of years, I came to understand that his views on Israel were founded on more than political expediency. My fears proved to be groundless."

Now, during the first seventy-two hours of combat, Israel made no urgent arms requests. It expected to roll back the Egyptians and Syrians, as in the past. By day four, though, optimism faded. Fighter plane and tank losses mounted, and front-line commanders hesitated to risk further losses in offensive operations. Soviet-supplied SAM-6 missiles and portable rocket launchers proved devastatingly effective. By air and sea, more Soviet supplies reached Cairo and Damascus daily. Briefed on the Jewish state's worsening position, Nixon declared, he later told Eban, "Israel must be saved."

Secretary of State Henry Kissinger supported bountiful military aid. The Department of Defense demurred, fearing Arab reaction. It wanted no more than three of its huge Galaxy transports committed. Eban quotes Nixon: "We have twenty-five; send them all at once—everything that can fly.... As for the Arabs, I'll have to pay the same political price for three as for twenty-five."

From military air bases in the Northeast, the great aircraft filled with tanks, munitions, helicopter parts, spare transmissions, electric jamming equipment, antiradar devices, and "smart bombs" began round-the-clock resupply operations. Nothing matched it since the Berlin Airlift of 1948.

The first cargo planes arrived on October 14, and their contents were quickly unloaded and sent to the front. Golda Meir later wrote in *My Life*,

"It not only lifted our spirits but also served to make the American position clear to the Soviet Union.... When I heard that the planes had touched down at Lydda, I cried.... I remember going to Lydda once to watch the Galaxies come in. They looked like some kind of prehistoric monster."

Soon, the Galaxies were landing at a rate of one every fifteen minutes. In less than six weeks, twenty-two thousand tons of equipment arrived on 570 flights. Meanwhile, beginning on October 13, Phantoms and A-14 Skyhawks were flown to Israel via the Azores. America's NATO allies had refused the Nixon administration's request to provide landing rights.

By late October, the tide having turned, Israeli forces surrounded and trapped Egypt's Third Army, causing Leonid Brezhnev to cable Nixon on October 25, urging him to "keep Israel in order." If not, the Soviets would act.

America's own interests did not include starving the Third Army into surrender, so it, too, was pressuring Israel to let food supplies through. But Soviet bullying called for a response. Nixon's was dramatic.

Within hours, Nixon ordered U.S. forces to go on worldwide alert— DEF CON III (Defense Condition Three). As in the earlier case of Johnson sending the Mediterranean Fleet toward Syria, the Soviets were checked. Brezhnev withdrew. Prime Minister Meir wrote, "Détente or no détente, he was not about to give in to Soviet blackmail. It was, I think, a dangerous decision, a courageous decision, and a correct decision."

Memoirs by other Israeli political and military leaders recall Nixon's role in the Yom Kippur War, before and after. In *Personal Witness*, Foreign Minister Eban affirmed, "whenever Israel's security was at issue or in hazard, he would supply our needs or lay down rules for effective cooperation with us." Washington Ambassador Yitzhak Rabin, in *The Rabin Memoirs*, wrote: "I cannot deny we had some tough arguments with Nixon's administration; but neither can I forget that Nixon provided Israel with more arms than any other American president." Defense Minister Moshe Dayan wrote in *Story of My Life:* "I hate to think what our situation would have been if the United States had withheld its aid."

Could an anti-Semitic president have been good for Jews? Maybe it's a matter of geography. Is the jury sitting in judgment in the United States or Israel?

From Asia Without Love

MOHANDAS K. GANDHI, 1869–1948

JAWAHARLAL NEHRU, 1889–1964
Prime Minister of India, 1947–1964

MAO TSE-TUNG, 1893–1976
Chairman, Chinese Communist Party, 1949–1976

CHOU EN-LAI, 1898–1976
Premier, 1949–1976

History's Conventional View

Remembered by his title Mahatma ("Great Soul"), the bald, bespectacled, hunched figure of Mohandas Gandhi forged civil disobedience into a potent weapon to loosen Britain's grip on India. He preached passive resistance, and practiced it personally by going on long hunger strikes. When the Union Jack was lowered in the British Raj, Gandhi's long struggle ended, his place in history assured. Albert Einstein said of him: "Generations to come will scarcely believe that such a one as this walked the earth in flesh and blood."

Jawaharlal Nehru, the less saintly, more pragmatic, ally of Gandhi in the Indian National Congress guided the new nation through its teething period. Economic uplift and social progress were his top priorities at home, while "nonalignment" kept India aloof of cold war stresses. This did not stop Western nations from all-too-often detecting a Soviet tilt. The United States, at times, found him less than a gracious recipient of foreign aid, and he was a strong advocate of Chinese Communist UN admission—until Chinese armed forces crossed the Indian-Chinese frontier, beginning a border war. Nehru's ongoing global influence came from his status as a Third-World leader.

Mao Tse-tung, the twentieth-century's model revolutionary, emerged as the Chinese Communist movement's unchallenged leader after a legendary six-thousand-mile trek (The Long March) to sanctuary in rugged northwest China. Only twenty thousand of its original one hundred thousand participants reached safety from the pursuing Nationalists of Chiang Kai-shek.

After victory in the Civil War, on October 1, 1949, Chairman Mao became paramount leader of the People's Republic of China, home to more than one-quarter of the world's population. He sent volunteers to throw back General MacArthur's UN forces in Korea, and directed the Great Leap Forward to restructure Chinese economic life. Blaming failure on bureaucratic foot-dragging, he embarked on the vast Cultural Revolution to bring Chinese society into harmony with his ideological vision. It, too, resulted in a period of economic chaos extending well beyond his passing.

Chou En-lai, unlike the thunderbolt-hurling deity Mao had become, ran China's day-to-day affairs. Of mandarin origin, he moved comfortably in diplomatic circles and handled contacts with the world beyond China's borders. A pragmatist, he sometimes fell from his ideologically-inclined chief's favor. But he remained Mao's perennial number two.

But From a Jewish Perspective

Most Jews, like most everybody else, remember Gandhi vaguely as a saintly, unreal figure. But at one point in time—November 1938, just after the Kristallnacht—his unreality, not his saintliness, caught Jewish attention. This followed his commentary on German Jewry in the Indian weekly *Harijan*.

"If the Jewish mind could be prepared for voluntary sacrifice," he wrote, "even the massacre I have imagined [by Nazis] could be turned into a day of thanksgiving that Jehovah had wrought deliverance of the race even at the hands of a tyrant. For to the God-fearing, death has no terror...the German Jews will score a lasting victory over the German gentiles in the sense that they will have converted the latter to an appreciation of human dignity."

The *Jewish Frontier* of New York pointed out, "A Jewish Gandhi in Germany, should one arise, could function about five minutes and would be promptly taken to the guillotine."

Saints are not necessarily stargazers, so Gandhi can be forgiven for a lack of prescience regarding the Holocaust's immensity. Less explicable is his response to biographer Louis Fischer in 1946, when statistics were complete. Yes, it was "the greatest crime of our time," admitted Gandhi, "but the Jews should have offered themselves to the butcher's knife. They should have thrown themselves into the sea from cliffs.... It would have aroused the world and the people of Germany."

Either Gandhi still didn't comprehend the meaning of the Holocaust, or there's a fine line between sainthood and something else.

Jawaharlal Nehru, weighing demographic factors rather than spiritual concepts, concluded early on that there were more Arabs in the world than Jews, more Moslems in India than Jews, and he framed his Middle East policy accordingly. At Israel's birth, he had been disposed to accept the new nation, especially after King Farouk's Egypt opposed India's position on Hyderabad. But Islamic pressure restrained his inclination to abstain when Israel's UN admission came to a vote, and he ordered India's representative to vote against it.

On May 5, 1949, biographer Sarvepalli Gopol writes, Nehru jotted down, "It is about time we made some of these Arab countries find that we are not going to follow them in everything in spite of what they do." A few months later, India officially recognized Israel, but there was no follow-up, no willingness to exchange high-level diplomats. Thereafter, Israeli Foreign Ministry official Gideon Raphael complained, India's "promises were as frequent as its evasions."

As preparations for the 1955 Bandung, Indonesia, conference of Asian and African nations got under way, Nehru told his foreign minister he would accept a Jewish presence only if the Arab states agreed. They didn't. In a January 4, 1955, telegram to all Indian missions, Nehru admitted that keeping Israel out was illogical, but he stuck to his decision. (Nehru showed sterner stuff in rejecting U.S. objections to Communist China's attendance.)

The year 1956 found the proudly "nonaligned" Nehru aligned solidly at Suez with Nasser's Egypt. He made no similar choice between the Soviet Union and the rebellious citizenry of Budapest.

In 1961, while attending a World Health Organization meeting at New Delhi, Ambassador Raphael sought out Nehru in an effort to move Indian-Israeli relations from their state of "stagnation." Nehru said India's sentiments toward Israel were good, but concern about Arab reactions barred closer contacts. Raphael later wrote, "Nehru preferred evasion to valor and expediency to principle."

When China invaded India in 1962, Nehru momentarily departed from form, announcing India was willing to accept arms from any source, including Israel. Talks to that end began, but broke off when Nasser made his displeasure known at New Delhi. It takes little imagination to picture the stance Nehru would have taken as moral leader of the third world, in June 1967 or October 1973, when Egypt and Israel clashed.

The presence of Chairman Mao is justified on these pages to the extent it is hardly likely that his number two man, Chou En-lai, would have said, "Let our Israeli policy be *this*" if his paramount leader said, "Let it be *that*." But Mao's attention was elsewhere, and his fingerprints are not found in foreign affairs as clearly as Chou's.

Early in 1950, Israel recognized the People's Republic of China, and David Hacohen, Israel's ambassador to Burma, came away from a meeting with Chou convinced the Chinese premier would welcome diplomatic relations. But the Korean War intervened, and in its wake, Israel, not China, showed hesitancy. Opportunity was lost.

By the time Israel proposed an exchange of ambassadors in April 1955, it was already too late. Chou, at the Bandung Conference earlier that month, had discovered the "potential of the Arab world," as Gideon Raphael put it. "From that time on, China embarked on a steady anti-Israel course of ever increasing harshness." Visiting Cairo in December 1964, Chou declared: "We are ready to help the Arab nations to regain Palestine. We are willing to give you anything and everything, arms and volunteers."

China's last communication with an Israeli leader had come in August 1963, when Chou sent all heads of government a letter concerning the Nuclear Test Ban Treaty. The Israeli prime minister, Levi Eshkol, responded to Chou, via China's Stockholm embassy, expressing agreement with his proposals and an interest in normalizing relations as well. Chou didn't respond. In 1965 Eshkol tried again, and invited Chou to send a delegation to Israel to discuss relations. Again, Chou never bothered to answer.

Golda Meir later wrote that the Chinese leaders were "totally committed to the Arab war against Israel" with "arms, money, and moral support." Wistfully, she added, "I, for one, have never really understood why and for years had been under the illusion that if we could only talk to the Chinese, we might get through to them."

One Jew eventually did—but after Mao and Chou had passed from the scene. In March 1997, at what resembled a state funeral, Prime Minister Benjamin Netanyahu paid tribute to financier Saul Eisenberg. "I will personally miss Eisenberg as the entire country will miss him," said Netanyahu.

Twenty years earlier, it was revealed, then prime minister Menachem Begin learned of Peking's need to modernize its armed forces as Sino-Soviet tensions mounted. With U.S. permission, he gave Eisenberg authority to arrange a $10 billion ten-year deal for Israel's aircraft and defense industries. The Chinese insisted on complete secrecy, but this was the Great Leap Forward toward the normalization in relations so elusive under the predecessors of Deng Xiaoing, who died one month before Eisenberg.

ANWAR EL-SADAT, 1918–1981
President of Egypt, 1970–1981

History's Conventional View

Four televised sequences highlight Anwar Sadat's notable place in history textbooks, except those read in Baghdad, Damascus, Tripoli, and Riyadh.

The first shows him descending an El Al ramp from a Boeing 707, with Republic of Egypt markings, at floodlit Ben-Gurion Airport on Saturday night, November 19, 1977. Welcomed by Israeli leaders present and past, Sadat receives the red carpet treatment, a twenty-one-gun salute, and hears the Egyptian national anthem played by an Israeli band. He had gone where no Arab head of state had ventured before, and, suddenly, Middle East peace seemed not so wild a dream.

In the second, he is at the rostrum of the Knesset on November 20, wiping perspiration from his forehead as he addresses its members on issues dividing them.

Next we see him on March 27, 1978, at the most astonishing of all diplomatic photo-ops, trading handshakes and smiles with the Israeli prime minister, Menachem Begin, and President Jimmy Carter in a White House lawn ceremony witnessed by everyone who was anyone in Cairo, Jerusalem, or Washington.

The fourth doesn't show Sadat at all, just rows of folding chairs in disarray on a reviewing stand, bloodstains marking the area where, moments before, on October 6, 1981, he had watched army troops pass by in a parade commemorating the 1973 Yom Kippur War.

Already given the highest mark for political daring, Sadat now received posthumous tributes for a personal courage that—given fundamentalist Arab fanaticism—inevitably proved suicidal.

But From a Jewish Perspective

Jews came to see a second Sadat eventually, but the first remained sharply in focus when he made his astounding journey across the frontier. On the eve of his arrival, Lt. Gen. Motta Gur, the Israeli chief of staff, warned of Egypt's preparations for a 1978 war "irrespective of Sadat's willingness to come to Jerusalem."

There was cause for skepticism. After succeeding the charismatic Nasser in 1970, Sadat, first lightly regarded as an interim figure, had shown wiliness in thwarting a palace coup. Later he lulled Israeli planners into semi-complacency by ousting fifteen thousand Soviet advisers, pilots, technicians, and other military personnel. When they departed in 1972, along with them went 150 combat planes and 300 SAM missile launchers. Superficially, he appeared to be retreating from a confrontation with Israel for which those Soviet arms were needed. In reality, he saw the cautious Russians exercising unwarranted restraint on his plan to strike across the Suez.

The following March, Sadat got what he wanted, minus strings. To advance its Arab world standing, Russia decided to pour military hardware into Cairo's war machine. The latest SAM missile launchers, also SCUDs and ground-to-ground missiles, plus two thousand late-model Soviet battle tanks were readied for action. When the attack came, it made October 6, 1973, a date that would live in infamy more than December 7, 1941. There were fifty-two Sundays in a year, but only one Yom Kippur. Religious Jews, forbidden to turn on radios on that most holy of days, learned of Sadat's sneak attack by world-of-mouth at their synagogues.

Now enter Sadat II, four years later. Frustrating months of on-again, off-again negotiations had brought Egypt no closer to reclaiming Sinai after its military reversals in the Yom Kippur War. As Yitzak Rabin saw it, the Egyptian president was nudged toward his spectacular journey to Jerusalem by fear of being pressured into an international conference where he would be further pressured to fall in line behind the more radical Syrians and Palestine Liberation Organization. Add to all that the meddlesome Soviets, and direct one-on-one negotiations with Israel seemed more profitable.

Sadat's quest for peace was spurred mightily by a domestic time bomb. Housing and food shortages accelerated since 1973, causing a growing undercurrent of unrest. Spiraling inflation reached nearly uncontrollable levels. One anti-Sadat refrain heard during demonstrations in the textile center of Mehilla al-Qubra went:

O Pasha, O Bey, we don't eat and shoes go for five pounds,
O Hero of October, where is our breakfast?

Professor Howard M. Sacher, an expert on Middle East affairs as well as Jewish history, wrote, "In truth, the social structure of the nation as a whole faced disintegration." Egypt *needed* peace.

Sadat deserves credit for ultimately revolutionizing Egyptian-Israeli relations. Negotiations advanced, faltered, fell back, and nearly broke off. Then the deal was struck at the U.S. presidential retreat of Camp David in Maryland's Cacoctin Mountains, Jimmy Carter presiding.

Sadat's narrowing of focus to primarily Egyptian-Israeli issues, relegating broader questions to the background, was not why other Arab leaders labeled him a traitor. True, as an Egyptian nationalist he saw removing the Israelis from Sinai and away from Suez as his top goal. But whether he weakly presented the Palestinian case or came across as its champion, their wrath was unquenchable. Destruction *of* Israel, not accommodation *with* Israel, remained their goal.

Before journeying to Jerusalem, Sadat had said he had every intention of pressing the Palestinians' case. Yet Hafad Assad's Syrian regime promptly proclaimed a day of national mourning, complete with "funeral eulogies" for Sadat.

After the Camp David Accords were signed, even those moderate Arab royals—Morocco's King Hassan and Jordan's King Hussein—kept their distance. Emissaries of Arab states meeting in Baghdad discussed sanctions to punish Egypt if it followed through with a peace treaty— severance of diplomatic relations, an embargo on Egyptian companies doing business with Israel, and removal of Egypt from the Persian Gulf oil states' dole. This last measure would cost Egypt a potential $15 billion over five years. Sadat went ahead with negotiations for a final peace treaty anyway, ignoring financial and personal threats.

From a Jewish perspective, the total concession of Sinai was a heavy price. It meant relinquishing agricultural settlements, factories, and one thousand miles of roadway. It would call for the dismantling of a $10 billion military infrastructure set up during the decade-long occupation, including ten air bases, two of which matched NATO's largest. It meant surrender of direct control of the Gulf of Aqaba shipping lanes. It would result in turning over the Alma oil field in southern Sinai, developed at a cost of $5 billion, which was currently supplying half of Israel's energy needs. But it also meant peace with the Jewish state's largest and potentially most dangerous neighbor, and for his partnership in that peace—which won him the Nobel Prize and cost him his life—Anwar Sadat was ultimately good for Jews.

The Four American Presidents Who Closed the Last Quarter Century of the Second Millennium

JIMMY CARTER, President, 1977–1981

RONALD REAGAN, President, 1981–1989

GEORGE BUSH, President, 1989–1993

BILL CLINTON, President, 1993–

Actually, there was a fifth, GERALD FORD, president from 1974–1977. But a Jewish perspective on chief executives of this twenty-five-year period—an eye-blink in our 2,300-year journey that began with Alexander the Great crossing Judea to get to the other side—may justifiably skip him. Consider Conor Cruise O'Brien's shrewd observation that, on Nixon's resignation, Ford "was happy not only to retain [Henry] Kissinger as secretary of state, but to leave him the conduct of international affairs." He allowed Kissinger to rule for the remainder of their term as a "virtually sovereign secretary of state." Kissinger, a Jew, is ineligible for these pages.

History's Conventional View

On the upside, the four-year presidency of Jimmy Carter—"Jimmy who?" when the 1976 campaign first began—is remembered for twelve tense days in the late summer of 1978. On September 5, Anwar Sadat and Menachem Begin arrived with their entourages at Camp David, hostile and suspicious. Getting the two principals to even talk to each other was an ordeal. Yet on September 17, the weary Egyptian president and Israeli prime minister, and an equally exhausted U.S. president, went before White House television cameras and announced agreement on plans for a peace treaty. All concerned regarded Carter the catalyst, indefatigably laboring to convert apparent deadlock into a last-moment success. It was his shining moment.

There were few others. Carter's downside included failure to end a hostage crisis that dragged along for fourteen months at the U.S. embassy in Teheran, unsuccessful measures to deal with Russia's invasion of Afghanistan, and an inability to halt "stagflation"—economic stagnation and inflation. A disenchanted electorate rejected him in 1980.

Ronald Reagan's electoral college victory—489 votes to Carter's 49—signaled a sweeping change to the political right. But it's unlikely that history textbooks a hundred years hence will dwell on the New Federalism and supply-side economics, or on controversies over prayer in schools, abortion-by-choice, or the Irangate and Federal Savings and Loans scandals. Instead, they will emphasize the major international story of his era. With the end of the 1980s came victory in the cold war and communism's impending collapse. Whether Reagan's escalation of military spending (e.g., "Star Wars") bankrupted the financially strapped Soviet Union is for pro- and anti-Reaganites to argue. The record will simply show that when he left office, the "Evil Empire" was no more, and, shortly afterward, the Soviet Union itself dissolved.

For Reagan's presidential heir, vice president George Bush, there came—as with Carter—one shining diplomatic moment. In Bush's case, it entailed making war, not peace. He arranged a coalition of European and Arab states to oust Saddam Hussein's Iraq from Kuwait. Thus, Desert Shield of 1990 evolved into 1991's Desert Storm, which was initiated with a bombing offensive and closed with a one-hundred-hour ground assault that pushed Iraq far back behind its own frontier.

But Bush could not long bask in reflected foxhole glory; domestic potholes were about to do him in. A recession lifted unemployment levels past 7 percent, affordable health care for middle- and low-income Americans became a top issue, and Bush lacked "the vision thing" to deal with them.

President Bill Clinton *did* have the vision, but not the same vision as many in Congress, on managed medical health care programs, North American free trade, relations with Japan, the size of the U.S. federal budget, and tax cuts. His personal morals and ethics became fair game for Republican attack, but voters in 1996 opted for four more years under the "Comeback Kid" rather than his septuagenarian foe. If any early historical consensus on Clinton is to embrace both Clinton partisans and Clinton critics, it won't happen until the twenty-first century is under way.

But From a Jewish Perspective

Jimmy Carter did not share 1978's Nobel Peace Prize with Anwar Sadat and Menachem Begin despite what many described as herculean labors at Camp David. Perhaps he deserved one, on his own, for what he accomplished *after* those twelve grueling days.

The accords reached were still fragile reeds, and in the weeks and months ahead, with Sadat and Begin back at their capitals, they began to wilt. Total collapse neared when Carter, on March 7, 1979, flew to Cairo and Jerusalem. Clearly, presidential prestige was on the line, and on a more personal level, Carter's political future: Could he resolve knotty disputes ranging from Israeli purchase of oil from surrendered Sinai fields, to the timing of ambassadorial exchanges, to the nature of Palestinian elections?

Carter spent five hectic days in the Middle East. Later that month, when a final treaty, three annexes, an appendix, agreed-upon minutes, and six letters of understanding passed between the participants, the principals recognized his essential role. At the official White House ceremony, Sadat said, "There came certain moments when hope was eroding and retreating in the face of crisis. However, President Carter remained unshaken in his confidence and determination." And Begin: "It was a great day in your life, Mr. President of the United States. You have worked so hard, so insistently, so consistently, to achieve this goal."

Despite this on-site praise, Carter's longer-range standing from a Jewish perspective is shakier. This stems from what came before, and what came after.

Carter's plan for a "reassessment" of Middle East policy aroused suspicions early in his administration. On March 8, 1977, he indicated that Israel should withdraw from territories acquired in the Six Day War, something neither presidents Johnson nor Nixon had pressed. Ten days later he spoke publicly in favor of a Palestinian homeland. To Yitzhak Rabin, this was "a further dramatic change in traditional U.S. policy."

Sometime later, Carter headed off for Europe. At a Geneva, Switzerland, press conference, after meeting Syria's Hafed Assad, he repeated his call for a "homeland for the Palestinians" and his willingness to talk to the Palestinian Liberation Organization (PLO) if it renounced terror and accepted Israel's existence. The PLO would not comply, so no talks took place. But in diary notes, Carter found Assad "very constructive...and somewhat flexible," while Saudi Arabia's Crown Prince Fahd "agreed to help in every way he could." The president concluded: "After meeting with these key Arab leaders, I was convinced that all of them were ready for a strong move on our part to find solutions to long-standing disputes and that with such solutions would come their recognition of Israel and the right of Israelis to live in peace."

Years earlier, Golda Meir had written of Nixon's first secretary of state, William Rogers: "He is a very nice, very courteous and extremely patient man," one she did not suspect "ever realized that the verbal reality of the Arab leaders was not, in any way, similar to his own...as is true of many other gentlemen I have known, Rogers assumed— wrongly, unfortunately, that the whole world was made up solely of other gentlemen."

Was Carter about to fall through the same trap door? More startlingly, he sought to draw the Soviet Union into the Middle East equation as a peacemaking partner. Prudent predecessors wanted no Russian Bear sniffing about.

Sadat's dramatic move, though, set the ground rules for further negotiations, and the president had to adjust to new facts. But on Palestinian questions, wrote George Ball, former undersecretary of state and no friend of Israel, Carter remained "more Arab than the Egyptians."

For disputes arising over language and interpretation, the president put more blame on Israel than its negotiating partner, and he was clearly irritated by Israeli development of the West Bank (Judea and Samaria, to Begin). On March 1, 1980, he ordered a yes vote on a Security Council resolution deploring new settlements there. According to National Security Adviser Zbigniew Brzezinski, he told Secretary of State Cyrus Vance, "I would be willing to lose my election because I will alienate the Jewish community but...if necessary, be harder on the Israelis."

Ezer Weizman, present at the 1977 Camp David marathon and an admirer of Carter's doggedness there, sadly noted, "Only fifty-four percent of Jewish voters opted for Carter [in 1980]—a relatively low proportion of Jewish backing for a Democratic candidate."

Ronald Reagan came to the White House already viewing Israel as a "stabilizing force," a deterrent to radical movements, and a military offset to Soviet influence. He had been "appalled" by the Carter administration's decision to abstain rather than veto a UN resolution condemning

Israel's proclamation of Jerusalem as its capital. On February 2, 1981, after two weeks in office, he stated his position on West Bank settlements: "I disagreed when the previous administration referred to them as illegal. They're not illegal."

Reagan *did* revive a Carter proposal to sell electronically advanced AWAC radar aircraft to Saudi Arabia, causing consternation among some Jewish-American groups. Presumably intended to monitor Iranian air operations, they could be used against Israel as well. Reagan overcame strong anti-AWAC lobbying to push through the $8.5-billion deal. Israel officially steered clear of the brouhaha, merely stating it would shoot down any AWAC violating its air space.

When Prime Minister Menachem Begin visited Reagan in September 1981, they greeted each other warmly. Closer military ties were charted, joint military exercises arranged, and an agreement reached on stockpiling American supplies on Israeli soil. Said Begin: "This is the warmest atmosphere I have ever enjoyed."

Israel's annexation of the Golan Heights later that year though, upset Reagan, and the United States joined in a unanimous UN vote declaring the act "illegal, null, and void." But when the Security Council met the following January to consider measures to punish Israel, the United States threatened to block the action.

Reagan's pronounced pro-Israeli stance did not deter criticism from American Jews when the president prepared for a state visit to Germany in 1985. At Chancellor Helmut Kohl's behest, he agreed to join his counterpart in laying a wreath at a German military cemetery. Discovery that Waffen SS troops also lay buried there led to passionate pleas by Holocaust survivor Eli Wiesel and others to bow out of the ceremony, but Reagan could not extract himself from this awkward commitment without embarrassing his NATO ally, so off he went to Bitburg, albeit reluctantly.

More important for Jews were two things Reagan did *not* do. He did not overreact to Israel's air assault of June 7, 1981, on Saddam Hussein's nearly completed Osirak nuclear reactor. Despite his denials, the Iraqi dictator was readying the facility to produce nuclear weapons. Israel's preemptive strike drew world condemnation down on Jerusalem, and in Washington, Arab ambassadors appeared en masse at the White House to confront Reagan.

The attack had been made by eight F-16 fighter bombers escorted by six F-15 fighters, all supplied to Israel under a U.S.-Israeli military pact barring their use in offensive operations. But other than telling the Arab ambassadors that the incident was "regrettable," he let the matter pass. Later, he told Israel's ambassador that the United States did not "anticipate any change" or "fundamental reevaluation" of their relationship.

Israel could expect no support from Washington, nor did it need any, when it crossed the Lebanese border in June 1982. Some fifteen thousand PLO guerrillas had turned the southern portion of that country into a state within a state, a vast armed camp and base from which mortar shells and Katyushka rockets whizzed toward northern Israeli towns. Eliminating their threat was worth presidential displeasure at conduct that the rest of the world would surely see as aggression—just as long as the president did not *act* on that displeasure.

Reagan complained, at one point by telephone to Begin, about Beirut's bombing. But overall relations with the White House remained unimpaired. Consider the consequences, by contrast, if the principals had not been Begin, Arafat, and Reagan, but Ben-Gurion, Nasser, and Eisenhower.

George Ball, who would surely have preferred otherwise, wrote in *The Passionate Attachment* that Reagan's "unrequited love for Israel led him to grant the Israelis more financial assistance than had all of his predecessors put together." But what Reagan chose to ignore politically and diplomatically during moments of crisis for Israel was perhaps just as important. In Reagan, the Jewish state had a friend at the White House.

George Bush, by virtue of background and oil business relationships, was not expected to be so favorably disposed to Israel as Reagan, and he wasn't. On West Bank issues he came down clearly on the Arab side. By way of example, Russian Jews—free at last to emigrate in early 1990—were pouring into Israel when a $400 million U.S. loan guarantee to house them came under congressional review. Bush's secretary of state, fellow Texan James Baker, said the loan should be conditional on Israel's agreement not to build further settlements on territory gained in the 1967 war. The following year, Bush again asked Congress delay considering loan guarantee requests by Israel to help absorb new arrivals.

Meanwhile, a "dialogue" between Washington and the PLO had begun, contingent, Israel was assured, on the PLO mending its terrorist ways. The PLO didn't, but talks continued anyway—even after the February 1990 attack on a tour bus in which nine Jews were murdered.

As strong congressional opposition to further talks grew, the Bush administration could not ignore another blatant massacre-in-the-making. A Palestinian death squad was caught before it could mount a murderous assault on civilians relaxing at a Mediterranean shoreline resort. PLO chief Yasir Arafat refused to condemn the near atrocity, and the United States called off talks.

A more imaginative president than George Bush might have scored peace-winning points in the Gulf War's wake. If ever there was a time when the United States was positioned to lean on Kuwait, Saudi Arabia, and the oil-rich Gulf states to make peace with Israel, this was the moment. They "owed" the United States, even though, at times, the Bush administration behaved as supplicant rather than savior, lest their cultural sensibilities be bruised.

By the same token, the United States "owed" Israel. Arab partners in the delicately crafted coalition might have bailed out if Israel demanded "in." And it had every right to, for Saddam Hussein's SCUD missiles began raining down over Israel, to the cheers of West Bank Arabs as they passed overhead.

According to General Colin Powell, chairman of the joint chiefs of staff, the SCUD was a "cheap, crude, inaccurate Soviet engine of destruction." And Israel, he wrote, "had survived for the past forty years by taking no guff from its enemies." Yet is was "clear to our side that we had to keep Israel out of this war."

In his memoirs, America's top uniformed officer left no doubt about Israel's role: "The forbearance of the Israelis, in the face of intense provocations, going completely against their grain, in my judgment helped keep the coalition intact."

Powell's civilian commander in chief knew this too, but despite his willingness to "go forward with new vigor and determination" to close the gap between Israel and the Arab states, expressed before Congress on March 6, 1991, little positive action can be traced to the efforts of George Bush. From a Jewish perspective, as well, he lacked "the vision thing."

On the White House South Lawn, on September 13, 1993, a pleased President Bill Clinton, Bush's successor, watched as Israeli prime minister Yitzhak Rabin and PLO chairman Yasir Arafat shook hands, sealing the Declaration of Principles, a framework for Palestinian autonomy on the West Bank and in the Gaza Strip. Henry Kissinger was there, and Jesse Jackson. So were Lubavitcher Jews, along with assorted senators and congressmen and reporters. The signing took place on the same table used by Begin and Sadat nearly two decades before. But Bill Clinton was no Jimmy Carter.

Clinton had not been told about this peace process when Israeli and PLO officials opened their secret channel in Norway. In fact, he was on another runway entirely. While face-to-face talks moved along in Oslo, an ineffectual indirect effort under U.S. auspices was chugging along in Washington.

However, the imprint of the leader of the world's only remaining superpower on any Middle East agreement—along with expected financial inducements to help the peace process—was a welcome plus. Clinton's White House would again be the setting on July 24, 1994, this time as Rabin and Jordan's King Hussein signed a declaration ending their forty-six-year-old official state of war. And again on September 28, 1995, when Rabin and Arafat paid a second call to put their signatures on another agreement expanding Palestinian self-rule.

Following Rabin's assassination that November, and the replacement of his Labor party by a harder-line Likud coalition, Clinton's peace-process role expanded. He became less the high-profile onlooker, more the hands-on manager and monitor.

On such issues as the opening of a tunnel near a Moslem religious site in East Jerusalem and the planned erection of new Jewish housing in that area (the 6,500-unit Har Homa project) he chastised Israel's new prime minister, Benjamin Netanyahu. "I would prefer the decision [on Har Homa] not have been made because I don't think it builds confidence," he said. "I think it builds mistrust."

Heavy-handed provocations were unwelcome, as well, in some Israeli and Jewish-American circles, but concern arose when Clinton criticized Israeli actions while downplaying conduct he could not downsize—a continuing stream of violence by the Palestinian side. Yasir Arafat disavowed acts of terrorism—but did little to contain them through his new Palestinian Authority. Events put in question Arafat's viability as a genuine peace partner and Clinton's reliability as an objective go-between.

Would Clinton, at some pivotal point, steel himself for a make-or-break confrontation with Arafat and the Palestinian Authority over his own insistence on "zero tolerance" for terrorism?

This question stirred American political juices, leading Republican Speaker of the House Newt Gingrich to complain, "When the Clinton-Gore [Albert Gore] Administration treats with moral equivalence Palestinian violence and Israeli housing, that undermines Israeli security."

From a Jewish perspective, Clinton's standing before history must await the first century of the third millennium, when we see whether he has contributed to true peace in the Middle East—or left it with half-sheathed swords.

BIBLIOGRAPHY

Adler, Michael. *Jews of the Middle Ages.* London, 1939.

Akbar, M. J. *Nehru: The Making of India.* London, 1988.

Bagger, Eugene. *Francis Joseph.* New York, 1927.

Balfour, Michael. *The Kaiser and His Times.* New York, 1972.

Ball, George W., and Ball, Douglas B. *The Passionate Attachment.* New York, 1992.

Barlow, Frank. *Willaim Rufus.* Berkeley, 1983.

Baron, Salo W. *The Russian Jews Under Tsars and Soviets.* New York, 1964.

Ben-Gurion, David. *The Jews in Their Land.* Jerusalem, 1966.

Ben-Sasson, H. H., ed. *A History of the Jewish People.* Cambridge, Mass., 1976.

Berkowitz, Jay R. *The Shaping of Jewish Identity in Nineteenth Century France.* Detroit, 1989.

Besterman, Theodore. *Voltaire.* Chicago, 1969.

Bled, Jean Paul. *Francois Joseph.* Cambridge, Mass., 1992.

Breitman, Richard, and Kraut, Alan M. *American Refugee Policy and European Jewry, 1933–1945.* Indiana, 1987.

Calimani, Riccardo. *The Ghetto of Venice.* New York, 1985.

Charques, R. D. *A Short History of Russia.* New York, 1956.

Chary Frederick B. *The Bulgarian Jews and the Final Solution, 1940–1944.* Pennsylvania, 1972.

Cobban, Alfred. *A History of Modern France,* vol. 2. New York, 1965.

Collard, George. *Moses: The Victorian Jew.* Oxford, 1990.

Conquest, Robert. *Stalin: Breaker of Nations.* New York, 1964.

Costain Thomas. *The Three Edwards.* New York, 1964.

Dayan, Moshe. *Story of My Life.* New York, 1976.

Dubnow, Simon. *History of the Jews,* 5 vols. New York, 1965.

Eban, Abba. *Personal Witness.* New York, 1992.

Eisenhower, Dwight D. *At Ease: Stories I Tell Friends.* New York, 1967.

Falconi, Carlo. *The Silence of Pius XII.* Boston, 1965.

Farago, Ladislas, and Sinclair, Andrew. *Royal Web.* New York, 1982.

Ferrell, Robert, ed. *The Eisenhower Diaries.* New York, 1981.

Fischer, Louis. *Gandhi.* New York, 1950.

Flender, Harold. *Rescue in Denmark.* New York, 1963.

Fraser, David. *Knight's Cross.* New York, 1994.

Friedman, Lee M. *Jewish Pioneers and Patriots.* New York, 1943.

Fuhrmann, Joseph. *Rasputin: A Life.* New York, 1990.

Gager, John G. *The Origins of Anti-Semitism.* New York, 1983.

Gerber, Jane S. *A History of the Sephardic Experience.* New York, 1992.

Gilman, Abraham. *The Emancipation of the Jews of England, 1850–1860*. New York, 1982.

Glassman, Samuel. *Epic of Survival*. New York, 1980.

Gottschalk, Louis, and Maddox, Margaret. *Lafayette in the French Revolution*. Chicago, 1973.

Graetz, Heinrich. *History of the Jews*. Philadelphia, 1946.

Grose, Peter. *Israel in the Mind of America*. New York, 1984.

Hadas, Moses, ed. *The Complete Works of Tacitus*. New York, 1942.

Haffner, Sebastian. *The Ailing Empire: Germany From Bismarck to Hitler*. New York, 1989.

Henriques, H. S. *The Return of the Jews to England*. London, 1905.

Hertzberg, Arthur. *The French Enlightenment and the Jews*. New York, 1968.

Herzl, Theodore. *The Complete Diaries of Theodore Herzl*. New York, 1960.

Hibbert, Christopher. *The Royal Victorians*. Philadelphia, 1976.

Hilberg, Raul. *The Destruction of the European Jews* (revised). New York, 1985.

Hitler, Adolf. *Mein Kampf*. Boston, 1943.

Holingdale, R. J. ed. *Nietzsche: The Man and His Philosophy*. Baton Rouge, 1965.

Horthy, Nicholas. *Memoirs*. New York, 1957.

Irving, David. *Hitler's War*. New York, 1977.

Isser, Natalie. *Anti-Semitism During the Second French Empire*. New York, 1991.

Johnson, Edgar. *Charles Dickens: His Tragedy and Triumph*. Boston, 1952.

Johnson, Lyndon. *The Vantage Point*. New York, 1977.

Jordan, William C. *The French Monarchy and the Jews: From Philip Augustus to the Last Capetians*. Philadelphia, 1989.

Josephus, Flavius. *The Jewish War*. New York, 1969.

Katz, Jacob. *The Darker Side of Genius*. Hanover, 1986.

Keller, Werner, *Diaspora*. New York, 1966.

Kersten, Felix. *The Memoirs of Doctor Felix Kersten*. New York, 1947.

Kesselring, Albert. *A Soldier's Record*. London, 1953.

Khrushchev, Nikita. *Khrushchev Remembers: The Glasnost Tapes*. Boston, 1990.

Kurenberg, Joachim. *The Kaiser*. New York, 1955.

Labarge, Margaret Wade. *Saint Louis: Louis IX, Most Christian King of France*. Boston, 1968.

Lacouture, Jean. *De Gaulle*. New York, 1991.

Lapide, Pinchas E. *Three Popes and the Jews*. New York, 1967.

Levin, Nora. *The Jews in the Soviet Union Since 1917*. New York, 1988.

Lincoln, W. Bruce. *The Romanovs*. New York, 1981.

Lipschitz, Chaim U. *Franco, Spain, the Jews and the Holocaust*. New York, 1984.

Liss, Peggy K. *Isabel the Queen*. New York, 1992.

Litvinoff, Barnet. *The Burning Bush*. New York, 1988.

Lloyd, Alan. *The Maligned Monarch: A Life of King John of England*. New York, 1972.

Longford, Elizabeth. *Wellington: Pillar of State*. New York, 1972.

Low, Alfred D. *Jews in the Eyes of the Germans*. Philadelphia, 1979.

Macintyre, Ben. *Forgotten Fatherland: The Search for Elizabeth Nietzsche*. New York, 1992.

Magnus, Philip. *King Edward the Seventh*. New York, 1964.

Magarschack, David. *Chekhov*. Westpoint, Conn. 1953.

Mannerheim, Gustav von. *The Memoirs of Marshal Mannerheim*. London, 1953.

Margolis, Max, and Marx, Alexander. *A History of the Jewish People*. Philadelphia, 1958.

Marrus, Michael R., and Paxton, Robert O. *Vichy France and the Jews*. New York, 1981.

May, Arthur J. *The Age of Metternich, 1814–1848*. New York, 1963.

McCullough, David. *Truman*. New York, 1992.

Meir, Golda. *My Life*. New York, 1975.

Michaelis, Meir. *Mussolini and the Jews*. Oxford, 1978.

Modder, Montagu. *The Jew in the Literature of England*. Philadelphia, 1939.

Morley, John. *The Life of William Ewart Gladstone*. London, 1903.

Morton, Frederic. *The Rothschilds*. New York, 1962.

Norgate, Kate. *Richard the Lion-Heart*. London, 1969.

Paget, R. T. *Manstein: His Campaigns and His Trial*. London, 1951.

Palmer, Alan. *The Kaiser: Warlord of the Second Reich*. London, 1978.

Parmet, Herbert S. *Richard Nixon and His America*. Boston, 1990.

Penkower, Monty Noam. *The Jews Were Expendable*. Chicago, 1983.

Poliakov, Léon. *History of Anti-Semitism*. New York, 1965.

Prestwich, Michael. *Edward I*. Berkeley, 1988.

Rabin, Yitzhak. *The Rabin Memoirs*. Boston, 1979.

Rafael, Gideon. *Destination Peace*. New York, 1981.

Richards, Jeffrey. *Consul of God: The Life and Times of Gregory the Great*. London, 1980.

Richter, Werner. *Bismarck*. New York, 1965.

Ridley, Jaspar. *Garibaldi*. New York, 1974.

Romain, Jonathan. A. *The Jews of England*. London, 1988.

Rose, Norman. *Chaim Weizmann*. New York, 1986.

Roth, Cecil. *A History of the Jews of England*. Oxford, 1949.

————. *A History of the Jews of Italy*. Philadelphia, 1946.

————. *The Jews of the Renaissance*. Philadelphia, 1957.

Sacher, Abram Leon. *A History of the Jews*. New York, 1975.

Sacher, Howard Morley. *The Course of Modern Jewish History*. New York, 1977.

————. *Egypt and Israel*. New York, 1981.

Salbstein, M. C. N. *The Emancipation of the Jews of Britain*. Rutherford, New Jersey, 1982.

Salzman, Louis F. *Edward I*. New York, 1968.

Schechter, Betty. *The Dreyfus Affair*. Boston, 1965.

Shannon, Richard. *Gladstone*, vol. I. London, 1982.

Shirer, William L. *Love and Hatred: The Troubled Marriage of Leo and Sonya Tolstoy.* New York, 1994.

Stern, Fritz. *Gold and Iron: Bismarck, Bleichroeder and the Building of the German Empire.* New York, 1977.

Stillman, Norma. *The Jews of Arab Lands: A History and Source Book.* Philadelphia, 1979.

Suetonius. *The Twelve Caesars.* New York, 1957.

Thayer, William. *The Life and Times of Cavour.* New York, 1971.

Tyler-Whittle, Michael. *The Last Kaiser.* New York, 1977.

Troyat, Henri. *Ivan the Terrible.* New York, 1984.

————. *Tolstoy.* New York, 1966.

Tusa, Ann, and Tusa, John. *The Nuremberg Trial.* New York, 1984.

Wasserstein, Bernard. *Britain and the Jews of Europe, 1939–1945.* New York, 1979.

Watson, Derek. *Richard Wagner.* New York, 1979.

Weintraub, Stanely. *Disraeli.* New York, 1993.

————. *Victoria: An Intimate Biography.* New York, 1987.

Williamson, G. A. *The World of Josephus.* London, 1964.

Wistrich, Robert S. *The Jews of Vienna in the Age of Franz Joseph.* New York, 1989.

Wolf, Lucien. *Sir Moses Montefiore: A Centennial Biography.* New York, 1985.

Wyman, David S. *The Abandonment of the Jews.* New York, 1984.

Yahil, Leni. *The Rescue of Danish Jewry.* Philadelphia, 1969.

Yarmolinsky, Avraham. *Dostoevsky.* New York, 1971.

Zuccotti, Susan. *The Holocaust, the French, and the Jews.* New York, 1993.

INDEX